A·N·N·U·A·L E·D·I·T·I·O·N·S

10 10 70

American Government

Thirty-First Edition

01/02

EDITOR

Bruce Stinebrickner
DePauw University

Professor Bruce Stinebrickner teaches American politics in the Department of Political Science at DePauw University in Greencastle, Indiana. He has also taught American politics at Lehman College of the City University of New York, at the University of Queensland in Brisbane, Australia, and in a DePauw program for Argentine students in Buenos Aires. He received his Ph.D. from Yale University in 1974. In his courses and publications on American politics, Professor Stinebrickner brings valuable insights gained from living, teaching, and lecturing abroad.

McGraw-Hill/Dushkin
530 Old Whitfield Street, Guilford, Connecticut 06437

Visit us on the Internet
http://www.dushkin.com

Credits

1. Foundations of American Politics
Unit photo—McGraw-Hill/Dushkin.
2. Structures of American Politics 2000
Unit photo—McGraw-Hill/Dushkin.
3. Process of American Politics
Unit photo—Associated Press photo by Ron Edmonds.
4. Products of American Politics
Unit photo—© 2001 by PhotoDisc, Inc.

Copyright

Cataloging in Publication Data
Main entry under title: Annual Editions: American Government. 2001/2002.
    1. U.S.—Politics and government—1945—Periodicals. I. Stinebrickner, Bruce, *comp*. II. Title: American government.
ISBN 0–07–243310–8   320.9′73′0924′05   76-180265   ISSN 0891-3390

© 2001 by McGraw-Hill/Dushkin, Guilford, CT 06437, A Division of The McGraw-Hill Companies.

Thirty-First Edition

Cover image © 2001 by PhotoDisc, Inc.

Printed in the United States of America   1234567890BAHBAH54321   Printed on Recycled Paper

To the Reader

In publishing ANNUAL EDITIONS we recognize the enormous role played by the magazines, newspapers, and journals of the public press in providing current, first-rate educational information in a broad spectrum of interest areas. Many of these articles are appropriate for students, researchers, and professionals seeking accurate, current material to help bridge the gap between principles and theories and the real world. These articles, however, become more useful for study when those of lasting value are carefully collected, organized, indexed, and reproduced in a low-cost format, which provides easy and permanent access when the material is needed. That is the role played by ANNUAL EDITIONS.

Annual Editions: American Government 01/02 is the thirty-first edition of a book that has become a mainstay in many introductory courses on American politics. The educational goal is to provide a readable collection of up-to-date articles that are informative, interesting, and stimulating to students beginning their study of the American political system.

In 1998 and 1999 we witnessed the dramatic revelation of President Bill Clinton's relationship with Monica Lewinsky, the resignation of Republican Speaker Newt Gingrich from the House of Representatives after the results of the 1998 mid-term congressional elections disappointed many in his party, the impeachment of the president under the leadership of House Judiciary chair Henry Hyde, and the president's acquittal in his Senate impeachment trial. After two tumultuous and polarizing years, the presidential and congressional elections in 2000 could well have been expected to return a semblance of normalcy to the functioning of the American political system.

By the summer of 2000, frontrunners George W. Bush, governor of Texas, and Al Gore, vice president, had won their respective parties' presidential nominations and had chosen running mates Dick Cheney and Joe Lieberman, respectively. As Election Day approached, the outcomes of the fall's general election campaigns for the presidency, House of Representatives, and one-third of the Senate remained very much in doubt. While trying to forecast winners and losers was difficult enough, no one could have predicted the turmoil and controversy that would arise from the razor-thin presidential election results in Florida and across the nation.

Unprecedented legal and public relations manipulation by both candidates and their supporters drew state and federal courts, the Florida state legislature, and various Florida executive branch officials into the controversy. Finally, after five weeks of seemingly endless media coverage, the United States Supreme Court issued a definitive ruling. Vice President Gore conceded and Governor Bush became president-elect. But, even with the resolution of the presidential election, the obvious flaws in the American electoral process, which surfaced during the Florida controversy, continue to be a serious concern. Whether or not electoral reforms will occur during the early years of the Bush presidency, as it co-exists with a House of Representatives with a narrow Republican majority and a Senate split 50-50 between the two parties, remains to be seen.

The inauguration of President Bush in January 2001 ended Bill Clinton's eight years as president. What an eight years they were! Besides the dramatic Lewinsky-impeachment events already mentioned, the Clinton presidency presided over the end of years of budget deficits amidst economic projections that the entire national debt would be eliminated within a decade or so. In addition, the welfare system that had been in place since the 1930s was substantially reformed in 1996. The 1990s also saw the increasing globalization of trade—facilitated by the NAFTA agreement of 1993—and the growing importance of computer technology and the Internet throughout the world. After the demise of the Soviet Union, U.S. foreign policy under Clinton did not—and perhaps could not—display the clear focus and direction of the simpler, bipolar cold war era. Peacekeeping efforts in Kosovo, Bosnia-Herzegovina, the Middle East, and elsewhere met with mixed and sometimes murky results. Whether the United States during the Bush administration, still in its infancy as of this writing, will experience as much far-reaching change as occurred during the Clinton administration remains to be seen.

The systems approach provides a rough organizational framework for this book. The first unit focuses on ideological and constitutional underpinnings of American politics, from both historical and contemporary perspectives. The second unit treats the major institutions of the national government. The third covers the "input" or "linkage" mechanisms of the system—political parties, elections, interest groups, and media—as well as having an entire section devoted to the 2000 presidential selection process. The fourth and concluding unit shifts the focus to policy choices that confront the government in Washington and resulting "outputs" of the political system. Also included in the book is a list of related *World Wide Web sites*, which are cross-referenced in the *topic guide* and which can be used to explore particular areas in greater depth.

Each year thousands of articles about American politics are published, and deciding which to reprint in a collection of readings such as this is not always easy. Since no position on the political spectrum has a monopoly on truth, articles are chosen with an eye toward providing viewpoints from left, right, and center. About half of the selections in this book are new to this year's edition.

Next year will bring another opportunity for change, and you, the reader, are invited to participate in the process. Please complete and return the postpaid *article rating form* on the last page of the book and let us know your reactions and your suggestions for improvement.

Bruce Stinebrickner

Bruce Stinebrickner
Editor

Contents

UNIT 1

Foundations of American Politics

The fourteen selections in this unit outline the foundations of American politics. In addition to primary documents, there are discussions of contemporary political ideals and viewpoints as well as recent commentaries on constitutional issues.

The concepts in bold italics are developed in the article. For further expansion please refer to the Topic Guide and the Index.

v

Overview

UNIT 2

Structures of American Politics 2000

Thirteen articles in this unit examine
the structure and present status of
the American presidency, Congress,
the judiciary, and bureaucracy.

The concepts in bold italics are developed in the article. For further expansion please refer to the Topic Guide and the Index.

vii

UNIT 3

Process of American Politics

In this unit, sixteen articles
review how political parties,
voters, election processes, interest
groups, and the media work within
the process of American politics.

The concepts in bold italics are developed in the article. For further expansion please refer to the Topic Guide and the Index.

The concepts in bold italics are developed in the article. For further expansion please refer to the Topic Guide and the Index.

The concepts in bold italics are developed in the article. For further expansion please refer to the Topic Guide and the Index.

UNIT 4

Products of American Politics

Five selections in this unit examine the domestic, economic, foreign, and defense policies that American government produces.

The concepts in bold italics are developed in the article. For further expansion please refer to the Topic Guide and the Index.

Topic Guide

This topic guide suggests how the selections in this book relate to the subjects covered in your course.

The Web icon (☉) under the topic articles easily identifies the relevant Web sites, which are numbered and annotated on the next two pages. By linking the articles and the Web sites by topic, this ANNUAL EDITIONS reader becomes a powerful learning and research tool.

TOPIC AREA	TREATED IN	TOPIC AREA	TREATED IN
Bureaucracy	5. What Good Is Government? 26. Turkey Farm 27. Finding the Civil Service's Hidden Sex Appeal: Why the Brightest Young People Shy Away From Government ☉ *1, 2, 4, 5, 10, 11, 12, 14, 15, 16, 17, 19, 20, 23*	**Economy/ Economic Policy**	7. New Power 45. $80,000 and a Dream: A Simple Plan for Generating Equal Opportunity ☉ *1, 2, 3, 6, 9, 14, 15, 17, 19, 20, 21, 25, 29*
Clinton, Bill	16. Hooked on Polls 17. Did Clinton Succeed or Fail? 18. Trivial Pursuits: Clinton's Record ☉ *1, 3, 4, 5, 6, 9, 10, 12, 14, 15, 16, 19, 20, 21, 22, 23, 24, 26*	**Elections and Nominations**	12. Drawing Legal Lines 21. Can It Be Done? 25. Up for Grabs: The Supreme Court and the Election 28. Running Scared 31. Making Every Vote Count 32. One Cheer for Soft Money: The Case for Strong Political Parties 39. Bush and Gore: Perfect Winners of a Perfect Race. Almost 40. Last Straw Poll: Seven Things From Campaign 2000 to Eliminate 41. Selling America to the Highest Bidder 42. Ten Observations on the 2000 Presidential Election Controversy in Florida 43. Old College Try: How We Pick the Prez ☉ *1, 3, 4, 6, 14, 15, 16, 19, 20, 21*
Congress	14. Disability Act's First 10 Years and the Challenges Ahead 15. Gone Are the Giants 19. Crackup of the Committees 20. King of the Roads 21. Can It Be Done? 22. Uninsured Americans Linger on Congress' Waiting List ☉ *1, 2, 3, 4, 5, 6, 7, 8, 9, 14, 15, 20, 21, 25*		
Constitution	2. Constitution of the United States, 1787 3. Size and Variety of the Union as a Check on Faction 10. Vigilante Justices 27. Gipper's Constitution ☉ *1, 3, 4, 5, 7, 8, 13*	**Federalism**	9. American Federalism: Half-Full or Half-Empty? ☉ *1, 3, 4, 5, 6, 7, 8*
Corporations	6. Chomp! ☉ *2, 23*	**Foreign and Defense Policy**	47. Musclebound: The Limits of U.S. Power 48. Longest War ☉ *1, 3, 7, 9, 10, 12, 14, 15, 16, 17, 24, 26, 27*
Courts	11. Guns and Tobacco: Government by Litigation 12. Drawing Legal Lines 25. Up for Grabs: The Supreme Court and the Election ☉ *1, 5, 6, 7, 13, 14, 15*	**Gun Control**	46. Yes and No to Gun Control ☉ *6, 12, 14, 15, 16*
		Historic Perspectives	1. Declaration of Independence, 1776 2. Constitution of the United States, 1787

● AE: American Government

The following World Wide Web sites have been carefully researched and selected to support the articles found in this reader. The sites are cross-referenced by number and the Web icon (●) in the topic guide. In addition, it is possible to link directly to these Web sites through our DUSHKIN ONLINE support site at *http://www.dushkin.com/online/*.

The following sites were available at the time of publication. Visit our Web site—we update DUSHKIN ONLINE regularly to reflect any changes.

General Sources

1. The Federal Web Locator
http://www.infoctr.edu/fwl/
Use this site as a launching pad for the Web sites of U.S. federal agencies, departments, and organizations. It is well organized and easy to use for informational and research purposes.

2. John F. Kennedy School of Government
http://www.ksg.harvard.edu
Starting from Harvard University's KSG page, you will be able to click on a huge variety of links to information about American politics and government, ranging from political party and campaign data to debates of enduring issues.

3. Library of Congress
http://www.loc.gov
Examine this Web site to learn about the extensive resource tools, library services/resources, exhibitions, and databases available through the Library of Congress in many different subfields of government studies.

Foundations of American Politics

4. American Studies Web
http://www.georgetown.edu/crossroads/asw/
This eclectic site provides links to a wealth of Internet resources for research in American studies, including agriculture and rural development, government, and race and ethnicity.

5. Federalism: Relationship Between Local and National Governments
http://www.infidels.org/~nap/index.federalism.html
Federalism versus states' rights has always been a spirited debate in American government. Visit this George Mason University site for links to many articles and reports on the subject.

6. Opinion, Inc.: The Site for Conservative Opinion on the Web
http://www.opinioninc.com
Open this site for access to political, cultural, and Web commentary on a number of issues from a conservative political viewpoint. The site is updated frequently.

7. Scanned Originals of Early American Documents
http://www.law.emory.edu/FEDERAL/
Through this Emory University site you can view scanned originals of the Declaration of Independence, the Constitution, and the Bill of Rights. The transcribed texts are also available, as are *The Federalist Papers*.

8. Smithsonian Institution
http://www.si.edu
This site provides access to the enormous resources of the Smithsonian, which holds some 140 million artifacts and specimens in its trust for "the increase and diffusion of

knowledge." Here you can learn about American social, cultural, economic, and political history from a variety of viewpoints.

9. The Written Word
http://www.mdle.com/WrittenWord/
This is an online journal of economic, political, and social commentary, primarily from a center or left-of-center viewpoint. The site provides links to governmental and political Web resources.

Structures of American Politics 2000

10. Department of State
http://www.state.gov
View this site for understanding into the workings of a major U.S. executive branch department. Links explain exactly what the Department does, what services it provides, and what it says about U.S. interests around the world, along with much more information.

11. Federal Reserve System
http://woodrow.mpls.frb.fed.us/info/sys/index.html
Consult this page to learn the answers to FAQs about the Fed, the structure of the Federal Reserve system, monetary policy, and more. It provides links to speeches and interviews as well as essays and articles presenting different views on the Fed.

12. Policy Digest Archives
http://www.public-policy.org/~ncpa/pd/pdindex.html
Through this site of the National Center for Policy Analysis, access discussions on an array of topics that are of major interest in the study of American government, from regulatory policy and privatization to economy and income.

13. Supreme Court/Legal Information Institute
http://supct.law.cornell.edu/supct/index.html
Open this site for current and historical information about the Supreme Court. The LII archive contains many opinions issued since May 1990 as well as a collection of nearly 600 of the most historical decisions of the Court.

14. United States House of Representatives
http://www.house.gov
This Web page of the House of Representatives will lead you to information about current and past House members and agendas, the legislative process, and more. You can learn about events on the House floor as they happen.

15. United States Senate
http://www.senate.gov
This U.S. Senate Web page will lead to information about current and past Senate members and agendas, legislative activities, and committees.

16. The White House
http://www.whitehouse.gov
Visit the White House home page for direct access to information about commonly requested federal services, the White House Briefing Room, and the presidents and vice presidents. The Virtual Library allows you to search White House documents, listen to speeches, and view photos.

Process of American Politics

17. The Henry L. Stimson Center
http://www.stimson.org
The Stimson Center, a nonprofit and self-described nonpartisan organization, focuses on issues where policy, technology, and politics intersect. Use this site to find assessments of U.S. foreign and domestic policy and other topics.

18. Influence at Work
http://www.influenceatwork.com
This commercial site focuses on the nature of persuasion, compliance, and propaganda, with many practical examples and applications. Students of such topics as the roles of public opinion and media influence in policy making should find these discussions of interest. The approach is based on the research and methods of influence expert Dr. Robert Cialdini.

19. LSU Department of Political Science Resources
http://www.artsci.lsu.edu/poli/
This extensive site will point you to a number of resources for domestic and international political and governmental news, including LSU's Political Science WWW Server, which is maintained by a dedicated group of professionals.

20. Marketplace of Political Ideas/University of Houston Library
http://info.lib.uh.edu/politics/markind.htm
Here is a collection of links to campaign, conservative/liberal perspectives, and political party sites. There are General Political Sites, Democratic Sites, Republican Sites, Third Party Sites, and much more.

21. NationalJournal.com
http://nationaljournal.com
This is a major site for information on American government and politics. There is discussion of campaigns, the congressional calendar, a news archive, and more for politicians and policy makers. Membership is required, however, to access much of the information.

22. Poynter Online
http://www.poynter.org
This research site of the Poynter Institute for Media Studies provides extensive links to information and resources about the media, including media ethics and reportage techniques. Many bibliographies and Web sites are included.

23. RAND
http://www.rand.org
RAND is a nonprofit institution that works to improve public policy through research and analysis. Links offered on this home page provide for keyword searches of certain topics and descriptions of RAND activities and major research areas.

Products of American Politics

24. American Diplomacy
http://www.unc.edu/depts/diplomat/
American Diplomacy is an online journal of commentary, analysis, and research on U.S. foreign policy and its results around the world.

25. Cato Institute
http://www.cato.org/research/ss_prjct.html
The Cato Institute presents this page to discuss its Project on Social Security Privatization. The site and its links begin from the belief that privatization of the U.S. Social Security system is a positive goal that will empower workers.

26. Clinton Foreign Policy Page
http://www.geocities.com/CapitolHill/8514/
For a change of pace from the sites of journals, think tanks, and government organizations, check out Eddie Robert's personal home page. Roberts, an individual who is very critical of President Bill Clinton's foreign policy, provides space for you to respond to his opinions.

27. Foreign Affairs
http://www.foreignaffairs.org
This home page of the well-respected foreign policy journal is a valuable research tool. It allows users to search the journal's archives and provides indexed access to the field's leading publications, documents, online resources, and more. Links to dozens of other related Web sites are possible from here.

28. The Gallup Organization
http://www.gallup.com
Open this Gallup Organization home page for links to an extensive archive of public opinion poll results and special reports on a variety of topics related to American society, politics, and government.

29. Tax Foundation
http://www.taxfoundation.org/index.html
Ever wonder where your taxes go? Consult the site of this self-described "nonprofit, nonpartisan policy research organization" to learn the history of "Tax Freedom Day," tax burdens around the United States, and other information about your tax bill or taxes in general.

30. STAT-USA
http://www.stat-usa.gov/stat-usa.html
This essential site, a service of the Department of Commerce, contains daily economic news, frequently requested statistical releases, information on export and international trade, domestic economic news and statistical series, and data bases.

31. U.S. Information Agency
http://usinfo.state.gov
This wide-ranging page of the USIA provides definitions, related documentation, and a discussion of topics of concern to students of American government. It addresses today's hot topics as well as ongoing issues that form the foundation of the field. Many Web links are provided.

We highly recommend that you review our Web site for expanded information and our other product lines. We are continually updating and adding links to our Web site in order to offer you the most usable and useful information that will support and expand the value of your Annual Editions. You can reach us at: *http://www.dushkin.com/annualeditions/*.

www.dushkin.com/online/

Unit Selections

1. **The Declaration of Independence, 1776**
2. **The Constitution of the United States, 1787**
3. **The Size and Variety of the Union as a Check on Faction,** James Madison
4. **Checks and Balances,** James Madison
5. **What Good Is Government?** William J. Bennett and John J. Dilulio Jr.
6. **Chomp!** Jim Hightower
7. **The New Power,** Robert B. Reich
8. **America's Ignorant Voters,** Michael Schudson
9. **American Federalism: Half-Full or Half-Empty?** Martha Derthick
10. **Vigilante Justices,** Antonin Scalia
11. **Guns and Tobacco: Government by Litigation,** Stuart Taylor Jr.
12. **Drawing Legal Lines,** David Byrd
13. **Speech Isn't Cheap,** Wendy Kaminer
14. **Disability Act's First 10 Years and the Challenges Ahead,** David Nather

Key Points to Consider

❖ What do you think would surprise the Founders most about the values and ideals held by Americans today?

❖ Which ideals, ideas, and values seem likely to remain central to American politics, and which seem likely to erode and gradually disappear?

❖ To what rights do you think all Americans are entitled? Do all Americans have these rights now? If not, why not?

❖ What provisions of the U.S. Constitution do you think are particularly wise and desirable? Which provisions, including ones that have been superseded by amendments, seem unwise and undesirable?

❖ What makes constitutional interpretation and reinterpretation necessary in the American political system? Why, at the same time, do the very words of the Constitution remain a respected foundation of the entire system of government? What groups seem most likely to become visible, active forces on the American political scene in the way that African Americans and women have in the recent past? Why?

❖ Do you consider yourself a conservative, a liberal, a socialist, a reactionary, or what? Why?

 **Links** **www.dushkin.com/online/**

4. **American Studies Web**
   http://www.georgetown.edu/crossroads/asw/
5. **Federalism: Relationship Between Local and National Governments**
   http://www.infidels.org/~nap/index.federalism.html
6. **Opinion, Inc.: The Site for Conservative Opinion on the Web**
   http://opinioninc.com
7. **Scanned Originals of Early American Documents**
   http://www.law.emory.edu/FEDERAL/
8. **Smithsonian Institution**
   http://www.si.edu
9. **The Written Word**
   http://www.mdle.com/WrittenWord/

These sites are annotated on pages 4 and 5.

This unit treats some of the less concrete aspects of the American political system—historic ideals, contemporary ideas and values, and constitutional and legal issues. These dimensions of the system are not immune to change. Instead, they interact with the wider political environment in which they exist, and they are modified accordingly. Usually this interaction is a gradual process, but sometimes events foster more rapid change.

Human beings can be distinguished from other species by their ability to think and reason at relatively high levels of abstraction. In turn, ideas, ideals, values, and principles can and do play important roles in politics. Most Americans value ideals such as democracy, freedom, equal opportunity, and justice. Yet the precise meanings of these terms and the best ways of implementing them are the subject of much dispute in the political arena. Such ideas and ideals, as well as disputes about their "real" meanings, are important elements in the practice of American politics.

Although the selections in this unit span more than 200 years, they are clearly related to one another. Understanding contemporary political viewpoints is easier if the ideals and principles of the past are also taken into account. In addition, we can better appreciate the significance of historic documents such as the Declaration of Independence and the Constitution if we are familiar with contemporary ideas and perspectives. The interaction of different ideas and values plays an important part in the continuing development of the "foundations" of the American political system.

The first section of this unit includes several historic documents from the eighteenth century. The first is the Declaration of Independence. Written in 1776, it proclaims the Founders' views of why independence from England was justified and, in so doing, identifies certain "unalienable" rights that "all men" are said to possess. The second document, the Constitution of 1787, remains in effect to this day. It provides an organizational blueprint for the structure of American national government, outlines the federal relationship between the national government and the states, and expresses limitations on what government can do. Twenty-seven amendments have

been added to the original Constitution in two centuries. In addition to the Declaration of Independence and the Constitution, the first section includes a selection from *The Federalist Papers,* a series of newspaper articles written in support of the proposed new Constitution. Appearing in 1787 and 1788, *The Federalist Papers* treated various provisions of the new Constitution and argued that putting the Constitution into effect would bring about good government.

The second section treats contemporary political ideas and viewpoints. As selections in this section illustrate, efforts to apply or act on political beliefs in the context of concrete circumstances often lead to interesting commentary and debate. "Liberal" and "conservative" are two labels often used in American political discussions, but political views and values have far more complexity than can be captured by these two terms.

Selections in the third section show that constitutional and legal issues and interpretations are tied to historic principles as well as to contemporary ideas and values. It has been suggested that, throughout American history, almost every important political question has at one time or another appeared as a constitutional or legal issue.

The historic documents and the other selections in this unit might be more difficult to understand than the articles in other units. Some of them may have to be read and reread carefully to be fully appreciated. But to grapple with the important material treated here is to come to grips with a variety of conceptual blueprints for the American political system. To ignore the theoretical issues raised would be to bypass an important element of American politics today.

Foundations of American Politics

The Declaration of Independence

WHEN in the Course of human events, it becomes necessary for one people to dissolve the political bands which have connected them with another, and to assume among the powers of the earth, the separate and equal station to which the Laws of Nature and of Nature's God entitle them, a decent respect to the opinions of mankind requires that they should declare the causes which impel them to the separation.—We hold these truths to be self-evident, that all men are created equal, that they are endowed by their Creator with certain unalienable Rights, that among these are Life, Liberty and the pursuit of Happiness.—That to secure these rights, Governments are instituted among Men, deriving their just powers from the consent of the governed.—That whenever any Form of Government becomes destructive of these ends, it is the Right of the People to alter or to abolish it, and to institute new Government, laying its foundation on such principles and organizing its powers in such form, as to them shall seem most likely to effect their Safety and Happiness. Prudence, indeed, will dictate that Governments long established should not be changed for light and transient causes; and accordingly all experience hath shewn, that mankind are more disposed to suffer, while evils are sufferable, than to right themselves by abolishing the forms to which they are accustomed. But when a long train of abuses and usurpations, pursuing invariably the same Object evinces a design to reduce them under absolute Despotism, it is their right, it is their duty, to throw off such Government, and to provide new Guards for their future security.—Such has been the patient sufferance of these Colonies; and such is now the necessity which constrains them to alter their former Systems of Government. The history of the present King of Great Britain is a history of repeated injuries and usurpations, all having in direct object the establishment of an absolute Tyranny over these States. To prove this, let Facts be submitted to a candid world.—He has refused his Assent to Laws, the most wholesome and necessary for the public good.—He has forbidden his Governors to pass Laws of immediate and pressing importance, unless suspended in their operation till his Assent should be obtained; and when so suspended, he has utterly neglected to attend to them.—He

has refused to pass other Laws for the accommodation of large districts of people, unless those people would relinquish the right of Representation in the Legislature, a right inestimable to them and formidable to tyrants only.—He has called together legislative bodies at places unusual, uncomfortable, and distant from the depository of their public Records, for the sole purpose of fatiguing them into compliance with his measures.—He has dissolved Representative Houses repeatedly, for opposing with manly firmness his invasions on the rights of the people.—He has refused for a long time, after such dissolutions, to cause others to be elected; whereby the Legislative powers, incapable of Annihilation, have returned to the People at large for their exercise; the State remaining in the meantime exposed to all the dangers of invasion from without, and convulsions within.—He has endeavoured to prevent the population of these States; for that purpose obstructing the Laws for Naturalization of Foreigners; refusing to pass others to encourage their migrations hither, and raising the conditions of new Appropriations of Lands.—He has obstructed the Administration of Justice, by refusing his Assent to Laws for establishing Judiciary powers.—He has made Judges dependent on his Will alone, for the tenure of their offices, and the amount and payment of their salaries.—He has erected a multitude of New Offices, and sent hither swarms of Officers to harass our people, and eat out their substance. He has kept among us, in times of peace, Standing Armies without the Consent of our legislatures.—He has affected to render the Military independent of and superior to the Civil power.—He has combined with others to subject us to a jurisdiction foreign to our constitution, and unacknowledged by our laws; giving his Assent to their Acts of pretended Legislation:—For quartering large bodies of armed troops among us:—For protecting them, by a mock Trial, from punishment for any Murders which they should commit on the Inhabitants of these States:—For cutting off our Trade with all parts of the world:—For imposing Taxes on us without our Consent:—For depriving us in many cases, of the benefits of Trial by Jury:—For transporting us beyond Seas to be tried for pretended offences:—For abolishing the free System of English Laws in a neighboring Province, establishing therein an Arbitrary government, and enlarging its Boundaries so as to render it at once an example and fit instrument for introducing the same absolute rule into these Colonies:—For taking away our Charters, abolishing our most valuable Laws and altering fundamentally the Forms of our Governments:—For suspending our own Legislatures, and declaring themselves invested with power to legislate for us in all cases whatsoever.—He has abdicated Government here, by declaring us out of his Protection and waging War against us.—He has plundered our seas, ravaged our Coasts, burnt our towns, and destroyed the lives of our people.—He is at this time transporting large Armies of foreign Mercenaries to compleat the works of death, desolation and tyranny, already begun with circumstances of Cruelty & perfidy scarcely paralled in the most barbarous ages, and totally unworthy the Head of a civilized nation.—He has constrained our fellow Citizens taken Captive on the high Seas to bear Arms gainst their Country, to become the executioners of their friends and Brethren, or to fall themselves by their Hands.—He has excited domestic insurrections amongst us, and has endeavoured to bring on the inhabitants of our frontiers, the merciless Indian Savages, whose known rule of warfare, is an undistinguished destruction of all ages, sexes and conditions. In every stage of these Oppressions We have Petitioned for Redress in the most humble terms: Our repeated Petitions have been answered only by repeated injury. A Prince, whose character is thus marked by every act which may define a Tyrant, is unfit to be the ruler of a free people. Nor have We been wanting in attentions to our British brethren. We have warned them from time to time of attempts by their legislature to extend an unwarrantable jurisdiction over us. We have reminded them of the circumstances of our emigration and settlement here. We have appealed to their native justice and magnanimity, and we have conjured them by the ties of our common kindred to disavow these usurpations, which would inevitably interrupt our connections and correspondence. They too have been deaf to the voice of justice and of consanguinity. We must, therefore, acquiesce in the necessity, which denounces our Separation, and hold them, as we hold the rest of mankind, Enemies in War, in Peace Friends.—

WE, THEREFORE, the Representatives of the UNITED STATES OF AMERICA, in General Congress, Assembled, appealing to the Supreme Judge of the world for the rectitude of our intentions, do, in the Name, and by Authority of the good People of these Colonies, solemnly publish and declare, That these United Colonies are, and of Right ought to be FREE AND INDEPENDENT STATES; that they are Absolved from all Allegiance to the British Crown, and that all political connection between them and the State of Great Britain, is and ought to be totally dissolved; and that as Free and Independent States, they have full Power to levy War, conclude Peace, contract Alliances, establish Commerce, and to do all other Acts and Things which Independent States may of right do.—And for the support of this Declaration, with a firm reliance on the protection of divine Providence, we mutually pledge to each other our Lives, our Fortunes and our sacred Honor.

The History of The Constitution of the United States

CONSTITUTION OF THE UNITED STATES. The Articles of Confederation did not provide the centralizing force necessary for unity among the new states and were soon found to be so fundamentally weak that a different political structure was vital. Conflicts about money and credit, trade, and suspicions about regional domination were among the concerns when Congress on February 21, 1787, authorized a Constitutional Convention to revise the Articles. The delegates were selected and assembled in Philadelphia about three months after the call. They concluded their work by September.

The delegates agreed and abided to secrecy. Years afterward James Madison supported the secrecy decision writing that "no man felt himself obliged to retain his opinions any longer than he was satisfied of their propriety and truth, and was open to the force of argument." Secrecy was not for all time. Madison, a delegate from Virginia, was a self-appointed but recognized recorder and took notes in the clear view of the members. Published long afterward, Madison's *Journal* gives a good record of the convention.

The delegates began to assemble on May 14, 1787, but a majority did not arrive until May 25. George Washington was elected President of the Convention without opposition. The lag of those few days gave some of the early arrivals, especially Madison, time to make preparations on substantive matters, and Gov. Edmund Jennings Randolph presented a plan early in the proceedings that formed the basis for much of the convention deliberations. The essentials were that there should be a government adequate to prevent foreign invasion, prevent dissension among the states, and provide for general national development, and give the national government power enough to make it superior in its realm. The decision was made not merely to revise the articles but to create a new government and a new constitution.

One of the most crucial decisions was the arrangement for representation, a compromise providing that one house would represent the states equally, the other house to be based on popular representation (with some modification due to the slavery question). This arrangement recognized political facts and concessions among men with both theoretical and practical political knowledge.

Basic Features. Oliver Wendell Holmes, Jr., once wrote that the provisions of the Constitution were not mathematical formulas, but "organic living institutions *[sic]* and its origins and growth were vital to understanding it." The constitution's basic features provide for a supreme law—notwithstanding any other legal document or practice, the Constitution is supreme, as are the laws made in pursuance of it and treaties made under the authority of the United States.

The organizational plan for government is widely known. Foremost is the separation of powers. If the new government were to be limited in its powers, one way to keep it limited would have been executive, legislative, and judicial power [given] to three distinct and non-overlapping branches. A government could not actually function, however, if the separation meant the independence of one branch from the others. The answer was a design to insure cooperation and the sharing of some functions. Among these are the executive veto and the power of Congress to have its way if it musters a super-majority to override that veto. The direction of foreign affairs and the war power are both dispersed and shared. The appointing power is shared by the Senate and the president; impeaching of officers and financial controls are powers shared by the Senate and the House.

A second major contribution by the convention is the provision for the judiciary, which gave rise to the doctrine of judicial review. There is some doubt that the delegates comprehended this prospect but Alexander Hamilton considered it in *Federalist* No. 78: "The interpretation of the laws is a proper and peculiar province of the Courts. . . . Wherever a particular statute contravenes the Constitution, it will be the duty of the judicial tribunals to adhere to the latter and disregard the former."

Another contribution is the federal system, an evolution from colonial practice and the relations between the colonies and the mother country. This division of authority between the new national government and the states recognized the doctrine of delegated and reserved powers. Only certain authority was to go to the new government; the states were not to be done away with and much of the Constitution is devoted to insuring that they were to be maintained even with the stripping of some of their powers.

It is not surprising, therefore, that the convention has been called a great political reform caucus composed of both revolutionaries and men dedicated to democracy. By eighteenth-century standards the Constitution was a democratic document, but standards change and the Constitution has changed since its adoption.

Change and Adaptation. The authors of the Constitution knew that provision for change was essential and provided for it in Article V, insuring that a majority could amend, but being restrictive enough that changes were not likely for the "light and transient" causes Jefferson warned about in the Declaration of Independence.

During the period immediately following the presentation of the Constitution for ratification, requiring assent of nine states to be effective, some alarm was expressed that there was a major defect: there was no bill of rights. So, many leaders committed themselves to the presentation of constitutional amendments for the purpose. Hamilton argued that the absence of a bill of rights was not a defect; indeed, a bill was not necessary. "Why," he wrote, in the last of *The Federalist Papers,* "declare things that shall not be done which there is no power to do?" Nonetheless, the Bill of Rights was presented in the form of amendments and adopted by the states in 1791.

Since 1791 many proposals have been suggested to amend the Constitution. By 1972 sixteen additional amendments had been adopted. Only one, the Twenty-first, which repealed the Eighteenth, was ratified by state conventions. All the others were ratified by state legislatures.

Even a cursory reading of the later amendments shows they do not alter the fundamentals of limited government, the separation of powers, the federal system, or the political process set in motion originally. The Thirteenth, Fourteenth, Fifteenth, and Nineteenth amendments attempt to insure equality to all and are an extension of the Bill of Rights. The others reaffirm some existing constitutional arrangements, alter some procedures, and at least one, the Sixteenth, states national policy.

Substantial change and adaptation of the Constitution beyond the formal amendments have come from national experience, growth, and development. It has been from the Supreme Court that much of the gradual significant shaping of the Constitution has been done.

Government has remained neither static nor tranquil. Some conflict prevails continually. It may be about the activities of some phase of government or the extent of operations, and whether the arrangement for government can be made responsive to current and prospective needs of society. Conflict is inevitable in a democratic society. Sometimes the conflict is spirited and rises to challenge the continuation of the system. Questions arise whether a fair trial may be possible here or there; legislators are alleged to be indifferent to human problems and pursue distorted public priorities. Presidents are charged with secret actions designed for self-aggrandizement or actions based on half-truths. Voices are heard urging revolution again as the only means of righting alleged wrongs.

The responses continue to demonstrate, however, that the constitutional arrangement for government, the allocation of powers, and the restraints on government all provide the needed flexibility. The Constitution endures.

—Adam C. Breckenridge, *University of Nebraska-Lincoln*

The Constitution of the United States

We the People of the United States, in Order to form a more perfect Union, establish Justice, insure domestic Tranquility, provide for the common defence, promote the general Welfare, and secure the Blessings of Liberty to ourselves and our Posterity, do ordain and establish this Constitution for the United States of America.

ARTICLE. I.

SECTION. 1. All legislative Powers herein granted shall be vested in a Congress of the United States, which shall consist of a Senate and House of Representatives.

SECTION. 2. The House of Representatives shall be composed of Members chosen every second Year by the People of the several States, and the Electors in each State shall have the Qualifications requisite for Electors of the most numerous Branch of the State Legislature.

No Person shall be a Representative who shall not have attained to the age of twenty five Years, and been seven Years a Citizen of the United States, and who shall not, when elected, be an Inhabitant of that State in which he shall be chosen.

Representatives and direct Taxes shall be apportioned among the several States which may be included within this Union, according to their respective Numbers, which shall be determined by adding to the whole Number of free Persons, including those bound to Service for a Term of Years, and excluding Indians not taxed, three fifths of all other Persons. The actual Enumeration shall be made within three Years after the first Meeting of the Congress of the United States, and within every subsequent Term of ten Years, in such Manner as they shall by Law direct. The Number of Representatives shall not exceed one for every thirty Thousand, but each State shall have at Least one Representative; and until such enumeration shall be made, the State of New Hampshire shall be entitled to chuse three, Massachusetts eight, Rhode-Island and Providence Plantations one, Connecticut five, New-York six, New Jersey four, Pennsylvania eight, Delaware one, Maryland six, Virginia ten, North Carolina five, South Carolina five, and Georgia three.

When vacancies happen in the Representation from any State, the Executive Authority thereof shall issue Writs of Election to fill such Vacancies.

The House of Representatives shall chuse their Speaker and other Officers; and shall have the sole Power of Impeachment.

SECTION. 3. The Senate of the United States shall be composed of two Senators from each State, chosen by the Legislature thereof, for six years; and each Senator shall have one Vote.

Immediately after they shall be assembled in Consequence of the first Election, they shall be divided as equally as may be into three Classes. The Seats of the Senators of the first Class shall be vacated at the Expiration of the second Year, of the second Class at the Expiration of the fourth Year, and of the third Class at the Expiration of the sixth Year, so that one third may be chosen every second year; and if Vacancies happen by Resignation, or otherwise, during the Recess of the Legislature of any State, the Executive thereof may make temporary Appointments until the next Meeting of the Legislature, which shall then fill such Vacancies.

No Person shall be a Senator who shall not have attained to the Age of thirty Years, and been nine Years a Citizen of the United States, and who shall not, when elected, be an Inhabitant of that State for which he shall be chosen.

The Vice President of the United States shall be President of the Senate, but shall have no Vote, unless they be equally divided.

The Senate shall chuse their other Officers, and also a President pro tempore, in the Absence of the Vice President, or when he shall exercise the Office of President of the United States.

The Senate shall have the sole Power to try all Impeachments. When sitting for that Purpose, they shall be on Oath or Affirmation. When the President of the United States is tried the Chief Justice shall preside: And no Person shall be convicted without the Concurrence of two thirds of the Members present.

Judgment in Cases of Impeachment shall not extend further than to removal from Office, and disqualification to hold and enjoy any Office of honor, Trust or Profit under the United States: but the Party convicted shall nevertheless be liable and subject to Indictment, Trial, Judgment and Punishment, according to Law.

SECTION. 4. The Times, Places and Manner of holding Elections for Senators and Representatives, shall be prescribed in each State by the Legislature thereof; but the Congress may at any time by Law make or alter such Regulations, except as to the Places of chusing Senators.

The Congress shall assemble at least once in every Year, and such Meeting shall be on the first Monday in December, unless they shall by Law appoint a different Day.

SECTION. 5. Each House shall be the Judge of the Elections, Returns and Qualifications of its own Members, and a Majority of each shall constitute a Quorum to do Business; but a smaller Number may adjourn from day to day, and may be authorized to compel the Attendance of absent Members, in such Manner, and under such Penalties as each House may provide.

Each House may determine the Rules of its Proceedings, punish its Members for disorderly Behaviour, and, with the Concurrence of two thirds, expel a Member.

Each House shall keep a Journal of its Proceedings, and from time to time publish the same, excepting such Parts as may in their Judgment require Secrecy; and the Yeas and Nays of the Members of either House on any question shall, at the Desire of one fifth of those Present, be entered on the Journal.

Neither House, during the Session of Congress, shall, without the Consent of the other, adjourn for more than three days, nor to any other Place than that in which the two Houses shall be sitting.

SECTION. 6. The Senators and Representatives shall receive a Compensation for their Services, to be ascertained by Law, and paid out of the Treasury of the United States. They shall in all Cases, except Treason, Felony and Breach of the Peace, be privileged from Arrest during their Attendance at the Session of their respective Houses, and in going to and returning from the same; and for any Speech or Debate in either House, they shall not be questioned in any other Place.

No Senator or Representative shall, during the Time for which he was elected, be appointed to any civil Office under the Authority of the United States, which shall have been created, or the Emoluments whereof shall have been encreased during such time; and no Person holding any Office under the United States, shall be a Member of either House during his Continuance in Office.

SECTION. 7. All Bills for raising Revenue shall originate in the House of Representatives; but the Senate may propose or concur with amendments as on other Bills.

Every Bill which shall have passed the House of Representatives and the Senate, shall, before it become a Law, be presented to the President of the United States; If he approve he shall sign it, but if not he shall return it, with his Objections to that House in which it shall have originated, who shall enter the Objections at large on their Journal, and proceed to reconsider it. If after such Reconsideration two thirds of that House shall agree to pass the Bill, it shall be sent, together with the Objections, to the other House, by which it shall likewise be reconsidered, and if approved by two thirds of that House, it shall become a Law. But in all such Cases the Votes of both Houses shall be determined by Yeas and Nays, and the Names of the Persons voting for and against the Bill shall be entered on the Journal of each House respectively. If any Bill shall not be returned by the President within ten Days (Sundays excepted) after it shall have been presented to him, the Same shall be a Law, in like Manner as if he had signed it, unless the Congress by their Adjournment prevent its Return, in which Case it shall not be a Law.

Every Order, Resolution, or Vote to which the Concurrence of the Senate and House of Representatives may be necessary (except on a question of Adjournment) shall be presented to the President of the United States; and before the Same shall take Effect, shall be approved by him, or being disapproved by him, shall be repassed by two thirds of the Senate and House of Representatives, according to the Rules and Limitations prescribed in the Case of a Bill.

SECTION. 8. The Congress shall have Power To lay and collect Taxes, Duties, Imposts and Excises, to pay the Debts and provide for the common Defence and general Welfare of the United States; but all Duties, Imposts and Excises shall be uniform throughout the United States;

To borrow Money on the credit of the United States;

To regulate Commerce with foreign Nations, and among the several States, and with the Indian Tribes;

To establish an uniform Rule of Naturalization, and uniform Laws on the subject of Bankruptcies throughout the United States;

To coin Money, regulate the Value thereof, and of foreign Coin, and fix the Standard of Weights and Measures;

To provide for the Punishment of counterfeiting the Securities and current Coin of the United States;

To establish Post Offices and post Roads;

To promote the Progress of Science and useful Arts, by securing for limited Times to Authors and Inventors the exclusive Right to their respective Writings and Discoveries;

To constitute Tribunals inferior to the supreme Court;

To define and punish Piracies and Felonies committed on the high Seas, and Offences against the Law of Nations;

To declare War, grant Letters of Marque and Reprisal, and make Rules concerning Captures on Land and Water;

To raise and support Armies, but no Appropriation of Money to that Use shall be for a longer Term than two Years;

To provide and maintain a Navy;

To make Rules for the Government and Regulation of the land and naval Forces;

To provide for calling forth the Militia to execute the Laws of the Union, suppress Insurrections and repel Invasions;

To provide for organizing, arming, and disciplining, the Militia, and for governing such Part of them as may be employed in the Service of the United States, reserving to the States respectively, the Appointment of the Officers, and the Authority of training the Militia according to the discipline prescribed by Congress;

To exercise exclusive Legislation in all Cases whatsoever, over such District (not exceeding ten Miles square) as may, by Cession of Particular States, and the Acceptance of Congress, become the Seat of the Government of the United States, and to exercise like Authority over all Places purchased by the Consent of the Legislature of the State in which the Same shall be, for the Erection of Forts, Magazines, Arsenals, dock-Yards, and other needful Buildings;—And

To make all Laws which shall be necessary and proper for carrying into Execution the foregoing Powers, and all other Powers vested by this Constitution in the Government of the United States, or in any Department or Officer thereof.

SECTION. 9. The Migration or Importation of such Persons as any of the States now existing shall think proper to admit, shall not be prohibited by the Congress prior to the Year one thousand eight hundred and eight, but a Tax or duty may be imposed on such Importation, not exceeding ten dollars for each Person.

The Privilege of the Writ of Habeas Corpus shall not be suspended, unless when in Cases of Rebellion or Invasion the public Safety may require it.

No Bill of Attainder or ex post facto Law shall be passed.

No Capitation, or other direct, Tax shall be laid, unless in Proportion to the Census or Enumeration herein before directed to be taken.

No Tax or Duty shall be laid on Articles exported from any State.

No Preference shall be given by any Regulation or Commerce or Revenue to the Ports of one State over those of another; nor shall Vessels bound to, or from, one State, be obliged to enter, clear or pay Duties in another.

No Money shall be drawn from the Treasury, but in Consequence of Appropriations made by Law; and a regular Statement and Account of the Receipts and Expenditures of all public Money shall be published from time to time.

No Title of Nobility shall be granted by the United States: And no Person holding any Office of Profit or Trust under them, shall, without the Consent of the Congress, accept of any present Emolument, Office, or Title, of any kind whatever, from any King, Prince, or foreign State.

SECTION. 10. No State shall enter into any Treaty, Alliance, or Confederation; grant Letters of Marque and Reprisal; coin Money; emit Bills of Credit; make any Thing but gold and silver Coin a Tender in Payment of Debts; pass any Bill of Attainder, ex post facto Law, or Law impairing the Obligation of Contracts, or grant any Title of Nobility.

No State shall, without the Consent of the Congress, lay any Imposts or Duties on Imports or Exports, except what may be absolutely necessary for executing its inspection Laws: and the net Produce of all Duties and Imposts, laid by any State on Imports or Exports, shall be for the Use of the Treasury of the United States; and all such Laws shall be subject to the Revision and Controul of the Congress.

No state shall, without the Consent of Congress, lay any Duty of Tonnage, keep Troops, or Ships of War in time of Peace, enter into any Agreement or Compact with another State, or with a foreign Power, or engage in War, unless actually invaded, or in such imminent Danger as will not admit of delay.

ARTICLE. II.

SECTION. 1. The executive Power shall be vested in a President of the United States of America. He shall hold his Office during the Term of four Years, and, together with the Vice President, chosen for the same Term, be elected as follows

Each State shall appoint, in such Manner as the Legislature thereof may direct, a Number of Electors, equal to the whole Number of Senators and Representatives to which the State may be entitled in the Congress: but no Senator or Representative, or Person holding an Office of Trust or Profit under the United States, shall be appointed an Elector.

The Electors shall meet in their respective States, and vote by Ballot for two Persons, of whom one at least shall not be an Inhabitant of the same State with themselves. And they shall make a List of all the persons voted for, and of the Number of Votes for each; which List they shall sign and certify, and transmit sealed to the Seat of Government of the United States, directed to the President of the Senate. The President of the Senate shall, in the Presence of the Senate and House of Representatives, open all the Certificates, and theVotes shall then be counted. The Person having the greatest Number of Votes shall be the President, if such Number be a Majority of the whole Number of Electors appointed; and if there be more than one who have such Majority, and have an equal Number of Votes, then the House of Representatives shall immediately chuse by Ballot one of them for President; and if no Person have a Majority, then from the five highest on the List the said House shall in like Manner chuse the President. But in chusing the President, the Votes shall be taken by States, the Representation from each State having one Vote; a quorum for this Purpose shall consist of a Member or Members from two thirds of the States, and a Majority of all the States shall be necessary to a Choice. In every Case, after the Choice of the President, the Person having the greatest Number of Votes of the Electors shall be the Vice President. But if there should remain two or more who have equal Votes, the Senate shall chuse from them by Ballot the Vice President.

The Congress may determine the Time of chusing the Electors, and the Day on which they shall give their Votes; which Day shall be the same throughout the United States.

No Person except a natural born Citizen, or a Citizen of the United States, at the time of the Adoption of this Constitution, shall be eligible to the Office of President; neither shall any person be eligible to that Office who shall not have attained to the Age of thirty five Years, and been fourteen Years a Resident within the United States.

In Case of the Removal of the President from Office, or of his Death, Resignation, or Inability to discharge the Powers and Duties of the said Office, the Same shall devolve on the Vice President, and the Congress may by Law provide for the Case of Removal, Death, Resignation or Inability, both of the President and Vice President, declaring what Officer shall then act as President, and such Officer shall act accordingly, until the Disability be removed, or a President shall be elected.

The President shall, at stated Times, receive for his Services, a Compensation, which shall neither be encreased nor diminished during the Period for which he shall have been elected, and he shall not receive within that period any other Emolument from the United States, or any of them.

Before he enter on the Execution of his Office, he shall take the following Oath or Affirmation:—"I do solemnly swear (or affirm) that I will faithfully execute the Office of President of the United States, and will to the best of my Ability, preserve, protect and defend the Constitution of the United States."

SECTION. 2. The President shall be Commander in Chief of the Army and Navy of the United States, and of the Militia of the several States, when called into the actual Service of the United States; he may require the Opinion, in writing, of the principal Officer in each of the executive Departments, upon any Subject relating to the Duties of their respective Offices, and he shall have Power to grant Reprieves and Pardons for Offences against the United States, except in Cases of Impeachment.

He shall have Power, by and with the Advice and Consent of the Senate, to make Treaties, provided two thirds of the Senators present concur; and he shall nominate, and by and with the Advice and Consent of the Senate, shall appoint Ambassadors, other public Ministers and Consuls, Judges of the supreme Court, and all other Officers of the United States, whose Appointments are not herein otherwise provided for, and which shall be established by Law: but the Congress may by Law vest the Appointment of such inferior Officers, as they think proper, in the President alone, in the Courts of Law, or in the Heads of Departments.

The President shall have Power to fill up all Vacancies that may happen during the Recess of the Senate, by granting Commissions which shall expire at the End of their next Session.

SECTION. 3. He shall from time to time give to the Congress Information of the State of the Union, and recommend to their Consideration such Measures as he shall judge necessary and expedient; he may, on extraordinary Occasions, convene both Houses, or either of them, and in Case of Disagreement between them, with Respect to the Time of Adjournment, he may adjourn them to such Time as he shall think proper; he shall receive Ambassadors and other public Ministers; he shall take Care that the Laws be faithfully executed, and shall Commission all the Officers of the United States.

SECTION. 4. The President, Vice President and all civil Officers of the United States, shall be removed from Office on Impeachment for, and Conviction of, Treason, Bribery, or other high Crimes and Misdemeanors.

ARTICLE. III.

SECTION. 1. The judicial Power of the United States, shall be vested in one supreme Court, and in such inferior Courts as the Congress may from time to time ordain and establish. The Judges, both of the supreme and inferior Courts, shall hold their Offices during good Behaviour, and shall, at stated Times, receive for their Services, a Compensation, which shall not be diminished during their Continuance in Office.

SECTION. 2. The judicial Power shall extend to all Cases, in Law and Equity, arising under this Constitution, the Laws of the United States, and Treaties made, or which shall be made, under their Authority;—to all Cases affecting Ambassadors, other public Ministers and Consuls;—to all Cases of admiralty and maritime Jurisdiction;—to Controversies to which the United States shall be a Party;—to Controversies between two or more States;—between a State and Citizens of another State;—between Citizens of different States;—between Citizens of the same State claiming Lands under Grants of different States, and between a State, or the Citizens thereof, and foreign States, Citizens or Subjects.

In all Cases affecting Ambassadors, other public Ministers and Consuls, and those in which a State shall be Party, the supreme Court shall have original Jurisdiction. In all the other Cases before mentioned, the supreme Court shall have appellate Jurisdiction, both as to Law and Fact, with such Exceptions, and under such Regulations as the Congress shall make.

The Trial of all Crimes, except in Cases of Impeachment, shall be by Jury; and such Trial shall be held in the State where the said Crimes shall have been committed; but when not committed within any State, the Trial shall be at such Place or Places as the Congress may by Law have directed.

SECTION. 3. Treason against the United States, shall consist only in levying War against them, or in adhering to their Enemies, giving them Aid and Comfort. No Person shall be convicted of Treason unless on the Testimony of two Witnesses to the same overt Act, or on Confession in open Court.

The Congress shall have Power to declare the Punishment of Treason, but no Attainder of Treason shall work Corruption of Blood, or Forfeiture except during the Life of the Person attained.

ARTICLE. IV.

SECTION. 1. Full Faith and Credit shall be given in each State to the public Acts, Records, and judicial Proceedings of every other State. And the Congress may by general Laws prescribe the Manner in which such Acts, Record and Proceedings shall be proved, and the Effect thereof.

SECTION. 2. The Citizens of each State shall be entitled to all Privileges and Immunities of Citizens in the several States.

A Person charged in any State with Treason, Felony, or other Crime, who shall flee from Justice, and be found in another State, shall on Demand of the executive Authority of the State from which he fled, be delivered up, to be removed to the State having Jurisdiction of the Crime.

No Person held to Service or Labour in one State, under the Laws thereof, escaping into another, shall, in Consequence of any Law or Regulation therein, be discharged from such Service or Labour, but shall be delivered up on Claim of the Party to whom such Service or Labour may be due.

SECTION. 3. New States may be admitted by the Congress into this Union; but no new State shall be formed or erected within the Jurisdiction of any other State; nor any State be formed by the Junction of two or more States, or Parts of States, without the Consent of the Legislatures of the States concerned as well as of the Congress.

The Congress shall have Power to dispose of and make all needful Rules and Regulations respecting the Territory or other Property belonging to the United States; and nothing in this Constitution shall be so construed as to Prejudice any Claims of the United States, or of any particular State.

SECTION. 4. The United States shall guarantee to every State in this Union a Republican Form of Government, and shall protect each of them against Invasion; and on Application of the Legislature, or of the Executive (when the Legislature cannot be convened) against domestic Violence.

ARTICLE. V.

The Congress, whenever two thirds of both Houses shall deem it necessary, shall propose Amendments to this Constitution, or, on the Application of the Legislature of two thirds of the several States, shall call a Convention for proposing Amendments, which, in either Case, shall be valid to all Intents and Purposes, as Part of this Constitution, when ratified by the Legislatures of three fourths of the several States, or by Conventions in three fourths thereof, as the one or the other Mode of Ratification may be proposed by the Congress; Provided that no Amendment which may be made prior to the Year One thousand eight hundred and eight shall in any Manner affect the first and fourth Clauses in the Ninth Section of the first Article; and that no State, without its Consent, shall be deprived of its equal Suffrage in the Senate.

ARTICLE. VI.

All Debts contracted and Engagements entered into, before the Adoption of this Constitution, shall be as valid against the United States under this Constitution, as under the Confederation.

This Constitution, and the Laws of the United States which shall be made in Pursuance thereof; and all Treaties made, or which shall be made, under the Authority of the United States, shall be the supreme Law of the Land; and the Judges in every State shall be bound thereby, any Thing in the Constitution or Laws of any State to the Contrary notwithstanding.

The Senators and Representatives before mentioned, and the Members of the several State Legislatures, and all executive and judicial Officers, both of the United States and of the several States, shall be bound by Oath or Affirmation, to support this Constitution; but no religious Test shall ever be required as a Qualification to any Office or public Trust under the United States.

ARTICLE. VII.

The Ratification of the Conventions of nine States, shall be sufficient for the Establishment of this Constitution between the States so ratifying the Same.

Done in Convention by the Unanimous Consent of the States present the Seventeenth Day of September in the Year of our Lord one thousand seven hundred and Eighty seven and of the Independence of the United States of America the Twelfth In witness whereof We have hereunto subscribed our Names,

Go. WASHINGTON—Presidt. and deputy from Virginia

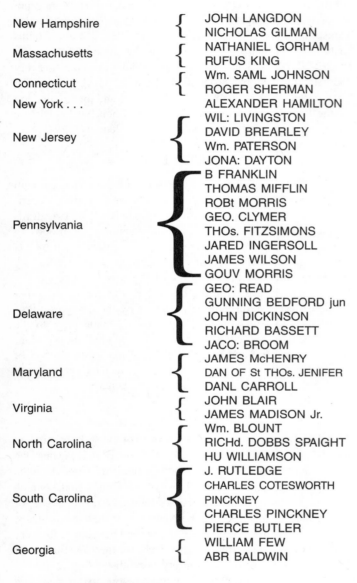

New Hampshire	{	JOHN LANGDON
		NICHOLAS GILMAN
Massachusetts	{	NATHANIEL GORHAM
		RUFUS KING
Connecticut	{	Wm. SAML JOHNSON
		ROGER SHERMAN
New York . . .		ALEXANDER HAMILTON
New Jersey	{	WIL: LIVINGSTON
		DAVID BREARLEY
		Wm. PATERSON
		JONA: DAYTON
Pennsylvania	{	B FRANKLIN
		THOMAS MIFFLIN
		ROBt MORRIS
		GEO. CLYMER
		THOs. FITZSIMONS
		JARED INGERSOLL
		JAMES WILSON
		GOUV MORRIS
Delaware	{	GEO: READ
		GUNNING BEDFORD jun
		JOHN DICKINSON
		RICHARD BASSETT
		JACO: BROOM
Maryland	{	JAMES McHENRY
		DAN OF St THOs. JENIFER
		DANL CARROLL
Virginia	{	JOHN BLAIR
		JAMES MADISON Jr.
North Carolina	{	Wm. BLOUNT
		RICHd. DOBBS SPAIGHT
		HU WILLIAMSON
South Carolina	{	J. RUTLEDGE
		CHARLES COTESWORTH PINCKNEY
		CHARLES PINCKNEY
		PIERCE BUTLER
Georgia	{	WILLIAM FEW
		ABR BALDWIN

In Convention Monday, September 17th 1787.
Present The States of
New Hampshire, Massachusetts, Connecticut, Mr. Hamilton from New York, New Jersey, Pennsylvania, Delaware, Maryland, Virginia, North Carolina and Georgia.

Resolved,

That the preceeding Constitution be laid before the United States in Congress assembled, and that it is the Opinion of this Convention, that it should afterwards be submitted to a Convention of Delegates, chosen in each State by the People thereof, under the Recommendation of its Legislature, for their Assent and Ratification; and that each Convention assenting to, and ratifying the Same, should give Notice thereof to the United States in Congress assembled. Resolved, That it is the Opinion of this Convention, that as soon as the Conventions of nine States shall have ratified this Constitution, the United States in Congress assembled should fix a Day on which Electors should be appointed by the States which shall have ratified the same, and a Day on which the Electors should assemble to vote for the President, and the Time and Place for commencing Proceedings under this Constitution. That after such Publication the Electors should be appointed, and the Senators and Representatives elected: That the Electors should meet on the Day fixed for the Election of the President, and should transmit their Votes certified, signed, sealed and directed, as the Constitution requires, to the Secretary of the United States in Congress assembled, that the Senators and Representatives should convene at the Time and Place assigned; that the Senators should appoint a President of the Senate, for the sole Purpose of receiving, opening and counting the Votes for President; and, that after he shall be chosen, the Congress, together with the President, should, without Delay, proceed to execute this Constitution.

By the Unanimous Order of the Convention
Go. WASHINGTON—Presidt.
W. JACKSON Secretary.

RATIFICATION OF THE CONSTITUTION

State	Date of ratification
Delaware	Dec 7, 1787
Pennsylvania	Dec 12, 1787
New Jersey	Dec 19, 1787
Georgia	Jan 2, 1788
Connecticut	Jan 9, 1788
Massachusetts	Feb 6, 1788
Maryland	Apr 28, 1788
South Carolina	May 23, 1788
New Hampshire	June 21, 1788
Virginia	Jun 25, 1788
New York	Jun 26, 1788
Rhode Island	May 29, 1790
North Carolina	Nov 21, 1789

ARTICLES IN ADDITION TO, AND AMENDMENT OF, THE CONSTITUTION OF THE UNITED STATES OF AMERICA, PROPOSED BY CONGRESS, AND RATIFIED BY THE SEVERAL STATES, PURSUANT TO THE FIFTH ARTICLE OF THE ORIGINAL CONSTITUTION.

AMENDMENT I.

Congress shall make no law respecting an establishment of religion, or prohibiting the free exercise thereof; or abridging the freedom of speech, or of the press; or the right of the people peaceably to assemble, and to petition the Government for a redress of grievances.

AMENDMENT II.

A well regulated Militia, being necessary to the security of a free State, the right of the people to keep and bear Arms, shall not be infringed.

AMENDMENT III.

No Soldier shall, in time of peace be quartered in any house, without the consent of the Owner, nor in time of war, but in a manner to be prescribed by law.

AMENDMENT IV.

The right of the people to be secure in their persons, houses, papers, and effects, against unreasonable searches and seizures, shall not be violated, and no Warrants shall issue, but upon probable cause, supported by Oath or affirmation, and particularly describing the place to be searched, and the persons or things to be seized.

AMENDMENT V.

No person shall be held to answer for a capital, or otherwise infamous crime, unless on a presentment or indictment of a Grand Jury, except in cases arising in the land or naval forces, or in the Militia, when in actual service in time of War or public danger; nor shall any person be subject for the same offence to be twice put in jeopardy of life or limb; nor shall be compelled in any criminal case to be a witness against himself, nor be deprived of life, liberty, or property, without due process of law; nor shall private property be taken for public use, without just compensation.

AMENDMENT VI.

In all criminal prosecutions, the accused shall enjoy the right to a speedy and public trial, by an impartial jury of the State and district wherein the crime shall have been committed, which district shall have been previously ascertained by law, and to be informed of the nature and cause of the accusation; to be confronted with the witnesses against him; to have compulsory process for obtaining witnesses in his favor, and to have the Assistance of Counsel for his defence.

AMENDMENT VII.

In Suits at common law, where the value in controversy shall exceed twenty dollars, the right of trial by jury shall be preserved, and no fact tried by a jury, shall be otherwise re-examined in any Court of the United States, than according to the rules of the common law.

AMENDMENT VIII.

Excessive bail shall not be required, nor excessive fines imposed, nor cruel and unusual punishments inflicted.

AMENDMENT IX.

The enumeration in the Constitution, of certain rights, shall not be construed to deny or disparage others retained by the people.

AMENDMENT X.

The powers not delegated to the United States by the Constitution, nor prohibited by it to the States, are reserved to the States respectively, or to the people.

AMENDMENT XI.

(Adopted Jan. 8, 1798)

The Judicial power of the United States shall not be construed to extend to any suit in law or equity, commenced or prosecuted against one of the United States by Citizens of another State, or by Citizens or Subjects of any Foreign State.

AMENDMENT XII.

(Adopted Sept. 25, 1804)

The Electors shall meet in their respective states and vote by ballot for President and Vice-President, one of whom, at least, shall not be an inhabitant of the same state with themselves; they shall name in their ballots the person voted for as President, and in distinct ballots the person voted for as Vice-President, and they shall make distinct lists of all persons voted for as President, and of all persons voted for as Vice-President, and of the number of votes for each, which lists they shall sign and certify, and transmit sealed to the seat of the government of the United States, directed to the President of the Senate;—The President of the Senate shall, in the presence of the Senate and House of Representatives, open all the certificates and the votes shall then be counted;—The person having the greatest number of votes for President, shall be the President, if such number be a majority of the whole number of Electors appointed; and if no person have such majority, then from the persons having the highest numbers not exceeding three on the list of those voted for as President, the House of Representatives shall choose immediately, by ballot, the President. But in choosing the President, the votes shall be taken by states, the representation from each state having one vote; a quorum for this purpose shall consist of a member or members from two-thirds of the states, and a majority of all the states shall be necessary to a choice. And if the House of Representatives shall not choose a President whenever the right of choice shall devolve upon them, before the fourth day of March next following, then the Vice-President shall act as President, as in the case of the death or other constitutional disability of the President.—The person having the greatest number of votes as Vice-President, shall be the Vice-President, if such number be a majority of the whole number of Electors appointed, and if no person have a majority, then from the two highest numbers on the list, the Senate shall choose the Vice-President; a quorum for the purpose shall consist of two-thirds of the whole number of Senators, and a majority of the whole number shall be necessary to a choice. But no person constitutionally ineligible to the office of President shall be eligible to that of Vice-President of the United States.

AMENDMENT XIII.

(Adopted Dec. 18, 1865)

SECTION 1. Neither slavery nor involuntary servitude, except as a punishment for crime whereof the party shall have been duly convicted, shall exist within the United States, or any place subject to their jurisdiction.

SECTION 2. Congress shall have power to enforce this article by appropriate legislation.

AMENDMENT XIV.

(Adopted July 28, 1868)

SECTION 1. All persons born or naturalized in the United States and subject to the jurisdiction thereof, are citizens of the United States and of the State wherein they reside. No State shall make or enforce any law which shall abridge the privileges or immunities of citizens of the United States; nor shall any State deprive any person of life, liberty, or property, without due process of law; nor deny to any person within its jurisdiction the equal protection of the laws.

SECTION 2. Representatives shall be apportioned among the several States according to their respective numbers, counting the whole number of persons in each State, excluding Indians not taxed. But when the right to vote at any election for the choice of electors for President and Vice President of the United States, Representatives in Congress, the Executive and Judicial officers of a State, or the members of the Legislature thereof, is denied to any of the male inhabitants of such State, being twenty-one years of age, and citizens of the United States, or in any way abridged, except for participation in rebellion, or other crime, the basis of representation therein shall be reduced in the proportion which the number of such male citizens shall bear to the whole number of male citizens twenty-one years of age in such State.

SECTION 3. No person shall be a Senator or Representative in Congress, or elector of President and Vice President, or hold any office, civil or military, under the United States, or under any State, who, having previously taken an oath, as a member of Congress, or as an officer of the United States, or as a member of any State legislature, or as an executive or judicial officer of any State, to support the Constitution of the United States, shall have engaged in insurrection or rebellion against the same, or given aid or comfort to the enemies thereof. But Congress may by a vote of two-thirds of each House, remove such disability.

SECTION 4. The validity of the public debt of the United States, authorized by law, including debts incurred for payment of pensions and bounties for services in suppressing insurrection or rebellion, shall not be questioned. But neither the United States nor any State shall assume or pay any debt or obligation incurred in aid of insurrection or rebellion against the United States, or any claim for the loss or emancipation of any slave; but all such debts, obligations and claims shall be held illegal and void.

SECTION 5. The Congress shall have power to enforce, by appropriate legislation, the provisions of this article.

AMENDMENT XV.

(Adopted March 30, 1870)

SECTION 1. The right of citizens of the United States to vote shall not be denied or abridged by the United States or by any State on account of race, color, or previous condition of servitude.

SECTION 2. The Congress shall have power to enforce this article by appropriate legislation.

AMENDMENT XVI.

(Adopted Feb. 25, 1913)

The Congress shall have power to lay and collect taxes on incomes, from whatever source derived, without apportionment among the several States, and without regard to any census or enumeration.

AMENDMENT XVII.

(Adopted May 31, 1913)

The Senate of the United States shall be composed of two Senators from each State, elected by the people thereof, for six years; and each Senator shall have one vote. The electors in each State shall have the qualifications requisite for electors of the most numerous branch of the State legislatures.

When vacancies happen in the representation of any State in the Senate, the executive authority of such State shall issue writs of election to fill such vacancies: *Provided,* That the legislature of any State may empower the executive thereof to make temporary appointments until the people fill the vacancies by election as the legislature may direct.

This amendment shall not be so construed as to affect the election or term of any Senator chosen before it becomes valid as part of the Constitution.

AMENDMENT XVIII.

(Adopted Jan. 29, 1919)

SECTION 1. After one year from the ratification of this article the manufacture, sale or transportation of intoxicating liquors within, the importation thereof into, or the exportation thereof from the United States and all territory subject to the jurisdiction thereof for beverage purposes is hereby prohibited.

SECTION 2. The Congress and the several States shall have concurrent power to enforce this article by appropriate legislation.

SECTION 3. This article shall be inoperative unless it shall have been ratified as an amendment to the Constitution by the legislatures of the several States, as provided in the Constitution, within seven years from the date of the submission hereof to the States by the Congress.

AMENDMENT XIX.

(Adopted Aug. 26, 1920)

The right of citizens of the United States to vote shall not be denied or abridged by the United States or by any State on account of sex.

Congress shall have power to enforce this article by appropriate legislation.

AMENDMENT XX.

(Adopted Feb. 6, 1933)

SECTION 1. The terms of the President and Vice President shall end at noon on the 20th day of January, and the terms of Senators and Representatives at noon on the 3d day of January, of the years in which such terms would have ended if this article had not been ratified; and the terms of their successors shall then begin.

SECTION 2. The Congress shall assemble at least once in every year, and such meeting shall begin at noon on the 3d day of January, unless they shall by law appoint a different day.

SECTION 3. If, at the time fixed for the beginning of the term of the President, the President elect shall have died, the Vice President elect shall become President. If a President shall not have been chosen before the time fixed for the beginning of his term, or if the President elect shall have failed to qualify, then the Vice President elect shall act as President until a President shall have qualified; and the Congress may by law provide for the case wherein neither a President elect nor a Vice President elect shall have qualified, declaring who shall then act as President, or the manner in which one who is to act shall be selected, and such person shall act accordingly until a President or Vice President shall have qualified.

SECTION 4. The Congress may by law provide for the case of the death of any of the persons from whom the House of Representatives may choose a President whenever the right of choice shall have devolved upon them, and for the case of the death of any of the persons from whom the Senate may choose a Vice President whenever the right of choice shall have devolved upon them.

SECTION 5. Sections 1 and 2 shall take effect on the 15th day of October following the ratification of this article.

SECTION 6. This article shall be inoperative unless it shall have been ratified as an amendment to the Constitution by the legislatures of three-fourths of the several States within seven years from the date of its submission.

AMENDMENT XXI.

(Adopted Dec. 5, 1933)

SECTION 1. The eighteenth article of amendment to the Constitution of the United States is hereby repealed.

SECTION 2. The transportation or importation into any State, Territory, or possession of the United States for delivery or use therein of intoxicating liquors, in violation of the laws thereof, is hereby prohibited.

SECTION 3. This article shall be inoperative unless it shall have been ratified as an amendment to the Constitution by conventions in the several States, as provided in the Constitution, within seven years from the date of the submission hereof to the States by the Congress.

AMENDMENT XXII.

(Adopted Feb. 27, 1951)

SECTION 1. No person shall be elected to the office of the President more than twice, and no person who has held the office of President, or acted as President, for more than two years of a term to which some other person was elected President shall be elected to the office of the President more than once. But this Article shall not apply to any person holding the office of President when this Article was proposed by the Congress, and shall not prevent any person who may be holding the office of President, or acting as President, during the term within which this Article becomes operative from holding the office of President or acting as President during the remainder of such term.

SECTION 2. This Article shall be inoperative unless it shall have been ratified as an amendment to the Constitution by the legislatures of three-fourths of the several States within seven years from the date of its submission to the States by the Congress.

AMENDMENT XXIII.

(Adopted Mar. 29, 1961)

SECTION 1. The District constituting the seat of Government of the United States shall appoint in such manner as the Congress may direct:

A number of electors of President and Vice President equal to the whole number of Senators and Representatives in Congress to which the District would be entitled if it were a State, but in no event more than the least populous State; they shall be in addition to those appointed by the States, but they shall be considered, for the purposes of the election of President and Vice President, to be electors appointed by a State; and they shall meet in the District and perform such duties as provided by the twelfth article of amendment.

SECTION 2. The Congress shall have power to enforce this article by appropriate legislation.

AMENDMENT XXIV.

(Adopted Jan. 23, 1964)

SECTION 1. The right of citizens of the United States to vote in any primary or other election for President or Vice President, for electors for President or Vice President, or for Senator or Representative in Congress, shall not be denied or abridged by the United States or any State by reason of failure to pay any poll tax or other tax.

SECTION 2. The Congress shall have the power to enforce this article by appropriate legislation.

AMENDMENT XXV.

(Adopted Feb. 10, 1967)

SECTION 1. In case of the removal of the President from office or of his death or resignation, the Vice President shall become President.

SECTION 2. Whenever there is a vacancy in the office of the Vice President, the President shall nominate a Vice President who shall take the office upon confirmation by a majority vote of both houses of Congress.

SECTION 3. Whenever the President transmits to the President pro tempore of the Senate and the Speaker of the House of Representatives his written declaration that he is unable to discharge the powers and duties of his office, and until he transmits to them a written declaration to the contrary, such powers and duties shall be discharged by the Vice President as Acting President.

SECTION 4. Whenever the Vice President and a majority of either the principal officers of the executive departments or of such other body as Congress may by law provide, transmit to the President pro tempore of the Senate and the Speaker of the House of Representatives their written declaration that the President is unable to discharge the powers and duties of his office, the Vice President shall immediately assume the powers and duties of the office as Acting President.

Thereafter, when the President transmits to the President pro tempore of the Senate and the Speaker of the House of Representatives his written declaration that no inability exists, he shall resume the powers and duties of his office unless the Vice President and a majority of either the principal officers of the executive department or of such other body as Congress may by law provide, transmit within four days to the President pro tempore of the Senate and the Speaker of the House of Representatives their written declaration that the President is unable to discharge the powers and duties of his office. Thereupon Congress shall decide the issue, assembling within forty-eight hours for that purpose if not in session. If the Congress within twenty-one days after receipt of the latter written declaration, or, if Congress is not in session, within twenty-one days after Congress is required to assemble, determines by two-thirds vote of both Houses that the President is unable to discharge the powers and duties of his office, the Vice President shall continue to discharge the same as Acting President; otherwise, the President shall resume the powers and duties of his office.

AMENDMENT XXVI.

(Adopted June 30, 1971)

SECTION 1. The right of citizens of the United States, who are 18 years of age or older, to vote shall not be denied or abridged by the United States or by any state on account of age.

SECTION 2. The Congress shall have the power to enforce this article by appropriate legislation.

AMENDMENT XXVII.

(Adopted May 7, 1992)

No law, varying the compensation for the services of the Senators and Representatives, shall take effect, until an election of Representatives shall have intervened.

THE SIZE AND VARIETY OF THE UNION AS A CHECK ON FACTION

FEDERALIST NO. 10

(MADISON)

To the People of the State of New York:

AMONG the numerous advantages promised by a well-constructed Union, none deserves to be more accurately developed than its tendency to break and control the violence of faction. The friend of popular governments never finds himself so much alarmed for their character and fate, as when he contemplates their propensity to this dangerous vice. He will not fail, therefore, to set a due value on any plan which, without violating the principles to which he is attached, provides a proper cure for it. The instability, injustice, and confusion introduced into the public councils, have, in truth, been the mortal diseases under which popular governments have everywhere perished; as they continue to be the favorite and fruitful topics from which the adversaries to liberty derive their most specious declamations. The valuable improvements made by the American constitutions on the popular models, both ancient and modern, cannot certainly be too much admired; but it would be an unwarrantable partiality, to contend that they have as effectually obviated the danger on this side, as was wished and expected. Complaints are everywhere heard from our most considerate and virtuous citizens, equally the friends of public and private faith, and of public and personal liberty, that our governments are too unstable, that the public good is disregarded in the conflicts of rival parties, and that measures are too often decided, not according to the rules of justice and the rights of the minor party, but by the superior force of an interested and overbearing majority. However anxiously we may wish that these complaints had no foundation, the evidence of known facts will not permit us to deny that they are in some degree true. It will be found, indeed, on a candid review of our situation, that some of the distresses under which we labor have been erroneously charged on the operation of our governments; but it will be found, at the same time, that other causes will not alone account for many of our heaviest misfortunes; and, particularly, for that prevailing and increasing distrust of public engagements, and alarm for private rights, which are echoed from one end of the continent to the other. These must be chiefly, if not wholly, effects of the unsteadiness and injustice with which a factious spirit has tainted our public administrations.

By a faction, I understand a number of citizens, whether amounting to a majority or minority of the whole, who are united and actuated by some common impulse of passion, or of interest, adverse to the rights of other citizens, or to the permanent and aggregate interests of the community.

There are two methods of curing the mischiefs of faction: the one, by removing its causes; the other, by controlling its effects.

There are again two methods of removing the causes of faction: the one, by destroying the liberty which is essential to its existence; the other, by giving to every citizen the same opinions, the same passions, and the same interests.

It could never be more truly said than of the first remedy, that it was worse than the disease. Liberty is to faction what air is to fire, an aliment without which it instantly expires. But it could not be less folly to abolish liberty, which is essential to political life, because it nourishes faction, than it would be to wish the annihilation of air, which is essential to animal life, because it imparts to fire its destructive agency.

The second expedient is as impracticable as the first would be unwise. As long as the reason of man continues fallible, and he is at liberty to exercise it, different opinions will be formed. As long as the connection subsists between his reason and his self-love, his opinions and his passions will have a reciprocal influence on each other; and the former will be objects to which the latter will attach themselves. The diversity in the faculties of men, from which the rights of property originate, is not less an insuperable obstacle to a uniformity of interests. The protection of these faculties is the first object of government. From the protection of different and unequal faculties of acquiring property, the possession of different degrees and kinds of property immediately results; and from the influence of these on the sentiments and views of the respective proprietors, ensues a division of the society into different interests and parties.

The latent causes of faction are thus sown in the nature of man; and we see them everywhere brought into different degrees of activity, according to the different circumstances of civil society. A zeal for different opinions concerning religion, concerning government, and many other points, as well of speculation as of practice; an attachment to different leaders ambitiously contending for pre-eminence and power; or to persons of other descriptions whose fortunes have been interesting to the human passions, have, in turn, divided mankind into parties, inflamed them with mutual animosity, and rendered them much more disposed to vex and oppress each other than to co-operate for their common good. So strong is this propensity of mankind to fall into mutual animosities, that where no substantial occasion presents itself, the most frivolous and fanciful distinctions have been sufficient to kindle their unfriendly passions and excite their most violent conflicts. But the most common and durable source of factions has been the various and unequal distribution of property. Those who hold and those who are without property have ever formed distinct interests in society.

Those who are creditors, and those who are debtors, fall under a like discrimination. A landed interest, a manufacturing interest, a mercantile interest, a moneyed interest, with many lesser interests, grow up of necessity in civilized nations, and divide them into different classes, actuated by different sentiments and views. The regulation of these various and interfering interests forms the principal task of modern legislation, and involves the spirit of party and faction in the necessary and ordinary operations of the government.

No man is allowed to be a judge in his own cause, because his interest would certainly bias his judgment, and, not improbably, corrupt his integrity. With equal, nay with greater reason, a body of men are unfit to be both judges and parties at the same time; yet what are many of the most important acts of legislation, but so many judicial determinations, not indeed concerning the rights of single persons, but concerning the rights of large bodies of citizens? And what are the different classes of legislators but advocates and parties to the causes which they determine? Is a law proposed concerning private debts? It is a question to which the creditors are parties on one side and the debtors on the other. Justice ought to hold the balance between them. Yet the parties are, and must be, themselves the judges; and the most numerous party, or, in other words, the most powerful faction must be expected to prevail. Shall domestic manufactures be encouraged, and in what degree, by restrictions on foreign manufactures? are questions which would be differently decided by the landed and the manufacturing classes, and probably by neither with a sole regard to justice and the public good. The apportionment of taxes on the various descriptions of property is an act which seems to require the most exact impartiality; yet there is, perhaps, no legislative act in which greater opportunity and temptation are given to a predominant party to trample on the rules of justice. Every shilling with which they overburden the inferior number, is a shilling saved to their own pockets.

It is in vain to say that enlightened statesmen will be able to adjust these clashing interests, and render them all subservient to the public good. Enlightened statesmen will not always be at the helm. Nor, in many cases, can such an adjustment be made at all without taking into view indirect and remote considerations, which will rarely prevail over the immediate interest which one party may find in disregarding the rights of another or the good of the whole.

The inference to which we are brought is, that the *causes* of faction cannot be removed, and that relief is only to be sought in the means of controlling its *effects.*

If a faction consists of less than a majority, relief is supplied by the republican principle, which enables the majority to defeat its sinister views by regular vote. It may clog the administration, it may convulse the society; but it will be unable to execute and mask its violence under the forms of the

Constitution. When a majority is included in a faction, the form of popular government, on the other hand, en-

3. Size and Variety of the Union

ables it to sacrifice to its ruling passion or interest both the public good and the rights of other citizens. To secure the public good and private rights against the danger of such a faction, and at the same time to preserve the spirit and the form of popular government, is then the great object to which our inquiries are directed. Let me add that it is the great desideratum by which this form of government can be rescued from the opprobrium under which it has so long labored, and be recommended to the esteem and adoption of mankind.

By what means is this object attainable? Evidently by one of two only. Either the existence of the same passion or interest in a majority at the same time must be prevented, or the majority, having such coexistent passion or interest, must be rendered, by their number and local situation, unable to concert and carry into effect schemes of oppression. If the impulse and the opportunity be suffered to coincide, we well know that neither moral nor religious motives can be relied on as an adequate control. They are not found to be such on the injustice and violence of individuals, and lose their efficacy in proportion to the number combined together, that is, in proportion as their efficacy becomes needful.

From this view of the subject it may be concluded that a pure democracy, by which I mean a society consisting of a small number of citizens, who assemble and administer the government in person, can admit of no cure for the mischiefs of faction. A common passion or interest will, in almost every case, be felt by a majority of the whole; a communication and concert result from the form of government itself; and there is nothing to check the inducements to sacrifice the weaker party or an obnoxious individual. Hence it is that such democracies have ever been spectacles of turbulence and contention; have ever been found incompatible with personal security or the rights of property; and have in general been as short in their lives as they have been violent in their deaths. Theoretic politicians, who have patronized this species of government, have erroneously supposed that by reducing mankind to a perfect equality in their political rights, they would, at the same time, be perfectly equalized and assimilated in their possessions, their opinions, and their passions.

A republic, by which I mean a government in which the scheme of representation takes place, opens a different prospect, and promises the cure for which we are seeking. Let us examine the points in which it varies from pure democracy, and we shall comprehend both the nature of the cure and the efficacy which it must derive from the Union.

The two great points of difference between a democracy and a republic are: first, the delegation of the government, in the latter, to a small number of citizens elected by the rest; secondly, the greater number of citizens, and greater sphere of country, over which the latter may be extended.

The effect of the first difference is, on the one hand, to refine and enlarge the public views, by passing them through the medium of a chosen body of citizens, whose wisdom may best discern the true interest of their country, and whose patriotism and love of justice will be least likely to sacrifice it to temporary or partial considerations. Under such a regulation, it may well happen that the public voice, pronounced by the representatives of the people, will be more consonant to the public good than if pronounced by the people themselves, convened for the purpose. On the other hand, the effect may be inverted. Men of factious tempers, of local prejudices, or of sinister designs, may, by intrigue, by corruption, or by other means, first obtain the suffrages, and then betray the interests, of the people. The question resulting is, whether small or extensive republics are more favorable to the election of proper guardians of the public weal; and it is clearly decided in favor of the latter by two obvious considerations:

In the first place, it is to be remarked that, however small the republic may be, the representatives must be raised to a certain number, in order to guard against the cabals of a few; and that, however large it may be, they must be limited to a certain number, in order to guard against the confusion of a multitude. Hence, the number of representatives in the two cases not being in proportion to that of the two constituents, and being proportionally greater in the small republic, it follows that, if the proportion of fit characters be not less in the large than in the small republic, the former will present a greater option, and consequently a greater probability of a fit choice.

In the next place, as each representative will be chosen by a greater number of citizens in the large than in the small republic, it will be more difficult for unworthy candidates to practise with success the vicious arts by which elections are too often carried; and the suffrages of the people being more free, will be more likely to centre in men who possess the most attractive merit and the most diffusive and established characters.

It must be confessed that in this, as in most other cases, there is a mean, on both sides of which inconveniences will be found to lie. By enlarging too much the number of electors, you render the representative too little acquainted with all their local circumstances and lesser interests; as by reducing it too much, you render him unduly attached to these, and too little fit to comprehend and pursue great and national objects. The federal Constitution forms a happy combination in this respect; the great and aggregate interests being referred to the national, the local and particular to the State legislatures.

The other point of difference is, the greater number of citizens and extent of territory which may be brought within the compass of republican than of democratic government; and it is this circumstance principally which renders factious combinations less to be dreaded in the former than in the latter. The smaller the society, the fewer probably will be the distinct parties and interests composing it; the fewer the distinct parties and interests, the more frequently will a majority be found of the same party; and the smaller the number of individuals composing a majority, and the smaller the compass within which they are placed, the more easily will they concert and execute their plans of oppression. Extend the sphere and you take in a greater variety of parties and interests; you will make it less probable that a majority of the whole will have a common motive to invade the rights of other citizens; or if such a common motive exists, it will be more difficult for all who feel it to discover their own strength, and to act in unison with each other. Besides other impediments, it may be remarked that, where there is a consciousness of unjust or dishonorable purposes, communication is always checked by distrust in proportion to the number whose concurrence is necessary.

Hence, it clearly appears, that the same advantage which a republic has over a democracy, in controlling the effects of faction, is enjoyed by a large over a small republic,—is enjoyed by the Union over the States composing it. Does the advantage consist in the substitution of representatives whose enlightened views and virtuous sentiments render them superior to local prejudices and to schemes of injustice? It will not be denied that the representation of the Union will be most likely to possess these requisite endowments. Does it consist in the greater security afforded by a greater variety of parties, against the event of any one party being able to outnumber and oppress the rest? In an equal degree does the increased variety of parties comprised within the Union, increase this security. Does it, in fine, consist in the greater obstacles opposed to the concert and accomplishment of the secret wishes of an unjust and interested majority? Here, again, the extent of the Union gives it the most palpable advantage.

The influence of factious leaders may kindle a flame within their particular States, but will be unable to spread a general conflagration through the other States. A religious sect may degenerate into a political faction in a part of the Confederacy; but the variety of sects dispersed over the entire face of it must secure the national councils against any danger from that source. A rage for paper money, for an abolition of debts, for an equal division of property, or for any other improper or wicked project, will be less apt to pervade the whole body of the Union than a particular member of it; in the same proportion as such a malady is more likely to taint a particular county or distinct, than an entire State.

In the extent and proper structure of the Union, therefore, we behold a republican remedy for the diseases most incident to republican government. And according to the degree of pleasure and pride we feel in being republicans, ought to be our zeal in cherishing the spirit and supporting the character of Federalists.

PUBLIUS

CHECKS AND BALANCES

FEDERALIST NO. 51

(MADISON)

To the People of the State of New York:

To what expedient, then, shall we finally resort, for maintaining in practice the necessary partition of power among the several departments, as laid down in the Constitution? The only answer that can be given is, that as all these exterior provisions are found to be inadequate, the defect must be supplied, by so contriving the interior structure of the government as that its several constituent parts may, by their mutual relations, be the means of keeping each other in their proper places. Without presuming to undertake a full development of this important idea, I will hazard a few general observations, which may perhaps place it in a clearer light, and enable us to form a more correct judgment of the principles and structure of the government planned by the convention.

In order to lay a due foundation for that separate and distinct exercise of the different powers of government, which to a certain extent is admitted on all hands to be essential to the preservation of liberty, it is evident that each department should have a will of its own; and consequently should be so constituted that the members of each should have as little agency as possible in the appointment of the members of the others. Were this principle rigorously adhered to, it would require that all the appointments for the supreme executive, legislative, and judiciary magistracies should be drawn from the same fountain of authority, the people, through channels having no communication whatever with one another. Perhaps such a plan of constructing the several departments would be less difficult in practice than it may in contemplation appear. Some difficulties, however, and some additional expense would attend the execution of it. Some deviations, therefore, from the principle must be admitted. In the constitution of the judiciary department in particular, it might be inexpedient to insist rigorously on the principle: first, because peculiar qualifications being essential in the members, the primary consideration ought to be to select that mode of choice which best secures these qualifications; secondly, because the permanent tenure by which the appointments are held in that department, must soon destroy all sense of dependence on the authority conferring them.

It is equally evident, that the members of each department should be as little dependent as possible on those of the others, for the emoluments annexed to their offices. Were the executive magistrate, or the judges, not independent of the legislature in this particular, their independence in every other would be merely nominal.

But the great security against a gradual concentration of the several powers in the same department, consists in giving to those who administer each department the necessary constitutional means and personal motives to resist encroachments of the others. The provision for defence must in this, as in all other cases, be made commensurate to the danger of attack. Ambition must be made to counteract ambition. The interest of the man must be connected with the constitutional rights of the place. It may be a reflection on human nature, that such devices should be necessary to control the abuses of government. But what is government itself, but the greatest of all reflections on human nature? If men were angels, no government would be necessary. If angels were to govern men, neither external nor internal controls on government would be necessary. In framing a government which is to be administered by men over men, the great difficulty lies in this: you must first enable the government to control the governed; and in the next place oblige it to control itself. A dependence on the people is, no doubt, the primary control on the government; but experience has taught mankind the necessity of auxiliary precautions.

This policy of supplying, by opposite and rival interests, the defect of better motives, might be traced through the whole system of human affairs, private as well as public. We see it particularly displayed in all the subordinate distributions of power, where the constant aim is to divide and arrange the several offices in such a manner as that each may be a check on the other—that the private interest of every individual may be a sentinel over the public rights. These inventions of prudence cannot be less requisite in the distribution of the supreme powers of the State.

But it is not possible to give to each department an equal power of self-defence. In republican government, the legislative authority necessarily predominates. The remedy for this inconveniency is to divide the legislature into different branches; and to render them, by different modes of election and different principles of action, as little connected with each other as the nature of their common functions and their common dependence on the society will admit. It may even be necessary to guard against dangerous encroachments by still further precautions. As the weight of the legislative authority requires that it should be thus divided, the weakness of the executive may require, on the other hand, that it should be fortified. An absolute negative on the legislature appears, at first view, to be the natural defence with which the executive magistrate should be armed. But perhaps it would be neither altogether safe nor alone sufficient. On ordinary occasions it might not be exerted with the requisite firmness, and on extraordinary occasions it might be perfidiously abused. May not this defect of an absolute negative be supplied by some qualified connection between this weaker department and the weaker branch of the stronger department, by which the latter may be led to support the constitutional rights of the former, without being too much detached from the rights of its own department?

If the principles on which these observations are founded be just, as I persuade myself they are, and they be applied as a criterion to the several State constitutions, and to the federal Constitution, it will be found that if the latter does not perfectly correspond with them, the former are infinitely less able to bear such a test.

There are, moreover, two considerations particularly applicable to the federal system of America, which place that system in a very interesting point of view.

First. In a single republic, all the power surrendered by the people is submitted to the administration of a single government; and the usurpations are guarded against by a division of the government into distinct and separate departments. In the compound republic of America, the power surrendered by the people is first divided between two distinct governments, and then the portion allotted to each subdivided among distinct and separate departments. Hence a double security arises to the rights of the people. The different governments will control each other, at the same time that each will be controlled by itself.

Second. It is of great importance in a republic not only to guard the society against the oppression of its rulers, but to guard one part of the society against the injustice of the other part. Different interests necessarily exist in different classes of citizens. If a majority be united by a common interest, the rights of the minority will be insecure. There are but two methods of providing against this evil: the one by creating a will in the community independent of the majority—that is, of the society itself; the other, by comprehending in the society so many separate descriptions of citizens as will render an unjust combination of a majority of the whole very improbable, if not impracticable. The first method prevails in all governments possessing an hereditary or self-appointed authority. This, at best, is but a precarious security; because a power independent of the society may as well espouse the unjust views of the major, as the rightful interests of the minor party, and may possibly be turned against both parties. The second method will be exemplified in the federal republic of the United States. Whilst all authority in it will be derived from and dependent on the society, the society itself will be broken into so many parts, interests and classes of citizens, that the rights of individuals, or of the minority, will be in little danger from interested combinations of the majority. In a free government the security for civil rights must be the same as that for religious rights. It consists in the one case in the multiplicity of interests, and in the other in the multiplicity of sects. The degree of security in both cases will depend on the number of interests and sects; and this may be presumed to depend on the extent of country and number of people comprehended under the same government. This view of the subject must particularly recommend a proper federal system to all the sincere and considerate friends of republican government, since it shows that in exact proportion as the territory of the Union may be formed into more circumscribed Confederacies, or States, oppressive combinations of a majority will be facilitated; the best security, under the republican forms, for the rights of every class of citizens, will be diminished; and consequently the stability and independence of some member of the government, the only other security, must be proportionally increased. Justice is the end of government. It is the end of civil society. It ever has been and ever will be pursued until it be obtained, or until liberty be lost in the pursuit. In a society under the forms of which the stronger faction can readily unite and oppress the weaker, anarchy may as truly be said to reign as in a state of nature, where the weaker individual is not secured against the violence of the stronger; and as, in the latter state, even the stronger individuals are prompted, by the uncertainty of their condition, to submit to a government which may protect the weak as well as themselves; so, in the former state, will the more powerful factions or parties be gradually induced, by a like motive, to wish for a government which will protect all parties, the weaker as well as the more powerful. It can be little doubted that if the State of Rhode Island was separated from the Confederacy and left to itself, the insecurity of rights under the popular form of government within such narrow limits would be displayed by such reiterated oppressions of factious majorities that some power altogether independent of the people would soon be called for by the voice of the very factions whose misrule had proved the necessity of it. In the extended republic of the United States, and among the great variety of interests, parties, and sects which it embraces, a coalition of a majority of the whole society could seldom take place on any other principles than those of justice and the general good; whilst there being thus less danger to a minor from the will of a major party, there must be less pretext, also, to provide for the security of the former, by introducing into the government a will not dependent on the latter, or, in other words, a will independent of the society itself. It is no less certain than it is important, notwithstanding the contrary opinions which have been entertained, that the larger the society, provided it lie within a particular sphere, the more duly capable it will be of self-government. And happily for the *republican cause,* the practicable sphere may be carried to a very great extent, by a judicious modification and mixture of the *federal principle.*

P   UBLIUS

What Good Is Government?

William J. Bennett & John J. DiIulio, Jr.

NOBODY NEEDS to persuade most Americans that their national government is too big, taxes and regulates too much, and fails to accomplish enough of genuine public value. Much of what emanates from Washington is an uneconomical, uncoordinated, unholy mess, and almost everyone knows it. When President Clinton declared, in his 1996 State of the Union address, that "the era of big government is over," he was belatedly responding to the political pressures generated by this deep-seated knowledge, which ever since the days of Ronald Reagan has been the motive force behind conservative and Republican victories at the polls. Indeed, Clinton himself won the presidency in 1992 and then won it again in 1996 largely by exploiting conservative themes about relimiting government and restoring civil society.

For conservatives, there would thus seem to be cause for satisfaction at this new coincidence of views between the leadership of both political parties. But of late, conservatives have been doing more fretting than celebrating. Some complain that today's Republican-led Congress is proving itself incapable of sustaining the "revolution" launched by its immediate predecessor after 1994. Others lament the "loss of political momentum" represented, for example, by the Clinton administration's slow but steady gutting of the work requirements in the 1996 welfare-reform law.

WILLIAM J. BENNETT *is co-director of Empower America and John M. Olin fellow in cultural-policy studies at the Heritage Foundation. His most recent book is* Our Sacred Honor. JOHN J. DIIULIO, JR. *is professor of politics and public affairs at Princeton and the co-editor (with Frank Thompson) of* Medicaid and the States, *forthcoming from Brookings.*

Still others carp that the latest bipartisan budget bill increases social spending by $70 billion in just its first year. The worry, in short, is that the fight against big government has no sooner begun than it is being toned down, qualified, or even abandoned, by Republicans and conservatives themselves no less than by Democrats and liberals.

There is something to this worry. But it also reflects the current state of confusion on both sides of the political aisle over exactly what our national government does, exactly what it can or should do, and what the American people want it to do. We are caught in one of those historic moments of transition, between one model of government, now 60 years old, with whose virtues and (especially) with whose defects we have become intimately familiar, and another model still very much in the making and yet to be adequately defined. In what follows we mean to contribute, however, tentatively, to such a definition, in the first place by dispelling some false ideas.

II

TO BEGIN at the beginning: *is* the era of big government over, and if not, is it likely to be over any time soon? The realistic answer to both questions is no.

Virtually every aspect of our lives is now touched by government. Washington underwrites support for the elderly and the disabled, for medical research, space missions, art museums, farmers, and mass transit. It subsidizes public television and mandates the number of hours that commercial networks must devote to "children's programs." It pays people to "volunteer" for national service. It builds prisons and supports public-housing projects and even midnight basketball. It provides food stamps, health care, college scholarships, loans, and grants. It involves itself in university admissions, hiring practices, family-leave policies, civil-rights laws, banking insurance and regulation, professional accrediting, air-traffic control, and parks administration. Among its obligations are protecting our air, water, and food; regulating tobacco and automobiles; constructing interstate highways; keeping out illegal immigrants and drugs; and providing pensions to our veterans.

This is only a partial list—and, needless to say, it all costs a lot. On the basis of the budget that has now become law, Americans will have at least $1.7 trillion-a-year's worth of national government as far as the fiscal eye can see. By every estimate, annual federal spending will top $2 trillion before the year 2003.

In order to get some earthly perspective on such astronomical figures, consider the humble fiscal facts behind the welfare-reform law, universally and deservedly acknowledged to be the single most far-reaching legislative action of the historic 104th Congress. This act abolished a means-tested federal-state program for low-income households, Aid to Families with Dependent Children (AFDC). But AFDC accounted for only about $22 billion a year in federal spending—much less than two cents of every federal dollar. And the act *continued* federal cash assistance via block grants to states, at funding levels largely comparable to AFDC.

Again: last June, members of the House commerce committee voted to cut $15 billion over five years from Medicaid, the joint federal-state program that provides health-care insurance to some 35 million low-income, elderly, and disabled Americans. But between 1988 and 1994, Medicaid spending *grew* by about $100 billion, roughly $77 billion of which were federal dollars, and will likely grow by another $40 billion or more by 2002. And incidentally, the same House panel that voted for the much-publicized $15 billion in cuts also approved a new $16-billion grant to the states to expand health-care coverage for uninsured children.

Where do the other hundreds of billions in federal money go every year? Roughly half goes to the "3 15's and a nickel"—15 percent each to national defense, grants to states and localities, and net interest payments, and 5 percent to other federal operations. The other half goes to payments to individuals. Of the latter, half again are made via entitlement programs that directly benefit the majority of all Americans, including many with annual incomes of $50,000 or more.

And what can be cut from all this? By the time the 104th Congress arrived in Washington in January 1995, the proportion of "big government" that consisted of nondefense discretionary spending, including such items as Head Start, public housing, and interstate highways, had already been squeezed by almost half in the 1990 Omnibus Budget Reconciliation Act and still further in its 1993 successor. In 1995 and 1996, as we have seen, programs for low-income families and individuals followed suit, absorbing over 90 percent of all cuts to entitlement programs.

The reason the only sizable cuts in the "nanny state" have fallen on programs for the poor rather than on those benefiting the middle class and the affluent is simple. In survey after survey, clear majorities of Americans have said that they would rather *prevent* cuts to most federal programs than balance the budget or shrink the deficit. As many as 80 percent or more favor maintaining or expanding Social Security and Medicare. For Medicaid the parallel figure is over 70 percent, and over 60 percent favor student loans, veterans' hospitals, environmental protection, unemployment insurance, and other programs. In a period like the present one, when economic growth has boosted tax revenues and shrunk the deficit, there is likely to be even less pressure for significant cuts to big-ticket entitlements and discretionary spending programs for the nonpoor.

III

THE LARGE majorities in favor of retaining government entitlement programs raise a question about what was in the mind of the American people when in 1994 they gave control of both the House and the Senate to the Republicans. Certainly many of those newly elected Senators and Congressmen read the results as a mandate to downsize government.

But the election results can also be read in other ways. For one thing, the Republican victory, which was in any case not the landslide it is sometimes depicted as being, may have had less to do with ideas than with long-term electoral trends. Thus, in every election from 1968 to 1992, the percentage of the vote going to Republicans in congressional battles had been higher than the percentage of seats actually won by Republicans. What happened in 1994 is that the party finally succeeded in closing the gap. In the words of the political scientist Gary C. Jacobson, "Most of the seats the [GOP] added in 1994 were seats a Republican should have held in the first place."

For Republicans, the good news is that the factors behind this trend are likely to continue. One such factor is the increasing suburbanization of the electorate. Another is the increasing consolidation of the Republican hold on the South. (In 1996, Republicans added Southern House seats even as they lost seats elsewhere, and the South was also the only region where Bob Dole's popular vote nosed out Bill Clinton's.) Finally, gathering Republican strength at the state level is a bellwether of greater strength at the national level.

We hardly mean to suggest that issues and ideas have played no role in all this: nobody who followed the course of Hillary Clinton's health-care fiasco could contend such a thing. More broadly, as the political analyst Everett Carll Ladd has written, Republicans have indeed benefited from an ongoing "philosophical realignment": ever larger majorities of voters have become more conservative, "especially in the sense of being far less inclined to accept claims that more government represents progress." As we noted above, when Bill Clinton won the presidency, he did so in large measure by playing to this growing conservative mood.

Nevertheless, Ladd argues, the continuities in voting behavior "are in many ways more striking than the . . . departures." So far, the philosophical realignment has produced no decisive party realignment and consolidated no conservative governing majority. In 1996, Ladd concludes,

> Voters again elected a President of one party and gave congressional majorities to the other. . . . They again signaled a desire to curb the growth of national government, though not to cut it greatly.

This seems to us to sum up the situation very well. The public may not have the scale of government it prefers, but there is little evidence that it wants government to withdraw from the *spheres* in which it is now involved, or to downsize simply for the sake of downsizing. This reading of the mood of the electorate was confirmed, moreover, when the

Republican majority in Congress did set out to cut government "greatly." In mid-1995, House Republicans proposed eliminating no less than $1.4 trillion in projected federal spending by the year 2002, while Senate Republicans proposed cuts of $961 billion. In 1996, a House budget-committee resolution called for terminating, turning into block grants, or privatizing 3 cabinet departments, 284 programs, 69 commissions, and 13 agencies.

The effect of these ambitious proposals was that, between December 1994 and June 1996, the 104th Congress's net approval rating fell like a rock. In the meantime, the President's steadily improved. In March 1995, according to an ABC News/*Washington Post* poll, almost twice as many people were worried that Republicans would go too far in cutting needed programs than that Democrats would go too far in defending wasteful ones.

THE SHIFT in public sentiment can be explained in part by willful Democratic exaggerations of the size and scope of the proposed Republican cuts. But that is only one element of the story. Another has to do with the inability of the Republican leadership to offer a persuasive defense of their plans against reasonable criticism and concerns.

Consider Medicare. When this program first became law in 1965, estimated spending for 1990 was projected at $8 billion. By the time 1990 rolled around, *actual* Medicare spending was nearly $160 billion and rising; by 1995, the system was (as it remains) headed for bankruptcy. In the words of the *Wall Street Journal,* "Medicare is growing so fast that by 2001 it will overtake all federal spending on defense; by 2005 it will exceed defense by $100 billion."

What to do? In the 104th Congress, the GOP proposed to cap overall Medicare spending. That proposal is now history. In the 105th Congress, the party has sought to modify the program by giving its beneficiaries financial incentives to economize (mostly by shifting from fee-for-service to so-called medical savings accounts). The elderly, Republicans argue, need more "choice," while future technologies will inevitably yield better care for all at less cost. But conservative lawmakers have so far failed to explain how we are to reduce the rate of growth in Medicare without causing millions of elderly Americans to receive less financial help from Washington, get worse care, or be thrown back on their own savings or the support of their often resistant or resourceless families.

It clearly will not do to assert that the public has already "voted for" cuts in Medicare or, for that matter, any of the other major entitlement programs. What the public has voted for is more complicated than that, and what it will stand for, it seems, is very little. In the absence of compelling alternatives, most Americans prefer the status quo, far from perfect though they know it to be, to radical retrenchment.

Faced with these apparently intractable facts, some conservatives have persuaded themselves that other means exist to solve the problem of big government. One, which goes by the name of devolution, is to kick things back from Washington to the states. Another is to hand them over to "civil society." Both these ideas are estimable in and of themselves; but as solutions to the perceived problem, they are partial at best.

IV

DEVOLUTION—VESTING as much decision- and policy-making power as possible in what Edmund Burke called the "little platoons" of society—is an idea for which a strong case can be made: philosophical, political, and practical. Why indeed should anyone assume that a Secretary of Health and Human Services in Washington knows better than the governor of Michigan what is good for the children of that state, or which welfare approach will work best there? Moreover, popular support for devolution is high, mirroring the popular disapproval of big government and bloated bureaucracy.

Best of all, evidence is accumulating that local initiative works. In the areas of welfare and education, what Governors Tommy Thompson of Wisconsin, John Engler of Michigan, and Arne Carlson of Minnesota have been able to accomplish in a few short years puts Washington to shame, and the same goes, in the area of criminal justice, for Mayor Rudolph Giuliani of New York City.

But for all its virtues, the paradoxical fact is that devolution *per se* does nothing to contain the size and scope of federal power. Many federal programs are already highly devolved to state and local governments through block grants. The real "Washington bureaucracy" is composed not of the two million nondefense

federal bureaucrats—about the same number as in 1960, before the fifteenfold growth in expenditures since the Great Society—but of the millions and millions of people who work indirectly for the national government as employees of state and local agencies, private firms, and nonprofit organizations that are largely if not entirely funded by federal dollars. About 90 percent of federal civilian workers live elsewhere than Washington and its environs, a reality brought home with tragic poignancy by the Oklahoma City bombing.

As the political scientist Donald F. Kettl has documented, today's national government is "government by proxy." Only about 4 percent of the federal budget, Kettl estimates, goes to programs or services that the federal government delivers directly. Mainly the tasks are performed by state and local governments, followed by private and nonprofit contractors. Indeed, every national domestic-policy initiative of the past six decades has been a version of government by proxy.

Thus, the interstate highway system was built through grants to state and local governments and contracts with private construction companies. Under the direction of state health and human-services officials, private financial intermediaries manage most of the Medicare and Medicaid programs. Contractors perform the clean-ups at the Superfund sites of the Environmental Protection Agency (EPA). Universities and other nonprofit organizations devise and direct federally-funded projects in areas ranging from biomedical research to juvenile justice. The federal prison system and the Federal Aviation Administration—two of the relatively few federal agencies that do directly administer federal laws—rely heavily on private contractors to perform many different functions. Even financing and payments under the Social Security Act are administered by the states (subject to review by the U.S. Department of Health and Human Services).

As for the now-defunct AFDC program, it was administered as a joint federal-state program on the basis of a legal commitment by Washington to match state spending; in effect, AFDC was an entitlement to state governments, and was accordingly managed under a mind-boggling array of local eligibility requirements, work provisions, and more. For well over a decade now, Medicaid too has been evolving into a highly decentralized program in which states take the lead in defining eligibility criteria, streamlining payment procedures, and deciding which, if any, costly auxiliary services get provided.

Supporters of devolution tend to speak of block grants not only as if they were something new but as if they were a proven device for cutting spending and/or a sure-fire way of improving performance. They are neither.

Between 1966 and 1993, there were 23 block-grant programs for the states, fifteen of which were still in effect when the 104th Congress was elected. Total federal aid to the states was $127 billion in 1980; in 1994, *after* the Reagan years with their ostensible commitment to cutting back, it was an estimated $170 billion.

Nor, as John P. Walters has shown, do block grants necessarily guarantee greater efficiency or even a greater degree of control on the part of citizens. Block grants can simply "transfer wealth and authority to state and local bureaucrats who are . . . often less efficient, less responsive, and more prone to corruption than federal bureaucrats." In addition, "devolving federal power" has often meant reducing the federal government's capacity to monitor and correct. It has helped produce fraud and record overpayments in Medicare; the flawed Hubble space telescope; some of the worst defense-procurement scandals ever; the illegal diversion of tens of millions of dollars in food stamps; spectacular defaults in the guaranteed student-loan program; excessive costs in the Superfund; the failure of the Internal Revenue Service's computer-modernization project; and malfeasance of Teapot Dome proportions in the Department of Housing and Urban Development.

In the proper hands, devolution can be a potent weapon in the arsenal of a society attempting to recover the habits of self-government. But it is only one weapon, and its utility is limited. In the wrong hands, moreover, devolution is just as likely to be a recipe for spending money that the federal government does not have, for purposes that no one has clearly specified, with results that cannot be measured or evaluated until it is too late.

V

THIS BRINGS us to the other great hope of conservatives: civil society. By this is meant the entire network of churches, charities, community groups, and other voluntary associations and institutions upon which our society has always depended for its successful functioning. According to at least one reading of the evidence, this network has been eviscerated by the growth and self-aggrandizement of government; families, churches, and community groups have been forced to surrender their authority to bureaucratic experts, with disastrous consequences not only for civility but for civilization itself. The retreat of government from the field would thus be a hopeful sign of progress, allowing these institutions to revive and resume their normal functions, which they have anyway always performed with far greater effectiveness.

Here, too, the evidence is in fact somewhat mixed. One thing still unclear, for example, is the degree to which government has indeed "crowded out" familial, communal, corporate, and philanthropic activity. In articles published in 1995 and 1996, the political scientist Robert Putnam contended that fewer and fewer Americans were voting, joining the PTA, going to church, or participating in other civic associations and group activities, while more and more were "bowling alone." But Putnam's thesis has come under severe challenge by analysts who assert that, to the contrary, the number of Americans volunteering for groups and causes remains huge and shows no signs of declining. Bowling leagues may be down, but soccer leagues are up.

An even tougher question to answer is whether volunteer programs can operate on a large enough scale to deal effectively with hard-core social problems. A few years ago, Public/Private Ventures, a policy-research organization with which one of us has been affiliated, completed a systematic evaluation of the Big Brothers Big Sisters of America program. The findings were remarkably encouraging: for low-income children, many of them abused or neglected, just a few hours a week with a "Big" yielded a 50-percent average reduction in first-time drug use, a 33-percent reduction in violent behavior, and measurable improvements in school performance. But the number of children who could benefit from this program or one like it remains far in excess of the number of adults who volunteer for it.

Whether such institutions are growing in number is again difficult to say. Most urban black churches, for example, run or participate directly in community-service activities that reach beyond their own membership—staffing day-care facilities, offering drug- and alcohol-abuse prevention programs, administering food banks, building shelters, serving as after-school safe havens, and more. But are such faith-based social programs more or less common today than they were ten, twenty, or thirty years ago?

In any case, the basic issue may be less one of numbers, or even of efficacy, than of sheer capacity. According to Princeton's Julian Wolpert, about 125,000 organizations in America operate as charities with receipts of at least $25,000 a year. Their combined revenues and expenditures are about $350 billion annually—roughly *one-seventh* of what is spent by federal, state, and local government. Moreover, a third of those revenues come from government itself. If all of America's grant-making private foundations gave away all of their income and all of their assets, they could cover only a year's worth of current government expenditures on social welfare. It is unlikely that Americans will donate much more than their present 2 percent of annual household income, or that corporate giving will take up any significant proportion of the slack in the event of further government reductions.

An energetic civil society is a blessing beyond compare, and government is no substitute for its myriad institutions. But getting government out of our lives would not *ipso facto* lead to a rebirth of those institutions, particularly ones that may have atrophied, and particularly if they have atrophied for reasons that are as much cultural (think, for instance, of the influence of television and the movies) as political. Nor, in the end, can civil institutions themselves, no matter how energetic, be a substitute for government.

VI

BUT WHAT sort of government do we need? In 1964, former President Eisenhower said:

> We Republicans believe in limited government, but also in effective government. We believe in keeping government as close to the people as possible.... But we do not shrink from a recognition that there are national problems that require national solutions.

Thirty-three years later, Eisenhower's words seem more relevant than ever, encapsulating a truly national view of our situation and suggesting not just a Republican but a republican way forward.

Perhaps the first lesson these words suggest is the need for all Americans, including those most offended by the depredations of big government, to make their peace with the persistent popular majorities whose duly-elected representatives have supported and sustained the national government's post-New Deal role. That role in itself is not the problem; however they may grumble, Americans want government to perform it, or something like it. Nor is the problem *simply* one of the size of government. Rather, partly on account of sheer size, but more on account of bad ideas in the hands of executors with arbitrary and unaccountable authority, our national government has fatally lost sight of what James Madison called the "permanent and aggregate interests of the community"— that is, of the public interest.

Only now, thanks to widespread disgust with what those ideas and that arbitrary authority have created, are we beginning to take stock of how badly the public interest has been served across the board: from law enforcement, to education, to family policy, to race relations, to tax law. Most saliently, unelected federal officials—whether bureaucrats or judges—have been permitted to define the public interest as they see fit and, through the reach of national power, to impose their understanding over and against the clearly expressed wishes both of representative institutions and of state and local governments, businesses, civic organizations, neighborhoods, and individuals. If our standard is to keep government "as close to the people as possible," then one of the most hopeful pieces of legislation passed by the 104th Congress was a little-noticed provision, authored by Senator Spencer Abraham, restricting the ability of federal judges to continue defying persistent public demands for laws prohibiting the arbitrary release of violent criminals. Similar sorts of restorative lawmaking are a prime desideratum.

Here is where the true value of devolution and civil society makes itself felt. For the foreseeable future, it seems, the social-policy "action" in America will be emanating less from Washington than from the states and localities, as well as from the sphere of private enterprise. That is all to the good. The seeds of a new reconstruction are being sown: from welfare reform to the revolution in health care, a whole array of promising initiatives, none of them conceived or directed by Washington (though some are at least partly subsidized by Washington), is beginning to undo the accumulated damage of a quarter-century and thereby to change the underlying relation of government and society. The eventual effect of these initiatives, if they are not impeded by the dead hand of the federal behemoth, will be to alter the definition not only of American politics, but of government itself.

In this period of experimentation, the role of responsible elected representatives in Washington is to monitor, to assess, to criticize, and even to propose—but first and foremost to foster and encourage. And in the meantime, there is plenty of other work to be done at the national level by a political class—in the nature of things, a conservative political class—bent not on dismantling but (to revert to Eisenhower's language) on limiting government and making it more effective. There may well be some federal agencies we would be better off without—the National Endowment for the Arts is one. On the other hand, calls to eliminate the EPA, for example, are unrealistic and out of touch with the wishes of the electorate; Americans want federal controls on the air they breathe as much as on the meat they consume. Still, *someone* has to start the decade-long task of bringing the morass of federal environmental regulations and the litigation they have spawned into line with the public interest properly understood. And the EPA is only one instance, if among the most egregious, of a much more pervasive problem.

IMPROVING THE performance of government hardly exhausts the matter, however. Perhaps the most pernicious legacy of the era of expanded government has been to engender widespread public mistrust of, precisely, government itself. This mistrust is founded on larger considerations than federal waste and inefficiency.

It has often been remarked how liberalism, by creating ever new categories of rights, and by relentlessly expanding the sphere of "entitlement," has devalued the habits of self-reliance and individual responsibility that are critical to economic and social advancement. What is less often remarked is the extent to which these same sturdy habits, the defining marks of a free citizenry, are and must be constitutive of the entire American political order. Should we really be surprised when people inculcated with the thoroughly infantilizing idea that government exists to take care of their "needs" begin to regard that government with increasing petulance and disrespect?

During the 1992 presidential debate in Richmond, Virginia, a middle-aged man stood up in the audience and asked the three candidates: "We're not under oath at this point, but could you make a commitment to the citizens of the United States to meet our *needs*?—and we have many." Neither George Bush, nor Ross Perot, nor, assuredly, Bill Clinton dared challenge the premise of the question. Every parent knows the symptoms of this insatiable disease; a wise one takes steps to prevent them from developing.

To this injury has been added still another: the breaking-down—the deconstruction—of our common American culture, of the American idea. Liberalism brought us not only the era of big government, now officially declared to be over, but the era of official, government-sponsored polarization. It was a bureau of the federal government that in the late 1960's began systematically to infiltrate our way of doing business and educating our young with the insidious practice of counting by race; and it is our national government that through its dogged adherence to these policies and a galaxy of related ones continues daily to go about dividing us by race, gender, and ethnicity, setting us each against the other and then wondering aloud why we cannot "talk."

No amount of devolution, no revival of civil society, can by themselves recreate this bedrock condition of our political existence: the knowledge that we are one nation, indivisible. To the contrary, the very act of draining authority away from Washington, and of encouraging the spirit of individual and civic initiative, may, in the absence of countervailing forces, tend rather to hasten than to impede the further atomizing of society. But neither is it imaginable that we can simply demand of citizens respect for a national government that has shown itself unworthy of their respect.

There is a trap here to which conservatives in particular may be susceptible. As Gertrude Himmelfarb has written in these pages,* in their impassioned and wholly understandable rush to decry big government and extol the virtues of civil society, many otherwise sensible conservatives have come perilously close to delegitimating the idea of government itself. Others, of a frankly libertarian stripe, have gone even farther; characterizing 60 years of expanded government programs as

---

*"For the Love of Country," [*Commentary*,] May 1997.

a kind of scam perpetrated on a society of native individualists yearning to breathe free, they not only seek to limit government but practically to do away with it.

THE TASK as we see it is instead to limit government; to make it more effective; and to keep it as close to the people as possible. But it is also to conserve, to rebuild, and to restore. The restoration of the American government as a true expression of the American idea cannot be achieved by an act of Congress, or triggered by a provision in a spending bill, or, alas, materialized in an act of will by the American people. It is a task for national leadership, and only national leadership can accomplish it. Ronald Reagan, who paradoxically came to office on a platform for re-limiting government, may have come closer than any statesman in living memory both to grasping what is required for the task and, in his person and spirit, to suggesting the elementary grounds for its realization.

It has been a long time since an American President could say with perfect assurance, as our first President did in his Farewell Address:

> This government, the offspring of our own choice uninfluenced and unawed, . . . has a just claim to your confidence and your support. Respect for its authority, compliance with its laws, acquiescence in its measures are duties enjoined by the fundamental maxims of true liberty.

Thanks to decades of often mindless expansion, and even more so to policies that have undermined the habits of freedom, respect for the authority of government is at a low point in our country. But in a fundamental sense, that government remains what it was 200 years ago: the "offspring of our own choice." Without destroying the institution itself, we should study to fashion a better one, of which we can more honestly say that it exercises "a just claim on [our] confidence and [our] support."

CHOMP!

How a 17th-century British scam morphed into a global monster—and what we can do about it

By Jim Hightower

They tell me advice sells, so here goes:
- Don't ever buy a pit bull from a one-armed man.
- Never sign nothin' by neon light.
- Always drink upstream from the herd.

Oh, and one more: Never, ever believe the "conventional wisdom," which is to wisdom what "near beer" is to beer. Only not as close.

This is especially true when it comes to our political system. The powers-that-be, for example, tell us over and over that we are not willing to undertake any significant political change. Americans are overwhelmingly middle-of-the-road, they say, and not interested in any kind of "ism."

This is a trick play designed to keep America's political debate from focusing on an insidious new "ism" that has crept into our lives: *corporatism.* Few politicians, pundits, economists, or other officially sanctioned mouthpieces for what passes as public debate in this country want to touch the topic, but—as most ordinary folks have learned—the corporation has gotten way too big for its britches, intruding into every aspect of our lives and forcing changes in how we live.

Less than a decade ago, for example, your medical needs rested in the hands of a doctor whom *you* got to choose. But quicker than a hog eats supper, America's health care system—including your personal doc—got swallowed damn-near whole by a handful of corporate mutants called HMOs, most of which are tentacles of Prudential, Travelers, and other insurance giants.

When did we vote on this? Did I miss the national referendum in which we decided that remote corporate executives with an army of bean counters would displace my handpicked doctor, and would decide which (if any) hospital I can enter, how long I can stay, what specialists I can consult? I know Congress did not authorize this fundamental shift. To the contrary, in 1994 Congress rightly trashed the Clinton health care plan on the grounds that it would do exactly what's being done to us now: put the bean counters in charge. Only back then we were warned by the infamous "Harry and Louise" televi-

sion spots that it would be government bean counters managing our health.

What irony. For years the very companies that financed the "Harry and Louise" ads have flapped their arms wildly to scare us about that old bugaboo, "socialized" medicine, while they blindsided us with something even harsher: corporatized medicine, a new form of "care" in which the Hippocratic Oath has been displaced by a bottom-line ethos. Now our health care is in the hands of people like Richard Scott, a mergers and acquisitions lawyer who headed up the Columbia/HCA Healthcare Corporation, a $20-billion-a-year HMO, until last July when he was forced out under a cloud of scandal about Medicare fraud. During Scott's tenure, Columbia/HCA demanded that its local hospital executives return a 20 percent annual profit to headquarters, or else. How did they meet his demand? By cutting back on services, on employees, and ultimately on us patients.

One place Scott did not cut back, however, was on his own paycheck. In 1995, he took a 43 percent salary hike, which meant he drew a million bucks from the till. Every *month.* But Scott is far less generous when it comes to taking responsibility for meeting the needs of America's sick. "Do we have an obligation to provide health care for everybody?" he recently asked rhetorically. "Where do we draw the line? Is any fast-food restaurant obligated to feed everyone who shows up?"

While it is true that corporations have long been a fact of life in America, since the 1970s they have metamorphosed into something different and disquieting. Corporations have become the governing force in our society, reshaping American life to fit nothing more enlightened than the short-term profile sheets of greedy CEOs. Everything from our amusements to our government, from our public schools to our popular culture—has become thoroughly corporatized.

The true symbol of America is no longer Old Glory, but the corporate logo. No public space, no matter how sacrosanct, is free from the threat of having "Mountain Dew," "Citibank," or "Nike" plastered on it. Not even space itself is off-limits:

From *Utne Reader*, March/April 1998, pp. 57-61, 102-103. Excerpted from *There's Nothing in the Middle of the Road But Yellow Stripes and Dead Armadillos* by Jim Hightower. © 1997 by Jim Hightower. Reprinted by permission of HarperCollins Publishers, Inc.

One visionary business enterprise is already working on launching a low-trajectory satellite equipped with what amounts to an extraterrestrial billboard that will be programmed to beam logos back to earth from the night sky. No matter where you live, from Boston to Bora Bora, you'll be able to gaze into the vast darkness, as humans have for thousands of years, and absorb the natural wonder of the moon, the Milky Way, and, yes, an orbiting ad for Mylanta. Lovely.

Every once in a while we come across a news item about a corporation acting contrary to form. For instance, the story of John Tu and David Sun, founders of Kingston Technologies in California, who sold a majority stake in their computer-chip enterprise for one and a half billion big ones and put $100 million of it into bonuses and special benefit programs for their 523 employees.

"What in the name of Ebenezer Scrooge are you two up to?" screeched their high-tech corporate peers. Nothing, it turns out. An amazed media found that this was not a publicity ploy or a tax dodge—it was, simply, sharing. Tu and Sun quietly explained that the hardworking people at Kingston are what made it possible for them as owners to prosper, so it felt right to reward them for their contribution.

Such acts of responsibility are so antithetical to accepted boardroom practice that when they occur it's big news. Indeed, immediately after the Kingston Technologies story broke, business analysts rushed forward to dump cold water on the fantasy that this is the way things should be done in today's complex corporate economy. Kingston Technologies, the critics scoffed, was a privately held company, so Messrs. Tu and Sun could be whimsical with company funds because they weren't subject to the short-term profit pressures from Wall Street investors. The "corporate system," the analysts explained, has no room for beneficence toward employees, communities, or the environment. None other than economist Milton Friedman himself, the patron saint of Wall Street excess, gave academic credence to such myopic thinking by asking and answering his own rhetorical question: "So the question is, do corporate executives, provided they stay within the law, have responsibilities in their business activities other than to make as much money for their stockholders as possible? And my answer to that is, no they do not."

So *my* question is, if the corporate structure exists only for stockholders, as Dr. Friedman makes clear, and since two-thirds of us are not stockholders, why should the larger public be so permissive toward this particular business structure? You don't have to be the brightest light on the block to figure out that if the "corporate system" makes John Tu and David Sun the anomalies (and, in some executive quarters, the pariahs) of American business, then it's time to fix the system. I know the wisdom of the oft-cited aphorism "If it ain't broke, don't fix it," but the equally sagacious corollary to that is "If it is broke, run get the toolbox."

What is this thing called the "corporation" and why is it here? It's time to put this basic question back into political play. The corporation has become a given in our culture, not unlike smog and Wayne Newton. It has been with us so long we assume it is part of the natural order.

Not so. Practically all of our nation's founders were appropriately anti-corporate (although you'll never find that in any standard textbooks of American history), and at the time of the Continental Congress, only about 40 corporations existed in our land, and they were kept on a very short leash.

Like powdered wigs and boiled beef, the corporation is a British invention, essentially created by the Crown as a vehicle to amass the capital needed to loot the wealth of its colonies. Of course, looting was nothing new, but this "joint stock" connivance was a devilishly radical scheme. For the first time, ownership of an enterprise was separated from responsibility for the enterprise. If an individual businessperson loots, pollutes, or otherwise behaves illegally, he or she is individually accountable to the community for those actions—that is, they get their sorry asses hauled into court, and get fined, put out of business, and/or tossed in the slammer. But the corporation is a legal fiction that lets the investors who own the business off the hook whenever the business behaves badly (read: steals, kills, poisons, pillages, corrupts, and so on), avoiding individual responsibility for illegal actions done in their name, even when such actions profit them enormously.

Like letting a cat loose in a fish market, this structure invites mischief, which is why the founders of our republic believed corporate charters should be granted only to serve the greater public interest. Through most of the 19th century, states typically limited each corporation they chartered to one kind of business, prohibited it from owning other businesses, strictly limited the amount of capital it could amass, required the stockholders to be local residents, spelled out specific benefits the corporation had to deliver to the community, and put a 20- to 50-year limit on the life of the charter. And, imagine this, legislatures were not shy about yanking charters when a corporation went astray from its stated mission or acted irresponsibly.

But just as America's founders clearly saw the dangers of the corporate entity, greedy hustlers saw its phenomenal potential to help them make a killing. And the latter began early on to lather up politicians with money to try to loosen up the chartering process. During the Civil War, numerous corporations were chartered to supply the Union Army, and the commander-in-chief, Abraham Lincoln, did not find it a positive experience. In an ominous foreboding of corrupt practices among today's Pentagon contractors, many of these corporations delivered shoddily made shoes, malfunctioning guns, and rotten meat. Honest Abe viewed the rise of corporations as a disaster, and warned in an 1864 letter that "as a result of the war, corporations have been enthroned and an era of corruption in high places will follow . . . until all wealth is aggregated in a few hands, and the Republic is destroyed."

Sure enough, during the next three decades, assorted industrialists and corporate flimflam artists known collectively as the robber barons were enthroned and took hold of both the economy and the government. Corruption did abound, from statehouses to the White House, and the concentration of wealth in the clutching hands of such families as the Astors,

TAMING THE CORPORATE BEAST

New strategies for making business work for all of us

For as long as there have been corporations, citizens have fought to limit their power and make them more accountable to the public. Two of the most innovative strategies to emerge in recent years—the corporate charter movement and social auditing—are encouraging, but they also demonstrate just how tough it can be to rein in megacorporations.

Corporate charters. This movement, led by environmentalist and labor activist Richard Grossman and his Provincetown, Massachusetts-based Program on Corporations, Law and Democracy, seeks to embolden citizens and lawmakers to toughen—or rather enforce—state corporate charter laws. These laws, which have been on the books for decades, give legislatures the power to limit corporations' activities and revoke their right to do business in their state.

Grossman acknowledges that, in an era of intense interstate competition for jobs and corporate tax revenues, few state governments are likely to pull the plug on any major employer. Still, he says, the question of who really governs the country—citizens or corporations—must be addressed. "By what authority are they participating in elections, by what authority are they lobbying politically, by what authority are they in our schools?" he asks. "We've been engaging people all over the country in these questions." And only when citizens begin looking seriously at reforming corporate charters will companies sit up and take notice.

To show how powerful these tools can be, Grossman points to the way some corporations have persuaded legislatures to write additional protections into state charter regulations to shield them from hostile takeovers. These particular charter changes, known as constituency statues, can now be used in 29 states to protect corporate directors from shareholder lawsuits if they make a decision—from mergers and acquisitions to plant closings—that may be beneficial to workers or the local community, but not necessarily to the pocketbooks of stockholders. In a 1987

Pennsylvania case, for instance, the court ruled that Commonwealth National Financial Corporation could approve a merger with Mellon Bank even though the bid was lower than that of its other suitor, Meridian Bancorp. Citing the state's constituency statute, the court ruled that the board was not shirking its fiduciary duties because its employees would have greater opportunities with Mellon than with Meridian.

This may not represent a radical transfer of power—citizens still don't have the right to sue if their needs are ignored—but, as Marjorie Kelly, editor and publisher of *Business Ethics,* has written, strengthening constituency statutes could usher in "a kind of Copernican revolution . . . [in which] stockholders are no longer the exact center of the corporate solar system."

Social audits. Not all corporations, of course, are slaves to the bottom line. In fact, some companies are so concerned about their impact on the world that they voluntarily undergo comprehensive evaluations of their operations by independent auditors. These audits, based primarily on social and environmental factors, were popularized three years ago by Ben & Jerry's and The Body Shop in response to criticism of their reputations as socially responsible companies. Now, a number of mainstream companies—including every major accounting firm—are embracing the concept as well.

The Body Shop's 1995 audit, which was performed by Kirk Hanson, longtime director of the Business Enterprise Trust at Stanford University, demonstrated both the promise and the perils of this trend. Hanson measured the Body Shop's performance using the so-called "social indicator" method pioneered by ethical investment firms. This method, which has been criticized by some for being too self-serving, gives greater weight to a company's policies on popular political issues (such as animal testing, human rights, energy conservation) than it gives to its performance in areas directly

affecting its stakeholders (such as employee relations, corporate governance, product quality). Hanson gave the company low marks in the more traditional areas of social responsibility—wages, working conditions, product quality, management accountability—while praising its environmental efforts and publicity campaigns about social issues.

Other social audit models can be used. Among the most popular are the social balance sheet (which integrates financial and social reporting by assigning a dollar value to a company's social impact) and benchmarking by objectives (which compares actual company performance with stated objectives). These methods are the primary tools of the accounting firms that are so aggressively pushing corporate social auditing into the mainstream business world, because they know a potential gold mine when they see one. None of these techniques are perfect, says Curtis Verschoor, an accounting professor at DePaul University, and in the absence of credible, recognized standards of ethical behavior, they will inevitably be inconclusive. Still, it's a positive step. "Even if these audits are only done by a few people on a voluntary basis," says Verschoor, "it will lead the way to more socially responsible behavior on the part of corporations."

— Craig Cox

Program on Corporations, Law & Democracy, 211.5 Bradford St., Provincetown, MA 02657; phone/fax 508/487-3151.

Institute for Social and Ethical Accountability, 1st Floor, Vine Court, 112 116, Whitechapel Rd., London EL 1JE, UK; phone 44 (0) 171/377-5866; fax 44 (0) 171/377-5720; Web site is located at www.accountability.org.uk; e-mail Secretariat@AccountAbility.org.uk.

the Vanderbilts, the Rockefellers, and the Morgans reached proportions unheard of . . . until today.

The power of the modern corporation dates back to this era, aided by two major legal shifts. First was the emasculation of the state "corporate charter," as power brokers goaded spineless and frequently corrupt politicians to remove, bit by bit and state by state, restrictions imposed to protect the public. Today the corporate chartering process is so perfunctory that it can be handled by a phone call.

The other big change came in 1886, when the U.S. Supreme Court essentially made the corporation bulletproof. In a stunning and totally irrational decision made without bothering to hear any formal arguments (indeed, the learned justices said they did not want to hear any arguments), the Court abruptly decreed in a case brought by a railroad company that a corporation is "a person," with the same constitutional protections that you and I have. Dr. Frankenstein could not have done better than the courts and legislators. In only a century, the corporation was transformed into a superhuman creature of the law, superior to you and me, because it has civil rights without any civil responsibilities. It is legally obligated to be selfish; it cannot be thrown into jail; it can deduct from its tax bill any fines it gets for wrongdoing; and it can live forever.

Corporations are the dominant institutions of our time, exercising the sort of power wielded by the church during the Middle Ages or by the nation-state in more recent times. In fact, some corporations are actually bigger than nations in terms of money. Mitsubishi is the 22nd largest economy on earth, ranked ahead of Indonesia. General Motors is number 26, bigger than Denmark or Thailand. Ford is 31st, ahead of South Africa and Saudi Arabia. Toyota, Shell, Exxon, Wal-Mart, Hitachi, and AT&T are all in the top 50.

If you read the business pages, you will find the captains of industry unabashedly declaring their independence from any social contract or community mores, and from nations themselves, even the most powerful nations. Ralph Nader told me about a telling moment at General Motors' stockholders meeting in 1996. The setting was appropriately ceremonious, with CEO John Smith and the board of directors arrayed like ministers of state across an elevated platform in a grand ballroom. At one point, a lone stockholder gained recognition to speak, and noting that GM had eliminated some 73,000 U.S. jobs in the past decade, asked politely if Smith and the members of the board would rise and join him in pledging allegiance to the American flag on display on the side of the platform. After some embarrassed tittering among the board members and scurrying of legal counsels back and forth behind the podium, Smith announced that the bottom line was no, they would not. Of course, even though there was a small army of reporters present, not a whisper of this revealing exchange made the news.

No single step, no magic fix-it, is going to deflate the arrogance of these elite investors and managers, but one strong hammer our democracy needs in its toolbox is a corporate charter with teeth. Just as the larger community specifies what it expects of welfare mothers, so must we set strict terms on the much more generous privileges bestowed on corporations. They must assume some individual responsibility for the malfeasance of their enterprises. And corporate charters, like politicians, should be subject to term limits. Such meaningful changes—along with a straightforward six-word constitutional amendment that says "a corporation is not a person"—would begin to mitigate the destructive, single-minded profit drive of the corporation and bring business back into balance with the greater goals of our society.

Challenging hegemonic corporate power head-on is made all the more difficult by the gutlessness that prevails among our present political leaders. This is a struggle that has to be organized and fought with no expectation of help from those in high positions. On the bright side, people already are focusing on the target, organizing, and fighting back, with newly aggressive groups like the Association of Community Organizations for Reform Now (ACORN), the AFL-CIO, the Alliance for Democracy, the Institute for Local Self-Reliance, the New Party, and the Program on Corporations, Law, and Democracy (see box, "Taming the Corporate Beast").

And when we think it is too difficult, even impossible, to win such a battle, it is worth remembering that Americans just like us have done this before—and won. Remember that everything Lincoln foresaw—entronement, corruption, aggregation, and destruction—came true over the next 40 years, except the last: destruction of the republic. This is because ordinary people rose up against the corporate giants and the corrupt politicians. In historic battles from the early 1880s into the early 1900s, the republic was saved from the robber barons by a coalition of the Populist Movement, the labor movement, African American activists, the muckraking press, and thousands of national and local leaders. Together they forged a new politics that elected populists, socialists, radicals, and other noncorporatists to legislative seats, governorships, and Congress. And while they never elected a president, they did force both the Democratic and the Republican parties to embrace their reform agenda, producing the nation's first trust-busting laws, the first minimum-wage-and-hour laws, laws about food purity, women's suffrage, the first national conservation program, the direct election of U.S. senators, and other populist, working people's reforms.

Yes, corporations today are more powerful than any robber baron could have dreamed, but they remain a creation of government. The Supreme Court also ruled in 1906 that "The corporation is a creature of the state. It is presumed to be incorporated for the benefit of the public." When it ceases to be a benefit—declaring itself above the common good—then we can cease to sanction incorporation.

As powerful as the corporation seems, remember this: No building is too tall for even the smallest dog to lift its leg on.

Jim Hightower, former Texas commissioner of agriculture, is now a radio talk show host and the editor of a newsletter called The Hightower Lowdown *(www.jimhightower.com).*

ROBERT B. REICH

The New Power

It seemed appropriate to begin my series of modest screeds with a short pre-millennial analysis of where power is moving to in America.

Here's who's losing it:

Giant corporations and their CEOs. They've made money in the current expansion, but they're losing clout. Vast industrial-age bureaucracies can't move fast enough. All are downsizing, and many CEOs are losing their jobs. Since 1990, heads have rolled at IBM, AT&T, General Motors, Sears, and other corporate behemoths. As the economy slows, expect more heads, lower profits, and downsizings on a monumental scale.

Labor unions. Even with the tough-minded John Sweeney at the helm of the AFL-CIO, the percentage of private-sector workers belonging to labor unions continues to drop. Unless the AFL-CIO succeeds in organizing vast numbers of low-wage service workers in hotels, hospitals, retail stores, restaurants, and laundries, as well as platoons of overworked and underpaid high-tech workers, organized labor is in danger of disappearing.

The federal government. When Bill Clinton said the "era of big government is over," he was understating. Without a Cold War to wage, a national crisis to manage, or a public aroused about anything loftier than the value of their 401(k) plans, the federal government has all but vanished from the public's mind. So long as right-wing Republicans and a centrist White House remain unwilling to do anything of importance about health care, education, Social Security, Medicare, or campaign finance, Washington's irrelevance will solidify into a gelatinous mass of indigestible spin.

The military-industrial complex. Dwight Eisenhower's farewell warning now seems quaint. Yes, military contractors are still collecting billions, but the money is really supporting the nation's largest jobs program, and

it can't last. The fanciest high-tech gadgets now come out of commercial firms, not from military contractors. Big weapons systems won't work against global terrorism. The International Monetary Fund has more influence over the world's fate than America's military muscle does.

Here's who's gaining it:

Big institutional investors. Forget the day traders. Giant pension funds and mutual funds are the major players on Wall Street. Some 44 percent of adult Americans are investing part of their savings in the stock market these days, and almost all this money is moving through these institutions. Fidelity, TIAA-CREF, CalPers, and a dozen others are telling global CEOs what to do and toppling those who won't listen.

Venture capitalists. Fewer than 100 of them are single-handedly creating the companies of the future. They're not only bankrolling the "dot.coms" (the stock-market value of Amazon.com is twice the value of the entire U.S. steel industry) but are also supplying most of their key talent.

The Federal Reserve Board's Open Market Committee. Alan Greenspan and 11 other people run the American economy. Now that fiscal policy (using government spending to fuel economic growth) is dead, monetary policy (raising and lowering interest rates to slow or accelerate the economy) is the only game in town, and the Fed is the sole player. They're largely responsible for America's Roaring '90s, and they'll be responsible for the great crash to come.

The telecommunications-entertainment complex. Eventually, almost everyone in America will be working directly or indirectly for MCI WorldCom, Microsoft, Disney, or AT&T. Only a handful of giant brands will have the scale to offer a full range of phone, wireless, data, Internet, and entertainment services. These giants will both define American culture and spread it around the world at the speed of an electronic impulse.

The new power centers are far less visible than the old. Big corporations, big labor, big government, and the military couldn't be missed. Almost everyone knew the likes of GM's Charlie Wilson, Walter Reuther of the United Auto Workers, Henry Kissinger, and the boys from Bechtel. The public didn't always know exactly what these guys were up to, but there was at least some semblance of accountability—if not directly through laws and regulations then indirectly through countervailing power, as John Kenneth Galbraith once termed it. Big labor, for example, provided a degree of balance with big business.

But institutional investors, venture capitalists, the Fed, and big entertainment-telecommunications companies all deal in intangibles, and they operate without anyone being particularly aware of what they're up to or how it affects everyone else. For the most part, reporters don't cover them. Who runs Fidelity? Who sits on the Fed's Open Market Committee other than Greenspan? Who's the CEO of MCI WorldCom? And what exactly are all these people doing? On the new frontiers of finance and technology, there are few laws or regulations, no oversight, and a total absence of countervailing power.

Americans' lives are affected no less by these new power centers, but Americans know far less about them than they did about the old. As long as the economy appears to be doing well for most of us, that doesn't seem to matter very much. But should a giant investment house go under and destabilize the world market, or should Wall Street crash, or should America's entire telecommunications system explode in a Y2K spasm, it would be well to discover whose actions or inactions precipitated these crises. There is also value, within a democracy, in citizens knowing where power lies and understanding how it is being exercised. It is when everything appears to be beyond anyone's control that all manner of bad things happen.

America's Ignorant Voters

This year's election is sure to bring more lamentations about voter apathy.
No less striking is the appalling political ignorance of the American electorate.

by Michael Schudson

Every week, the *Tonight Show's* Jay Leno takes to the streets of Los Angeles to quiz innocent passersby with some simple questions: On what bay is San Francisco located? Who was president of the United States during World War II? The audience roars as Leno's hapless victims fumble for answers. Was it Lincoln? Carter?

No pollster, let alone a college or high school history teacher, would be surprised by the poor showing of Leno's sample citizens. In a national assessment test in the late 1980s, only a third of American 17-year-olds could correctly locate the Civil War in the period 1850–1900; more than a quarter placed it in the 18th century. Two-thirds knew that Abraham Lincoln wrote the Emancipation Proclamation, which seems a respectable showing, but what about the 14 percent who said that Lincoln wrote the Bill of Rights, the 10 percent who checked the Missouri Compromise, and the nine percent who awarded Lincoln royalties for *Uncle Tom's Cabin?*

Asking questions about contemporary affairs doesn't yield any more encouraging results. In a 1996 national public opinion poll, only 10 percent of American adults could identify William Rehnquist as the chief justice of the Supreme Court. In the same survey, conducted at the height of Newt Gingrich's celebrity as Speaker of the House, only 59 percent could identify the job he held. Americans sometimes demonstrate deeper knowledge about a major issue before the nation, such as the Vietnam War, but most could not describe the thrust of the Clinton health care plan or tell whether the Reagan administration supported the Sandinistas or the contras during the conflict in Nicaragua (and only a third could place that country in Central America).

It can be misleading to make direct comparisons with other countries, but the general level of political awareness in leading liberal democracies overseas does seem to be much higher. While 58 percent of the Germans surveyed, 32 percent of the French, and 22 percent of the British were able to identify Boutros Boutros-Ghali as secretary general of the United Nations in 1994, only 13 percent of Americans could do so. Nearly all Germans polled could name Boris Yeltsin as Russia's leader, as could 63 percent of the British, 61 percent of the French, but only 50 percent of the Americans.

How can the United States claim to be a model democracy if its citizens know so little about political life? That question has aroused political reformers and preoccupied many political scientists since the early 20th century. It can't be answered without some historical perspective.

Today's mantra that the "informed citizen" is the foundation of effective democracy was not a central part of the nation's founding vision. It is largely the creation of late-19th-century Mugwump and Progressive reformers, who recoiled from the spectacle of powerful political parties using government as a job bank for their friends and a cornucopia of contracts for their relatives. (In those days before the National Endowment for the Arts, Nathaniel Hawthorne, Herman Melville, and Walt Whitman all subsidized their writing by holding down federal patronage appointments.) Voter turnout in the late 19th century was extraordinarily high by today's standards, routinely over 70 percent in presidential elections, and there is no doubt that parades, free whiskey, free-floating money, patronage jobs, and the pleasures of fraternity all played a big part in the political enthusiasm of ordinary Americans.

The reformers saw this kind of politics as a betrayal of democratic ideals. A democratic public, they believed,

From *The Wilson Quarterly*, Spring 2000, pp. 16-22. © 2000 by Michael Schudson. Reprinted by permission.

A tradition of ignorance? Making sober political choices wasn't the top priority of these Kansas Territory voters in 1857.

must reason together. That ideal was threatened by mindless enthusiasm, the wily maneuvers of political machines, and the vulnerability of the new immigrant masses in the nation's big cities, woefully ignorant of Anglo-Saxon traditions, to manipulation by party hacks. E. L. Godkin, founding editor of the *Nation* and a leading reformer, argued that "there is no corner of our system in which the hastily made and ignorant foreign voter may not be found eating away the political structure, like a white ant, with a group of natives standing over him and encouraging him."

This was in 1893, by which point a whole set of reforms had been put in place. Civil service reform reduced patronage. Ballot reform irrevocably altered the act of voting itself. For most of the 19th century, parties distributed at the polls their own "tickets," listing only their own candidates for office. A voter simply took a ticket from a party worker and deposited it in the ballot box, without needing to read it or mark it in any way. Voting was thus a public act of party affiliation. Beginning in 1888, however, and spreading across the country by 1896, this system was replaced with government-printed ballots that listed all the candidates from each eligible party. The voter marked the ballot in secret, as we do today, in an act that affirmed voting as an individual choice rather than a social act of party loyalty. Political parades and other public spectacles increasingly gave way to pamphlets in what reformers dubbed "educational" political campaigns. Leading newspapers, once little more than organs of the political parties, began to declare their independence and to portray themselves as nonpartisan commercial institutions of public enlightenment and public-minded criticism. Public secondary education began to spread.

These and other reforms enshrined the informed citizen as the foundation of democracy, but at a tremendous cost: Voter turnout plummeted. In the presidential election of 1920, it dropped to 49 percent, its lowest point in the 20th century—until it was matched in 1996. Ever since, political scientists and others have been plumbing the mystery created by the new model of an informed citizenry: How can so many, knowing so little, and voting in such small numbers, build a democracy that appears to be (relatively) successful?

There are several responses to that question. The first is that a certain amount of political ignorance is an inevitable byproduct of America's unique political environment. One reason Americans have so much difficulty grasping the political facts of life is that their political system is the world's most complex. Ask the next political science Ph.D. you meet to explain what government agencies at what level—federal, state, county, or city—take responsibility for the homeless. Or whom he or she voted for in the last election for municipal judge. The answers might make Jay Leno's victims seem less ridiculous. No European country has as many elections, as many elected offices, as complex a maze of overlapping governmental jurisdictions, as the American system. It is simply harder to "read" U.S. politics than the politics of most nations.

The hurdle of political comprehension is raised a notch higher by the ideological inconsistencies of American political parties. In Britain, a voter can confidently cast a vote without knowing a great deal about the particular candidates on the ballot. The Labor candidate generally can be counted on to follow the Labor line, the Conservative to follow the Tory line. An American voter casting a ballot for a Democrat or Republican has no such assurance. Citizens in other countries need only dog paddle to be in the political swim; in the United States they need the skills of a scuba diver.

If the complexity of U.S. political institutions helps explain American ignorance of domestic politics, geopolitical factors help explain American backwardness in foreign affairs. There is a kind of ecology of political ignorance at work. The United States is far from Europe and borders only two other countries. With a vast domestic market, most of its producers have relatively few dealings with customers in other countries, globalization notwithstanding. Americans, lacking the parliamentary form of government that prevails in most other democracies, are also likely to find much of what they read or hear about the wider world politically opaque. And the simple fact of America's political and cultural superpower status naturally limits citizens' political awareness. Just as employees gossip more about the boss than the boss gossips about them, so Italians and Brazilians know more about the United States than Americans know about their countries.

Consider a thought experiment. Imagine what would happen if you transported those relatively well-informed Germans or Britons to the United States with their cultural heritage, schools, and news media intact. If you checked on them again about a generation later, after long exposure to the distinctive American political environment—its geographic isolation, superpower status, complex political system, and weak parties—would they have the political knowledge levels of Europeans or Americans? Most likely, I think, they would have developed typically American levels of political ignorance.

L ending support to this notion of an ecology of political knowledge is the stability of American political ignorance over time. Since the 1940s, when social scientists began measuring it, political ignorance has remained virtually unchanged. It is hard to gauge the extent of political knowledge before that time, but there is little to suggest that there is some lost golden age in U.S. history. The storied 1858 debates between Senator Stephen Douglas and Abraham Lincoln, for example, though undoubtedly a high point in the nation's public discourse, were also an anomaly. Public debates were rare in 19th-century political campaigns, and campaign rhetoric was generally overblown and aggressively partisan.

Modern measurements of Americans' historical and political knowledge go back at least to 1943, when the *New York Times* surveyed college freshmen and found "a striking ignorance of even the most elementary aspects of United States history." Reviewing nearly a half-century of data (1945–89) in *What Americans Know about Politics and Why It Matters* (1996), political scientists Michael Delli Carpini and Scott Keeter conclude that, on balance, there has been a slight gain in Americans' political knowledge, but one so modest that it makes more sense to speak of a remarkable stability. In 1945, for example, 43 percent of a national sample could name neither of their U.S. senators; in 1989, the figure was essentially unchanged at 45 percent. In 1952, 67 percent could name the vice president; in 1989, 74 percent could do so. In 1945, 92 percent of Gallup poll respondents knew that the term of the president is four years, compared with 96 percent in 1989. Whatever the explanations for dwindling voter turnout since 1960 may be, rising ignorance is not one of them.*

As Delli Carpini and Keeter suggest, there are two ways to view their findings. The optimist's view is that political ignorance has grown no worse despite the spread of television and video games, the decline of political parties, and a variety of other negative developments. The pessimist asks why so little has improved despite the vast increase in formal education during those years. But the main conclusion remains: no notable change over as long a period as data are available.

Low as American levels of political knowledge may be, a generally tolerable, sometimes admirable, political democracy survives. How? One explanation is provided by a school of political science that goes under the banner of "political heuristics." Public opinion polls and paper-and-pencil tests of political knowledge, argue researchers such as Arthur Lupia, Samuel Popkin, Paul Sniderman, and Philip Tetlock, presume that citizens require more knowledge than they actually need in order to cast votes that accurately reflect their preferences. People can and do get by with relatively little political information. What Popkin calls "low-information rationality" is sufficient for citizens to vote intelligently.

TUNING OUT THE NEWS?

In 1998 a Gallup poll asked respondents where they got their news and information. The results paint a portrait of a less-than-enlightened electorate. Other indicators are discouraging: daily newspaper circulation slid from 62 million in 1970 to 56 million in 1999.

	Every day	Several times/week	Occasionally	Never
Local newspapers	53%	15%	22%	10%
National newspapers	4	11	26	59
Nightly network news	55	19	19	7
CNN	21	16	33	29
C-SPAN	3	4	25	65
National Public Radio	15	12	25	47
Radio talk shows	12	9	21	58
Discussions with family or friends	27	26	41	6
On-line news	7	6	17	70
Weekly news magazines	15	6	27	52

Source: The Gallup Organization. (*Not shown: those answering "no opinion."*)

This works in two ways. First, people can use cognitive cues, or "heuristics." Instead of learning each of a candidate's issue positions, the voter may simply rely on the candidate's party affiliation as a cue. This works better in Europe than in America, but it still works reasonably well. Endorsements are another useful shortcut. A thumbs-up for a candidate from the Christian Coalition or Ralph Nader or the National Association for the Advancement of Colored People or the American Association of Retired Persons frequently provides enough information to enable one to cast a reasonable vote.

Second, as political scientist Milton Lodge points out, people often process information on the fly, without retaining details in memory. If you watch a debate on TV—and 46 million did watch the first presidential debate between President Bill Clinton and Robert Dole in 1996—you may learn enough about the candidates' ideas and personal styles to come to a judgment about each one. A month later, on election day, you may not be able to answer a pollster's detailed questions about where they stood on the issues, but you will remember which one you liked best—and that is enough information to let you vote intelligently.

The realism of the political heuristics school is an indispensable corrective to unwarranted bashing of the general public. Americans are not the political dolts they sometimes seem to be. Still, the political heuristics approach has a potentially fatal flaw: It subtly substitutes *voting* for *citizenship*. Cognitive shortcuts have their place, but what if a citizen wants to persuade someone else to vote for his or her chosen candidate? What may be sufficient in the voting booth is inadequate in the wider world of the democratic process: discussion, deliberation, and persuasion. It is possible to vote and still be disenfranchised.

Yet another response to the riddle of voter ignorance takes its cue from the Founders and other 18th-century political thinkers who emphasized the importance of a morally virtuous citizenry. Effective democracy, in this view, depends more on the "democratic character" of citizens than on their aptitude for quiz show knowledge of political facts. Character, in this sense, is demonstrated all the time in everyday life, not in the voting booth every two years. From Amitai Etzioni, William Galston, and Michael Sandel on the liberal side of the political spectrum to William J. Bennett and James Q. Wilson on the conservative side, these writers emphasize the importance of what Alexis de Tocqueville called "habits of the heart." These theorists, along with politicians of every stripe, point to the importance of civil society as a foundation of democracy. They emphasize instilling moral virtue through families and civic participation through churches and other voluntary associations; they stress the necessity for civility and democratic behavior in daily life. They would not deny that it is important for citizens to be informed, but neither would they put information at the center of their vision of what makes democracy tick.

Brown University's Nancy Rosenblum, for example, lists two essential traits of democratic character. "Easy spontaneity" is the disposition to treat others identically, without deference, and with an easy grace. This capacity to act as if many social differences are of no account in public settings is one of the things that make democracy happen on the streets. This is the disposition that foreign visitors have regularly labeled "American" for 200 years, at least since 1818, when the British reformer and journalist William Cobbett remarked upon Americans' "universal civility." Tocqueville observed in 1840 that strangers in America who meet "find neither danger nor advantage in telling each other freely what they think. Meeting by chance, they neither seek nor avoid each other. Their manner is therefore natural, frank, and open."

Rosenblum's second trait is "speaking up," which she describes as "a willingness to respond at least minimally to ordinary injustice." This does not involve anything so impressive as organizing a demonstration, but something more like objecting when an adult cuts ahead of a kid in a line at a movie theater, or politely rebuking a coworker who slurs a racial or religious group. It is hard to define "speaking up" precisely, but we all recognize it, without necessarily giving it the honor it deserves as an element of self-government.

We need not necessarily accept Rosenblum's chosen pair of moral virtues. Indeed a Japanese or Swedish democrat might object that they look suspiciously like distinctively American traits rather than distinctively democratic ones. They almost evoke Huckleberry Finn. But turning our attention to democratic character reminds us that being well informed is just one of the requirements of democratic citizenship.

The Founding Fathers were certainly more concerned about instilling moral virtues than disseminating information about candidates and issues. Although they valued civic engagement more than their contemporaries in Europe did, and cared enough about promoting the wide circulation of ideas to establish a post office and adopt the First Amendment, they were ambivalent about, even suspicious of, a politically savvy populace. They did not urge voters to "know the issues"; at most they hoped that voters would choose wise and prudent legislators to consider issues on their behalf. On the one hand, they agreed that "the diffusion of knowledge is productive of virtue, and the best security for our civil rights," as a North Carolina congressman put it in 1792. On the other hand, as George Washington cautioned, "however necessary it may be to keep a watchful eye over public servants and public measures, yet there ought to be limits to it, for suspicions unfounded and jealousies too lively are irritating to honest feelings, and oftentimes are productive of more evil than good."

If men were angels, well and good—but they were not, and few of the Founders were as extravagant as Benjamin Rush in his rather scary vision of an education that would "convert men into republican machines." In theory, many shared Rush's emphasis on education; in practice, the states made little provision for public schooling in the early years of the Republic. Where schools did develop, they were defended more as tutors of obedience and organs of national unity than as means to create a watchful citizenry. The Founders placed trust less in education than in a political system designed to insulate decision making in the legislatures from the direct influence of the emotional, fractious, and too easily swayed electorate.

All of these arguments—about America's political environment, the value of political heuristics, and civil society—do not add up to a prescription for resignation or complacency about civic education. Nothing I have said suggests that the League of Women Voters should shut its doors or that newspaper editors should stop puffing politics on page one. People may be able to vote intelligently with very little information—even well-educated people do exactly that on most of the ballot issues they face—but democratic citizenship means more than voting. It means discussing and debating the questions before the political community—and sometimes raising new questions. Without a framework of information in which to place them, it is hard to understand even the simple slogans and catchwords of the day. People with scant political knowledge, as research by political scientists Samuel Popkin and Michael Dimock suggests, have more difficulty than others in perceiving differences between candidates and parties. Ignorance also tends to breed more ignorance; it inhibits people from venturing into situations that make them feel uncomfortable or inadequate, from the voting booth to the community forum to the town hall.

What is to be done? First, it is important to put the problem in perspective. American political ignorance is not growing worse. There is even an "up" side to Americans' relative indifference to political and historical facts: their characteristic openness to experiment, their pragmatic willingness to judge ideas and practices by their results rather than their pedigree.

Second, it pays to examine more closely the ways in which people do get measurably more knowledgeable. One of the greatest changes Delli Carpini and Keeter found in their study, for example, was in the percentage of Americans who could identify the first 10 amendments to the Constitution as the Bill of Rights. In 1954, the year the U.S. Supreme Court declared school segregation unconstitutional in *Brown v. Board of Education*, only 31 percent of Americans could do so. In 1989, the number had moved up to 46 percent.

Why the change? I think the answer is clear: The civil rights movement, along with the rights-oriented Warren Court, helped bring rights to the forefront of the American political agenda and thus to public consciousness. Because they dominated the political agenda, rights became a familiar topic in the press and on TV dramas, sitcoms, and talk shows, also finding their way into school curricula and textbooks. Political change, this experience shows, can influence public knowledge.

This is not to say that only a social revolution can bring about such an improvement. A lot of revolutions are small, one person at a time, one classroom at a time. But it does mean that there is no magic bullet. Indeed, imparting political knowledge has only become more difficult as the dimensions of what is considered political have expanded into what were once nonpolitical domains (such as gender relations and tobacco use), as one historical narrative has become many, each of them contentious, and as the relatively simple framework of world politics (the Cold War) has disappeared.

In this world, the ability to name the three branches of government or describe the New Deal does not make a citizen, but it is at least a token of membership in a society dedicated to the ideal of self-government. Civic education is an imperative we must pursue with the full recognition that a high level of ignorance is likely to prevail—even if that fact does not flatter our faith in rationalism, our pleasure in moralizing, or our confidence in reform.

---

*There is no happy explanation for low voter turnout. "Voter fatigue" is not as silly an explanation as it may seem: Americans have more frequent elections for more offices than any other democracy. It is also true that the more-or-less steady drop in turnout starting in about 1960 coincided with the beginning of a broad expansion of nonelectoral politics that may have drained political energies away from the polling places: the civil rights movement, the antiwar demonstrations of the Vietnam years, the women's movement, and the emergence of the religious Right. The decline in turnout may signify in part that Americans are disengaged from public life, but it may also suggest that they judge electoral politics to be disengaged from public issues that deeply concern them.

MICHAEL SCHUDSON, *a professor of communication and adjunct professor of sociology at the University of California, San Diego, is the author of several books on the media and, most recently,* The Good Citizen: A History of American Civic Life *(1998).*

American
FEDERALISM
Half-Full or Half-Empty?

By Martha Derthick

Last August the *Wall Street Journal* noted that some taxpayers were claiming that they did not have to pay federal income tax because they were residents of a state, not the United States. A few weeks earlier the *New York Times* carried a story describing Vice President Albert Gore's plan to have detailed positions on a wide range of issues in his quest for the Democratic presidential nomination in 2000. At the top of his list was education, a function not long ago considered a preserve of state and local governments.

Gore's "blizzard of positions" included preschool for all children, a ban on gang-style clothing, teacher testing, "second-chance" schools for trouble-prone students, back-to-school parent-teacher meetings where a strict discipline code would be signed, and "character education" courses in the schools. Gore proposed to amend the Family and Medical Leave Act to permit parents to attend the parent-teacher meetings during working hours.

As these contrasting conceptions suggest, American federalism is a highly protean form, long on change and confusion, short on fixed, generally accepted principles. In the event, a tax court judge fined the taxpayers who claimed not to be citizens of the United States. And the *Times* reporter hinted that many actions Gore planned to "require" would need local school board cooperation to take effect.

As the 20th century ends, public commentators often suggest that this is a time of decentralization in the federal system. The view derives mainly from a series of Supreme Court decisions that have sought to rehabilitate the states in constitutional doctrine and from passage of a welfare reform act in 1996 that office-holders and analysts alike interpreted as radically devolutionary.

But matters are more complicated than that. American federalism was born in ambiguity, it institutionalizes ambiguity in our form of government, and changes in it tend to be ambiguous too.

To sort out what is happening, I will distinguish among three spheres of activity: constitutional interpretation by the Supreme Court; electoral politics; and the everyday work of government as manifested in policies and programs.

The Supreme Court

A narrow majority of the Rehnquist Court led by the chief justice attaches importance to preserving federalism. To that end, it has made a series of daring and controversial decisions that purport to limit the powers of Congress or secure constitutional prerogatives of the states.

In *Printz v. U.S.* (1997) the Court invalidated a provision of the Brady Handgun Violence Prevention Act that required local law enforcement officers to conduct background checks on all gun purchasers. The Court objected that the provision impermissibly violated the Tenth Amendment by commandeering the state

From the *Brookings Review*, November 6, 2000, pp. 25-27. © 2000 by the Brookings Institution. Reprinted by permission.

government to carry out a federal law. An earlier opinion, *New York v. U.S.* (1992), had begun to lay the ground for the anticommandeering principle. In another leading case, *U.S. v. Lopez* (1995), the Court held that Congress had exceeded its commerce clause power by prohibiting guns in school zones. Still other decisions signaled a retreat from federal judicial supervision of school desegregation, prison administration, and the judgments of state courts. Another line of cases has secured the state governments' immunity from certain classes of suits under federal law.

Some analysts profess to see a revolutionary development here, but qualifications are in order. The Court decides many cases in which it does not give primacy to federalism, as for example a 7–2 ruling in 1999 that state welfare programs may not restrict new residents to the welfare benefits they would have received in the states from which they moved. This ruling struck down a California law and by implication a provision of federal law that had authorized it. Moreover, the majority that has decided the leading federalism cases is narrow (often 5–4) and tenuous, inasmuch as it includes some of the oldest members of the Court. The decisions have not exactly been hailed by legal scholars, even some who might be thought sympathetic. Charles Fried of the Harvard Law School, a former solicitor general in the Reagan administration, denounced the series of decisions last June on immunity from suits as "bizarre" and "absurd."

If this is a revolution, it is one that may not last.

Electoral Politics

Speaker Thomas P. O'Neill's famous aphorism that "all politics is local" applied to virtually all structural aspects of U.S. electoral politics for a very long time. Determining electoral districts and voter qualifications, mobilizing voters, and financing campaigns were the province mainly of state laws and customs and were locally rooted well into this century. But that has ceased to be true under the impact of 20th-century constitutional amendments extending the electorate, as well as federal statutes and judicial decisions governing apportionment and voting rights. Federal supervision now extends even to such matters as ward-based versus at-large elections in local governments. And changes in technology and in social and economic structures mean

that candidates for congressional seats or even lesser offices do not depend exclusively on funds raised from local constituencies. Candidates may get help from party committees and interest groups organized on a national scale.

Nationalization of electoral practices proceeds apace at century's end. The Motor Voter Act of 1993 requires states to allow all eligible citizens to register to vote when they apply for or renew a driver's license. It also requires states to allow mail-in registration forms at agencies that supply public assistance, such as welfare checks or help for the disabled. The costs are borne by the states.

Nevertheless, one hesitates to insist that our electoral processes are being comprehensively nationalized at a time when governors seem to have gained an advantage in access to the presidency, growing, arguably, out of the public's now chronic distrust of the national government. Of the four last presidents in this century, three were governors before they were elected, and in the run-up to the 2000 election, a governor, George W. Bush of Texas, has secured a large and early advantage over other Republican candidates. He owes his success partly to other Republican governors—of whom there were 32 after the election of 1998—who have backed him under the lead of Michigan's John Engler. To find a presidential nomination that originated in the action of elected state officials, one must go all the way back to 1824, when several state legislatures put forth candidates.

Policies and Programs

It is necessary to be selective because there are so many policies and programs. I will concentrate on three sets—welfare, schools, and criminal justice—that have traditionally been regarded as quite decentralized. Indeed, for decades they constituted the bedrock of local government activity.

The welfare reform legislation of 1996 is everyone's leading example of decentralization in action. The law converted what had been an open-ended matching grant, with federal funds tied to the number of cases, to a fixed-sum ("block") grant and explicitly ended individuals' entitlements to welfare. States gained freedom to design their own programs, a change already largely effectuated by White House decisions during the Reagan, Bush, and Clinton administrations to grant waivers of certain federal requirements to individual states. The decentralization of program authority in this case was an important change in intergovernmental relations. Still, its significance must be put in perspective.

Whatever may have happened with welfare in 1996, income support, which is the core function of the modern welfare state, has been largely federalized in the United States in the six decades since 1935. Social Security, Supplemental Security Income (SSI), and food stamps accounted for $431 billion in federal spending in 1998, compared with $22 billion for welfare, now known as TANF (or Temporary Assistance for Needy Families). I pass over the earned income tax credit, weighing in at a volume comparable to that for welfare, a use of federal tax law for income support that would take us too far afield here.

Welfare could be decentralized in 1996 in large part because, unlike income support for the aged and the disabled, it had never been fully centralized. The main change in 1996 was a national policy change that strongly discouraged dependency and certain behavior, especially out-of-wedlock pregnancies and lack of child support from fathers, that had come to be associated with welfare. To carry out this policy change, the new law imposed some stringent federal requirements, such as time limits for receipt of welfare, on the states. Surprisingly, a liberal president and conservative members of the new Republican minority in Congress coalesced in support of legislation, but the national coalition was so frail and incomplete that it became necessary to lodge discretion in the states to achieve a result.

That is one of the traditional functions of American federalism: in the absence of agreement at the national level, discretion can be left to the states. Typically, through *inaction* by Congress, matters are left with the states, which have initial jurisdiction. What was new in 1996 was that AFDC (Aid to Families with Dependent Children) had become sufficiently centralized in the generation since the mid-1960s that giving discretion to the states required an affirmative act. It required giving back some portion of what had been taken away, as much by federal courts as by Congress. "No more individual entitlement," the most arresting phrase in the act, was directed at altering relations between Congress and the federal judiciary. I would argue that the law had at least as much significance for what it said about interbranch relations at the federal level as about relations among governments in the federal system.

Elementary and secondary education, far from being off limits to national politicians as a local matter, has risen to the top of their rhetorical agenda. It took a year for Congress to reauthorize the Elementary and Secondary Education Act in 1993–94. The resulting law consumed 14 titles and 1,200 pages, covering subjects as wide-ranging as academic standards, racial desegregation, language assessments, migrant education, teacher training, math and science equipment, libraries, hate-crime prevention, vouchers, school prayer, sex education, gay rights, gun control, the handicapped, English as a second language, telecommunications, pornography, single-sex schools, national tests, home schooling, drugs, smoking—and more. The level of detail was minute. Any state receiving federal funds had to require that any student who brought a gun to school would be expelled for at least a year. Local officials could, however, modify the requirement on a case-by-case basis. School districts also had to refer offenders to local law enforcement officials. Developmentally disabled students were subject to the expulsion rule, but if school officials established that their behavior was related to their disability, the students could be placed in an alternative educational setting for up to 45 days instead.

In 1999, when the act was again up for reauthorization, Congress by wide margins enacted "Ed-Flex," the Educational Flexibility Partnership Demonstration Act, which authorized the Secretary of Education to implement a nationwide program under which state educational agencies could apply for waivers of certain federal rules. To be eligible for Ed-Flex, states had to develop educational content and performance standards and procedures for holding districts and schools accountable for meeting educational goals. One could point to this law, of course, as an example of decentralization; members of Congress naturally did so. But in education as in welfare, the subject of waivers would never have arisen had not a vast body of law and regulation developed from which relief had to be sought.

In criminal justice, it remains true that most police and prosecutors are state and local officials. Ninety-five percent of prosecutions are handled by state and local governments. Yet federal criminal law has grown explosively as Congress has taken stands against such offenses as carjacking and church burning, disrupting a rodeo and damaging a livestock facility. A 1999 task force report of the American Bar Association documented and decried this development but is unlikely to stop, let alone reverse it.

The "Mores" of Intergovernmental Relations

In everyday affairs, how do we and our officials think and talk about governments in the federal system? Without having any evidence to support my point, I would argue that citizens and journalists routinely refer to "the government" as if there were only one—the Big One. That this is a country of many governments, though a patent fact, is nonetheless a fact that it takes a pedant or a lawyer to insist on.

Moreover, we are now accustomed to reading that Washington is giving orders to the states, or at least exhorting them to act in regard to one or another matter in which they have been found deficient. Some sample headlines from end-of-century stories in the *New York Times* would appear very odd to a student of American government who had gone to sleep in, say, 1955 and just awakened: "Clinton to Require State Efforts to Cut Drug Use in Prisons" (January 12, 1998); "White House Plans Medicaid Coverage of Viagra by States" (May 28, 1998); "Clinton to Chide States for Failing to Cover Children" (August 8, 1999). None of this is to say that the states promptly act on orders or admonitions from Washington, only that Washington is accustomed to giving them, without pausing to question the appropriateness of doing so—as is evident from an executive order on federalism that the Clinton administration issued, suspended when state officials angrily protested, and then issued in much revised form.

The offending order, issued in May 1998, contained a set of criteria for policymaking by federal agencies that was broad and inclusive enough invariably to justify federal government action: "(1) When the matter to be addressed by federal action occurs interstate as opposed to being contained within one State's boundaries. (2) When the source of the matter to be addressed occurs in a State different from the State (or States) where a significant amount of the harm occurs. (3) When there is a need for uniform national standards. (4) When decentralization increases the costs of government thus imposing additional burdens on the taxpayer. (5) When States have not adequately protected individual rights and liberties. (6) When States would be reluctant to impose necessary regulations because of fears that regulated business activity will relocate to other States. . . ." Only the most obtuse and indolent federal administrator could not have put this list to use.

The revised executive order, issued following consultation with state officials, was completely different. The section on policymaking criteria called for "strict adherence to constitutional principles," avoiding limits on policymaking discretion of the states except with constitutional and statutory authority, granting "maximum administrative discretion" to the states, encouraging states to "develop their own policies to achieve program objectives," where possible deferring to the states to "establish standards," consulting with appropriate state and local officials "as to the need for national standards," and consulting with them in developing national standards when such were found to be necessary.

It is hard to imagine a more complete about-face. It is also hard to know how to interpret the event. One can cite the original order as evidence of the imperious attitudes that high federal officials actually bring to intergovernmental relations, or one can cite the revision as evidence of the continuing power of the states. In studying American federalism, the analyst is forever asking whether the glass is half-empty or half-full. That is the appropriate question as the century turns, and the answers are to be found more in the day-to-day operations of intergovernmental relations than in either Supreme Court decisions or executive orders. It requires a blind eye to call ours an era of devolution. But even with two sharp eyes, it is hard to detect a plain answer. Everywhere one looks, the answer remains murky and many-sided.

Martha Derthick is professor of government and foreign affairs emeritus at the University of Virginia. She is the editor of Dilemmas of Scale in America's Federal Democracy *(Cambridge, 1999).*

THE DYING CONSTITUTION

Vigilante Justices

As the Court ignores the Constitution in favor of its conscience, it tramples on democracy—and the rights of the minority.

ANTONIN SCALIA

THE argument most frequently made in favor of The Living Constitution is a pragmatic one: Such an evolutionary approach is necessary in order to provide the "flexibility" that a changing society requires; the Constitution would have snapped if it had not been permitted to bend and grow. This might be a persuasive argument if most of the "growing" that the proponents of this approach have brought upon us in the past, and are determined to bring upon us in the future, were the *elimination* of restrictions upon democratic government. But just the opposite is true. Historically, and particularly in the past 35 years, the "evolving" Constitution has imposed a vast array of new constraints—new inflexibilities—upon administrative, judicial, and legis-

lative action. To mention only a few things that formerly could be done or not done, as the society desired, but now cannot be done:

— admitting in a state criminal trial evidence of guilt that was obtained by an unlawful search;

— permitting invocation of God at public-school graduations;

— electing one of the two houses of a state legislature the way the United States Senate is elected, i.e., on a basis that does not give all voters numerically equal representation;

— terminating welfare payments as soon as evidence of fraud is received, subject to restoration after hearing if the evidence is satisfactorily refuted;

— imposing property requirements as a condition of voting;

— prohibiting anonymous campaign literature;

— prohibiting pornography.

And the future agenda of constitutional evolutionists is mostly more of the same—the creation of new restrictions upon democratic government, rather than the elimination of old ones. *Less* flexibility in government, not *more*. As things now stand, the federal and state governments may either apply capital punishment or abolish it, permit suicide or forbid it—all as the changing times and the changing sentiments of society may demand. But when capital punishment is held to violate the Eighth Amendment, and suicide is held to be protected by the Fourteenth Amendment, all flexibility with regard to those matters will be gone. No, the reality of the matter is that, generally speaking, devotees of The Living Constitution seek not to facilitate social change but to *prevent* it.

There are, I must admit, a few exceptions to that rule—a few instances in which, historically, greater flexibility *has* been the result of the process. But those exceptions serve only to refute another argument of the proponents of an evolving Constitution: that evolution will always be in the direction of greater personal liberty. They consider that a great advantage, for reasons that I do not entirely understand. All government represents a balance between individual freedom and social order, and it is not true that every alteration of that balance in the direction of greater individual freedom is necessarily good. But in any case, the record of history refutes the proposition that the evolving Constitution will invariably enlarge individual rights. The most obvious refutation is the modern Court's limitation of the constitutional protections afforded to property. The provision prohibiting impairment of the obligation of contracts, for example, has been gutted. I am sure that We the People agree with that development; we value property rights less than did the Founders. So also, we value the right to bear arms less than did the Founders (who thought the right of self-defense to be absolutely fundamental), and there will be few tears shed if and when the Second Amendment is held to guarantee nothing more than the state National Guard. But this just shows that the Founders were right when they feared that some (in their view misguided) future generation might wish to abandon liberties that they considered essential, and so sought to protect those liberties in a Bill of Rights. We may *like* the abridgment of property rights and *like* the elimination of the right to bear arms; but let us not pretend that these are not *reductions* of rights.

My pointing out that the American people may be satisfied with a reduction of their liberties should not be taken as a suggestion that the proponents of The Living Constitution *follow* the desires of the American people in determining how the Constitution should evolve. They follow nothing so precise; indeed, as a group they follow nothing at all. Perhaps the most glaring defect of Living Constitutionalism, next to its incompatibility with the whole anti-evolutionary purpose of a constitution, is

that there is no agreement, and no chance of agreement, upon what is to be the guiding principle of the evolution. *Panta rhei* is not a sufficiently informative principle of constitutional interpretation. What is it that the judge must consult to determine when, and in what direction, evolution has occurred? Is it the will of the majority, discerned from newspapers, radio talk shows, public-opinion polls, and chats at the country club? Is it the philosophy of Hume, or of John Rawls, or of John Stuart Mill, or of Aristotle? As soon as the discussion goes beyond whether the Constitution is static, the evolutionists divide into as many camps as there are individual views of the good, the true, and the beautiful. I think that is inevitably so, which means that evolutionism is simply not a practicable constitutional philosophy.

I DO not suggest, mind you, that originalists always agree upon their answer. There is plenty of room for disagreement as to what the original meaning was, and even more as to how that original meaning applies to the situation before the Court. But the originalist at least knows what he is looking for: the original meaning of the text. Often—indeed, I dare say usually—that is easy to discern and simple to apply. Sometimes (though not very often) there will be disagreement regarding the original meaning; and sometimes there will be disagreement as to how that original meaning applies to new and unforeseen phenomena. How, for example, does the First Amendment guarantee of "the freedom of speech" apply to new technologies that did not exist when the guarantee was created—to sound trucks, or to government-licensed over-the-air television? In such new fields the Court must follow the trajectory of the First Amendment, so to speak, to determine what it requires—and assuredly that enterprise is not entirely cut-and-dried but requires the exercise of judgment.

But the difficulties and uncertainties of determining original meaning and applying it to modern circumstances are negligible compared with the difficulties and uncertainties of the philosophy which says that the Constitution *changes;* that the very act which it once prohibited it now permits, and which it once permitted it now prohibits; and that the key to that change is unknown and unknowable. The originalist, if he does not

have all the answers, has many of them. For the evolutionist, on the other hand, every question is an open question, every day a new day. No fewer than three of the Justices with whom I have served (Justices Brennan, Marshall, and Blackmun) have maintained that the death penalty is unconstitutional, *even though its use is explicitly contemplated in the Constitution.* The Due Process Clause of the Fifth and Fourteenth Amendments says that no person shall be deprived of life without due process of law; and the Grand Jury Clause of the Fifth Amendment says that no person shall be held to answer for a capital crime without grand-jury indictment. No matter. Under The Living Constitution the death penalty may have *become* unconstitutional. And it is up to each Justice to decide for himself (under no standard I can discern) when that occurs.

In the last analysis, however, it probably does not matter what principle, among the innumerable possibilities, the evolutionist proposes to use in order to determine in what direction The Living Constitution will grow. Whatever he might propose, at the end of the day an evolving constitution will evolve the way the majority wishes. The people will be willing to leave interpretation of the Constitution to lawyers so long as the people believe that it is (like the interpretation of a statute) essentially lawyers' work—requiring a close examination of text, history of the text, traditional understanding of the text, judicial precedent, and so forth. But if the people come to believe that the Constitution is not a text like other texts; that it means, not what it says or what it was understood to mean, but what it should mean, in the light of the "evolving standards of decency that mark the progress of a maturing society"—well, then, they will look for qualifications other than impartiality, judgment, and lawyerly acumen in those whom they select to interpret it. More specifically, they will look for judges who agree with them as to what the evolving standards have evolved to; who agree with them as to what the Constitution ought to be.

It seems to me that that is where we are heading, or perhaps even where we have arrived. Seventy-five years ago, we believed firmly enough in a rock-solid, unchanging Constitution that we felt it necessary to adopt the Nineteenth Amendment to give women the vote. The battle was not fought in the courts,

Court Jesters

THE men who wrote the U.S. Constitution dreaded an imperial President, and they feared an unrestrained Congress. Either could destroy the new democratic Republic. So they established an ingenious system of checks and balances to prevent either branch from encroaching too far on the prerogatives of the other. But the Founders considered the judiciary to be inherently the weakest branch of government. They never contemplated what has happened—a willful judiciary that is fencing voters and their elected representatives out of the decision-making process.

Abuse of power by the Supreme Court has long been a serious concern. But the stakes are magnified by the re-election of President Bill Clinton. Mr. Clinton is likely to have the opportunity to nominate one or more members of the High Court. Presumably, he will be inclined to appoint activist Justices whose presence on the Court would aggravate an already untenable situation.

Fortunately, however, members of the U.S. Senate still can prevent our worst fears from being realized. Senators have the right to deny confirmation of activist nominees to the Supreme Court and, for that matter, other courts. Senators should decide that, henceforth, judicial nominees will be required to pledge publicly that they will interpret the Constitution and statutes in accordance with the original intent of the documents and their authors. As the High Court veers further and further from the text and intention of the Constitution, it seems clear that such a promise should be a precondition to confirmation of judicial appointees.

Most Americans paid little attention when Supreme Court Justices first began to substitute their own values for the express provisions of the Constitution. After all, Justices continued to support their decisions by references to the written law even while subverting it. Lately, however, even the pretense that the Court is abiding by the words of the Constitution has worn thin.

"The most important moral, political, and cultural decisions are steadily being removed from democratic control," Judge Robert Bork points out. "A majority of the court routinely enacts its own preference as the command" of the Constitution.

Professor Russell Hittinger terms the situation a "crisis of legitimacy," while Charles W. Colson regards recent trends as the "systematic usurpation of ultimate political power by the American judiciary." Justice Scalia, never one to mince words, is even more direct: "day by day, case by case, [the Court] is busy designing a Constitution for a country I do not recognize."

Some will be dismayed by such characterizations. But what else can be said when the Court changes laws from what was intended and written by the authors? Citizens can appeal directly to their elected representatives in state legislatures and Congress; they can request changes in existing laws; if frustrated by elected officials they can seek to replace them next election day. In a democratic society, this is the way the people govern, the way old laws are updated or repealed and new laws enacted.

But when Justices—an unelected elite—arbitrarily substitute their own preferences for the preferences of those who are elected to make laws, they are, in effect, repealing or modifying existing laws or inventing new ones. They be-

come, in George Will's memorable phrase, "our robed masters."

Instinctively most of us shrink from thinking this could be true. But innumerable Supreme Court decisions support Professor Hittinger's contention that "we live today under an altered constitutional regime, where the rules are no longer supplied by a written document but by federal courts defining the powers of government ad hoc."

The Founding Fathers considered it dangerous to leave each state with complete power to regulate commerce. The nation could not long endure if states could discriminate against one another by erecting tariff barriers. Therefore Article I of the Constitution gives to Congress "the power to regulate commerce . . . among the several states." The Constitution could have been written to grant Congress complete power to control all commerce including that which affects only one state or the people within a single state. The Founders decided not to write it that way.

However, the Supreme Court consistently ignores the intent of the Constitution in this area. In the strange case of *Wickard* v. *Filburn,* the Court upheld federal limits on production of wheat even though the crop was never sold in interstate commerce. In fact, the wheat in question was never sold at all. It was consumed at home by the grower. The Court upheld the conviction of Mr. Filburn for violating the limits. In doing so, a majority of the Justices established the bizarre principle that by planting and harvesting wheat on his own property for home consumption, a farmer could substantially affect interstate commerce. With such a precedent that is hard to imagine any form of commerce—for that matter, any human activity—which might not be deemed to "affect" interstate commerce and therefore be subject to federal regulation. Constitutional limitations on the scope of the national government have been effectively repealed by the Court.

When Congress passed the Civil Rights Act of 1964, it was plainly never intended that that Act would require racial quotas in business, education, etc. The law does not provide for such quotas. Indeed, Senator Hubert Humphrey and other backers of the legislation vehemently denied that such an outcome was possible. But within a few years the courts had implemented precisely the quota regime sponsors said could never result.

FROM their own experience, the Framers of the Constitution feared the establishing of an official religion for Americans. So they drafted a very simple and clear prohibition on the power of Congress to do so. But in *Everson* v. *Board of Education, McCollum* v. *Board of Education, Engle* v. *Vitale,* and many other cases, the Court has tortured the First Amendment to produce judicial outcomes which the amendment's authors would have found inconceivable. So prayers and Bibles are banned from public schools; displays of religious symbols are forbidden; postal workers are prohibited from wishing one another "Merry Christmas"; and schoolchildren are taught that the Pilgrims instituted the first Thanksgiving Day because they wished to commemorate their gratitude to . . . the Indians!

In *Romer* v. *Evans,* the Court struck down a provision of the Colorado Constitution which prohibited Colorado cities from adopting civil-rights ordinances predicated on sexual

(Continued)

preference. In a ruling one scholar termed "indecipherable," not only did the Court overrule the people of the state, who had adopted the provision in 1992, the Justices also totally ignored their own ruling in the 1986 case of *Bowers* v. *Hardwick*. *Bowers* affirmed that the state of Georgia had the constitutional right to provide criminal penalties for homosexual conduct. But *Romer* says the state may not deny special rights to those who engage in the very behavior it is permitted to criminalize.

Some applaud these cases. Among our fellow citizens are some who believe the national government should have unlimited power to regulate commerce, that racial quotas are a good idea and school prayers are not. But the main point is not whether one is pleased or distressed by the outcome of specific cases. What is worrisome is the process by which Justices are hijacking our democratic system of government. We can well recall with apprehension the boast of Chief Justice Charles Evans Hughes that "the Constitution is what judges say it is."

Before the situation gets any worse, senators should put the White House on notice that no judicial nominee—especially for the Supreme Court—will win confirmation unless the nominee will publicly promise to judge cases in accordance with the meaning intended by the authors of the Constitution and of the various statutes. Such notification will, of course, provoke howls of outrage. The Administration, the American Bar Association, and apologists for the welfare state will be apoplectic. Some TV and newspaper pundits—fortunately not all—will decry any effort to strengthen the Senate's traditional "advice and consent" role in this way.

Insistence on an "original intent" pledge could also delay filling vacancies on various courts. The White House will strongly resist such efforts, and the resulting tensions may make it more difficult for Congress and the President to cooperate on balancing the budget, reforming entitlement programs, etc. If senators were forced to filibuster the confirmation of recalcitrant nominees, it could put a crimp in the whole legislative schedule.

Most senators aren't likely to have the stomach for such a fight. But those who do may prevail. The public is exceedingly cynical about our judicial system. If the issue is properly framed—as a showdown between democracy and elitism—it is very possible the nation will enthusiastically support efforts to curb the abuse of power by "our robed masters." If the public gets behind the idea, then, sooner or later, a majority of senators will also. In the meantime, merely raising the issue will have a beneficial effect on the thought life of nominees and sitting judges.

Cynics may wonder if judicial nominees can be counted on to keep their word if they make an original-intent promise. If they do not, then their faithlessness will merely encourage more drastic reforms.

And what if the effort to extract such promises from nominees should initially fail? In that case, the nation nonetheless will owe a debt of gratitude to any senators who raise the issue. By bringing up this fundamental question, senators can give the whole country an opportunity to participate in the decision. Ultimately, the people are supposed to decide such issues. But they can do so only if the question is put squarely before them.

—WILLIAM L. ARMSTRONG

Mr. Armstrong, a Colorado businessman, was a U.S. senator from 1979 to 1991.

and few thought that it could be, despite the constitutional guarantee of Equal Protection of the Laws; that provision did not, when it was adopted, and hence did not in 1920, guarantee equal access to the ballot but permitted distinctions on the basis not only of age but also of property and of sex. Who can doubt that if the issue had been deferred until today, the Constitution would be (formally) unamended, and the courts would be the chosen instrumentality of change? The American people have been converted to belief in The Living Constitution, a "morphing" document that means, from age to age, what it ought to mean. And with that conversion has inevitably come the new phenomenon of selecting and confirming federal judges, at all levels, on the basis of their views regarding a whole series of proposals for constitutional evolution. If the courts are free to write the Constitution anew, they will write it the way the majority wants; the appointment and confirmation process will see to that. This, of course, is the end of the Bill of Rights, whose meaning will be committed to the very body it was meant to protect against: the majority. By trying to make the Constitution do everything that needs doing from age to age, we shall have caused it to do nothing at all.

Mr. Scalia is a Justice of the U.S. Supreme Court.

GUNS AND TOBACCO: GOVERNMENT BY LITIGATION

Stuart Taylor Jr.

"The legal fees alone are enough to bankrupt the industry."

—John Coale, one of the private lawyers suing gunmakers on behalf of municipalities, as quoted in *The Washington Post* after the March 17 settlement in which Smith & Wesson agreed to adopt various safety measures that have stalled in Congress.

In its March 21 ruling that the Clinton Administration lacked authority to regulate the tobacco industry, no matter how great the need for regulation, the Supreme Court reaffirmed the broad principle that the power to set national policy on such hotly contested issues belongs to Congress. But the Justices have taken little note of other bold efforts to bypass Congress—and short-circuit the judicial process to boot—by using the threat of ruinous litigation to impose de facto regulation and taxation on targeted industries, including guns and tobacco. As *The Wall Street Journal* observed, the gun law-

suits could bring about "a more sweeping round of gun regulation than any single piece of legislation in 30 years."

And the far larger tobacco companies, which seem to have been sued by almost everyone alive, could be bankrupted by litigation, including a pending class action by smokers in Florida and a Clinton Administration lawsuit that invokes far-fetched legal theories to seek many billions of dollars to compensate the government for the cost of treating smokers covered by Medicare. Also in the dock are HMOs, companies that sold lead paint more than 40 years ago, and makers of latex gloves. Later may come purveyors of liquor, beer, fatty foods, and, someday, maybe even fast cars and violent videos.

(For a fuller taste of these and other peculiar workings of our legal system, with copious links to news reports, check out an amusingly depressing Web site called *Overlawyered.com,* created and edited by Walter K. Olson of the conservative-libertarian Manhattan Institute.)

From the *National Journal*, March 25, 2000, pp. 929-930. © 2000 by National Journal Group, Inc. All rights reserved. Reprinted by permission.

The alliance of would-be lawmakers behind many of these broad legal assaults includes the Clinton Administration, state attorneys general, and municipalities, working closely with public interest activists and wealthy private lawyers who started it all. Their incentives to sue variously include hopes of raising vast new revenues, bringing unpopular industries to heel, protecting public health and safety, and reaping billions of dollars in fees for the lawyers, who also tend to be big campaign contributors.

This public-private alliance's most recent triumph illustrates the combination of policy-making ambitions and financial incentives that drives such litigation. The triumph was the March 17 decision by British-owned Smith & Wesson, the nation's largest maker of handguns, to abide by a long list of restrictions on gun sales demanded by the Clinton Administration. Smith & Wesson entered the agreement to extricate itself from some or all of the lawsuits against the industry by 29 cities, counties, and other plaintiffs.

The gun lawsuits were bankrolled by contingent-fee lawyers who are also prominent in the more-lucrative tobacco wars and have lots of money to invest in multifront attacks on other industries. They recruited municipalities as clients by dangling the prospect of imposing previously unimagined liability on gunmakers for selling unnecessarily dangerous guns, and selling them to the wrong people, thus allegedly contributing to governmental costs associated with murders, accidental shootings, and other gun violence. Every shooting by a spouse, a child, an armed robber, or a drug dealer is at least theoretically a potential source of liability to the gunmakers. Seizing on the fact that many such shootings occur in federally subsidized housing projects, President Clinton and Housing and Urban Development Secretary Andrew Cuomo jumped in by pressing the gun companies to accept new restrictions or face "death by a thousand cuts," as Cuomo put it.

THE FOUNDERS CREATED CONGRESS TO SET NATIONAL POLICY. THEY DIDN'T INTEND FOR POLICY TO BE FASHIONED BY LAWSUITS.

The plaintiffs have never had to prove their flimsy theories of liability in court. Indeed, judges have dismissed some of the lawsuits. But in this era of astronomical jury awards, a few losses could bankrupt the gun companies even if they win most of their cases. And the legal fees alone are potentially crushing, given the plaintiffs' strategy of deploying massive firepower on multiple fronts, the better to force the companies to settle.

This strategy forced Smith & Wesson to raise the white flag. The restrictions drafted by Administration officials and agreed to by the company require it to develop "smart gun" technology within three years, so that only authorized users can fire new handguns; to limit bulk purchases; to bar dealers from selling at gun shows unless the buyers have passed background checks; to include trigger locks with all new handguns (which Smith & Wesson was already doing); and more. Others may be driven to make similar concessions.

If the plaintiffs' divide-and-conquer strategy forces the rest of the industry to fall into line, the effect would be the de facto imposition of new, nationwide gun-control rules much like those that President Clinton has urged but that Congress has refused to pass. This is reminiscent of the far richer tobacco industry's $246 billion in settlements with state attorneys general in 1998: The intent, and effect, was to finance the payments (and the billions in legal fees) by sharply raising cigarette prices, in what was the functional equivalent of a new nationwide tax on smokers—a tax that neither Congress nor state legislatures had voted to impose.

Will restrictions like those in the Smith & Wesson settlement reduce the number of shooting deaths? There's great dispute about that. Even some advocates of more-radical controls such as banning all handguns worry that "smart gun" technology might increase total gun deaths by stimulating the sale of tens of millions more guns to people who mistakenly think them safe. The National Rifle Association and other, more scholarly opponents of the new gun controls sought by the Administration argue that they would not have prevented the rash of highly publicized shootings since the Littleton, Colo., massacre last year, and that "smart guns" might fail when most needed for legitimate self-defense.

I suspect that restrictions such as those agreed to by Smith & Wesson would save some lives, and so I would like to see Congress pass most, or all, of the Administration's proposals. But with scholarly experts, detailed empirical studies, and millions of people on all sides of the issue, I can't be sure.

One thing I am sure of is that the Framers of the Constitution created Congress—and assigned to it "all legislative powers herein granted"—to set policy for the nation on such complex questions of social engineering. They also made it hard to enact legislation unless backed by a fairly broad national consensus. That's a far cry from what's going on now, with the Clinton Administration and its allies boasting of using lawsuits to bypass partisan gridlock in Congress.

Do the ends justify the means? After all, these lawsuits represent just the latest in a succession of mushrooming theories of liability, expansive constitutional doctrines, and other trends that have led to deep intrusions by the judicial and executive branches into what was once the province of Congress. Why stop now, when so much needs to be done, and Congress is so unhelpful?

But the gun litigation represents a deeply disturbing way of making public policy. It was started by private lawyers and municipalities with big financial interests at stake. The courts have largely been bystanders as the Clinton Administration and its allies have sought to bludgeon gunmakers into settling before trial. And in the words of Robert B. Reich, Clinton's former Labor Secretary, in *The American Prospect:* "If I had my way, there'd be laws restricting cigarettes and handguns. [But] the White House is launching lawsuits to succeed where legislation failed. The strategy may work, but at the cost of making our frail democracy even weaker. . . . You might approve the outcomes in these two cases, but they establish a precedent for other cases you might find wildly unjust."

After the Supreme Court's 5–4 ruling that the federal Food and Drug Administration lacks the power to regulate tobacco without new legislation, President Clinton appropriately stressed that the Justices had been unanimous in asserting that "tobacco use . . . poses perhaps the single most significant threat to public health in the United States." He also called on Congress to pass a new law incorporating the now-voided FDA rule. Senate Majority Leader Trent Lott, R-Miss., immediately announced his opposition. It will be a bitter election-year struggle, with all players attending closely to how the voters will react to whatever they do.

That's called democracy. It's not always the quickest or easiest way to get things done. But it's the best way.

Drawing Legal Lines

BY DAVID BYRD

The 1990s witnessed a revolution in the law underlying redistricting. The Supreme Court dramatically limited the ability of states to take race and ethnicity into account when drawing new electoral boundaries, and new rules determined how census data may be used for redrawing districts. But sharply divided Court decisions since the last redistricting a decade ago have raised more questions than they've answered. And the forecast for this brave new world of redistricting after 2000? Even more litigation.

In the 1993 landmark decision *Shaw vs. Reno,* the Supreme Court declared that excessive and unjustified use of race in drawing state electoral districts violates the equal

protection clause of the Constitution's 14th Amendment. At the same time, though, the Court held that states could conduct redistricting "with consciousness of race." Adding some meat to the meager bones of its rulings on race and redistricting, the Court struck down North Carolina's 12th Congressional District, which snaked from Charlotte to Durham along Interstate 85, in an effort, according to one judge, to "gobble in enough enclaves of black neighborhoods" to consolidate African-American voting strength in a string of urban areas. The Court ruled that the district's noncontiguous "serpentine" shape—coupled with the fact that the district was 53 percent black—was an unconstitutional use of race in redistricting. The Court held that "reapportionment is one area in which appearances *do* matter." It sent North Carolina back to the drawing board.

But the Court left the matter of race in redistricting somewhat unclear, because it also said that a regular shape is not constitutionally required. A "bizarre" or "irregular" shape in conjunction with certain racial demographics, the Court explained, may serve as "persuasive circumstantial evidence that race for its own sake, and not other districting principles, was the legislature's dominant and controlling rationale in drawing its district lines." On the

WHAT SHOULD A DISTRICT LOOK LIKE? SUPREME COURT DECISIONS KEEP THE QUESTION ALIVE.

other hand, those districts with large populations of African-Americans that have been drawn more compactly—"satisfactorily tidy," as the Court characterized one challenged district—have survived the Court's scrutiny.

The Court has also signaled that other nonracial factors might justify a large minority population. They include how tightly the district is drawn; the plan's respect for political subdivisions, such as towns, cities, and counties; the maintenance of an existing partisan balance; and the consideration shown for communities of common interest, such as shared socioeconomic interests. If such factors lie at the heart of a legislature's efforts to redraw a state's districts, a district with a high percentage of minority residents stands a better chance of surviving a court challenge, said Gerry Hebert, the general counsel for the Democrats' national redistricting project and a former deputy chief of the Justice Department's voting rights section.

The Court has at least said clearly that race may not be the *controlling* principle in how a district is drawn. In 1995, the Court struck down Georgia's redistricting plan on the

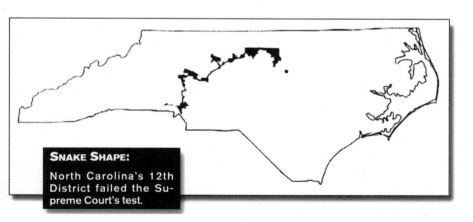

SNAKE SHAPE:
North Carolina's 12th District failed the Supreme Court's test.

ground that race had been "the predominant factor motivating the legislature's decision to place a significant number of voters within or without a particular district." The Court cited comments and admissions made by those drafting the districting plan that they purposefully used race to enhance African-American voting strength in one district.

Nevertheless, states are required in some instances to take race into account. Under the Voting Rights Act of 1965, the Court has said that states with a history of discrimination against minority voters *must* take race into account in redistricting, because the Voting Rights Act prohibits a "retrogression" in minority voting rights. "As a result," Hebert says, "there is now this tension between how states must take race into account in order to comply with the Voting Rights Act, vs. how states, under *Shaw,* should not consider race too heavily."

Race will play a particularly critical role in redistricting after 2000. Most states likely to lose congressional seats—Illinois, Mississippi, New York, Ohio, and Pennsylvania—have sizable minority populations; race will be a major factor in how those states' districts are redrawn to accommodate fewer congressional seats. And in most of those states that are certain to gain congressional seats (Arizona, California, Florida, Georgia, and Texas) Hispanics and blacks play an equally critical role.

Another key to this evolving drama: After the 1990 census, minorities complained that blacks and Hispanics were not adequately represented in districts where minorities made up a majority of the voters, which made it harder to elect their candidates. But this time around, Republicans control the legislatures in most of the states that are losing or gaining seats. Now minorities fear that Republicans might try to consolidate minority populations in one district, "wasting" their

votes by overrepresenting or corralling them. And corralling would deny minorities the opportunity to influence surrounding districts.

In Virginia, for example, the GOP won control of both houses and the governor's mansion last November for the first time since the Civil War. The Republican domination raises concerns among blacks that the state's redistricters may draw boundaries to over-include blacks in one district. The Supreme Court, however, has repeatedly said that "packing" minorities into one district would be a violation of the Voting Rights Act. "The politics of race in 2000 redistricting has reached a boiling point that can't get much higher," Hebert warns.

Race also becomes a factor in determining whether a state uses unadjusted census data or "sampled" numbers for drawing its districts. The Census Bureau initially collects data that are unadjusted for what is known as an "undercount." Because of the difficulty of actually counting every person in the country, the last census in 1990 undercounted the U.S. population by more than 8 million people, the vast majority of whom were minorities and the poor. As a result, states with large populations of minorities and poor people—both pillars of Democratic strength—were underrepresented and therefore received fewer federal dollars. According to the General Accounting Office, for example, Texas, where 25 percent of the population is Hispanic, has lost close to $1 billion in federal aid since the 1990 census.

To address the undercount, the Census Bureau employs a sampling technique to produce population figures widely regarded as more accurate than the census' traditional head count. Under the Bush Administration, the Census Bureau refused to release such data. Under the Clinton Administration, the Census Bureau has stated it will release such sampled data for states to use in redistricting.

But in a 5–4 decision last year, the Supreme Court ruled that a 1976 amendment to the statute on conducting the census prohibits Congress from using sampled data for apportioning congressional seats among the states. Republicans and Democrats vehemently disagree about whether sampled census data can be used for redistricting *within* the state, which differs from Congress apportioning seats *among* the states. The Court did not answer this question, and both parties agree that this is the next great battle in redistricting law.

It is up to each state to decide which data to use for drawing its districts. A number of states, particularly those controlled by Republicans, have started passing laws requiring the use of unsampled census data in redistricting. Democrats argue that this method will result in an undercounting of minority and poor populations.

On March 24, however, the Justice Department signaled in a letter to Arizona's attorney general that no matter which type of census data a state chooses to use, Justice would use the data the Census Bureau deems most accurate—that is, sampled data—in analyzing whether a state's redistricting plans violate the Voting Rights Act. It was an unmistakable warning to those states that plan to use the unsampled census data that undercount minorities. But this issue will surely turn on who wins the presidency in November: Unlike the Clinton-Gore Administration, George W. Bush has said that he opposes using sampled data, and he would probably instruct his Justice Department and Census Bureau accordingly.

While both parties disagree on the law, they agree on its effect: "This is a litigation bonanza," said Tom Hoffeller, the redistricting director for the Republican National Committee. "The dispute over which set of data to be used is the Full Employment Act for redistricting attorneys."

Speech Isn't Cheap

WENDY KAMINER

Despite the materialism that defines American culture and our reverence for financial success, a suspicion that money really is the root of all evil retains its appeal, especially among progressives. The association of wealth with corruption is particularly clear in debates about campaign finance reform. Reformers are self-proclaimed proponents of "clean elections"; their opponents are presumed to favor dirty politics. Even centrist politicians eager to occupy the moral high ground (along with the occasional conservative like John McCain) fulminate against "big money" and "special interests."

Of course, the view that political contributions exert undue influence on policy is not exactly unfounded. Bribery, or what one Tammany Hall figure called "illegal graft" (as opposed to "honest graft"), is an especially sturdy political tradition. Voters, as well as politicians, are subject to being bought (however unwittingly) by the political ads and image-making machines that contributions finance. But fear and loathing of concentrated wealth does sometimes blind "clean election" advocates to the complexities of campaign regulations and the role of money in politics.

Nothing seems to irritate reformers more than the assertion that limits on money—whether campaign contributions or expenditures—are the equivalent of limits on speech. Money isn't speech; it's property, Supreme Court Justice Stevens declared in a recent case upholding a Missouri law limiting campaign contributions. His insistence that money isn't speech has visceral ap-

> ## Bribery is an especially sturdy political tradition.

peal; it seems so egalitarian, so democratic. But it's also wishful thinking.

Money isn't speech? Try telling that to the folks at National Public Radio the next time they beg you for donations to keep their programming on the air. Money makes speech possible. *The American Prospect* now publishes biweekly, thanks to the generous support of wealthy benefactors. If Congress passed a law limiting the amount of money we could spend annually on books or newspapers, we would probably not say, "Never mind. Money isn't speech."

In our society, money facilitates the exercise of rights. Children who attend schools in poor districts don't receive equal educations unless schools throughout the state are equitably funded. Poor women don't exercise abortion rights if they can't afford abortions, unless Medicaid provides funding. Often, people need public subsidies to achieve some measure of equality, which is why progressives advocate expanding our notions of individual rights so that they protect basic economic needs, like housing or health care.

Like it or not, this relationship between money and the enjoyment of rights is an American fact of life, and as a practical matter (absent a revolution), it is essentially immutable. It is an argument for public financing of campaigns designed to subsidize candidates who do not have personal fortunes or major party support, and an argument against limits on contributions and expenditures.

When the government restricts our ability to spend money, it restricts our ability to speak. That fact doesn't end debates about campaign finance reform, but it does complicate them. They become debates about balancing individual rights (free speech) with other social goods that some presume will follow from reform—expanded access to the electoral process and increased public faith in it.

On balance, the damage done to First Amendment rights seems much greater than the promised benefits of reform proposals to limit the flow of money in and out of campaigns. Expanded access can be facilitated by public financing systems that establish a financial floor, but not a ceiling, for candidates. (Public subsidies generally provide minimum support for poor people without dictating maximum expenditures for the rich.) The promise of increased faith in the system is quite speculative. Advocates of reform claim that campaign finance abuses cause voter apathy; the claim is plausible, but I've never seen much evidence to support it. The counterclaim that these abuses have little effect on voter participation seems equally plausible. Politics has long been regarded as a scoundrel's game. Regardless of campaign finance laws, people seem to expect a certain amount of thievery from elected officials. At the same time, they manage to put their faith in quite a few.

The harms of reform to free speech (and political discourse), however, are clear. Existing restrictions on campaign contributions have already created more problems than they have solved. As almost everyone knows, federal reforms passed in 1974 limited both campaign contributions and expenditures. The Supreme Court struck down the limits on expenditures but upheld the limits on contributions. This ruling greatly advantaged incumbents, who don't need to buy as much speech as insurgents. In the 1996 congressional election, for example, all incumbents who spent less than half a million dollars were re-elected, while only 3 percent of all challengers who spent less than half a million dollars succeeded in knocking off an incumbent.

Still, the Supreme Court remains somewhat blindly sympathetic to reform efforts. It recently upheld limits on contributions, in a case that clearly demonstrated their dangers. *Nixon v. Shrink Missouri Government PAC,* which was decided in January, involved a challenge to Missouri's campaign limits by a third-party candidate who was substantially disadvantaged by the cap on individual contributions. Major party candidates had much greater visibility and access to soft money— money contributed to the parties ostensibly for party-building purposes. The law provides that soft money can be used for issue advocacy, not in support of particular candidates, but in this respect, the law is practically unenforceable. In political campaigns, it's not always possible to distinguish between advocating for issues and advocating for candidates.

Reformers propose solving access problems for insurgents by restricting soft money (the market for which was created by the 1974 reforms). But we know what new

> **It's an American fact of life that money facilitates the exercise of rights.**

problems will follow from soft-money restrictions. Dissatisfied with the disclosure requirements that accompany contributions to political parties, wealthy contributors are already forming their own not-for-profit issue advocacy groups, which are not required to disclose their donors. These are stealth groups whose political interests or agendas aren't clear, which operate under vague names like Americans United for Good Things, and groups like Republicans for Clean Air (organized by a wealthy Bush ally, it ran anti-McCain ads in New York prior to the Republican primary).

As Supreme Court Justice Kennedy observed in his dissent in *Nixon v. Shrink,* limits on campaign contributions have greatly increased incentives for a new kind of "covert" political speech. Campaign finance reform "forced a substantial amount of speech underground."

Of course, covert speech can be made overt with effective disclosure requirements. Prohibiting anonymous contributions to political parties or advocacy groups does raise First Amendment concerns: Anonymity is an important element of free speech. On balance, however, the danger of a secret campaign finance system outweighs the danger of restricting the right to speak anonymously through large political contributions.

But reformers are not necessarily content with stringent disclosure requirements. Many want to limit in-

dependent expenditures and to prohibit issue advocacy groups from advertising within 30 or 60 days of an election. A provision limiting independent expenditures was originally included in the McCain-Feingold bill and in the Massachusetts Clean Elections law. It was dropped from the final proposals, partly because it cut the heart out of individual rights to political speech. Imagine being prohibited by the government from buying television time or taking out an ad in your local newspaper arguing for or against particular public policies or criticizing particular candidates a month or two before an election, when people are actually paying attention.

This is the dilemma for reformers: If they limit independent expenditures, they deprive private citizens of First Amendment rights during political campaigns; if they don't, they cannot hope to limit effectively the influence of "big money" on elections.

Now imagine that we have accepted restrictions on independent expenditures as necessary evils of campaign reform. Who would be left to speak? Mort Zuckerman could write an editorial in the *New York Daily News* the week before the New York Senate election, endorsing Rick Lazio. But the government would prohibit you and the public interest groups you support from buying an ad in his paper criticizing Lazio and the policies of the Republican Congress. It's not surprising that *The New York Times* supports restrictions on fundraising by independent groups. Taken to its logical extreme, campaign finance reform will give media moguls, pundits, and elected officials exclusive rights to effective political speech in the crucial month or two before an election. I doubt that will open up our democracy in ways that reformers have in mind.

Disability Act's First 10 Years and the Challenges Ahead

Congress tries to balance demands for change with businesses' fears of runaway lawsuits

By David Nather

A bumper sticker sums up the positive view most people with disabilities have of the changes wrought by the 1990 Americans with Disabilities Act: "To boldly go where everyone else has gone before."

To business owners, however, these changes have come at a price. Just ask Clint Eastwood. Angered by a lawsuit that claimed his Mission Ranch Hotel in Carmel, Calif., was not accessible to people with disabilities, the actor urged Congress to crack down on attorneys he believes have gotten trigger-happy filing ADA lawsuits over problems that could have been easily fixed.

"These lawyers cloak themselves under the guise they're doing a favor for the disabled when they really are doing a disservice," Eastwood said at a May 18 House Judiciary hearing. "They end up driving off in a big Mercedes and the disabled person ends up riding off in a wheelchair."

Civil rights landmark or lawsuit mill? Ten years after President George Bush signed it into law, the ADA (PL 101–336) is under fire: A House bill would require people to give businesses 90 days' notice before suing, and the act faces a constitutional challenge before the Supreme Court this fall.

Fearing a backlash that could undermine the law, a familiar face has stepped in. Former Senate Majority Leader Bob Dole, R-Kan. (1968–96)—who lost the use of one arm in World War

Since the Americans with Disabilities Act was enacted in 1990, disability policy has become more complicated. Congress' next challenges range from employment and housing to making computers and the Internet more accessible to people with disabilities.

II and was one of the law's strongest supporters as minority leader in 1990–has been circulating a proposal to his former colleagues that would let businesses obtain advisory opinions from the government to determine whether they are in compliance before they get sued.

Measuring Quality of Life

Education and employment opportunities for individuals with disabilities have improved since 1986, according to a Harris poll in May and June that surveyed 997 adults with disabilities and 953 adults without disabilities. However, people with disabilities say they still face greater problems overall than people without disabilities, according to the poll, which was released July 19.

■ Employment rate for people with disabilities who are able to work:
1986: 46 percent
2000: 56 percent

■ People **with** disabilities working full-time or part-time: **32 percent**
■ People **without** disabilities working full-time or part-time: **81 percent**

■ People **with** disabilities who did not get needed health care on at least one occasion in 1999: **19 percent**
■ People **without** disabilities who did not get needed health care on at least one occasion in 1999: **6 percent**

■ High school graduation rate for people with disabilities:
1986: 61 percent
2000: 77 percent

■ Adults **with** disabilities who have not completed high school: **22 percent**
■ Adults **without** disabilities who have not completed high school: **9 percent**

■ People **with** disabilities who have inadequate access to transportation:
30 percent
■ People **without** disabilities who have inadequate access to transportation:
10 percent

SOURCE: 2000 National Organization on Disability/Harris Survey of Americans with Disabilities.

"I don't want to short-circuit [the ADA] . . . I worked too hard to get it done," Dole, now special counsel to a Washington law firm, said July 19. "It just seems to me that there ought to be some kind of middle ground."

As they prepare to mark the 10th anniversary of the law's signing July 26, supporters in Congress and the disability community want Americans to focus on the good things they say the law has accomplished. The ADA, they say, merely lets individuals with disabilities lead the same kind of lives as everyone else.

"Members of Congress don't remember what it was like when we couldn't get around," Patrisha A. Wright, director of governmental affairs for the Disability Rights Education and Defense Fund, said July 18. "They hear a lot from businesses, but they don't hear a lot from real people."

Their voices will have to be heard if they want Congress to tackle the remaining challenges people with disabilities face. Just as racial issues became more complex and the targets more abstract after the passage of the 1964 Civil Rights Act, disability pol-icy has become more complicated since the passage of the ADA.

Those brewing issues range from health care and personal attendant services to special education, transportation and housing costs. Some groups are also concerned about the other "digital divide"–the one that locks many people with disabilities out of the technological revolution.

"Civil rights was the first barrier. You'd literally get to the door and the employer would say, 'Sorry, we don't need you,'" said Tony Young, manager of governmental affairs for NISH, an organization that helps people with severe disabilities find jobs.

Now, Young said July 13, "the targets have become more difficult."

The Next Steps

There is not another bill on the same scale as ADA looming in the future, but there are other issues on the congressional agenda that could affect people with disabilities–as well as issues disability groups say are not on the agenda but should be.

Health care. Sens. Charles E. Grassley, R-Iowa, and Edward M. Ken-nedy, D-Mass., are sponsoring a bill (S 2274) to let the parents of children with disabilities buy into Medicaid.

It is a sequel of sorts to last year's Ticket to Work and Work Incentives Improvement Act (PL 106–170), which is supposed to ensure that adults with disabilities keep federal health insurance after they go to work. The law allows people with disabilities to stay on Medicare longer and allows states to create an option for them to buy into Medicaid. *(1999 CQ Weekly, p. 2762)*

The new bill, the Family Opportunity Act, would help parents who often quit jobs to meet Medicaid's strict income limits by giving their children another track into the program, which offers more generous coverage for children with special needs than many private health plans. The bill would encourage parents to obtain private insurance first and then use Medicaid as a "wraparound" benefit to pay for services their private plan does not cover.

About 850,000 children are eligible for Medicaid coverage through the Supplemental Security Income program.

Compliance on the Hill

When Max Cleland, D-Ga., first came to the Senate in 1997, he had to use the women's bathroom just off the floor because the men's bathroom was not wheelchair accessible.

"I used [the women's room] for four or five months," Cleland said in a July 19 interview, before the men's room was redesigned to accommodate his wheelchair.

The predicament faced by Cleland, a triple amputee, came seven years after Congress passed, and President George Bush signed, the Americans With Disabilities Act of 1990 (PL 101–336), which requires employers to make "reasonable accommodations" for disabled workers. *(1990 Almanac, p. 447)*

Today, Congress is slowly coming into full compliance with the act. Among the changes that have taken place in recent years are the lowering of elevator call buttons and control panels to be within the reach of wheelchair users, the installation of Braille informational signs for the blind and the construction of hundreds of curb ramps to allow travel by wheelchairs throughout the Capitol.

According to the congressional Office of Compliance, which surveys Hill facilities at least once each session, all major congressional buildings now have at least one entrance where wheelchair users can "get in the door."

Rep. Mark Foley, R-Fla., a member of the Ways and Means Human Resources Subcommittee, said Congress should not have taken 10 years to come into compliance.

"Congress can't even set an example," Foley said in a July 19 interview. "How do they expect cities to do so? . . . It's like a parent talking to a child. 'Do as I say, not as I do'."

Cleland says he is able to maneuver around Capitol Hill fairly easily these days and is relatively satisfied with Congress' gradual phasing-in of ADA compliance, although he admits that his arrival on Capitol Hill may have "accelerated their schedule a little bit."

"These old buildings, especially government buildings, become the biggest obstacle to your existence," Cleland said. "But just like with heating and air conditioning, you can blend accessibility with overall surroundings."

—Karen Foerstel

say it would create an expensive new entitlement.

Harkin does not buy that argument. "On the average, it will be cheaper. There will be some severely disabled people for whom it will be more expensive," he said July 12. "But even if it's a wash, we should do it because it will bring Medicaid into compliance with the letter and spirit of the ADA."

The other digital divide. When President Clinton and members of Congress talk about closing the "digital divide," they generally mean the gap between people who can afford computers and those who cannot.

There is another divide, however, between people with disabilities who need accommodations to use computers—often expensive ones—and those who do not.

According to a March study by the Disability Statistics Center at the University of California in San Francisco, only 23.9 percent of people with disabilities have access to a computer at home and only 11.4 percent are able to connect to the Internet. By comparison, 51.7 percent of people without disabilities have home computers and 31.1 percent connect to the Internet.

The gap has several causes, but the biggest is that people with disabilities tend to be less able to afford computers or specialized software and hardware, says Bonnie O'Day, who handles technology issues for the National Council on Disability. The council is a federal agency that advises Congress and the president on disability policy.

People who are blind or visually impaired, for example, may need a screen reader, which translates text in a synthesized voice; a Braille display that uses a set of pins to convert screen text into raised dots; or a screen magnifier.

Such devices are not cheap—a screen reader or magnifier can run $500 to $800 and a Braille printer may cost $2,000 to $3,000. That is why O'Day says Congress should consider passing legislation to offer low-interest or no-interest loans to

The bill is unlikely to move this year, but the Senate Budget Committee gave it a boost with a July 12 hearing. Eventually, Grassley told reporters, he expects it to have as much bipartisan support as the Work Incentives legislation did last year.

"The government forces these parents to choose between work and their children's health care," Grassley said at the hearing. "That's a terrible choice."

Personal attendants. A big priority for the disability community is the Medicaid Community Attendant Services and Supports Act (S 1935), proposed by Sen. Tom Harkin, D-Iowa, who sponsored the ADA.

The bill would let Medicaid recipients get long-term care at home rather than in nursing facilities. It would help people with disabilities pay for community-based attendant services—help with activities such as eating, dressing and moving from the wheelchair to the bed—so they could live independently.

Supporters say the legislation would correct a biased system that requires Medicaid to pay for nursing homes but not for the kind of home-based care that gives people with disabilities the freedom they want. To offer community-based care under Medicaid, states now have to apply for waivers from the federal government.

"You're employing somebody to help you . . . when you're in a very vulnerable position," said Max J. Starkloff, president of Paraquad, an independent living center in St. Louis. "You really have to be able to trust people and know you can count on them. And to do that, you have to be able to pay them."

The legislation is opposed by many of the nation's governors, who help people with disabilities get technology they need.

"You can have all the technology you want," said O'Day, "but if you can't afford it and you don't have the training to use it, you're still no better off than if it didn't exist."

Congress already has taken a first step to narrow the divide. The 1998 Rehabilitation Amendments Act (PL 105–220) requires the federal government to make electronic and information technology accessible to people with disabilities. As of Aug. 7, individuals with disabilities will be able to sue the government if they have access problems. A debate already has started about whether there should be accessibility standards for Internet sites.

Employment. Congress eventually will have to address the issue of how to help more people with disabilities enter the work force because the Social Security Administration's Disability Insurance (SSDI) program is running out of money.

The program, which provides benefits to about 4.9 million people who have paid into Social Security and can no longer work because of severe and long-term disabilities, is under just as much stress as the rest of Social Security. Its caseload has grown by 67 percent over the past 15 years, according to the General Accounting Office, and its benefit payments have nearly tripled in that time. In seven years, the SSDI trust fund will be paying out more than it takes in, and by 2023 it will not be able to pay full benefits.

The Basics

In 1990, supporters of the ADA simply wanted to end discrimination,

The law that eventually passed requires employers to make "reasonable accommodations" for workers with disabilities as long as they do not create an "undue hardship" for the businesses. Public services such as mass transportation and all kinds of private businesses that serve the public—hotels, restaurants, bars, movie theaters, retail stores and shopping

centers—have to be just as accessible to people with disabilities as they are to able-bodied people. *(1990 CQ Almanac, p. 447)*

"It has opened up great new worlds compared to where we were 10 years ago," said Harkin. "Now people with disabilities have a lot to back them up. It makes them feel like they're powerful."

Dole agrees. "I think generally the law has worked pretty well," he said. "It's helped a lot of people who couldn't have gotten into a restaurant before because they were in a wheelchair."

Mostly, people with disabilities say the law has changed the nation's attitudes and made businesses and governments more willing to eliminate the hundreds of indignities they face every day.

"When I go to work and make phone calls, I use the telecommunications relay services enacted by the ADA," Kelby Nathan Brick, an attorney in Greenbelt, Md., who is deaf, wrote in an e-mail exchange July 18. "In the afternoon I go to the doctor's office and am able to communicate with my doctor because the ADA has required the presence of a sign interpreter. . . . The ADA [has] had a major impact on almost every facet of my life."

Another person who believes the ADA has made a big difference in attitudes is J. Marque Moore, who worked as a law clerk this summer in the Office of Personnel Management.

Paralyzed from the neck down in a bull-riding accident 10 years ago, Moore found an eager employer in OPM, which is trying to serve as a role model for how the private sector should put the ADA to use. The law, Moore said in a July 14 interview, "provides an environment in which people are more willing to work with you."

The biggest expense OPM had was a personal assistant, at a cost of $480 a week, to help Moore with everything from taking notes and running office errands to such basic needs as helping him periodically adjust his position in his wheelchair.

The rest of the accommodations were relatively easy. To get started every morning, the 28-year-old University of Texas law student needed someone to punch in the security code, open the door to his office and put on his headset so he could make phone calls. He used voice-recognition software to dictate memos and e-mails and manipulated a special stick placed in his mouth to dial phone numbers and open applications on his computer.

"Once you get past the physical access" of being able to get into the building, into elevators and into offices, Moore said, "the rest of the costs aren't that high."

According to a survey by the Job Accommodation Network, an ADA service run by the federal government, businesses reported spending an average of $943 on accommodations for each worker with a disability since the law took effect in 1992. For every dollar employers spent, they estimated they got almost $35 back in other benefits, such as retaining a qualified employee and saving on workers' compensation costs.

While business groups agree the law has had numerous benefits, they say there is another side of the story.

"The difficulty is that the ADA is written in such a vague and ambiguous way that businesses never know whether they've complied with the law completely until they wind up in court," Mary Leon, a lobbyist with the National Federation of Independent Business, said in a July 11 interview.

State governments have joined the fight. In October, the Supreme Court is scheduled to hear oral arguments in *University of Alabama Board of Trustees v. Garrett*, a lawsuit that challenges the constitutionality of ADA lawsuits against states over discrimination in employment and public services.

If the court strikes down that part of the law, "it could not help but encourage the people who would like to repeal the whole thing," Justin Dart, former vice chairman of the National Council on Disability, said July 10.

Disability groups say the threat of lawsuits is overblown and that most people with disabilities have neither the will nor the money to sue anybody. They get what they need, the groups say, simply by mentioning the ADA, a gentle but effective reminder that the law is on their side.

That is why Congress and the disability groups keep talking past each other on the ADA subject of the moment—how to help businesses comply with the law and stay out of court.

Fair Warning?

The bill that brought Eastwood to Capitol Hill, and has alarmed the disability community, is the ADA Notification Act (HR 3590). The proposal by Reps. Mark Foley and E. Clay Shaw Jr., Florida Republicans, would require people to give 90 days' notice before filing a lawsuit under the ADA.

To Foley and the bill's supporters, it is a simple, common-sense measure that would help well-meaning business owners comply with the law by giving them time to fix whatever accessibility problems they have.

"This is simply about fairness, not weakening the ADA," Foley said in a July 19 interview. "All we're saying is, let's not start active litigation until they've been notified of the problem."

To disability groups, it is a harmless-sounding first step toward chipping away at the ADA's protections.

The issue is so sensitive that some disability groups recently fired off a series of e-mails warning that Republicans wanted to slip the bill through the House quietly as a suspension item, a designation normally reserved for such non-controversial measures as renaming post offices.

Foley wants to pass the bill as a suspension item, but he said that is to ensure that it could not be amended on the House floor to weaken the ADA in other areas. "Unless it's a suspension, I will not let it go to the floor," Foley said. "I don't want the 90-day notice badly enough to have the ADA go down in flames."

'Drive-by Lawsuits'

The problem, according to the law's critics, is not the government lawsuits but the private ones. The Equal Employment Opportunity Commission, which enforces the employment discrimination protections, filed 369 lawsuits between fiscal 1992–the year the law went into effect–and fiscal 1999. The Justice Department's Civil Rights Division, which enforces the public accommodations and public services provisions, had filed or intervened in 202 ADA lawsuits as of July 7.

The federal government does not track private suits. Business groups say it is impossible to estimate how many they have faced, but they believe the number is growing.

At the May 18 subcommittee hearing where Eastwood testified, Christopher G. Bell, an attorney and former EEOC employee, said the law has produced a blizzard of "drive-by suits in South Florida and other areas."

In one case, Bell said, his Minneapolis law firm defended a business owner who was sued because the toilet paper dispenser in the men's room was an inch off the accessibility standards.

If the Foley bill had been law at the time, Bell said, "the owner presumably would have taken a screwdriver and lowered the toilet paper dispenser by an inch rather than face a lawsuit."

Lee Culpepper of the National Restaurant Association, which supports the Foley bill, agrees. "The goal [of ADA] was to reach some common-sense accommodations with litigation really being the last option," he said. Now, "lawsuits have become the first option."

That argument has worn thin with disability groups. "The act is 10 years old. People have had lots of notice," said Stephanie Thomas, a national organizer for the disability rights group ADAPT, in a July 17 interview.

Unit 2

Key Points to Consider

❖ Read Articles I, II, and III of the U.S. Constitution to get a picture of the legislative, executive, and judicial branches as painted by the words of the Framers. How does that picture compare with the reality of the three branches as they operate today?

❖ How might the presidency and Congress change in the next 100 years?

❖ What advantages and disadvantages do each of the following have for getting things done: The president? The vice president? A cabinet member? The Speaker of the House of Representatives? The Senate majority leader? The chief justice? A top-ranking bureaucrat in an executive branch agency? A congressional aide?

❖ Which position in American government would you most like to hold? Why?

❖ Do you think Bill Clinton was a successful president in getting things done? A *good* president? Defend your answers.

❖ In what way(s) does President Bush function differently as president than his predecessor, Bill Clinton, did? So far, has George W. Bush's performance as president surprised you or has he performed about as you had expected?

 **Links**   # www.dushkin.com/online/

These sites are annotated on pages 4 and 5.

James Madison, one of the primary architects of the American system of government, observed that the three-branch structure of government created at the Constitutional Convention of 1787 pitted the ambitions of some individuals against the ambitions of others. Nearly two centuries later, contemporary political scientist Richard Neustadt wrote that the structure of American national government is one of "separated" institutions sharing powers. These two eminent students of American politics suggest an important proposition: the very design of American national government contributes to the struggles that occur among government officials who have different institutional loyalties and potentially competing goals.

This unit is divided into four sections. The first three treat the three traditional branches of American government and the last one treats the bureaucracy. One point to remember when studying these institutions is that the Constitution provides only a bare skeleton of the workings of the American political system. The flesh and blood of the presidency, Congress, judiciary, and bureaucracy are derived from decades of experience and the shared expectations of today's political actors. A second point to keep in mind is that the way a particular institution functions is partly determined by those who occupy relevant offices. The presidency will operate differently with George W. Bush in the White House than it did when Bill Clinton was president. Similarly, Congress and the Supreme Court also operate differently according to who serve as members and who hold leadership positions within the institutions. There were significant changes in the House of Representatives after Republican Newt Gingrich succeeded Democrat Tom Foley as Speaker of the House in 1995 and lesser changes in the Senate after Trent Lott replaced fellow Republican Bob Dole as majority leader in mid-1996. With Speaker Dennis Hastert succeeding Gingrich in January 1999, additional changes occurred in the way the House of Representatives functions.

The first section contains articles on the presidency. After 12 straight years of Republican presidents (Ronald Reagan and George Bush), Democrat Bill Clinton assumed the presidency in 1993. For the first two years of his presidency, the Democrats also held a majority of seats in the House of Representatives and Senate. But in the 1994 and 1996 congressional elections, Republicans won control of the House and Senate, a development that inevitably led to changes in the way Clinton functioned as president. When George W. Bush became president in 2001, Republicans had a narrow majority in the House of Representatives and the U.S. Senate was split 50-50 between Republicans and Democrats. An important point to remember is that neither the presidency nor any other institution operates in isolation from the other institutions of American national government.

The second section addresses Congress. The legislative branch underwent substantial changes in recent decades under mostly Democratic control. Reforms in the seniority system and the budgetary process in the 1970s brought an unprecedented degree of decentralization and, some would say, chaos to Capitol Hill. In addition, during the 1970s and 1980s, both the number of staff and special-interest caucuses in Congress increased. The unexpected Republican takeover of the House of Representatives as a result of the November 1994 elections brought even more changes to that body. The new Republican speaker, Newt Gingrich, reduced the power of committees, consolidated power in the Speaker's office, and became a prominent figure on the national scene. But 1998 brought the downfall of Gingrich as a result of the November congressional elections and, for the second time in history, the impeachment of a president. And the 2000 congressional elections narrowed the Republican majority in the House to a handful of seats and resulted in a historic 50-50 split of Democrats and Republicans in the Senate. These events will likely affect the functioning of Congress (and the presidency) for some time to come.

The Supreme Court sits at the top of the U.S. legal system and is the main topic of the third section in this unit. The Court is not merely a legal institution; it is a policymaker whose decisions can affect the lives of millions of citizens. The Court's decisive role in determining the outcome of the 2000 presidential election showed its powerful role in the American political system. Like all people in high government offices, Supreme Court justices have policy views of their own, and observers of the Court pay careful attention to the way the nine justices interact with one another in shaping decisions of the Court.

The bureaucracy of the national government, the subject of the fourth and last section in this unit, is responsible for carrying out policies determined by top-ranking officials. The bureaucracy is not merely a neutral administrative instrument, and bureaucratic waste and inefficiency often seem excessive. On the other hand, government bureaucracies also share credit for many of the accomplishments of American government. Most presidents claim that they want to make the bureaucracy perform more efficiently, and it remains to be seen how effective President Bush will be in this regard.

For many readers, the selections in this unit will rank among the most enjoyable in the book. Not surprisingly, most of us are more comfortable on familiar territory, and the separate branches of government are likely to be familiar from earlier study in school or from media coverage of politics. Nevertheless, the selections in this unit should provide additional and more sophisticated insights into how the institutions of American national government actually work.

Gone Are the Giants

TODAY IN THE WHITE HOUSE, CONGRESS, AND THE SUPREME COURT, THE NATION SEEMS TO LACK THE LARGER-THAN-LIFE FIGURES WHO RULED THE CAPITAL IN EARLIER ERAS. WHY?

BY BURT SOLOMON

Listen to the somber reflections of an eminent historian and statesman: "The ordinary American voter does not object to mediocrity. . . . The best men do not go into politics. . . . Great men have not often been chosen Presidents, first because great men are rare in politics; secondly, because the method of choice may not bring them to the top; thirdly, because they are not, in quiet times, absolutely needed."

How could James Bryce, a professor of law at Oxford University and later a British ambassador to the United States, have possibly known of the presumptive American presidential nominees in 2000 when he penned *The American Commonwealth* in 1888? He knew that the Presidents between Andrew Jackson and Abraham Lincoln, and again during the decades following the Civil War, had been—as he spelled it—"intellectual pigmies." Was he imagining Texas Gov. George W. Bush, a Republican who smirks while discussing his decision to send a murderer to her death, and Vice President Al Gore, a Democrat whose pandering meanderings on Elián González suggest that he has no political core? "They are underwhelming, aren't they?" says presidential scholar Fred I. Greenstein of Princeton University.

Yet either of them could turn out to be a very capable 43rd President, says historian Alonzo L. Hamby of Ohio University, a biographer of Harry S. Truman. This era of peace and prosperity, he points out, "is probably the easiest time to be President, ever." And it's dangerous to predict how history will ultimately judge. As Truman's case shows, politicians scorned in their own time may rise in reputation later.

Still, it seems as if pygmies have come to dominate American political life. In all three branches of the federal government, the giants—officials with vast influence, foreseeable historic importance, or merely a larger-than-life presence—have practically vanished from the scene.

In the past quarter-century, the White House has arguably had only one, a simple-thinking ex-actor. The sort of giants who prevailed in the Senate (and occasionally in the House) during the 1950s and 1960s are, with one or two exceptions, history. Even the Supreme Court has, at most, a single Justice, Antonin F. Scalia, who may be remembered by educated citizens a century hence. Around the statehouses, ex-wrestler (and Minnesota Gov.) Jesse Ventura may be literally larger-than-life, but the Al Smiths and Huey Longs and Nelson A. Rockefellers are gone. The only truly powerful American public official with a worldwide sweep may be Alan Greenspan, the taciturn Federal Reserve Board chairman who has never been elected to anything.

What's going on? Why have we entered the land of the pygmies—or, at least, of the absence of giants? It isn't just coincidence, venerable Washington-watchers say. A lot of it is the times we're in. It's almost a cliché that it takes a great crisis to make a great President; in this lovely era of peace and prosperity, we're out of true crises—and we should thank our stars for it.

Also, the political system has changed. The near death of the political parties as power brokers has left every politician to his or her own devices, shorn of the natural stature that comes from being bolstered by—and identified with—a mighty institution. At the same time, the capital's unrelenting partisanship has produced a dearth of officeholders willing to work across party lines, the sort of for-the-greater-good behavior that magnifies a politician's enduring reputation. And if the opposition won't tear a politician down, the news media will. Anyone running for political office must expect to "have every human flaw, pimple, and boil lanced," says former Sen. Alan Simpson, R-Wyo., now the director of Harvard University's Institute of Politics. Such scathing treatment not only cuts officeholders down to size but also discour-

From the *National Journal*, May 27, 2000, pp. 1668-1673. © 2000 by National Journal Group, Inc. All rights reserved. Reprinted by permission.

ages many potential candidates from trying. Not only are the giants gone, laments the 6-foot-7-inch Simpson, but they're never coming back.

Of course, as Bryce suggested more than a century ago, the lack of giants is nothing new. Harry McPherson, an aide to President Lyndon B. Johnson who became a prominent Washington lawyer, says he first noticed this in the early 1970s, amid the Watergate scandal, when he was riding downtown on the bus past a labor union headquarters and realized that labor bosses were a dying breed. So, too, were the giants of politics, literature, civil rights, and education. He blamed Americans' characteristic suspicion of leadership—"a paucity of followers," as he wrote at the time—and media overexposure. Sound familiar?

Maybe the only thing that has changed is that the nation's political leadership matters even less to Americans now than it did in 1974. After all, it is Silicon Valley and Wall Street—not Washington—that are driving American life. "The society is about making money right now," says Leon E. Panetta, who served eight terms in Congress and two and a half years as President Clinton's chief of staff before going home to California. "The public has basically written off Washington. They don't think that it impacts on their lives."

It may not be the political figures who have shrunk so much as the political times. The great issues are gone, at least for the moment. The Cold War is kaput. So, it seems, is any longing to use the government to do ambitious things. Grand crusades are a shadow of what they were; the most passionate race-related issue right now is a symbolic dispute in South Carolina over flying the Confederate flag.

"It's the politics of small issues—isn't it?" says Richard Fenno, an expert on Congress at the University of Rochester. The biggest issue that Washington now faces is the rescue of federal entitlement programs, notes Michael J. Boskin, a Stanford University economist who chaired President Bush's Council of Economic Advisers. It's "a vital issue," he adds, "[but] it's not Pearl Harbor."

There may be some nostalgia involved in judging the older generations of notables as grander than the current incumbents. But truly, the mega-issues of World War II and its aftermath—the Marshall Plan, nuclear weaponry, the Cold War between capitalism and socialism—brought outsized actors to the fore. Small issues, though, make decision-makers look, well, small. Had Franklin D. Roosevelt become President in 1993, history might come to consider him as something other than great. Or had Bill Clinton taken the oath of office in 1933, he might have become a top-rank President.

Political giants may rise again when giant issues return, as surely they must. This suggests, in turn, that some of the apparent pygmies who stand before us may harbor a latent greatness that has yet to be glimpsed.

Perhaps. But there's also some evidence that the quality of the individuals who run the country has suffered.

"Certainly, in my judgment," says Robert S. Strauss, who has counseled Presidents of both political parties, "the demise of civility, combined with the press mentality, has made it exceedingly difficult to attract top people, whether it's to elective or appointive office." Trent Lott is no Everett M. Dirksen, as Senate Republican leaders go. Among the chamber's Democratic leaders, Thomas A. Daschle isn't a Lyndon B. Johnson or even a Mike Mansfield. And House Speaker J. Dennis Hastert, R-Ill., isn't Newt Gingrich. Quiet times seem to bring leaders to power who don't need to lead, and quite possibly can't.

PRESIDENTS OF HUMAN SCALE

When it came to the quality of its political leaders, a young nation was spoiled early on. Historians speak of the *golden* and *silver* generations of American statesmen—respectively, the Founding Fathers and the pre-Civil War giants of Congress such as Henry Clay, John C. Calhoun, and Daniel Webster.

But too soon, the nation learned that its luck wouldn't last. From Lincoln's death to around 1900, the national government was run by what Keith W. Olson, a historian at the University of Maryland, describes as "a bunch of second-raters." The reasons weren't very different when Bryce wrote than they are now. Inventors and titans of commerce—the likes of Thomas A. Edison and John D. Rockefeller, the Bill Gateses of their day—dominated the nation's course. By comparison, Presidents and politicians didn't matter much. This proved true again during the 1920s, as peace and prosperity prevailed, and the voters elected a succession of forgettable Presidents.

Great Presidents "tend to come very sporadically, under very particular conditions," explains Stephen Skowronek, a presidential scholar at Yale University. And now, he adds, "we're in kind of a lull period."

Becoming a giant in the presidency takes a strong will and the fortune to hold office in politically momentous times. Theodore Roosevelt's vivid personality, in part, earned him a place on Mount Rushmore. Princeton's Greenstein describes TR as "Giuliani on acid," comparing the current New York City mayor, Rudolph W. Giuliani, with the city's one-time police commissioner who conducted splashy midnight raids, later served as assistant Navy Secretary, quit to ride up San Juan Hill, then (in 1901) became a President who invited in reporters to watch him shave. While in the White House, the first Roosevelt never had to fight a war or an economic depression. But his trust-busting progressivism was meant to tame the Industrial Revolution so that capitalism might survive, and his big-stick internationalism projected the United States as a world power.

Leading the nation through imminent peril is a more reliable route to becoming a giant. Woodrow Wilson led America in a war intended to end all wars; Franklin D.

Roosevelt commanded the next war, which ended the Great Depression. FDR's greatness was a stroke of timing, in more ways than one. Suppose James Cox, the Democratic candidate in 1920, had won the presidency and then—like the man who defeated him, Warren G. Harding—died. His successor, Hamby wrote in the latest issue of *The Key Reporter,* a quarterly newsletter of Phi Beta Kappa, would have been "his charming lightweight of a Vice President, Franklin D. Roosevelt." Even in 1932, after polio had deepened FDR's character, pundit Walter Lippmann portrayed him as a pleasant, indecisive man—a smart judgment at the time, political historians say today.

The next five Presidents, from Truman through Richard M. Nixon, also led the nation through war, whether it was hot or cold. Some of them led in domestic policy, too. LBJ pushed through the landmark civil rights law of 1964 and sought to abolish poverty. Nixon opened the way to China and made the environment a federal concern. "He had a concept" of how to govern with a Democratic-run Congress, says Charles O. Jones, a retired political scientist at the University of Wisconsin. "Nixon was impressive."

It may have been Nixon's overreaching for power, however, that broke the string. The next two Presidents, Gerald R. Ford and Jimmy Carter, acted as pygmies, and purposely so, in reaction to the disgraced Nixon's imperial ways. Ever since, the White House has been home to "a pretty unmemorable lot," says John Milton Cooper, a historian at the University of Wisconsin. "The only memorable President since Nixon," he adds, "is, maybe, Ronald Reagan." Reagan's tough-minded, effective approach toward the Soviet Union and his success in changing many of the premises of domestic politics have moved him onto some historians' list of near-great Presidents.

His successor's tenure, however, inspired a book-length recounting called *Marching in Place: The Status Quo Presidency of George Bush.* And then there's Clinton, a President of large talents but middling accomplishments. Cass Sunstein, a law professor at the University of Chicago, argues that Clinton will rank as a historically important President because of his "Third Way," the use of government as a catalyst instead of a bludgeon in dealing with social ills. But Sunstein's view is in the minority. John R. Hibbing, a political scientist at the University of Nebraska, says he "can't see any tremendously lasting legacy" in either Clinton's foreign policy or his "nickel-and-dime approach" to domestic policy. Even Panetta has his doubts. Clinton helped to balance the federal budget and bring on prosperity, the former aide says, but he "probably" won't be compared to FDR or Wilson a century hence. Impeachment will be "always a shadow," he explains, and Clinton has fallen short in another way: "Reagan took risks. Clinton hasn't, very much."

But it isn't as if giants would have occupied the White House if Bush and Clinton had lost the elections they won. President Dukakis? President Dole? Tomorrow's political historians would probably have yawned.

TIMIDITY IN BLACK ROBES

Judicial biographers, too, may be in for a rough time. Who among the current nine Justices on the Supreme Court might be remembered a century hence? "No one," says John Hart Ely, a constitutional scholar at the University of Miami. The Court is crowded with smart, capable Justices, Court-watchers say. But it includes nobody like Oliver Wendell Holmes, Louis Brandeis, Felix Frankfurter, Earl Warren, or—most recently—William J. Brennan Jr.

The only serious prospect, Ely and others say, seems to be Antonin Scalia, an eloquent judicial minimalist with a libertarian streak. Sunstein describes him as the sole sitting Justice "with a large concept of where the law should be taken." He is so out of step, though, with most of the Court—and probably most of the public—that a lot would have to change for Scalia's closely reasoned dissents to ultimately prevail.

It isn't because of trivial issues that the Court lacks giants. To the contrary. In their current session, the Justices have taken up a range of consequential matters, including assisted suicide, affirmative action, prayer in schools, and the rights of criminal suspects. "They do have great questions," says Sunstein, "but they give small answers to them."

This isn't, of course, an accident of history. It dates to 1987, when an angrily divided Senate rejected the nomination of Robert Bork precisely because they feared that he would become a giant by undoing some of the Warren Court's crucial holdings. Ever since, Presidents have usually aimed low in their Supreme Court choices. President Bush nominated the self-effacing David H. Souter, in part because his judicial career had left no paper trail of controversial opinions. Clinton named a pair of sober moderates, Ruth Bader Ginsburg and Stephen G. Breyer.

"The process filters out the kind of Justices who would tend to think in grand terms," says A.E. Dick Howard, a law professor at the University of Virginia. The current Justices, he suggests, show the incrementalist temperament of former appellate court judges, which all but one of them were, instead of the broader vision of the politicians who dominated the Warren Court (including an ex-governor as Chief Justice, an ex-Senator, a former Securities and Exchange Commission chairman, and an FDR brain-truster). "We may never see [such giants] again," Howard says, "at least for the foreseeable future."

THE MORTALS ON CAPITOL HILL

Soon after he published the Pulitzer Prize-winning *Profiles in Courage* in 1957, Sen. John F. Kennedy chaired an elaborate process to pick five legendary Senators and to have their portraits painted in alcoves just off the Senate floor. The 19th century was represented by Clay, Calhoun, and Webster; the 20th by Wisconsin progressive Robert M. La Follette Sr. and Ohio conservative Robert A. Taft, who had died a few years earlier.

Now the search for immortals is beginning again. Last November, the Senate approved a proposal by Lott to choose two more deceased Senators for portraits by the time Congress finishes its work this year. Excluded are any Senators who had a Senate office building named for them, became Vice President, or served during the past 21 years. This leaves out LBJ, Hubert H. Humphrey, Dirksen, Richard Russell, and Philip Hart.

That still leaves plenty to choose from. The 1950s and 1960s alone saw a multitude of other Senate giants, including—just among Democrats—Paul Douglas of Illinois, J. William Fulbright of Arkansas, Henry "Scoop" Jackson of Washington state, Lister Hill of Alabama, Estes Kefauver of Tennessee, Robert Kerr of Oklahoma, Mansfield, and Wayne Morse of Oregon. The Republicans of the period include John Sherman Cooper of Kentucky, Barry Goldwater of Arizona, Jacob Javits of New York, and—depending upon one's criteria—Joseph R. McCarthy of Wisconsin. Even the House of Representatives, which offers less of a stage for its egos, boasted the likes of Speaker Sam Rayburn of Texas, Emanuel Celler of New York, and Wilbur Mills of Arkansas, all Democrats.

Today, you don't even need the fingers on one hand to count up the giants; flashing a peace symbol will probably do. How does Jesse Helms stack up as a chairman of the Senate Foreign Relations Committee against Arthur Vandenburg, who helped a President of the opposite party enact the Marshall Plan, or against Fulbright, who fought a President of his own party over a war? The list of giants has shriveled to almost nothing. The House doesn't have an obvious one right now, since Newt Gingrich quit as Speaker after the 1998 elections. In bringing the Republicans to power in 1994 after decades of Democratic control, Gingrich changed the nation's political landscape. The longer the Republicans keep control of the House, the likelier that history will judge Gingrich a giant. But he also made it harder for anyone else to qualify. He shifted power from the committee chairmen into the Speaker's hands and also left House Republicans longing for someone weaker at the helm. Hastert was chosen as Gingrich's successor largely because he was Gingrich's antithesis and would leave much of the Speaker's authority unasserted. Only Henry J. Hyde, R-Ill., the white-maned Judiciary Committee chairman, is oft cited as a congressional lion—though his handling of Clinton's impeachment "didn't do him any favors," says Burdett A. Loomis, a political scientist at the University of Kansas. Rep. John D. Dingell of Michigan, long the dominant Democrat on the Commerce Committee, could refurbish his own claim if his party regains control of the House.

A couple of prospective giants quit the arena—Democratic Sens. George J. Mitchell of Maine and Sam Nunn of Georgia—apparently because so little was getting done. Close observers of the current Congress can only come to a consensus on one remaining giant—Sen. Edward Kennedy, D-Mass. Once Kennedy became convinced that his transgressions at Chappaquiddick would prevent him from ever winning the White House, he became what Loomis describes as "a serious Senator of the first order," one who has "affected the tides of the Senate [as] a strong polar force" and embodied the liberal viewpoint on a wide range of domestic policies. On any issue except maybe agriculture or the environment, says Fenno, the Senate "can't have debate" without taking Kennedy into account. His joint legislative ventures with Republicans to enact bills on health insurance, job training, immigration, and judicial issues have added to his reputation as a legislative heavyweight.

Sen. Daniel Patrick Moynihan, D-N.Y., is considered by some to be a giant, though to a lesser extent than Kennedy. Legislative craftsmanship isn't Moynihan's forte, despite his years as the Finance Committee chairman and his pivotal role in brokering a compromise to rescue Social Security in 1983. Instead, he's thought of as an intellectual giant, a one-time Harvard University urban studies professor who (while an adviser to President Nixon) famously suggested treating the race problem with "benign neglect." As a Senator, people want to know what he thinks—colleagues, journalists, and policy wonks. "Any debate he entered, he became part of it," Fenno says. Once he retires in January, after four terms, he'll probably stand a better chance of ultimately being judged a giant if an economic recession finds children asleep on heating grates, as he forewarned during the 1996 debate over welfare reform.

Many other members of Congress are considered competent and, on occasion, courageous. (Ask ex-Rep. Marjorie Margolies-Mezvinsky, D-Pa., who lost her seat for backing Clinton's 1993 economic package.) Congresswatchers say that, given the right circumstances, others may qualify someday. They offer scattered votes for Republican Sens. Pete V. Domenici of New Mexico, Phil Gramm of Texas, Orrin G. Hatch of Utah, and—"on some days," says Loomis—Fred D. Thompson of Tennessee, and for Democratic Sens. Robert C. Byrd of West Virginia and Joseph I. Lieberman of Connecticut.

But the circumstances, quite clearly, aren't right. The Senate, notably, isn't the autocracy it used to be—rife with powerful fiefdoms and run by Senators-for-life. Instead, the world's supposedly greatest deliberative body has become a chaotic and even occasionally childish democracy. Richard A. Baker, the Senate's in-house historian, traces what he calls "the fragmentation of power" to the looser style that Mansfield used after he took over as Senate Majority Leader in 1961 from the intimidatingly powerful LBJ. Filibusters are more frequent, and committee chairmen are weaker. What McPherson described years ago as a Senate of "whales and minnows" has now become "a lot of speckled trout," says Bruce Oppenheimer, a Vanderbilt University scholar of the Senate.

There are other reasons, too, for the Senators' shrinking stature. In the Senate's midcentury heyday, they weren't "campaigning or running for President as the end-all and be-all in politics," says McPherson. Nor were they always running so scared for re-election. Many seats used to be safe, so Senators could act like statesmen—ignoring the will of the people, if need be, to do the right thing—at least during the first three or four years of a six-year term. But now "it's harder to drive colleagues into dangerous terrain," says Ross K. Baker, a political scientist at Rutgers University. The daunting cost of campaigns and Senators' vulnerability to well-financed challengers have increased the political risks of thoughtful independence. "Nobody can be idiosyncratic anymore," sighs Stephen Hess, a senior fellow at the Brookings Institution and the author of *The Little Book of Campaign Etiquette*.

Surely something has been lost. Charles D. Ferris, who spent 14 years as Mansfield's top legislative aide, remembers the "genuine agonizing" that lawmakers endured in judging Nixon's fate after the Watergate scandal, compared with the rote, party-line debate over Clinton's fate, which changed few minds. Are shallower people in charge now? Not necessarily, in Ferris' mind. "The environment has changed so drastically," he says, "that it is much more difficult for them to act" as they once did—from time to time—for the greater good.

PERSONAL GLORY

Ah, yes, the greater good—remember that? The giants of old, "when the national interest was involved, they found a compromise," says Panetta. He and others say they can't imagine Trent Lott signing on to the 1964 civil rights bill after opposing it for years, as Dirksen did, or conversely, Dirksen telling the public not to answer questions they found offensive in the federal census forms, as Lott recently did. "Dirksen took a risk," Panetta recounts. "Ultimately, leadership is about taking risks."

Part of the problem may be generational. The people in power in the '50s and '60s, shaped by privation and war, "were institutionalists—the institution really meant something," Ferris recalls. "It wasn't personal glory [they] sought." But ironically, acting on behalf of the greater good increased, not diminished, their stature.

Structural reasons also help explain why giants in Washington are rare. Weaker political parties have made officeholders, more than ever, into independent entrepreneurs. A politician tied to the vagaries of public opinion polls isn't likely to look larger-than-life. Also, the trust in government that bolsters giants has sagged under a constant media glare. Often, mediagenic politicians are happy to oblige, down to revealing (as Clinton did) their preferred style of underwear. Suppose Dirksen showed up regularly on CNN's *Crossfire* or CNBC's *Hardball*, says Jones of Wisconsin. "Familiarity breeds smallness."

Of course, if Washington mattered more than it seems to, politics might draw more giants. "Colin Powell would have been [a giant]," says Hess, "and still might be." Possibly his wife would consent to letting the popular ex-chairman of the Joint Chiefs of Staff run for President (or Vice President) were the stakes higher. But, Nebraska's Hibbing suggests, "once he started taking positions, and people started probing, he wouldn't look like a giant."

Still, there's evidence that Americans yearn for giants, or think that they do. Much of the appeal of Sen. John McCain, R-Ariz., in his recent presidential surge, came from his larger-than-life story and the perception that he needed no one to tell him what he thought. If we faced a foreign crisis, or if the political times seemed more dramatic, Republican primary voters might have chosen McCain over Bush. In both parties, the quality of candidates seems to be declining. George W. Bush apparently lacks the depth of his father, who had lost a child and several political races before winning the presidency. Gore has nothing of Clinton's political verve.

Maybe we should be grateful, though, that political giants will not be running our lives. They usually show up, after all, in the presence of crisis. In happier times, amid peace and prosperity, pygmies will do.

---

nationaljournal.com *Internet links and background information related to this article are available to all* National Journal *subscribers on our Web site.*

Hooked on Polls

BY CARL M. CANNON

THEY'RE BEING USED LIKE NEVER BEFORE. WHATEVER HAPPENED TO REPRESENTATIVE GOVERNMENT?

In 1992, Ross Perot brought a radical idea to American presidential politics: the real-time plebiscite. In Perot's world, decisions on the great issues of the day, from federal budget policies to war-making, could be reached instantaneously by the American people through the use of high-tech referendums conducted by telephone or the Internet. This voting would follow televised presentations on the issues in which various policy options would be explained to the public.

Perot called his concept the "electronic town meeting," but what he really was describing was elevating the public opinion polls to the status of a kind of super-Congress and president-in-chief that would trump the desires and machinations of Washington's elected leaders.

"With interactive television every other week, we could take one major issue, go to the American people, cover it in great detail, have them respond, and show by congressional district what the people want," Perot explained. "If we ever put the people back in charge of this country and make sure they understand the issues, you'll see the White House and Congress, like a ballet, pirouetting around the stage getting it done in unison."

Perot placed a lot of faith in "experts" to explain to the public what needed to be done, but most experts in politics and government tended to view his electronic town hall idea as simplistic and unworkable, if not an affront to the Constitution.

"It just gives me the shudders, the potential for manipulation, the one-sidedness, that a thing like this could do," said Norman Bradburn, director of the polling center at the University of Chicago.

Vice President Dan Quayle asserted that Perot's plan entailed nothing less than "nullifying representative democracy with a bizarre scheme of government by polls." And President Bush said Perot "was out of touch with reality" when he suggested Bush could have used the electronic town hall to build a mandate for liberating Kuwait.

Perhaps most scathing was liberal journalist Sidney Blumenthal, who now works in the Clinton White House. "Thus the Madisonian system would be replaced by the Geraldo system; checks and balances by applause meter," Blumenthal wrote.

In hindsight, however, the most instructive response to Perot's idea was the one offered by the Democratic presidential nominee in 1992. Asked about Perot's electronic town hall ideas—on CNN's *Larry King Live*, fittingly—Bill Clinton replied, "Oh, I think it's a good idea." Clinton went on to make the obligatory comments about how polls don't absolve elected officials from their responsibilities, but the most animated part of his answer was this: He took credit for holding electronic town hall meetings before Perot did.

Today, barely six years after the putative rise and demise of Ross Perot, polls are being used more aggressively than ever before by the president and his loyalists, he and they, both, endless consumers and endless peddlers of polls. "They become addictive," said a former White House official. "They work once, and then they become a crutch; you don't do anything without them."

As president, Clinton has commissioned polls on issues ranging in gravity from whether he ought to stop genocide in Bosnia (the public gave a qualified thumbs-up) to whether it was better public relations to vacation in Wyoming or Martha's Vineyard (voters preferred he go out West). It is now common for polling results to be offered

From *National Journal*, October 17, 1998, pp. 2438-2441. © 1998 by National Journal Group, Inc. All rights reserved. Reprinted by permission.

as validation in themselves, an argument—sometimes the primary argument—for such disparate positions as whether tax cuts are warranted, what an independent counsel should properly investigate, what the president's legal strategy should be, whether he should apologize for having sex with an intern, how much coverage the media should devote to the topic, and, of course, the dominant political question of the day: whether Bill Clinton should be impeached.

"On [impeachment], polls are our religion," said a Clinton loyalist. "We cite them, we flog them, we beat people over the head with them." Some Democrats, in fact, say polling numbers are more definitive than election returns. This postulate was advanced by the president and his press secretary as recently as Oct. 7. That day, the president said on the question of his own impeachment that "ultimately, it's going to be up to the American people to make a clear statement there."

Hours later, at the regular White House briefing, Clinton spokesman Joe Lockhart reiterated this point. Lockhart was asked if he and the president had the upcoming November elections in mind. Oh no, Lockhart said, adding that congressional elections are usually decided on local considerations. So then, Lockhart was asked, was he talking about the public opinion polls? "Yes," he replied. "People in Congress, people in elective office do, properly, stay in touch with their constituents."

One member who seems to have taken this doctrine literally is Rep. Ted Strickland of Ohio, one of the 31 Democrats who voted for the sweeping GOP impeachment inquiry. "It was not a particularly courageous vote," he told *The Washington Post*. "I think I did what my constituents wanted me to do."

How did he know what they wanted him to do? He commissioned a poll.

It's almost impossible to resist comparing this approach with the stance taken by Sen. Edmund G. Ross of Kansas in 1866 as pressure mounted on him back home to vote for conviction in the impeachment proceedings against President Andrew Johnson. No scientific public opinion surveys existed back then, but public opinion certainly did, and on the eve of Ross' fateful vote, he received this telegram from well-connected Republicans back home:

Kansas has heard the evidence and demands the conviction of the President. [signed] D.R. Anthony and 1,000 Others.

The morning of the vote, May 16, 1866, Ross sent a telegram back:

To D.R. Anthony and 1,000 Others: I do not recognize your right to demand that I vote either for or against conviction. I have taken an oath to do impartial justice according to the Constitution and laws, and trust that I shall have the courage to vote according to the dictates of my judgment and for the highest good of the country. [signed] E.G. Ross.

To David W. Moore, a Gallup Organization vice president and political scientist by training, the dichotomy of their two approaches has echoes in the venerable civics debate over how much pure democracy a representative form of government ought to have. Are the voters back home supposed to choose representatives whose judgments they trust, and who are then free—indeed, obligated—to exercise their wisdom as they see fit? Or are officeholders bound to vote the prejudices, viewpoints and passions of the majority in their districts?

> **MARK PENN:**
> At a Tuesday morning staff meeting, he assured everyone that Clinton's Lewinsky speech had struck just the right tone.

"In political science, we call these two approaches the 'trustee model' and the 'delegate model,'" notes Moore. "I would be perfectly willing to debate either side of the question."

But there are several possible problems with the 'delegate model.' One is that despite the mythic faith pollsters and political consultants put in polls, they aren't infallible. They are also often misinterpreted and misused. And, finally, there are times when leadership is needed, not polls.

HOW ACCURATE?

Today polls are taken on subjects ranging from the profound to the profoundly silly. Is O.J. Simpson guilty or innocent? Whom do you want to break Roger Maris' home run record? Would a woman rather be married to a man who looked like Danny DeVito and did the dishes or a man who looked like Robert Redford and did no dishes? Do you approve of Monica Lewinsky?

But polling's origins, and its bread and butter, have always been the business of predicting elections. The question traditionally asked is basic: "If the election were held today, would you vote for x or for y?" The tricky part is ensuring that question is asked of a representative sample. Since the Truman-Dewey debacle of 1948, polling firms, led by the Gallup Organization, have refined their techniques for gathering this information to a fine art and have compiled an impressive record for accuracy. In the early 1990s, however, venerated California pollster Mervin Field began to notice a troubling trend: the plummeting response rates in his polls.

This phenomenon seems to be caused by a variety of factors, including the availability of call-screening devices, the fact that polling is not a novelty anymore and, probably more than anything else, the vast increase in telemarketing that has left the public surlier and less cooperative. With response rates dipping below 40 percent—half what he sought when he started out—Field said he feared that eventually the industry was going to be simply wrong about an election.

That election happened, in 1996, though nobody seemed to notice. As late as Oct. 23 of that year, the major polling organizations said Clinton had a huge lead over Bob Dole that ranged from the mid-teens to nearly 20 percentage points. The final numbers were 49 percent for Clinton, 41 percent for Dole and 8 percent for Perot. The only pollster who was right was an unknown named John Zogby, who polled for Reuters. For his efforts, Zogby found his methods harshly attacked—he is still attacked to this day—by the pollsters he'd embarrassed.

The 1996 results were hardly in the league of 1948—at least the pollsters picked the right winner—but they sent alarm bells ringing at Gallup, which concluded that it had waited far too long to start polling only "likely voters" instead of registered voters.

But was this lesson really learned?

In recent months, the airwaves have been inundated with polls showing a significant majority of the American people do not want Bill Clinton impeached over lies he told about Monica Lewinsky. From that fact, all kinds of other theories emanate: that the Republicans are overplaying their hand, that Clinton is out of the woods, that this issue will actually work in Democrats' favor in the upcoming elections.

But a closer examination of the numbers, what pollsters call the "internals," raise doubts. For starters, who is being polled? Well, it turns out that it is not likely voters or even registered voters, but the general public. This is quite relevant. Zogby, who polls only likely voters year-round, consistently finds an approval rating for Clinton that's 10 points lower than the other major polls find. "The demographics of all adults is very different from the demographics of likely voters," Zogby says.

Underscoring this point is a new Gallup poll in which the impeachment question is broken down by likely voters. The results are interesting: Whereas the general population opposes impeachment 62 percent to 34 percent, the likeliest voters are against it only 54 to 42. If you add party affiliation to the mix (registered Republicans *favor* impeachment by more than 2-to-1) one can see how unlikely it is that a Republican candidate in a solidly Republican district could be hurt by making Clinton's life difficult.

Take another frequently bandied-about poll number—Clinton's approval rating. Gallup and others have this figure in the mid-60s. Assume for a moment that number is accurate. What does it really tell us? Well, it's 10 points higher than Clinton's normal number, even when things are going well. Not to put too fine a point on it, but even White House officials concede privately that nothing Clinton has done in the policy arena in his second term can really explain the upward spike in support that came after the Lewinsky story broke.

So here's a postulate: It's no coincidence that the approval rating and the anti-impeachment numbers are vir-

tually the same; voters are substituting one question for the other because they know how polls are used today to try to win debates.

USE AND ABUSE

The day after Clinton's disastrous pseudo-apology on the Monica Lewinsky matter, Clinton Pollster Mark Penn assured everyone at the Tuesday morning staff meeting that the president had struck just the right tone—because 58 percent of those polled in Penn's surveys told him this, according to one participant in the session.

But those polls didn't take into account—and couldn't, really—a host of other factors, including that Clinton's new story meant he had personally lied to the very Democrats who could give him cover, including Cabinet members and Capitol Hill leaders. In other words, as every reputable pollster readily admits, there are limits to what polling can tell us. "There are just things you can't poll," said one White House aide, with a laugh. "But we try."

They aren't alone. The last president who didn't employ polling was Herbert Hoover. Jimmy Carter actually began the tradition of having an in-house pollster, and Ronald Reagan's extensive polling operation was the model for the Clinton White House.

The first president to study polls, to commission his own private polls and, ultimately to ignore the polls, was Franklin D. Roosevelt. In 1940, FDR desperately wanted to help Britain stave off Nazi aggression, but Americans were in an isolationist mind-set. According to Robert Eisinger, assistant professor of political science at Lewis & Clark College, Roosevelt began quietly obtaining poll data from Gallup and another Princeton pollster with ties to Gallup named Hadley Cantril.

Roosevelt consulted polls on everything from support for Lend-Lease to whether Catholic voters would be offended if strategic bombing by the Allies harmed religious sites in Italy. In the end, however, Roosevelt scholars say that FDR set his own course. "I don't think there's any evidence that he relied on polls," said Eisinger. "They are feeding into his policy decisions, but they are not driving them."

Two, more recent, examples of presidents and polls are also instructive. In 1990, after Iraqi tanks overran Kuwait, polls showed Americans overwhelmingly opposed to the idea of American ground troops being deployed to the Arabian peninsula. But President Bush, asserting that national security was at stake, decided to send troops anyway. The following winter, 10 days before the ground war began, only 11 percent of Americans were in favor of launching one. A month later, this figure was closer to 90 percent—and so was Bush's approval rating.

A third example is Clinton's 1995 decision to send troops to the Balkans to halt ethnic genocide. After ago-

> **DICK MORRIS:**
>
> "You don't use a poll to reshape a program, but to reshape your argumentation for the program so the public supports it."

nizing over this issue for a year, Clinton finally decided to act. Deeply concerned about public opinion polls that were running 2-to-1 against committing American ground troops, the White House pollsters delved deeply into exactly what the public would accept. Clinton pollster Dick Morris insists that the purpose of these polls was to know how to explain the Bosnian commitment to the public, but it also seems that the American public helped set the parameters of the military mission. The public told Clinton's pollsters it didn't want American troops scouring mountainsides looking for war criminals or disarming the Bosnian militias, and that it wanted a firm timetable for withdrawal. All these elements ultimately became conditions of the deployment.

"Clinton does polls to decide what to do," says Republican pollster Frank Luntz, who tested the GOP "Contract With America" in surveys. "That's not what they should be used for. When we did the contract, we used polls to decide what to say, not what to do."

Morris insists that this is what Clinton does as well.

"A misuse of polls is when a politician switches positions because of a poll," Morris said. "You don't use a poll to reshape a program, but to reshape your argumentation for the program so that the public supports it and it works." Morris points out that Bosnia was not the first time Clinton bucked the polls, and he rattles off a litany of issues, ranging from the International Monetary Fund bailout and the rescue of the Mexican peso to support for late-term abortion and affirmative action.

Clinton also uses polls to tell people what they want to hear about a policy—sometimes even when the language doesn't actually describe the policy. In the case of affirmative action, for instance, Clinton's polling told him what to say—"mend it, don't end it"—and he said it, but he made no real changes in policy.

Lawrence Jacobs, a political scientist at the University of Minnesota, says this example highlights the real abuse of polling. Jacobs argues that since 1980, presidents and members of Congress have charted their courses mostly on the basis of special-interest pressure, campaign contributions and ideology, while using polls to help them put a (sometimes false) face on their policies. "They use polls to learn how to manipulate the language and to employ buzzwords and symbols," he says. Thus voters get the worst of both worlds. They don't believe their elected officials are listening to them, and when the politicians pretend to listen, it's merely to learn how to fool them.

So where does this leave us on impeachment?

One possible answer is that on this issue, the public knows it has a right to be consulted and is taking back some of the power of politicians, pollsters and the media to spin.

Republican House members keep stressing "the rule of law," and holding out hopes that they can bring public opinion along with them. But this issue is not as remote as understanding the menace of the Third Reich—or even of Saddam Hussein. Infidelity (and lying about it) is domestic policy, literally, and the public seems to believe it knows as much about it as do members of Congress, the media and these lawyers who keep popping up on television. "I'm not saying we should have a national referendum on it, clearly that's not what the Constitution and the Founders had in mind," White House Press Secretary Joe Lockhart said in an interview. "But the public ought to be heard on this, on what constitutes an impeachable offense. They have a right to be heard."

Certainly the facts are in the public domain—Independent Counsel Kenneth W. Starr and the Republicans made sure of that—and on this issue, at least, the polls are probably accurate. "If there's one clear message in all this data," said Gallup's David Moore, "it's that they don't want him impeached."

Sydney J. Freedberg Jr. contributed to this report.

Did Clinton Succeed or Fail?

The editors of the British magazine *Prospect* invited *American Prospect* co-editor
Robert Kuttner and columnist E.J. Dionne to have a friendly debate on whether the Clinton
presidency was a success. An adaptation of that exchange follows.

BY ROBERT KUTTNER AND E.J. DIONNE

Dear E.J. Dionne:

Did Clinton succeed or fail? It depends on how you define success. We need to consider him as a president, as a party man, as a world leader, and as a political figure who we hoped would rebuild confidence in the enterprise of democratic government.

The U.S. economy certainly boomed during his presidency. For this, Clinton shares credit with Alan Greenspan, and with fortunate timing. Thanks to information technology and the disinflation of the 1990s, these were likely to be good years. Clinton had the wit to strike a deal with Greenspan and the markets: a lower federal budget deficit in exchange for eased interest rates. Early in his presidency, when the Democrats controlled Congress, Clinton even achieved his deficit reduction by raising taxes on the rich rather than by slashing public services.

But also, during his first two years, Clinton made big mistakes as a partisan—two in particular. First, he contrived a national health insurance scheme in a manner more befitting a parliamentary government. Congress was not much involved in the design or political management of his plan. Worse, Clinton bungled the interest-group and popular politics of health reform. The managed competition scheme was complex, and it did not fire the public imagination. Politically, Clinton hoped to make a deal with the big employers and insurance companies, but this proved naïve. In the end, both turned on him—and he didn't have public opinion on his side as a counterweight.

Worse still, Clinton spent what remained of his political capital in 1993-1994, to ram the NAFTA deal through Congress. The plan was a leftover from the Bush administration. It badly split the Democrats, and it was not even wise geopolitics. In the end, Clinton got NAFTA enacted with heavy Republican support, dispiriting his own party. Republicans took control of Congress in the 1994

midterm elections, and Clinton deserves some of the blame.

What followed was of course a turn to the right. Clinton did play a weak hand well, helping Newt Gingrich's Republican Congress to overreach itself. But during the mid-1990s, Clinton himself tacked further to the right than the situation required. He embraced a Republican view of welfare reform. He went along with a brutal immigration bill and assaults on civil liberty in the name of crime control. He accepted the idea of a balanced budget—and then when an economic boom pushed the budget into surplus, he declared that he would pay off the entire national debt.

To a point, all this was a kind of tactical Dunkirk: a strategic retreat to enable the Democrats to fight another day. But this particular Dunkirk moved the fleet not just to Dover but to Bermuda. The entire center of gravity moved to the right. On most aspects of domestic policy, Bill Clinton has been to the right of Richard Nixon.

Today, there is a government budget surplus projected at $200 billion a year as far as the eye can see. But the Democrats have so distanced themselves from public spending that the most imaginative thing Clinton and Gore can think to do is to pay off the national debt a year earlier.

The welfare state, thanks to Roosevelt and LBJ, does a fair job of taking care of the elderly. It gives little to working families except tax bills. Now is surely the time for increased spending on child care, lifelong training, first-time homeownership, and universal health insurance. This would give working-age voters, as well as the elderly, a reason to vote Democratic. But Clinton has made the politics of budget balance sacrosanct, and Gore will needlessly lose liberal votes to Ralph Nader.

In fairness, Clinton is not alone with this problem. Throughout the West, men and women of the center-left are governing on center-right programs. In general, cen-

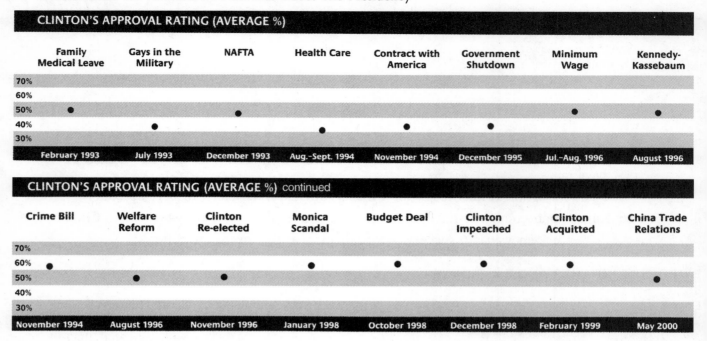

ter-left parties have failed to rein in the global market. In Europe, at least, this is seen to be a problem.

On foreign policy, Clinton's presidency has been a mixed bag. He did well to advance peace in Ireland and in the Middle East. He intervened late in the former Yugoslavia—but better late than never. His Russian policy has been a failure, and his effort to launch a new World Trade Organization round was naïve. His International Monetary Fund and World Bank policies are too solicitous of investors and too casual about the stability of the global system.

Domestically, Clinton did take some risks for unpopular causes, as in the Elián González case. By doing so, he sometimes made them popular. He defended affirmative action for blacks when it would have been easy to abandon it. He backed tolerance for gays. He went out of his way to find talented women and minorities for senior jobs. Yet he also left government and politics blemished by personal and financial scandal. The Lewinsky disgrace had some benefits: Americans decided that they would rather be governed by Casanova than by Torquemada. But most people would rather not have to make that choice. So while Clinton survived, even thrived, the party and the government he led both continued to fall in public esteem. After Clinton, American progressivism is weaker: more centrist, less imaginative, less inspiring to voters. As I have observed elsewhere, Clinton became the Typhoid Mary of U.S. politics—a carrier who maintained his own health while infecting others. Al Gore may contract the fatal rash.

Best, Bob Kuttner

Dear Bob Kuttner:
Almost everything you say about Clinton is true—and so is its opposite. Did his failures in the first two years lead to the 1994 Republican sweep that weakened the Democrats at every level? Yes. Did Clinton beat back Gingrich's revolution and push American politics so far away from the right that George W. Bush is forced to defend government? Yes.

Did Clinton preside over a golden age of capitalist growth and create a climate in which the public imagination is dominated by stock ownership and high-tech millionaires? Yes. Did he make taxes far more progressive? Yes. Did he sign a Republican-sponsored welfare bill that ended public assistance as an entitlement? Yes. Did he preside over unprecedented increases in public spending for the working poor (expanding the Earned Income Tax Credit, Medicare, and child care for the low paid)? Yes. In sum, did he move the United States to the right? Yes. Did he move it to the left? Yes. Welcome to the Clinton paradox.

The paradox is that a politician of extraordinary talent missed the opportunity to be an extraordinary president. A Republican opponent who knows him well has said that Clinton was "Roosevelt without the steel." This Republican sees Clinton as the most talented American politician since FDR, but without the discipline and the toughness (and, in fairness, without a war and a depression to create opportunities for heroism).

The paradoxes of Clintonism have a parallel: the paradoxes of interpreting Clinton. Where people stand now often depends on where they stood in 1992. If you believe that the Democrats needed to make strategic corrections—on crime, welfare, family policy, defense, and fiscal prudence—you're inclined to be sympathetic to what Clinton tried to do (even if, as in my case, you opposed his signing the welfare bill and dislike his embrace of the death penalty). But if you thought that New

Democrats were always and everywhere sellouts, you probably start out being tough on Clinton.

Clinton never fully governed as either a New Democrat or an old one. He understood that a Democratic president needed to blend the two. So he went for a balanced budget, but courtesy of progressive taxation; he sought to establish national health insurance, but with a plan that tried to balance state and market; he spoke more respectfully of religion and tradition than most liberals, but favored gay rights.

Yes, he may have made all the mistakes on national health insurance that you suggest, but he was the first president since Truman to make a serious effort to close the largest gap in America's social insurance state. On the health care fiasco, Clinton is assailed from the left (he made too many concessions to the market), from the right (his plan involved too much government), and from the center (he bungled his dealings with Congress). Still, if he had pulled off health care reform, his presidency would have been very different.

It would have been different, too, if he had ignored the leaders of the 1993 Democratic Congress and insisted on political reform. Democrats should be ashamed that Republican John McCain is identified by the public as the leading foe of big money in politics. Democrats have embraced the cause now, but because they blew their chance of enacting reform when they had the opportunity to do so, their current claims ring hollow. (And the campaign finance abuses during Clinton's re-election effort hardly make it easy for Democrats to stand as the party of clean government.)

Did the fleet really withdraw to Bermuda? It is plausible to argue that the net result of the Clinton term has been to move the political debate slightly toward the left. If you doubt that, remember that Reagan's slogan was "Government isn't the solution; government is the problem." George W. Bush says, "Government if necessary, but not necessarily government." Bush underscores this shift in rhetoric—described as "the fourth way" by Bush's chief domestic policy adviser—when he says, "Too often, my party has confused the need for limited government with a need for government itself."

My favorite comment from the right came from a young conservative writer, Ramesh Ponnuru of the *National Review*. "Whatever they may say, conservatives know in their bones that their position is weak," he wrote last autumn. "What these conservatives sense is that, at a level of politics deeper than the fortunes of the political parties, the ground is shifting away from them . . . . The 2000 election is shaping up not to be a ratification of conservatism, but of Clintonism—and will be even if the Republicans win."

So, is the United States, on balance, better-off now than it was nearly eight years ago? The answer, for most Americans, is yes. Could Clinton have accomplished more? The answer, for this American, is also yes. How you judge Clinton depends on which question you judge to be the more important.

Yours, E.J.

Dear E.J.:

As always with our Bill, we can emphasize the half-full or the half-empty glass. Is American liberalism stronger or weaker as a result of eight years of Clinton? Can Clinton be faulted for tacking further to the right than he tactically needed to? On these questions, you judge him more kindly than I do. It was not inevitable that the Democrats had to lose both houses of Congress in 1994. It was not inevitable that Clinton had to make budget surplus the test of virtue, much less to pledge to retire the entire national debt.

You say that he moved the country both to the right and to the left. On tolerance issues, we have moved to the left. But on the big issues of political economy, the choices today are further to the right than when Clinton took office. In 1992 no politician was talking about paying off the entire national debt. Nobody was talking about privatizing Social Security—even in part. Universal health insurance was on the agenda. The share of GDP devoted to nondefense spending other than Social Security was larger then—it has been steadily cut during the Clinton years. Meanwhile, big money dominates political life to an unprecedented degree, and political participation continues to dwindle.

Yes, the Earned Income Tax Credit and higher minimum wage laws have helped ordinary people—although the latter was foisted on Clinton by Ted Kennedy, Robert Reich, and the unions; it proved too popular for even the Republicans to resist. Even so, inequality continues to widen, despite full employment.

The budget surplus is not, as you claim, mostly the result of the 1993 tax increase on the top-income bracket. It is mostly the result of the 10-year spending cuts in the 1997 budget, together with higher-than-projected growth. You say that the Democrats needed to make strategic corrections on crime, welfare, family policy, defense, and fiscal prudence. I agree. But in each case, Clinton moved further into conservative territory than he needed to. Besides disliking his welfare bill, what do you think of his views on gun laws? Or the death penalty? Or immigrants' rights? Or habeas corpus?

With a Republican Congress, he certainly had to compromise. But why didn't he try to lead public opinion in a more liberal direction? With an economic boom fattening tax revenues and a big federal budget surplus, I can imagine a liberal Democratic candidate for president declaring that now is the time to put universal health coverage back into the debate; to inject serious federal funds into failing schools; to construct rules of engagement for global commerce that include rights for workers as well as for capital. Clinton's shift to the center-right has made it more difficult for a successor to run for office on these themes and still seem mainstream. To the extent that

Gore is sounding more progressive, Ralph Nader probably deserves more credit than Clinton.

The problem with the third way, in the style of Bill Clinton and Tony Blair, is that you begin by meeting the conservatives halfway. When that doesn't quite succeed, you meet them halfway again. And again. Soon, you have two conservative parties. You can narrowly win elections by being a little less conservative than the other guy, but it rouses no passion in the electorate. So while even George W. Bush grudgingly concedes that there is some role for government, Clinton's legacy is a diminished faith in democratic politics. To the extent that government and politics are the sources of economic redress for those in the bottom two-thirds, I am not so sure that most of America is better-off after Clinton.

Best, Bob

Dear Bob:

On many of the specifics, I am with you. You are right that the Democrats didn't have to lose Congress. But here, I think the fault lies not just with Clinton, but with the Democratic Congress. It was wrong for congressional Democrats to resist campaign finance reform. It was wrong of liberals to resist Clinton's earlier efforts at welfare reform, which were more socially generous than the bill that was ultimately enacted. Clinton not only lost the health insurance battle as a result of his own mistakes; he also lost because liberal groups did not realize until too late how powerful were the forces arrayed against them. Moreover, the Democratic majority in Congress was not coherent. It was badly split among conservative Democrats who resisted the health insurance plan, liberal Democrats who thought Clinton didn't go far enough, and the rest. Congressional Democrats share with Clinton the responsibility for the failures of those first two years. (Most of them know it, which is why the party is more coherent now than it was then.)

On the budget: Yes, the tax increases were not the only factor in balancing the budget. But I find it remarkable that liberals give Clinton so little credit for making the tax code more progressive. He increased taxation on the wealthy and increased benefits for the working poor. And by making the tax code highly progressive, Clinton made it very complicated for advocates of lower taxes on the rich. Now, all across-the-board tax cuts give most benefit to the very well-to-do, which is why Republicans struggle to pass them.

I am with you on the death penalty and habeas corpus. (A lot of the anti-immigrant provisions of the welfare bill were eventually knocked out.) On gun laws, we disagree: The cause of gun control is much more advanced now than it was in 1992. Indeed, one reason the Democrats lost Congress was the willingness of both Clinton and many House members to support stronger gun laws, which proved unpopular in many rural constituencies. And by the way, the falling crime rate has allowed many Americans to rethink their position on the death penalty. The proportion favoring capital punishment has dropped from 80 percent in 1994 to 66 percent now. It is a positive legacy for progressives that many of the old "wedge" issues that so divided the United States along racial and cultural lines are no longer so powerful. And it is useful, as Richard Parker argued in *The American Prospect,* that liberals have dropped some of their prejudgments against religion. Isn't that part of the cultural transformation which occurred in the Clinton era?

As for growing inequality, the current boom—whether it is Clinton's doing or not—has proven a point progressives (you especially) have made for years: If unemployment went low enough, at least inequality would stop growing. To the extent that a welfare reform bill we both opposed has worked, it is because opportunities for the poor exist now that did not exist before. Isn't 4 percent unemployment the essence of Truman liberalism?

You say that the third way leads to the existence of two conservative parties. But New Dealish, progressive social democratic parties have all, one way or another, concluded that there is no alternative to the market economy. This leaves all such parties confronting three big questions. First, what can the social insurance state do to correct the injustices markets inevitably leave in their wake? Second, what forms of regulation can national governments—separately or in cooperation—impose to protect workers' rights, the environment, and other values not naturally protected by the market? Third, how can governments, through both action and strategic retreat, protect the civic institutions that citizens build independently of government and market?

Clinton could have gone farther on all three fronts. But I'm not convinced that the Clinton era has left us as bereft of democratic possibilities as you suggest. Part of our problem is that we won't really know how to assess him until we know what comes after. If Social Security is partially privatized, if there is no movement whatever toward universal health insurance and decent child care, if little more is done for those left out of the boom, then you will be proved right. If we succeed in building on the achievements of this era, we'll look back more kindly on our Bill—even as he continues to frustrate and mystify us.

Yours, E.J.

Dear E.J.:

Like so many other Americans, you are more charmed by this guy than I am. You cut him more slack than I do. I will credit Clinton with much that you credit him for, but the whole is less than the sum of its parts.

Clinton has the gift of being a superb public teacher. He has educated Americans on the fact that gays are people, too, that the struggle for racial justice isn't over, that the revolution in gender equality is incomplete. Suppose he had used some of those gifts to provide a more complex view of the virtues and limits of markets. Suppose he had proposed more than token initiatives in health and education, if he had said positive things about trade unions as well as the new economy. He might have inspired a real popular movement, as Roosevelt, Truman, and the Kennedy brothers did.

You say that there is no alternative to the capitalist economy, but a capitalist economy need not be a laissez-faire one. Capitalism can and should be housebroken so that it provides a measure of security to temper the famous creative destruction. This requires, as you say, decent social welfare, government regulation, and a strengthened civil society. But above all, this enterprise of building strong countervailing public institutions requires a politics.

With his gifts, Clinton might have helped define and animate that politics. Mostly, he didn't. So his aspiring successor faces resurgent laissez-faire ideologues and institutions far more bereft of popular counterweights than might have been the case. Today, a newly reinvented, populist Al Gore is trying to contrive such a politics from scratch. But Gore as Clinton's vice president necessarily starts from a center-right posture, facing a cynical electorate. This makes it hard for him to credibly seem the pocketbook champion of the workaday voter. Bill Clinton is an extraordinary politician. But his signal failure as a progressive was, ironically, political.

Best, Bob

Dear Bob:

To the extent that we disagree, I don't believe it's because of Clinton's charm. And I don't think the troubles of the first two years can be attributed only to a failure of progressive will, but rather to a poorly organized administration, some bad choices (what if Clinton had tried health care in cooperation with Congress, including some Republicans, as part of his 1993 budget?), and the difficulties congressional Democrats had in dealing with a president of their own party.

While I don't much like it when others harp on them, I think that the twin scandals—Monica Lewinsky and campaign fundraising —are the biggest scars on Clinton's legacy, in part because they turned people off public engagement at a moment when they were ready to be turned on. A new generation was prepared to be excited by social commitment, much as Clinton's generation was inspired by John Kennedy. Americans under 30 are far more inclined than their forebears to volunteer in social service activities. But for now, such good work is seen as an alternative to politics, where—under more promising circumstances—it might be connected to a larger project of social reconstruction. That is a loss for which Clinton bears some blame.

My sense is that at the end of these eight years, there is less hostility to government, more open questioning about what the market can accomplish all by itself, a larger willingness to deal with the problems of the poor, significantly greater social tolerance, and an abatement of cultural warfare in which elites often sneered at the values of average Americans. Those changes create political opportunities. You, Bob, will be the first to take advantage of them. If you succeed, you will have to revise your opinion of this era upward. Let's meet in five or 10 years and figure out who was right.

Yours, E.J.

First published in the August issue of the London-based *Prospect* magazine.

E.J. DIONNE is a senior fellow at the Brookings Institution and a columnist at *The Washington Post*.

Trivial Pursuits

Clinton's record

RAMESH PONNURU

Bill Clinton is in the process of proving that a presidential legacy is like individual happiness or national greatness: something achieved mostly as a byproduct of activities undertaken for other ends, rather than as part of a self-conscious design. His is a negative proof. Never has a president mused as much, or as openly, about his place in history as our Solipsist-in-Chief has. But rarely has it been harder to determine what that place should be.

Part of the difficulty, as liberal columnist E. J. Dionne Jr. has pointed out, is that almost anything one could say about Clinton's presidency is true—and so is its opposite. Did he move the country right or left? Yes. Strengthen the Democrats or weaken them? Both. Was he the perfect president for the times, or a historical accident? A case could be made either way. He was larger than life, and so, so small.

We'll have a better picture of his presidency in a few years' time, after we will have seen what further fruits his policies will bear and how his successor will govern. If, say, China were to nuke Los Angeles next year, the defects of Clinton's foreign and defense policies would presumably get more space in the encyclopedia entry on him. But we can essay some judgments right now.

Clinton's economic record, it has to be said, is pretty good. Not, to be sure, as good as the conventional wisdom would have it: A recovery from the brief recession of the early

1990s was already underway when Clinton was elected, and his tax increase of 1993 was followed by a few years of sub par growth. But Clinton deserves credit for promoting free trade, allowing Alan Greenspan to vanquish inflation, and acceding to Republican demands for a reduction in the capital gains tax. The combination of these policies more than compensated for the tax hike. Hillary Rodham Clinton should take a bow, too. Her rigidity doomed the administration's health-care plan and thus was a boon for the economy.

Clinton's biggest contribution to the economy was not to do much to screw it up. This is not the faint praise it sounds like: It is a boast that could not be made by most recent presidents, including Republicans Richard Nixon, Gerald Ford, and George Bush.

Moreover, the positive aspects of Clinton's economic record are likely to endure. The inflationary wing of the Democratic party, strong as recently as a decade ago, hardly exists any more. In the late 1980s, leading Democratic intellectuals wanted the government to direct economic development and to channel subsidies to prominent industries. They were itching for a trade war with our major allies. Nobody serious believes any of that any more. Clinton consolidated a Reaganite consensus on these issues, just as President Eisenhower ratified FDR's New Deal.

Clinton moved right on moral and cultural issues, too, though this truth has sometimes been obscured

by his trysts. Previous Democrats had suffered for their liberal attitudes on work and welfare, sex and family, race, crime, and religion. But Clinton declared that abortion should be rare. He decried illegitimacy. He signed a Republican bill ending the federal welfare entitlement. He even funded abstinence-education programs. Michael Dukakis had fairly radiated an aggressive secularism; Clinton's rhetoric was steeped in religion, and sometimes delivered from the pulpits of black churches.

In some respects, the country became more socially conservative under Clinton. Rates of abortion, illegitimacy, divorce, and teen sexual activity all began to decline. But social liberalism comes in bourgeois and antibourgeois varieties, and the former—the liberalism of niceness and tolerance—also made strides. Public acceptance of homosexuality grew, probably helped along by the president's association with gay lobbies. But this is yet another feature of the Clinton years that cannot simply be described as a shift to the left or right. Gays and lesbians have spent the Clinton years trying to join the army, to marry, and to lead Boy Scout troops. They have sought, in other words, to be integrated into society's most conservative institutions; to lead the sort of square lives that most heterosexuals long ago grew tired of. It is because of such shifts that after three decades of culture wars, a measure of peace has broken out. (Granted, conservatives

From *National Review*, November 20, 2000, pp. 16, 18. © 2000 by National Review, Inc., 215 Lexington Avenue, New York, NY 10016. Reprinted by permission.

cannot be wholly pleased by the terms of this peace.)

America's racial politics are relatively placid as well. To the extent Clinton deserves credit for the good economy, he also deserves credit for the reduction in both black unemployment and racial tensions that economy has produced. On the other side of the ledger must be set Clinton's occasional race-baiting, as when he accuses Republicans of having a policy of holding up black and Hispanic judicial nominees. And while it may be argued that Clinton ended divisive political arguments over immigration and racial preferences, his policies may be storing up racial trouble for the future.

Clinton ended, at least temporarily, a final set of battles: those over the role of the federal government, which, it is now clear, will neither expand dramatically nor shrink at all. Welfare reform helped to religitimize the federal government. Clinton was also shrewd to expand tax credits for the working poor. Previous Democrats ran into trouble by taxing other Democrats; by taking them off the tax rolls, Clinton was able to tax Republicans for the benefit of Democrats. As a result, it's been much harder to cut tax rates.

Blunting the conservative attack on the welfare state was Clinton's greatest achievement for liberalism. In 1996, he said that the era of big government was over. But it may be truer to say that the era of arguing about big government is over, except in the most abstract of terms. Newt Gingrich was the last politician who railed against the "liberal welfare state"; not even conservative writers use such terms any more. Republicans no longer make principled objections to a federal role in education policy.

But liberals paid a steep price for this victory. They had to become

The question left for Clinton's successor is what to make of a diminished thing.

more statist as well, buying popularity by abandoning libertarian positions on crime, foreign policy, and civil liberties. They lost their moral authority and, perhaps, some portion of their self-respect by becoming apologists for Clinton's compromises and his abuses. Clinton made the Democrats competitive again in presidential races, but devastated them down the ticket. The Democrats are a minority in Congress and the states, and they are more dependent than ever on a labor movement that is itself declining.

Moreover, Clinton's triumph for liberalism was a matter of politics much more than of policy. In many respects, Clinton's has been a bystander presidency. It may be true that if not for Clinton welfare would not have been reformed, capital-gains taxes not cut, and NAFTA not passed. But Newt Gingrich was at least as indispensable for each achievement. Most of the rest of Clinton's policy legacy is trivia: paid volunteerism for kids and unpaid leave for new parents.

It is tempting to suggest that this is in fact Clinton's real legacy: the trivialization of the presidency, of the government, of politics. The presidency may have grown more powerful by some measures: the independent-counsel law is dead, and it has become more acceptable to govern through executive order and regulatory fiat. But the presidency has never had less respect. Washington has never seemed more irrelevant. Clinton suggests, deceptively,

that he has reduced the federal workforce. But it is surely true that the government's place in the American imagination has been downsized. Politics is now a spectator sport, which is to say a television show.

But this judgment may be too harsh—or, to put it another way, even the view that Clinton's chief legacy was to shrink the presidency may ascribe too much importance to him. The end of the Cold War was bound to alter the nature of the presidency. (Neither Clinton nor George W. Bush would have won a presidential nomination if the Soviet Union were still a menace.) It's not Clinton's fault that television's cultural influence peaked during his tenure.

Clinton probably contributed to these trends, but he didn't cause them. The empathetic style with which he is identified has been gaining force for three decades, as his generational cohort advanced through their careers. His presidency, and particularly the Lewinsky scandal, coarsened the culture; the stain on her dress is a stain on his record. But by the mid '90s, radios were already broadcasting stuff that would have shocked listeners ten years before. (Hard as it is to remember, there was a national controversy over whether stations would play George Michael's song "I Want Your Sex" when it came out in 1987.)

Bill Clinton was a man of many firsts: the first Democrat to be reelected to a second full term as president since FDR; the first president to talk about his underwear in public, or apologize for an affair. But the era of Bill Clinton is ending. It is impossible to say how much his presidency reflected his times, and how much they reflected it. The question left for Clinton's successor is what to make of a diminished thing.

Crackup of the Committees

A MAJOR REASON FOR THE CHAOS PERVADING CAPITOL HILL IS THAT COMMITTEE POWER HAS ERODED TO THE POINT OF COLLAPSE

BY RICHARD E. COHEN

From the scant handful of major bills passed by the House and the Senate this year, one unmistakable fact emerges: The congressional committees have lost their long-standing pre-eminence as the center of legislative ideas and debates. A major reason for the chaos pervading Capitol Hill is that committee power has eroded to the point of collapse.

During May and June, for example, both the House and the Senate considered major gun control proposals that were not written or reviewed by either chamber's Judiciary Committee. Earlier this month, Senate Majority Leader Trent Lott, R-Miss., after bowing to Democratic demands for action on patients' rights, took the unusual step of selecting as the focus of the floor debate a bill crafted by key Democrats. Republicans offered an alternative measure that was initially prepared by a Senate GOP task force and was modified only slightly by the committee with jurisdiction. Meanwhile, key House committees are so splintered over their managed care legislation that Speaker J. Dennis Hastert, R-Ill., this week devised a plan to bypass them altogether.

Also in recent days, both chambers have taken up major tax cuts that were cleared by the tax-writing committees, but were not really the handiwork of a majority of their members. The chairmen of the House Ways and Means and Senate Finance committees wrote their tax legislation in consultation chiefly with a handful of senior aides. The committees then spent only a few hours on token review of the major budgetary and tax-policy consequences and made modest changes before the full House and Senate advanced the bills with little debate and amid grumbling, even from some Republicans.

Publicly and privately, "there was virtually no discussion of the [tax] bill with members," complained moderate Rep. Michael N. Castle, R-Del., who forced last-minute changes in the House proposal. "Everything has been fed to everybody."

This ad hoc legislating flouts the textbook model for how Congress makes laws. As generations of high school students have learned in civics courses, legislation is supposed to result when thorough hearings are followed by

a committee review of alternatives in an attempt to build consensus, and then by a second and third round of those same debates on the House and Senate floors. Such a framework was described more than a century ago by a respected political scientist who initially framed his ideas as a Princeton University undergraduate and later became President.

"Congress in session is Congress on public exhibition, whilst Congress in its committee rooms is Congress at work," wrote Woodrow Wilson in his classic 1885 study, *Congressional Government.* "Whatever is to be done must be done by, or through, the committee."

For most of the 20th century, Wilson's doctrine remained the rule on Capitol Hill. Small groups of members working in committees typically won deference for their expertise on particular policy matters. Generally, committee chairmen were recognized as first among equals. Their legislation was carefully crafted after extensive debate and deal-making and was rarely challenged on the House or Senate floor.

Over the past 30 years, however, committee power has eroded to the point where it now has largely collapsed. In many respects, this process has been both gradual and purposeful. It began during the era of Democratic control and has been greatly accelerated by both parties during the past decade. The death warrant for the old system came in 1995, when Newt Gingrich, R-Ga., assumed power as House Speaker. As part of his top-down management style, Gingrich circumvented and intentionally undermined the committee process by creating Republican task forces and demanding that they write legislation reflecting his own views.

With Gingrich gone, this legislative year began with promises that a more mature and steady Republican ma-

From *National Journal,* July 31, 1999, pp. 2210-2217. © 1999 by National Journal Group, Inc. All rights reserved. Reprinted by permission.

WOODROW WILSON:

"Whatever is to be done must be done by, or through, the committee."

jority would pay greater homage to committee perquisites. Upon taking over as House Speaker in January, Hastert embraced a return to the "regular order." More comfortable than Gingrich with the committee system, Hastert promised to give the panels free, or at least freer, rein to achieve his general goals.

To be sure, some of the same chairmen who meekly ducked decisions under Gingrich have sought to impose their own marks on legislation in Hastert's House. "There is a stronger sense that our members are charting their own course," said a veteran House GOP aide. But Hastert often has found that implementing his lofty goal of a return to legislating-as-usual hasn't worked out smoothly.

In the Senate, Lott, now in his fourth year as Majority Leader, seems more settled in his post and less inclined to create party task forces to guide the work of committee chairmen. Nevertheless, Senate committees, like their counterparts in the House, routinely find that they, too, suffer because of their own ineffectiveness or lack of deliberation—or simply are ignored by party leaders. In both chambers, this has been the case in recent months with the gun control, tax cut, and patients' rights legislation. A similar scenario is likely to develop this fall on campaign finance reform.

Democrats, for their part, have been eager to criticize the Republicans for their continued efforts to detour around the conventional committee process. "It's an everyday occurrence now for committees to lose control," said Rep. Martin Frost of Texas, the chairman of the House Democratic Caucus.

Even GOP allies see little prospect for resolving the problem. Committees "will become increasingly irrelevant from the standpoint of legislation," veteran conservative activist Gordon S. Jones wrote last September in *The World & I,* a magazine published by *The Washington Times.*

That judgment may sound radical, but it is really only what has been obvious for some time. Despite occasional bursts of nostalgia from chairmen seeking to reclaim what they view as their due prerogatives, the arrangements that Woodrow Wilson described are as dated as quill pens and snuffboxes. And as the century ends, the breakdown of the committee system has become a major factor in the chaos that pervades Capitol Hill. Congressional leaders repeatedly have encountered difficulties with party-driven legislation that was hastily brought to the House or Senate floor without a thorough vetting—or any attempts at bipartisan compromise—among the experts at the committee level.

Republican leaders, said Frost, "have danced on the edge several times and are flirting with disaster. You can't always cram for the final exam and get A's. Plus, their incompetence emboldens our side to go after them."

The increasing use of the filibuster in the Senate is one indicator that objectionable legislation is being scheduled more frequently for floor consideration, thus boosting combativeness. In a paper presented this month to a Capitol Hill conference on civility in the Senate, congressional scholar Barbara Sinclair, a political science professor at the University of California (Los Angeles), wrote that in the Senate during 1997–98, "half of all major measures ran into filibuster problems." During June, the Senate was hamstrung by simultaneous gridlock on managed care reform, appropriations, and steel-import legislation.

Moreover, the disruptive nature of the current legislative process has left the Republican majority struggling to effectively enunciate a party message. Consultant Steven Hofman, a House Republican leadership aide during the 1980s who became a senior Labor Department official in the Bush Administration, noted that in contrast to the congressional GOP, President Clinton often "produces a proposal and then goes to the country to talk about it." Hofman contended: "With divided government, narrow majorities, and a cynical public, moving policy forward requires public support. If I were a strategist for Hastert, I'd bring in our committee and subcommittee chairmen to see how we can engage issues with the country and have a dialogue."

Although there has been little serious discussion of institutional alternatives, the coming years may dictate a search for new models of legislative order—no matter who is elected President and who controls Congress.

BARONIES UNDER SIEGE

Democrats these days are well-positioned to criticize Republican operations, but they had plenty of their own problems in running the House and Senate committees while they held the majority. And the Democrats were responsible for major changes in the committee system that have had a lingering impact on the GOP-controlled Congress.

For most of the 20th century—following the Republicans' 1911 revolt against their domineering Speaker Joseph G. Cannon, who was called "czar"—the majority party in the House under both Democratic and GOP control gave the committees broad authority to dictate the agenda. The seeds for the destruction of that system were planted in the 1960s, when the mostly Southern and conservative Democratic committee chairmen in both the House and the Senate resisted large parts of President Kennedy's "New Frontier" program.

The views of most of these conservative Democratic chairmen ran counter to those of most of their party col-

■ FILLIBUSTER-HAPPY

As Senate committees and leaders increasingly send party-driven legislation to the floor, opposition forces have mounted a growing number of filibusters. Many of these filibusters have succeeded in killing the bills, since Senate rules require 60 votes to invoke cloture and limit further debate. By the 1990s, according to Barbara Sinclair, a political science professor at the University of California (Los Angeles), "The Senate's big workload and limited floor time made threats to filibuster a potent weapon, and Senators increasingly employed such threats." The data at right, compiled by Sinclair, showed the increased numbers of filibusters and cloture votes during the past half-century.

YEARS	FILIBUSTERS PER CONGRESS	CLOTURE VOTES PER CONGRESS
1951–60	1.0	0.4
1961–70	4.6	5.2
1971–80	11.2	22.4
1981–86	16.7	23.0
1987–92	26.7	39.0
1993–94	30.0	42.0
1995–96	25.0	50.0
1997–98	29.0	53.0

leagues, who wanted to increase the role of the federal government on economic and social issues. But during the early 1960s, Democratic congressional leaders lacked the muscle to break the deadlocks that resulted.

The old-style Democratic committee barons changed course and went along with President Lyndon B. Johnson's "Great Society" initiative only when LBJ's huge election victory in 1964 allowed him to define the terms of debate the following year. Perhaps the best example occurred in 1965, when Wilbur D. Mills, D-Ark., the masterful consensus builder who chaired the Ways and Means Committee, abandoned his longtime opposition to government-sponsored medical care for the elderly and took the lead in painstakingly building a bipartisan coalition to enact what became the Medicare program. "Generally, the committee system accommodated change," Hofman said. "Committees knew where the wind was blowing."

Even in those days, however, the committee system hardly functioned perfectly. Segregationist Chairman James O. Eastland, D-Miss., and other Southern Democrats who controlled the Senate Judiciary Committee opposed civil rights legislation so ferociously that Democratic leaders were forced to take those bills directly to the Senate floor.

Eventually, President Johnson's popularity waned, and the coalition of Southerners and cautious Northern Democrats who took their cues from the big-city political machines regained control of the House and its committees. They engaged in a titanic struggle with liberal Democratic reformers who demanded a more activist federal government. The struggle continued until after the 1974 election, when the "Watergate babies" eliminated the final vestiges of the old system—including the iron-clad seniority rules, closed-door deal-making, and Southern dominance among congressional Democrats. Another key step in 1974 was passage of the Congressional Budget Act, which created an annual budgeting process that supersedes the committees' role.

What followed was the democratization of the Democratic Caucus and of House committees: Subcommittee chairmen gained vast new influence; junior members won seats on the most powerful committees; party leaders—notably Speaker Thomas P. "Tip" O'Neill Jr., D-Mass.—became national figures.

With the introduction of C-SPAN coverage of the House in 1978, Hofman said, "members viewed themselves as much more independent, through the use of modern communications techniques." A prime early example was the move in 1982 by two young lawmakers—then-Sen. Bill Bradley, D-N.J., and Rep. Richard A. Gephardt, D-Mo.—to craft a massive tax reform plan and sell it to the nation. Slowly, reluctantly, the old-style committee chairmen accommodated themselves to the changes.

During the Reagan years of politically divided government, important legislation was written largely in informal settings outside of the committee process. This was the case with the crafting of Social Security reform in 1983 and the so-called Gramm-Rudman-Hollings deficit reduction scheme in 1985.

In 1994, the final year of the Democratic majority, the committee system collapsed under the combined weight of its own decrepitude and the Clinton Administration's legislative naivete. The Administration's insistent demand for action on a costly, indigestible plan for national health care coverage triggered the final, whimpering end: Neither House nor Senate committees were able to produce credible legislative proposals.

TRANSFORMING THE WAY CONGRESS WORKS

When the Republicans took control of Congress in January 1995, armed with their ready-made legislative agenda, the Contract With America, the committees became all but superfluous. The document, signed by nearly all Republican House candidates in 1994, committed a Republican-controlled House to voting on 10 main planks and a variety of sub-topics, ranging from balancing the budget to congressional term limits.

What the committee chairmen may have thought about those goals simply did not matter. Gingrich was viewed by colleagues, and saw himself, as the political revolution's paramount leader. Members of the large and feisty GOP freshman class in each chamber emphasized that they would oppose a return of domineering committee chairmen of the type that had flourished during the era of Democratic control.

MY WAY OR THE HIGHWAY:

Newt Gingrich circumvented committees by demanding that GOP task forces write bills for him.

Especially in the House, Republicans "rightly sensed that their enemies were not just the Democrats' policies, but also their prevailing policy-making structures," wrote University of Maryland political scientist Roger H. Davidson in a recently published book, *New Majority or Old Minority?* The book, an assessment of the GOP-controlled Congress, was edited by Nicol C. Rae and Colton C. Campbell.

In keeping with the Contract With America's promise to "transform the way Congress works," House Republicans during early 1995 approved significant procedural reforms to weaken the grip of committee chairmen, including a six-year term limit for full-committee and subcommittee chairmen. (In the Senate, a similar six-year rule for committee chairmen, which has received less public attention, took effect in 1997.)

Other significant changes that weakened the power of House chairmen include the elimination of proxy voting in committees and the enhancement of the Speaker's authority to refer legislation to committees. In addition, Republicans cut committee staff positions by one-third in the House and by one-sixth in the Senate. They also eliminated three minor House committees and merged or eliminated several dozen House and Senate subcommittees.

"The corporate party leadership, and the Speaker in particular, gained substantial power at the expense of committees and committee chairs," wrote Christopher Deering, a George Washington University professor, in the Rae-Campbell anthology.

During the Gingrich years, Republicans also moved away from the Democratic majority's practice of calling in federal agency officials for oversight hearings to pinpoint bureaucratic failures. Rather than focus on programmatic oversight, Republicans trained their committee guns on investigative oversight to uncover scandal, especially among Clinton Administration officials.

Rep. Barney Frank of Massachusetts, a senior Democrat on both the Banking and Financial Services and the Judiciary committees who has been a Clinton loyalist during GOP investigations, said that Republicans have spent less time in committees on programmatic oversight because they oppose many of those programs in the first place. "To blame an Administration for a program not working, you have to believe the program *should* work," Frank said.

According to official records, the Democratic-controlled House committees issued reports on 55 federal programs and related matters in 1991–92, while the comparable total from the GOP majority in 1997–98 was a mere 14. Republicans concede that their cutback in committee staffing has left them with few aides experienced in conducting oversight. Indeed, the House Rules Committee recently has been working with the Congressional Research Service to assist Capitol Hill staffers in learning how to conduct program oversight.

The committees' supervisory role also has been diminished by the Clinton Administration's unusually aggressive efforts to deny or at least limit oversight. At a recent hearing of a House Rules subcommittee chaired by Rep. John Linder, R-Ga., five House GOP chairmen recounted their difficulties in securing information from the Clinton Administration.

"Trying to get the facts out of this Administration is some trick," said Judiciary Committee Chairman Henry J. Hyde, R-Ill., who voiced frustration with White House responses to his impeachment inquiry last fall. Linder said that the panel may seek a House rules change to improve compliance with committee inquiries.

THE BUMPY ROAD TO REGULAR ORDER

The regimen of the early Gingrich years gradually broke down following the unpopular federal government shutdowns during the winter of 1995–96, the House reprimand of the Speaker for ethics violations in early 1997, and an aborted coup attempt against him in mid-1997. These incidents crippled Gingrich, weakened his command of his leadership team, and gave committees an opportunity to regain legislative primacy.

Yet members still complain of an absence of true debate and thoughtfulness in most committee actions. "The deliberative process does not happen very often," said GOP Rep. Castle.

In recent years, a growing number of members seeking to learn about issues have often found committee hearings so stage-managed as to be useless, and these members have stopped relying on the committees as a source for education and deliberation. In one alternative approach, small groups of members get together and call experts to their offices for private discussions. Likewise, the failure of many committees to promote serious debates on issues has created pressure—especially in the clubbier Senate—for bipartisan closed-door meetings in party leaders' offices.

Moreover, the past two years have seen recurring examples of committee chairmen on both sides of Capitol Hill who have been unprepared for the task and have documented their irrelevance by failing to act. For instance, House Commerce Committee Chairman Tom Bliley, R-Va., has become a prime target of criticism from his own party because his committee, despite its broad jurisdiction, has had a very limited output during the past four years.

Bliley has repeatedly failed to move managed care reforms because of disagreements among committee Republicans on the scope of the legislation. With Bliley's panel deadlocked, the action shifted several months ago to the House Education and the Workforce Committee, which had been largely dormant on health care issues. Hastert this week said that he would follow through on his private warning that if Republicans can't settle their differences soon, he will bypass the committees altogether and bring one or more "patient protection" bills directly to the House floor. Critics also point to embarrassing setbacks that Bliley suffered in June, when his panel took up the banking reform bill, on privacy and thrift-regulation issues. "Bliley is out of his element," said one House GOP leadership source. "John Dingell [the Michigan Democrat who is the panel's ex-chairman] runs circles around him." The source, like other detractors, would not speak for attribution about the chairman, whom they regard as thin-skinned.

At other times, committee chairmen have had problems when their views have run counter to a majority of their party. For instance, House Armed Services Committee Chairman Floyd Spence, R-S.C., sparked an uproar on July 1, when he made what is usually a routine motion on the House floor to send the defense authorization bill to a House-Senate conference committee. In doing so, Spence backed what appeared to be an innocuous effort by committee Democrats to "recognize the achievement of goals" by U.S. forces and the Clinton Administration in the Kosovo conflict.

GOP hard-liners seized the opportunity to launch another rhetorical attack on Clinton's handling of the war, which had ended weeks earlier. Rep. Randy "Duke" Cunningham, R-Calif., termed the legislative commendations of the Administration "sickening." Although the House—including Hastert and Spence—voted for the language, 261-162, most Republicans were opposed.

This incident underscores a larger point: Congress's entire debate on Kosovo this spring occurred largely outside of the committee process, again because of divisions among Republicans on the key panels and weak leadership by their chairmen, who couldn't settle differences. Debate resulted chiefly when GOP leaders called measures directly to the House or Senate floor. Rep. Tom Campbell, R-Calif., took the unusual route of filing proposals under the 1973 War Powers Resolution in what became a futile effort to force the House to take a position.

On gun control, which gained great urgency this spring following the high school massacre in Littleton, Colo., the key House committee of jurisdiction was also circumvented because of its inability to resolve splits among Republicans. In May—after Democrats forced the GOP to move the issue directly to the Senate floor, where Vice President Gore cast the tie-breaking vote to give his party a ringing victory—Hastert voiced support for some gun control steps.

Hyde favored action akin to the Senate-passed measure, but most of the predominantly Southern and Western Republicans on his panel strongly opposed new gun restrictions. The Judiciary Committee lost control of the issue, and House Majority Whip Tom DeLay, R-Texas, worked with Dingell to produce a weak alternative; then the Rules Committee structured the House debate to permit votes on various alternatives. In the end, the House rejected the Dingell amendment and other gun control provisions, and instead approved several steps designed to address moral decay and to expand juvenile justice programs. Since then, procedural objections have delayed efforts to craft a limited House-Senate compromise.

After the House vote, DeLay proclaimed, "I think the process moved very well." Likewise, Rules Committee Chairman David Dreier, R-Calif., praised the GOP's handling of the issue and blamed the failure on Democratic partisanship. "It was a brilliant process," Dreier said in an interview. "It allowed the House to work its will. . . . I would have preferred a different outcome. But we still may get something in a conference committee."

The most successful House chairman under Republican rule has been Bud Shuster, R-Pa., the head of the Transportation and Infrastructure Committee, who has frequently defied party leaders by pressing for public works spending that far exceeds their budget plans. Shuster generally has prevailed because—unlike other House chairmen—he works assiduously to develop bipartisan consensus on his 75-member committee, and he is willing to challenge current GOP dogma. "He embarrasses the leadership, but I admire the ways he gets things done," said a victim of Shuster's exploits.

Even when House and Senate committees manage to handle their legislation in a relatively routine fashion, they often face setbacks later in the process at the hands of Republican leaders. For instance, in resolving differences between two competing bank reform proposals before House floor debate began, committee chairmen and other senior Republicans dropped controversial amendments—one, from the Banking and Financial Services Committee, to restrict redlining (refusal to do business in poor neighborhoods) by insurance companies; the other, from the Commerce Committee, to strengthen privacy of banking records.

Neither proposal was debated on the House floor, even though each was supported by committee majorities that included Democrats and some Republicans. "In each case, the Rules Committee dictated the winner," charged a Rules Committee Democratic aide.

TAXING MATTERS

The House Ways and Means and Senate Finance committees, though long regarded as two of the most powerful panels on Capitol Hill, recently have been something less than models of legislative effectiveness.

This spring, the two committees behaved haphazardly when a bipartisan congressional coalition of steel-industry allies demanded action on steps to limit steel imports. Most Ways and Means and Finance members tend to oppose protectionist measures, so Republican leaders, having made commitments for floor votes, circumvented the committees. Ways and Means reported a steel import quota bill to the floor "adversely," but the House approved it anyway. Then the proposal was placed directly on the Senate calendar to avoid the prospect of committee delay; an attempt to force Senate action was stymied on a cloture vote in June.

The two committees' handling of tax cut legislation this summer has been haphazard as well. Ways and Means Chairman Bill Archer, R-Texas, unveiled his bill to both committee Republicans and Democrats on July 12—the day that Congress returned from its Fourth of July recess and less than 24 hours before the panel began its debate.

"Tax legislation is so complex that one word can change the entire meaning," said Rep. Robert T. Matsui of California, a Ways and Means Democrat. With so little time for review, "you don't have the opportunity to find unintended, or intended, consequences," Matsui said. "This wasn't a fair process." Rep. Sander M. Levin, D-Mich., added that Archer's lack of interaction with committee members conveyed the attitude that "he was telling us what was written on the tablets."

Although Ways and Means Republicans conceded that they, too, had little time to examine the bill, many said that Archer had kept them informed of his general direction and that the result included no real surprises. "Most of us had a pretty good idea of what was in it," said Rep. Rob Portman, R-Ohio. "You need to approach a tax bill with a lot of discretion for the chairman to make tough choices. Otherwise, it leaks out by dribs and drabs." In addition, members—especially those who do not sit on the committee—usually don't focus on the details until the final days before the vote, Portman said. "A lot of things around here don't get done until crunch time."

But after Ways and Means approved the tax package on a party-line vote, clusters of GOP moderates and conservatives met and identified an armful of problems with Archer's proposal. The issues ranged from the proposal's failure to completely eliminate the "marriage penalty" on certain middle-income couples to excessive benefits for the wealthy by means of a reduction in the capital gains tax rate and the phase-out of the estate tax. Other Republicans complained that the tax cuts did not leave enough money to restore the fiscal soundness of Social Security and Medicare. "People don't understand this bill," Rep. Ray LaHood, R-Ill., complained two days before the House floor debate.

Republican leaders were forced to postpone the floor vote by a day as they worked in a last-minute frenzy to round up their dissidents. To appease GOP moderates, the leaders agreed to condition the 10 percent, across-the-board income tax cut in Archer's bill on a commitment to reduce interest payments on the public debt. In addition, the Rules Committee wrapped highly technical—and perhaps ineffectual—tax-policy changes to Archer's proposal into the separate resolution setting the terms of debate on the overall bill. In the end, on July 22 the House passed the tax bill, 223-208, with all but four Republicans on board.

"The Republicans are operating by the seat of their pants," complained Frost, a Rules Committee Democrat. "Either they can't count, or they are not competent." Even a senior House GOP aide complained that the tax bill was "not deftly handled" and that Archer had placed party leaders in an awkward position because "he didn't reach out to many Republicans."

Like Archer, Senate Finance Committee Chairman William V. Roth Jr., R-Del., unveiled his tax cut proposal after only limited exchanges of views with other panel members—mostly by letter or through staff discussions. "He didn't have many discussions with Senators," said Virginia K. Flynn, Roth's spokeswoman. "But he's been signaling for months what are his plans."

Unlike Archer, Roth included provisions that were designed to reach out to Democrats, two of whom voted for the measure in committee on July 21. However, some Finance Committee Republicans complained about Roth's details, even though they voted for his bill. Four of the panel's most conservative Republicans, including Lott, offered an alternative modeled after Archer's proposal, but it was defeated, 13-7. GOP leaders hope to resolve House-Senate differences before the August recess.

The effort to finalize the tax legislation is sure to be a major headache during the remainder of the session. But also still looming is a related conflict that will probably prove the most difficult to resolve—how to pass the 13 appropriations bills to finance federal operations in fiscal 2000. Both problems stem directly from policy assumptions laid out by the House and Senate Budget committees in their budget resolutions earlier this year and approved on the floors in April in nearly party-line votes.

Although House Budget Committee Chairman John R. Kasich, R-Ohio, held listening sessions to seek the views of other Republicans on his budget resolution, it has become apparent that many members did not fully understand or embrace the consequences of the plan they approved—which included the large tax cut, tight spending caps in keeping with the 1997 balanced-budget agreement, and a "lockbox" that Republicans said will direct $1.8 trillion of the budget surplus to the Social Security trust funds during the next 10 years.

"The numbers don't work out in the long run," Rep. Fred Upton, R-Mich., complained on the eve of the House vote on the tax bill. When Hastert privately reminded the tax measure's GOP critics that they had supported the budget, Upton—who voted for the final version of the budget plan with all but three House Republicans—said he responded that other budget details, including more money for education, had not been fulfilled.

Now Republican members of the House and Senate Appropriations committees are desperate to avoid a repeat of last year's budget endgame, in which Gingrich took control of decisions. Complaining that their pool of money is inadequate, they say that they will be forced to engage in fiscal sleight of hand to meet the political prerequisites for enacting their budget. Other Republicans, however, bitterly respond that the free-spending Appropriations committees have gone off the party reservation.

In recent weeks, House and Senate Republicans have deferred committee and floor action on various appropriations measures because they feared that they lacked a majority to approve them. "We're suffering from inadequate internal communications," said a House Republican aide who has been actively engaged in the budget debate. "When no one has a standard understanding [of the spending legislation details], it's hard to grow the vote."

FLOUNDERING TO EXERT CONTROL

Despite the setbacks that House and Senate committees have encountered this year, congressional Republican leaders contend that, with some exceptions, they have restored legislative power to the committees. The leaders also emphasize their continuing desire for a less active federal government and make clear that they would not sanction a return to the old system of omnipotent chairmen.

Republicans, to be sure, have been handicapped by the nearly hopeless dynamics of the 106th Congress. They currently have only five-seat control in both the House and the Senate, and they must contend with a wounded Democratic President bent on reasserting his political primacy and leaving a legacy of peace and prosperity. Their dual challenge is keeping their diverse forces unified while confronting Democrats—especially in the House—who have become increasingly confident that they will regain control in next year's election. It is easy to see why Republican leaders, when confronted with difficult legislation, might surmise that the only way to exert control in the current climate is to move decisively, without waiting for often-wayward committees to work their will.

For their part, Gephardt and other Democrats have said that they will promote closer party coordination with the committees if they regain the majority. At the start, at least, the Democrats' desire to effectively manipulate the levers of power most likely would override some of their past excesses. But the prospect that most of the Democrats' House chairmen would be strong liberals could soon pose the same kinds of problems that Republicans have had since 1995.

Few in the House or Senate—or, for that matter, in the news media or academia—give much thought to the committee system's problems. With most lawmakers spending only three or four days a week in Washington and focusing mainly on the crisis of the week, they find little reward in thinking about seemingly intractable dilemmas. In the meantime, the problem deepens.

King of the Roads

HOW BUD SHUSTER PAVED HIS PATH TO POWER WITH FOCUS, GOOD TIMING, AND SHEER WILL

BY MARK MURRAY

When you drive on Interstate 99 through central Pennsylvania, the first things you notice are the gentle, tree-clad Allegheny Mountains that surround the highway. The view almost compels you to pull over, get out of the car, and take in the scenery.

But to an inside-the-Beltway eye, there's something else striking about I-99: its name, the Bud Shuster Highway. State officials named it after Shuster—the 14-term Republican congressman from Pennsylvania who chairs the powerful House Transportation and Infrastructure Committee—because he played a key role in securing $270 million over more than 20 years to transform an old two-lane road into this 58-mile, four-lane highway. After all, the interstate was what the residents of this hardscrabble area wanted from the millionaire computer-business owner they sent to Congress in 1972. "When he was first elected to office, he came to the local business community and said, 'Where do you want me to place my emphasis in Washington?'" recalls local business leader Marty Marasco. "And, basically, they told him, 'Bud, we need highways, we need improved air accessibility, and we need infrastructure.'"

All agree that as a member of the House Transportation Committee, Shuster has delivered. In addition to the highway, he has helped central Pennsylvania win federal dollars for bridges, water and sewer projects, a bus-testing center, and airports. According to critics, these infrastructure improvements have been a little *too* much for this mostly rural district. Its largest city is Altoona, with a population of just over 51,000.

As you head north on picturesque I-99 near its midpoint in East Freedom, Pa., it's hard to miss another landmark bearing the Shuster name: the Shuster Chrysler dealership.

In 1990, Maurice Lawruk, an Altoona millionaire developer, became the guarantor of a $260,000 lease for Shuster Chrysler, which is headed by the Transportation Committee chairman's two sons, Robert and William. Lawruk also invested $30,000 in the dealership. But Lawruk, it seems, wasn't your typical business partner.

DRIVEN TO DELIVER:
Shuster helped secure $270 million for I–99, and state officials named the road after him.

As first reported by the Capitol Hill newspaper *Roll Call*, less than two years before Lawruk's involvement with Shuster Chrysler, Bud Shuster—along with the late Sen. H. John Heinz III, R–Pa.—helped the businessman win a $3 million low-income housing contract with the Department of Housing and Urban Development.

Moreover, two months after Lawruk became the dealership's guarantor, Shuster intervened on Lawruk's behalf in a labor dispute the developer was having with the Bush Administration. Shuster again intervened for Lawruk the following year. In 1996, in a formal complaint to the House Standards of Official Conduct (Ethics) Committee, the Congressional Accountability Project (a Ralph Nader-affiliated organization) questioned whether Shuster should have assisted someone who had given him generous campaign donations and helped his family. This complaint, which contains several other charges involving Shuster's ties to special interests, is still pending before the Ethics Committee.

Shuster, 68, has chaired the House Transportation Committee since the Republicans took over Congress in 1995. But due to the term limits that Newt Gingrich and his GOP revolutionaries imposed on House committee chairmen, this year is most likely Shuster's final one as full committee chairman. And nothing has symbolized his six-year tenure more than the Bud Shuster Highway and the car dealership that sits beside it.

As chairman, Shuster has had a hand in passing two of the most important and expensive pieces of legislation since the GOP takeover. In 1998, he helped to pave the way for a six-year, $218 billion highway and mass transit construction bill. This year, he helped to pass a $40 billion bill to fund airport construction projects. "When you build infrastructure, you create jobs," Shuster told *National Journal*. "You create economic prosperity."

Indeed, Shuster has chalked up a remarkable record. At a time when congressional rancor is the norm, he has made his committee the most bipartisan on Capitol Hill. As the power of committee chairmen has diminished, he has been able to frustrate, and often defeat, his party's leadership. And as critics have slapped Congress with the "Do-Nothing" label, Shuster's committee has been responsible for a flurry of legislative activity. Not surprisingly, his colleagues regard him as one of the last great chairmen on Capitol Hill. "He's probably one of a dying breed," said Rep. Ray LaHood, R-Ill., who sits on Shuster's panel.

But the car dealership stands as a reminder of Shuster's ties to special interests. In fact, a federal investigation into favors for property owners in Boston led to an indictment of and misdemeanor guilty plea from Ann Eppard, Shuster's former chief of staff, who's now one of Washington's most powerful lobbyists.

Shuster has also been attacked for being Washington's pork barrel king, and he's been accused of threatening to eliminate his opponents' transportation projects. Perhaps more than any other member since Dan Rostenkowski, D-Ill., who ruled the House Ways and Means Committee, Shuster represents the best and worst of Congress. And it's not surprising: To get legislation passed, members often have to twist arms, intimidate opponents, and win colleagues' support with pork barrel projects. To amass power and rank (not to mention win re-election), members have to raise considerable sums of campaign money, and fund raising often involves cozying up to lobbyists and returning favors to large donors. "The reality is, in this legislative system, the people are the combination of the good and bad," says Meredith McGehee of Common Cause, a liberal watchdog group.

But Fred Wertheimer, president of the campaign finance reform group Democracy 21, believes that the American political system should be better than that. "There obviously are better ways to do business than through the corrupt practices that benefit large donors at the expense of average citizens," he said. "I would give minimum weight that [Shuster] practices the best of politics and maximum weight that he practices the worst."

THE TRUST FUND WARS

Shuster's two great legislative triumphs as chairman have been the highway and aviation bills. More than anything else, they were battles over the heart and soul of the budget process.

In 1956, to help build the interstate highway system, the federal government created the Highway Trust Fund, which was to be financed by gasoline taxes. The logic

was simple: Gasoline taxes that motorists paid would be dedicated to road construction and improvement.

But in the late 1960s, the Johnson Administration—in a move, some say, to help pay for the escalating war in Vietnam—decided to make the Highway Trust Fund and all other trust funds part of the unified federal budget. The change became effective in 1969. Consequently, cash reserves from gasoline taxes were used to make the federal budget bigger. So when Washington embarked on its budget-balancing crusade in the 1990s, trust fund dollars that weren't spent on highways went toward other discretionary spending.

Shuster recalls that when he wanted to join the Transportation Committee (then called the Public Works Committee) as a freshman in 1973, he had to first pass a trust

> ### OLD SCHOOL:
> "With all the baloney that goes on around this town," says Shuster, "we're building America."

fund litmus test from former Rep. William Harsha, R-Ohio, who was then the committee's ranking member. "'Where do you stand on protecting the Highway Trust Fund?'" Shuster remembers Harsha asking. "And that was an easy one for me," Shuster says, "because I believe deeply in protecting the trust funds. . . . It's fraudulent [for the government] to take your gas tax money and not spend it for the purpose intended."

In his 1998 highway reauthorization bill, Shuster proposed taking the trust fund "off-budget" in order to pay for a massive increase in funding road improvements. "I am not a big spender. I am a fiscal conservative," he argued during the House debate over his bill. "But there is a fundamental difference between spending tax dollars to build assets and pouring money down a rat hole."

Shuster's quest wasn't easy, and it didn't succeed without compromises. Appropriations and Budget committee members have always resisted off-budget moves because such tactics reduce the amount of spending that these members control. Other opponents—including the Clinton Administration—objected to Shuster's bill because it would have significantly increased transportation spending, and that would have meant reducing spending on other programs. "Will education suffer? Will the environment suffer? Will housing suffer?" asked Rep. Michael N. Castle, R-Del., during the House floor debate.

But Shuster was able to strike a deal with his opponents, with considerable help from Sens. Christopher S. Bond, R-Mo.; Robert C. Byrd, D-W.Va.; Phil Gramm, R-Texas; and John W. Warner, R-Va. Under the compromise, the trust fund was to remain "on-budget," meaning that the money in it could still be used to prop up the federal budget. But a fire wall was erected around the trust fund.

This ensured that the money couldn't be used on anything other than highways. The fire wall also eliminated appropriators' authority to limit highway spending. On June 9, 1998, President Clinton signed into law the $218 billion Transportation Equity Act for the 21st Century (TEA–21)—the largest public works bill in U.S. history.

That a Republican congressman would work to pass such a mammoth spending bill still infuriates fiscal conservatives. "That was the low point in the Republicans' control of Congress, because it established that it was business as usual," said Marshall Wittmann, a senior fellow in governmental studies at the conservative Hudson Institute.

The next year, 1999, Shuster once again frustrated fiscal conservatives—this time with his Aviation Investment and Reform Act for the 21st Century (AIR–21). As he did with the highway bill, Shuster proposed taking the aviation trust fund (which consists of revenues from taxes on airline tickets and aviation fuel) off-budget to finance increased spending for airport projects.

But the appropriators and budgeteers—particularly Senate Budget Committee Chairman Pete V. Domenici, R-N.M.—were determined not to give in to Shuster. "It stuck in their craw that he had beat them on the highway bill," an aviation lobbyist said. So for almost six months after the House and Senate had passed their respective aviation bills, Shuster wrangled with Domenici. Finally, Senate Majority Leader Trent Lott, R-Miss., stepped in and helped broker a compromise. "Trent was crucial in the Senate," Shuster admitted.

The deal that was struck, which President Clinton signed into law in April, resulted in a three-year, $40 billion bill. Under the agreement, Shuster wasn't able to take the aviation trust fund off-budget, nor did he get a fire wall that was similar to the highway compromise. And although the aviation deal promised a general-fund contribution for the Federal Aviation Administration's operations, the money would be subject to the annual appropriations process. The day the agreement was reached, Domenici's spokeswoman declared victory: "[Shuster] capitulated, so we're pretty happy."

Yet, as it turned out, Shuster got what he always wanted: a guarantee (through congressional points of order) that the money from the aviation trust fund would be dedicated exclusively to paying for significant increases in aviation infrastructure. "Shuster won on money, and Domenici won on process," one observer remarked after the deal was made. "Shuster's laughing all the way to the bank."

Roping off the highway and aviation trust funds was not an easy task. "Every single fight was a downright bloodbath," said T. Pete Ruane, a Shuster ally and president of the American Road and Transportation Builders Association. Former Rep. Robert A. Roe, D-N.J., who chaired the Transportation Committee from 1991–92, expressed amazement at Shuster's feats. "For him to be able to work that out is [nothing] short of a miracle."

TIMING, FOCUS, AND POWER

Why did Shuster succeed in the trust fund wars when other chairmen had failed? Part of the answer is good timing. A key argument for keeping the transportation trust funds part of the unified budget was to keep the nation's soaring deficit under control, notes Stan Collender, a federal budget expert at Fleishman Hillard. But in the era of budget surpluses, he says, "you take away that last remaining argument. Shuster was at the right place at the right time."

According to Shuster's friends and foes, another reason for his success is focus. Shuster has devoted most of his energies to unlocking the trust funds. In the battle over the aviation bill, Shuster simply cared about it more

ETHICS AT ISSUE:

A complaint against shuster cited his ties to a developer who backed a dealership owned by Shuster's two sons.

than Domenici and the other budget hawks did, notes Todd Hauptli, the senior vice president for legislative affairs at the American Association of Airport Executives and the Airports Council International. "He just made it clear from the beginning that he was not going to go away," Hauptli said. "The dirty little secret about Washington is, persistence pays off."

Shuster agrees that his focus on transportation has played a large role in his legislative triumphs, and it has since he came to Congress. "While I like to think I was the best freshman member of the Transportation Committee," he recalled, "I may well have been the worst member of the Education and Labor Committee because I simply didn't give time to it. I focused my time on the Transportation Committee."

Another reason for Shuster's success is the bipartisan nature of the committee. Shuster works very well with the committee's ranking member, Rep. James L. Oberstar, D-Minn. "There is a great reservoir of trust between us that makes a whale of a difference in getting stuff done," Oberstar said.

When crafting any large piece of legislation, Shuster works to reach a deal with Oberstar, the subcommittee chairman who has jurisdiction over the bill, and the subcommittee's ranking member. Once the "Big Four" agree to the compromise, they vote together for and against amendments to the bill. They also try to keep contentious labor and environmental provisions out of the legislation. In addition, Shuster goes out of his way to work with other committee members, says William J. Hughes, a former committee staffer who now works in the

---

ANN EPPARD:

Admitted receiving illegal payments while she was Shuster's chief of staff.

Speaker's office. "He will accommodate members on the committee. . . . Because he has taken care of everyone else, if he can't work out a deal with you, you are going to be beat."

Shuster's staff is regarded as one of the best on the Hill. In particular, observers have lauded the work of Chief of Staff Jack Schenendorf, who has worked on the Transportation Committee for more than 20 years. "I call him the half-million-dollar man," said former Shuster staffer Jeffrey P. Nelligan, who now works at the General Accounting Office. "Any lobbying association, any group would just give their eyeteeth to have that guy."

But critics point to another reason for Shuster's success: sheer strength. "He's not winning his debates on intellectual arguments. And he's not winning the debates on 'It's the right thing to do for America,'" said a senior Senate aide. "He's winning those debates on pure power. Bud Shuster's politics are about power, and he's good at it."

Much of Shuster's power comes from the size of his committee, which, at 75 members, is the biggest committee in the history of Congress. With Republicans having such a slim majority in the House, the chairman has been able to use this gigantic, bipartisan committee to have his way with the GOP leadership. "At any given time, on any given issue, Shuster can command at least 40 Republican votes," Hauptli said. "And as a result, Shuster's gotten the leadership to go along with him on issues that they might not otherwise be supportive of."

Shuster's power also resides in his ability to entice potential supporters with spending earmarks, which are more commonly known as pork barrel projects. The final highway bill contained almost 2,000 spending earmarks totaling $9 billion—between 4 percent and 5 percent of the $218 billion piece of legislation. (An analysis by Gannett News Service found that Pennsylvania benefited more from these earmarks than any other state. The state received 186 projects totaling $801 million.) "If we have to [round up] the tough votes to raise money, then it's not unreasonable for the members who are casting those votes . . . to be able to have a voice in how 5 percent of that money is spent," Shuster explained.

Critics have attacked Shuster's predilection for distributing pork. Rep. Tom Coburn, R-Okla., complained about Shuster's tactics during the 1998 highway bill debate. Coburn cited a voice mail left for one of his aides by a Shuster staffer as evidence: "'Matt, this is

Darrell Wilson with the Transportation Committee. I'm calling about the [highway] bill. . . . We have a deal for you on the funding levels for that. I originally spoke with your office last September, and we said there was $10 million in this bill for your boss. Well, we are now upping that by $5 million. . . . I just want to know where your boss wants to spend that money.'" Rep. John Shadegg, R-Ariz., who spoke after Coburn, said, "It is pure and simple bribery."

But Shuster stresses that earmarked projects still must be vetted by state transportation departments before they can proceed. He also points out that most highway dollars are distributed to the states, and that this process is just as political and suspect. "Angels in heaven don't decide where highways or airports are going to be built."

Shuster has also been criticized for taking pork away. For example, during the 1995 House debate over the Line-Item Veto Act, former Rep. William H. Orton, D-Utah (who's currently running for governor of that state), had offered an amendment that would have made transportation projects subject to the line-item veto. On the floor, Orton made it clear that a member of Shuster's staff had threatened Orton not to offer the amendment. "The staff of the chairman, the gentleman from Pennsylvania, had let it be known that they are looking at transportation projects in my district, and if I offered the amendment, there will be retaliation," Orton said. The amendment was soundly defeated, 65–360.

As it turned out, a $1 billion highway project in Provo, Utah, lost its funding, but the money was eventually restored. "Members were scared to death with what Bud Shuster did to us," said a former Orton staffer. Furthermore, Reps. Pete Hoekstra, R-Mich., and Dan Miller, R-Fla., charged in 1998 that funding for their transportation projects had been significantly cut because they voted against the highway bill.

Shuster denies any acts of retaliation. "I have never threatened a single member," he said. "And I challenge the media and anybody else to name one person [that] I have ever threatened." Shuster admits, however, that his supporters tend to get more funding for their transportation projects than his opponents do.

Roe, the former Transportation Committee chairman, says complaints of retaliation are nothing new. "People said the same thing about me," he said. But Roe believes that denying the spoils to opponents can be justified:

MEREDITH McGEHEE:

Shuster "does not seem to have sensitivity whatsoever to his relationships with these lobbyists."

"[They] can't ask for help if [they] vote against the legislation."

ETHICS TROUBLES

Shuster's abilities as a legislator are strikingly similar to those of another larger-than-life committee chairman: former House Ways and Means Chairman Dan Rostenkowski. From 1981–94, Rostenkowski ruled the committee and built his reputation as a master legislator.

But there's another similarity between the two chairmen: ethics troubles. In 1994, Rostenkowski was indicted on 17 counts, chief among them the charge that he traded official stamps from the House post office for cash. He eventually pleaded guilty to two lesser counts and spent 15 months in prison. Unlike Rosty, Shuster has never been indicted or convicted of a crime. But throughout his tenure as chairman, Shuster has been plagued by a series of charges and press reports—many of which focus on his ties to former longtime aide Ann Eppard—alleging that he has crossed the line of ethical propriety. For example:

• The ties between Shuster and Altoona developer Maurice Lawruk (especially those involving the Shuster Chrysler dealership) spurred one of several charges in the Congressional Accountability Project's complaint against Shuster, which was filed to the House Ethics Committee in 1996. Shuster's spokesman, Scott Brenner, says there is nothing wrong with Lawruk's business association with the dealership that's owned by the chairman's sons. "It's a small town, and people know each other very well," he said. "These are the things that happen."

• The Congressional Accountability Project's complaint also focused on Shuster's relationship with Eppard, who since leaving Shuster's office in 1994 has become one of Washington's most powerful transportation lobbyists (last year, her firm received more than $2 million in fees). She makes $3,000 a month serving as Shuster's political consultant. Among other things, the complaint charged that Shuster had received an illegal gratuity by staying overnight at Eppard's Alexandria, Va., home.

• On April 9, 1998, a federal grand jury in Boston indicted Eppard and Vernon A. Clark, a Washington lobbyist, for corruption and illegal payments. The central charge was that Clark and his two clients—who were worried that Boston's billion–dollar Central Artery transportation project, known as the Big Dig, would harm their property—gave Eppard and her son more than $200,000 in illegal payments from 1989–93, when Eppard was serving as Shuster's chief of staff. As it turned out, Shuster helped intervene on behalf of the two Boston businessmen, and they later settled their road-building disputes with the federal government. At one time, Shuster was reported to be a target of this federal investigation. On Nov. 1, 1999, federal prosecutors dropped their case after Eppard and Clark pleaded guilty to misdemeanor charges. Eppard admitted receiving payments totaling $15,000, an interest-free $30,000 loan, and other gratuities from Clark. Eppard was fined $5,000. Later that week, Rep. John P. Murtha, D-Pa., hosted a reception on Capitol Hill celebrating the end of the federal investigation.

Shuster's ties to Eppard and other special interests have sparked protests from watchdog groups. "The real unseemly part is that [Shuster] does not seem to have sensitivity whatsoever to his relationships with these lobbyists," said Common Cause's McGehee. "He's as clueless about that as Dan Rostenkowski was about being wined and dined at Morton's."

Yet what truly disturbs McGehee and other watchdogs is how Eppard's close ties to Shuster have benefited Eppard and her lobbying clients. In particular, the Congressional Accountability Project's 1996 complaint detailed how Eppard's clients, such as Federal Express Corp., Frito-Lay, and the Outdoor Advertising Association of America, have received assistance from Shuster and his committee. "These . . . alliances between a member of Congress and a lobbyist," complained Gary Ruskin, director of the Congressional Accountability Project, "lead to the appearance that those wealthy enough to pay the pricey fees of top lobbyists may receive special legislative favors or benefits." (Eppard did not return phone calls for this article.)

While Shuster acknowledges that Eppard's clients have won battles before his panel, he also points out that some have lost. Moreover, he stresses that a lobbyist who happens to have a close tie to a member of Congress is nothing new. "It's very clear to us that had she not been a woman, [these complaints] never would have surfaced. The sad reality I think Ann has come to—and if [I] were to advise any new member of Congress—is don't promote a woman into a senior position, particularly if she's not ugly. Maybe if she's ugly you can get away with doing it. . . . You see lobbyists camping out in members' offices. Chiefs of staff who have worked for years with members are looked upon as the political gurus for the members. It happens all the time."

When asked in his interview with *National Journal* why he thought Eppard had been singled out, Shuster took his defense one step further and responded to allegations that his relationship with Eppard goes beyond work and friendship: "Of course, there was a [*Roll Call*] story a couple of years ago. The reporter said I was seen coming out of her house at 6:30 a.m. That's true. What he didn't

TODD HAUPTLI:

"The dirty little secret about Washington is, persistence pays off."

write, and finally they had to acknowledge two weeks later, was that my family was there, my wife was there, my friend was there. We invited the reporter into the house, and the reporter sat there for 30 minutes talking to my son." Timothy J. Burger, who wrote that story for *Roll Call,* and now works for the New York *Daily News,* admits that Shuster's son was present, but says that he never saw his wife. "If Mrs. Shuster was actually in the building, I would have loved to have met her and chatted with her," he said.

HIS LEGACY AND FUTURE

Sometime in the next few weeks, Shuster will probably pound his last gavel as chairman of the Transportation Committee. When asked what he thought his legacy as chairman would be, he said, "With all the baloney that goes on around this town, we're the building committee. We're building America. We're doing something constructive."

Collender, the budget expert, points out that Shuster has "put transportation spending—and particularly highway spending—at a whole different level. He brought it up five or six notches on the priority list."

But critics have noted that the increased spending for highways and airports has resulted in less money for other programs, such as the U.S. Coast Guard and Amtrak. In addition, others contend that Shuster's trust fund victories have complicated the budget process and have made transportation more important than other types of spending. "In order to do a bipartisan approach during the [budget] process, you have to have numbers that make sense. TEA–21 and AIR–21 make that a lot more difficult," said a Republican Hill staffer. "They set priorities that they are not willing to pay for."

Other members of Congress have begun to mimic the way Shuster has roped off federal money for his programs, and that imitation may be Shuster's greatest legacy. Rep. Don Young, R-Alaska, is one example. Young, who chairs the House Resources Committee and most likely will succeed Shuster as Transportation chairman if the Republicans keep control of the House, recently helped pass a bill that stops offshore oil and gas royalty payments from going directly to the federal Treasury. Instead, the revenues will be set aside for conservation, wildlife, recreation, and historic-preservation programs.

"I had a bunch of people come to me and say that what they want to get for their programs is what Shuster got, a Shuster type of program," Collender said. "They want a separate cap just for their programs."

Shuster's influence on the Transportation panel will continue; indeed, that story is perhaps the best illustration of his power. Last year, Shuster created one of the most powerful subcommittees ever by fusing his committee's surface transportation and railroad subcommittees. And because term-limited chairmen may still head their panel's subcommittees, Shuster will more than likely sit atop that super-subcommittee if the Republicans keep control of Congress. If they don't, he'll likely serve as the ranking Republican on the full committee.

Some are already voicing concerns about a possible Young takeover of the committee. Peter Loughlin, a former Shuster staffer and currently a lobbyist at the Associated General Contractors of America, worries that Young might purge Shuster's committee aides—such as Chief of Staff Schenendorf and General Counsel Roger Nober, who are regarded as among the finest on Capitol Hill—and replace them with his own staffers. "If Don Young comes on and doesn't keep those people, then he loses a lot of institutional knowledge," Loughlin said. "The well-oiled machine will be at least changed."

One Republican Senate aide was confident that things would remain the same under Young. "Don Young is very creative, he is very innovative, he's politically very sharp, and he knows how to cut a deal. That sounds to me like I just described Bud Shuster." But some wonder about how much power Young will actually have if Shuster chairs the new super-subcommittee. "I think Don Young's biggest challenge," the GOP aide said, "is how do you run a committee that has Bud Shuster holding 80 percent of the jurisdiction of the committee in a single subcommittee?" Young, however, says he's not bothered by Shuster's presence.

Whether he's in the majority or the minority on the committee, observers say that Shuster will play an important role in reauthorizing the next highway bill in 2003—giving him a large role in distributing billions of dollars worth of federal funds and pork barrel projects. Oberstar, the likely chairman of the Transportation Committee if the Democrats take back the House, compares Shuster's future presence on the committee to a hurricane or an earthquake. "Whoever becomes chairman has to live with the reality that the force majeure in the Republican conference is Bud Shuster."

There's even speculation that, after sitting out for two years, Shuster could possibly return to the chairman's seat. Asked about this potential maneuver, Shuster replied: "I'll cross that bridge when I come to it." Knowing Shuster, he just might round up the funds to build it.

Can It Be Done?

**CONGRESS SEEMS RELUCTANT TO TRY TO ABOLISH THE ELECTORAL COLLEGE,
AND SMALL STATES PROBABLY WOULDN'T GO ALONG ANYWAY. STILL,
SOME HOLD OUT HOPE FOR A PUBLIC GROUNDSWELL.**

BY RICHARD E. COHEN
AND LOUIS JACOBSON

For Congress, junking the Electoral College appears to be an idea whose time has passed or hasn't yet arrived. At this stage, only a handful of lawmakers or top aides are even remotely interested in or familiar with the proposal's lengthy history and far-reaching consequences. And even those few are pretty dubious about overcoming the steep challenges of changing the Constitution.

To be sure, the controversy over the Electoral College's role in this year's presidential election has already resonated across the country and in Congress, and public officials may well undertake a serious debate over the issue in the months and years to come. A Nov. 11–12 Gallup survey for *USA Today* and CNN found that 61 percent of those surveyed favor a popular-vote system that directly elects the President. Moreover, interest groups are launching petition drives and Internet campaigns to try to stir up significant interest at the grassroots level for abolishing the Electoral College.

Several lawmakers, in turn, have stepped forward since the election with calls for action. Some, such as Sen.-elect Hillary Rodham Clinton, D-N.Y., Sen. Richard J. Durbin, D-Ill., and Rep. Ray LaHood, R-Ill., want to eliminate the Electoral College altogether. Others have taken a more measured approach by calling for commissions to study the Electoral College, or for modernizing and standardizing the way that the nation votes.

It's also true that in 1969, the House—at the urging of President Nixon—voted overwhelmingly to replace the Electoral College with a popular-vote system, only

30 YEARS AGO:

In 1969, the House voted to eliminate the Electoral College, but in the Senate, foes of the proposal, led by Sen. Sam Ervin prevailed over proponents, such as Sen. Birch Bayh.

to see the proposal subsequently die in the Senate. But even among the current lawmakers and aides who are interested in the issue, few remember what happened three decades ago. "I'm not aware that it passed the House" in 1969, said a senior House Republican legislative aide who has worked on Electoral College reform. "That's ancient history."

Why do the prospects for congressional action appear so slim? The short answer is that would-be proponents recognize that it might be impossible to persuade states with small populations to relinquish the disproportionate power that they believe they hold in the Electoral College. By constitutional design, those states also have disproportionate influence in the Senate, and that body has stifled past attempts at reform.

Ratifying an amendment to the Constitution requires two-thirds approval in the House and in the Senate, followed by a majority vote by legislatures in three-fourths of the states. Only 17 amendments have been ratified since the basic framework, including the Bill of Rights,

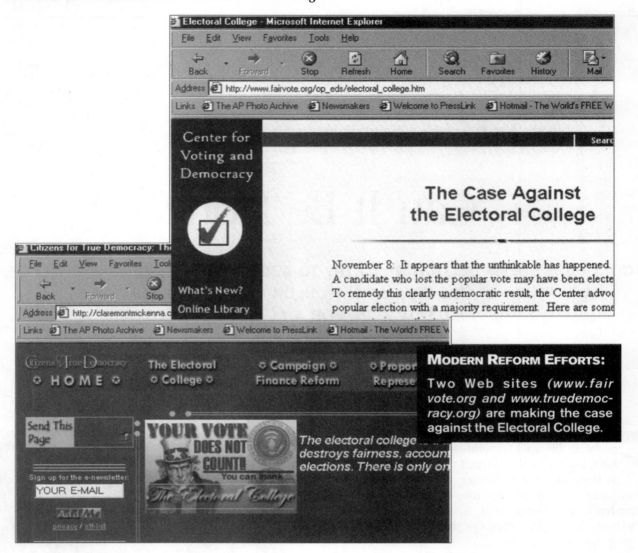

was completed in 1791. "Some of the states would be in favor of it, but it would be an uphill battle to get to three-quarters of the legislatures," said Tim Storey, an elections specialist with the National Conference of State Legislatures, which is neutral on Electoral College reform.

Under the current system, small-state proponents contend, each state's votes are important. That has become apparent in recent days as the world has breathlessly monitored the tally of a few hundred stray votes in, for instance, New Mexico, which has five electoral votes. (New Mexico's 1 percent of the total Electoral College vote is nearly twice its share of the nation's population.) Were the presidential election to hinge on a single nationwide popular vote, these small-state advocates contend, presidential candidates would focus their attention where the most votes are available—chiefly, in large metropolitan areas and on television.

"If this country elected a President on the basis of a popular vote, New Hampshire's sentiments would be entirely irrelevant," the state's Manchester *Union-Leader* editorialized this week. "An American President should

be beholden to all 50 states, not just two," said the newspaper, referring to the "teeming metropolises of Los Angeles and New York." During this year's presidential campaign, Al Gore and George W. Bush fought actively over New Hampshire's four electoral votes, and Bush eked out a narrow victory.

Direct-election proponents counter that the mathematics of the Electoral College give a lot of influence to the big-population states anyway. They cite the fact that Bush and Gore spent most of the campaign's final weeks battling for several large "swing" states, such as Florida and Michigan, and ignored most other states. (The two candidates, however, waged only limited campaigns in California and New York, because of Gore's big advantage in those states.)

Regardless of the fine points of the dichotomy between large and small states, Electoral College reform "won't happen, because the small states won't agree to it," said Rep. Jerrold Nadler, D-N.Y., a Judiciary Committee member who this week proposed a commission to examine how the nation conducts elections, with the

SPLIT SENATORS;

Dick Durbin wants to repeal the Electoral College, while Arlen Specter now just wants to study voting procedures.

goal of modernizing voting procedures. Nadler, an outspoken liberal, says he has "qualms" about holding a single national count because, as the current "mess in Florida" shows, "if we had to count 100 million votes and we had a close contest, we'd have a real problem."

Rep. Tom Davis of Virginia, the chairman of the National Republican Congressional Committee, voiced a similar fear. "A recount in 50 states wouldn't simplify the election," he said. Like other lawmakers, Davis added that he hasn't thought much about Electoral College reform. At least not yet.

PAST AS PROLOGUE

Not that long ago, the drive to abolish the Electoral College was on America's front burner. Throughout the 1960s, the proposal generated extensive public support, partly because of John F. Kennedy's razor-thin victory in the 1960 election, which runner-up Richard Nixon decided not to challenge.

Support grew further following the 1968 election, in which then-Gov. George C. Wallace of Alabama won six states, giving him 46 electoral votes. That was potentially enough to swing that year's contest between Nixon and Vice President Hubert Humphrey, the Democratic nominee, each of whom had won 43 percent of the total vote. The immediate problem was avoided when Nixon won 301 electoral votes, but leaders of both parties envisioned the nightmare scenario in which Wallace or another fringe candidate could have won enough support to throw a presidential election into the House.

In September 1969, the House voted 338-70 for a proposed constitutional amendment to do away with the Electoral College and substitute direct election of the President. Following the House vote, Nixon said the need for reform was "urgent and should be our controlling consideration."

But the constitutional amendment died a year later, the victim of a Senate filibuster by a coalition of Southern Democrats and conservative Republicans, many from small states. Their leader was Sen. Sam J. Ervin Jr., D-N.C., who would gain renown in 1973 for chairing the investigation of the Watergate break-in. That inquiry led to Nixon's resignation a year later, and Ervin became a liberal icon. But Ervin's opposition to Electoral College reform left him with a negative legacy as a retrograde states' righter.

Proponents continued to press the issue following the 1970 setback, but public interest gradually faded, and the political battlefield has since changed radically. During a Senate debate in 1979, the measure was rejected 51–48, 15 votes short of the required two-thirds majority.

As years passed, and several presidential elections were decided by wide margins, calls for reform of the Electoral College became outdated. In 1992, when Ross Perot received 19 percent of the vote as a third-party candidate, his vote was spread relatively evenly across the nation, and he was no threat to the Electoral College count. And Bill Clinton that year defeated President Bush 43 percent to 38 percent in the popular vote.

"Because recent elections have not been close in their popular-vote margin, there has been no hue and cry," said former Sen. Birch Bayh, D-Ind., who devoted much of his 18-year Senate career to advocacy of constitutional amendments, including one for direct election of the President, and was a key player during the chamber's Electoral College debates of the 1970s. "The feeling has been that we looked the tiger in the face."

Meanwhile, many interest groups turned to other government-reform causes or decided to trim their budgets. The American Bar Association, for example, had played a leading role in what Bayh called his "consortium" of supporters for abolishing the Electoral College. But that position was "archived"—or set aside—several years ago, according to an ABA spokesman, because the issue had lain fallow for too long without discussion.

The League of Women Voters, which has actively advocated campaign finance reform in recent years, has remained a consistent if relatively quiet voice for Electoral College reform. "We're hearing from our grass roots, and they seem pretty keyed up," Paul Boertlein, the group's senior director of communications, said this week.

Newer groups have also entered the debate. Since 1992, the Center for Voting and Democracy has urged the abolition of the Electoral College. The Takoma Park, Md.-based group, whose president is former third-party presidential candidate John Anderson, boasts a staff of roughly a half-dozen and a membership spanning the ideological spectrum.

In addition, a two-year-old group called Citizens for True Democracy has also seized the day with its call to abolish the Electoral College. The Los Angeles-based group is the brainchild of David Enrich, a Claremont-McKenna College graduate who's in his "early 20s" and dabbled early on in Ralph Nader's third-party campaign. He said he hopes to expand his mailing list of "probably a couple thousand supporters" by reaching out to voters over the Internet.

The main voices defending the Electoral College have historically been scholars, who are usually not really media-savvy. But philosophical conservatives might also rally, especially over talk radio, to retain the Electoral College, said John Samples, a supporter of the current system who directs the Center for Representative Government at the libertarian Cato Institute.

"I've appeared on 15 talk shows in the last three days," Samples said. "I've been struck by the level of phone calls and the intelligence of the comments by the callers and hosts" who oppose abolishing the Electoral College.

In a national debate over eliminating the Electoral College, another voice supporting the current system would be the American Legislative Exchange Council, an association of conservative state legislators. "State legislatures would more than likely oppose such [a constitutional] amendment, the reason being that it would be an erosion of state power," said spokesman Bob Adams.

ORRIN VS. HILLARY

On Capitol Hill, defenders of the Electoral College have a powerful ally in Senate Judiciary Committee Chairman Orrin G. Hatch, R-Utah, who vigorously opposes eliminating the institution. Hatch plans extensive hearings next year on proposals to abolish the Electoral College, and said he is confident that "reason will prevail" once the topic is fully debated. The fact that Hillary Clinton, in particular, already has announced her support for such proposals has grabbed his attention. "She needs to study this," Hatch admonished.

Nevertheless, the problems with this year's election clearly have registered with many members of Congress. In interviews this week, a broad cross section of lawmakers voiced support for exploring the states' disparate voting procedures and unreliable ballot-counting mechanisms, and said that a strong possibility exists for congressional action in these areas in the next two years.

Hatch himself said he would support steps to assist local governments in upgrading their voting machinery, as Nadler has proposed. "We can provide the financial wherewithal to purchase machines so that we have uniform action," Hatch said. "I can imagine that happening, even though it would be expensive." He also said he is open to reviewing proposals for a uniform poll-closing time across the nation, partly to deal with problems in the West resulting from televised coverage of early election returns.

Even before the current brouhaha, a handful of members of Congress already were pushing—with persistence but little impact—for eliminating the Electoral College. According to Thomas, which is the Library of Congress database, lawmakers in the past two years filed three proposed constitutional amendments calling for abolishing the Electoral College. By contrast, 265 such constitutional amendments were proposed between 1947 and 1968, according to a Congressional Research Service study.

The most active recent proponents of abolishing the Electoral College have been Durbin and LaHood. When they held a pre-election press conference at the Capitol,

JERROLD NADLER:

Electoral College reform "won't happen because the small states won't agree to it."

coverage was greater than they expected, probably because of the prospect for a close presidential election. Since then, interest has grown exponentially, both said this week. "When it comes to issues, you have to take advantage of the moment," said Durbin, who has sponsored similar legislation since 1993, when he was serving in the House.

Durbin plans to press for Senate action next year, starting in Hatch's Judiciary Committee, although he would not predict the outcome. LaHood, meanwhile, said that he will urge House Speaker J. Dennis Hastert, R-Ill., a home-state colleague, to commit to scheduling a House vote on the issue during the 107th Congress. "I've been interested in the issue since I was a junior high school teacher," LaHood said. "I've always said that there needs to be a controversy to stir up the American people."

Back in 1997, LaHood got a hearing on his proposal in the House Judiciary Constitution Subcommittee. Rep. Charles J. Canady, R-Fla., the panel's chairman, opened the hearing by stating, "There are indeed potential problems with the current manner in which we elect our President," and he added that the public "would not understand the election of a President who had not received the most votes in the election." But Canady concluded that the system "seems to have served the nation fairly well," and his panel took no further action.

During that 1997 hearing, House Judiciary Committee Chairman Henry J. Hyde, R-Ill., strongly opposed La-Hood's direct-election plan. "I like the system that recognizes competing interests, differing interests, and that synthesizes them into *E pluribus unum*," Hyde said. "By having to win this state and this state and this state, I think that consensus is better served" in electing a President.

CRUSADE OR PASSING FAD?

For the Electoral College reform issue to regain real currency, proponents would need to mount a new national crusade. That prospect depends, in part, on the extent of public unhappiness with the outcome of this year's presidential election. In addition, both parties will have to weigh the partisan implications of abolishing the current system.

For now, most Republicans have apparently become reluctant to discuss Electoral College reform, because such a step might be seen as undermining the legitimacy of a Bush victory, especially if he does not win a plurality of the popular vote.

This GOP skittishness has been evident in the recent maneuvers of Sen. Arlen Specter, R-Pa. On Nov. 8, the day after the election, Specter told reporters in Philadelphia that he would return to Washington the following week and file legislation to repeal the Electoral College, which he called "an anachronism . . . which doesn't make sense now" and is contrary to democratic principles.

But within a week's time, Specter retreated to the position of simply calling for a commission to study voting procedures. He told the Senate on Nov. 14 that the popular election of the President "appears to be unrealistic because there are so many smaller states."

Meanwhile, Rep. Christopher Shays, R-Conn., a leading GOP advocate of campaign finance reform, said that abolishing the Electoral College would be "a big mistake" because it would lead presidential candidates to focus on selected regions of the nation. If they could win "with a simple majority of the popular vote, they can play to a single area," Shays said. He also voiced fear that a tight race producing a national recount could create the "potential for civil unrest."

Democrats also are split on the issue. Durbin noted that he received a phone call after he held his pre-election press conference on his Electoral College reform plan from "a friend in the Gore campaign who asked why I was doing this."

During the Senate's debate in 1979, current Sens. Joseph R. Biden Jr., D-Del., and Daniel Patrick Moynihan, D-N.Y., opposed abolishing the Electoral College. And at a press conference in recent days, Sen. Robert G. Torricelli, D-N.J., said he, too, supports the institution, even though his home state presumably would benefit from reform. He depicted himself as an advocate of federalism and embraced the argument of the small-staters in calling the current voting system "an important element" for the nation. "Our sense of union and everyone's inclusion has now been based on this Electoral College," Torricelli said.

But Sen. Edward Kennedy, D-Mass., is a strong advocate of closing down the Electoral College. And although House Democratic Caucus Chairman Martin Frost of Texas has not taken a position on one side or the other on the Electoral College, he said "we ought to seriously look at the issue, with hearings," and noted that the public is clearly interested.

A congressional Democratic leadership aide speculated that Electoral College reform is merely the "flavor of the day" in political debate. Likewise, freshman Sen. Evan Bayh, D-Ind.—son of Birch Bayh—cautioned, "The prospects for change probably are not that good, once current passions cool."

It's impossible to predict whether these naysayers are right. And even if a significant movement develops to abolish the Electoral College, the prospects for ultimate success seem dim. But it is clear that the consequences of a close presidential election have once again registered on the American psyche.

Uninsured Americans Linger On Congress' Waiting List

Potential price of benefits unnerves lawmakers, but lack of coverage also has its costs

By Mary Agnes Carey

For the last three years, vast political and policy differences between Republicans and Democrats have stopped Congress from passing legislation to give millions of Americans more clout with their health insurers. Those same splits will likely block any action on broadening Medicare to include prescription drugs—even a scaled-down, $20 billion package introduced by Senate Finance Committee Chairman William V. Roth, Jr., R-Del., to help low-income beneficiaries.

With Congress in disarray over how to help people who already have insurance, it is no surprise that legislators have been unable to reach consensus on a far more sweeping problem—what to do about the nation's 44 million uninsured. Since President Clinton's plan for universal health care crashed in Congress in 1994, the number of Americans without health coverage has steadily increased. Experts predict as many as 55 million may be without medical insurance policies by 2008.

The staggering price tag for covering the uninsured—estimates range as high as $80 billion a year—frightens lawmakers, who would rather use the budget surplus for initiatives with more tangible election-year appeal, such as tax cuts or a hefty package of funding increases for Medicare providers. There is also dissent over how to approach the problem, with some lawmakers favoring tax-related solutions and others pushing to expand existing federal health programs.

The uninsured, many of whom are poor, do not have the same kind of political clout as senior citizens and consumer groups, who are well-financed and can afford to take their concerns to Congress every year, so their cause is easily forgotten. "Uninsured people don't vote," said Thomas A. Scully, president and chief executive officer of the Federation of American Hospitals, a trade group representing for-profit hospitals.

Congress' reluctance also stems in part from the lingering political damage of the Clinton health-care debacle. Confident that voters oppose a government-run health care system, House Republicans are reportedly planning an advertising campaign to link Democratic nominee Vice President Al Gore's prescription drug proposal to Clinton's failed Health Security Act.

"The Clinton plan scared the heck out of people," Dr. Michael T. Rapp, president of the American College of Emergency Physicians, said in a Sept. 1 interview. "It was too big, too much regulation." First Lady Hillary Rodham Clinton, who is seeking to replace retiring Democrat Sen. Daniel Patrick Moynihan of New York, has even joked about the disaster in her campaign. *(1994 CQ Almanac, p. 319)*

The GOP hunch might be on target. In Washington state, for example, supporters of a universal health-care initiative did not collect enough signatures to get the measure on the November ballot. "It's a lot harder than we expected it would be," psychiatrist Dr. Stuart Bramhall, president of the Health Care 2000 campaign, told the Seattle Times in May.

Yet a number of recent surveys suggest that many people view providing health insurance to all Americans as a priority for Congress:

- Respondents to a Pew Research Center for the People and the Press poll of 1,411 registered voters conducted last October ranked providing health insurance for those who cannot afford it a higher policy priority than efforts to bring more federal regulation to managed-care insurers.
- Half of the 1,020 people surveyed in October by The Washington Post said the rising number of people without insurance bothered them "a great deal."
- A July poll of 1,183 registered voters by the Post, the Henry J. Kaiser Family Foundation and Harvard University found that increasing the number of Americans with health insurance was

 From *CQ Weekly*, September 9, 2000, pp. 2062-2065. © 2000 by Congressional Quarterly, Inc. Reprinted by permission.

the second most important health care issue among those surveyed, just behind making Medicare "financially sound."

Though lawmakers and both major presidential candidates are steering clear of government-run universal health care, they are making feints at addressing at least part of the issue because they have seen how the price of providing care for the uninsured increases costs for consumers and the health care industry alike.

Republican nominee Gov. George W Bush of Texas advocates a refundable tax credit and the lifting of federal regulations he deems onerous to insuring more Americans, such as the current cap on medical savings accounts, which allow people to pay for medical expenses with pre-tax dollars.

Gore would expand government programs to cover the uninsured. He advocates broadening of both the Children's Health Insurance Program (CHIP) and Medicaid to cover more children and would permit parents of CHIP-eligible children to purchase coverage through the program. Gore also would give tax credits to companies with fewer than 50 employees whose workers join "purchasing coalitions," which would allow businesses to form pools to receive more affordable rates for health insurance.

Democrats and Republicans alike have sponsored bills that would alter the tax code to help people afford insurance or broaden existing federal health programs to help cover the uninsured. Rep. John D. Dingell, D-Mich., has introduced a universal health care measure every year since 1956. *(See chart: Bills to Help the Uninsured).*

A package of so-called access provisions, which include tax deductions and insurance purchasing groups, is part of the House and Senate managed-care bills (HR 2990, S 1344) now stuck in a bicameral conference, *(CQ Weekly, p. 1391)*

"[Helping the uninsured] is the $64,000 question, isn't it?" Karen M.

Ignagni, president and chief executive officer of the American Association of Health Plans, said in an Aug. 31 interview.

An Incremental Approach

With the Clinton failure in mind, lawmakers have focused on more incremental approaches, such as CHIP, which was created as part of the 1997 budget law (PL 105-33). While the law has made some progress in covering children, it has done nothing to solve the vexing problem of how to provide coverage to millions of other Americans. *(Children's insurance, 1997 Almanac, p. 6–3)*

Broader steps will not occur unless public demand for congressional action intensifies, said David Butler, a spokesman for the group Consumers Union. "It's unlikely that any lawmakers will tackle it. . . . It's the proverbial hot potato," he added.

Marcia Comstock, a health care policy and workplace issues fellow for the U.S. Chamber Foundation, an affiliate of the National Chamber of Commerce, said in an Aug. 30 interview that many Americans with coverage are unwilling to sacrifice their benefits to help provide coverage to those who do not have it.

Workers are spending more time, Comstock said, focusing on "what else can I get?" in health benefits rather than recognizing that some of those resources could be used to provide coverage to the uninsured.

Rapp said people mistakenly believe that if they have coverage, they are not affected by the growing number of uninsured. He noted, for example, that large numbers of uninsured patients slow an emergency room's speed and efficiency—the cases are often more medically complex because medical treatment has been delayed.

The rising ranks of the uninsured also may reduce workers' paychecks as overall health care costs rise, according to a January report from the Employee Benefit Research Institute, a nonprofit organization based in Washington. If employers feel pres-

sure to pass on those costs, that could mean higher health insurance premiums. Many employers are absorbing rising insurance costs in today's tight job market, but that is likely to change if the economy worsens.

Part of the problem in helping the uninsured is that they are a diverse and diffuse group. Some cannot afford coverage—even though their employers offer it—and others may work for small employers who do not provide it. Most people over 65 have Medicare, which provides health care to nearly 40 million disabled and elderly Americans.

Several reports combine to paint a telling picture of the uninsured. According to a May report from the Kaiser Family Foundation's Commission on Medicaid and the Uninsured, nearly three-quarters of the uninsured are in families where at least one person is working full time. Kaiser also found that:

- 10 percent of the uninsured are in families with at least one part-time worker and 16 percent of the uninsured are in families in which no one is employed.
- More than half of the uninsured population is low-income, which Kaiser defines as those who earn less than 200 percent of the federal poverty level, or $27,300 for a family of three in 1998.
- Nearly a third of workers earning under $20,000 a year are uninsured, while just 5 percent of workers earning over $50,000 a year do not have coverage.

Kaiser found that people with employer-sponsored insurance saw their average share of premiums rise from 20 percent in 1988 to 27 percent in 1998.

Members of minority groups are more likely to be uninsured than whites, according to the federal Agency for Healthcare Research and Quality, a division of the Department of Health and Human Services.

In early 1998, almost one-third of all Hispanics and one-fifth of all

Bills to Help the Uninsured

Bill	Sponsor	Focus
HR 16	John D. Dingell, D-Mich.	Create a national health insurance program. Dingell has introduced this bill every session since 1956, continuing a tradition begun by his father in 1943.
HR 1819	Jim McDermott, D-Wash.	Allow individuals who are ineligible to participate in employer-subsidized health plans a refundable tax credit of up to 30 percent of their yearly health insurance costs, and limit the full credit to taxpayers whose income is less than $50,000 for a joint return.
HR 2185	Peter Stark, D-Calif.	Allow a refundable tax credit of $1,200 for an individual and up to $3,600 for a family for insurance costs and establish an Office of Health Insurance in the Department of Health and Human Services.
HR 2261	Nancy L. Johnson, R-Conn.	Create a tax credit for qualified health insurance coverage up to or equal to 60 percent of the premium paid and allow a deduction for the costs of health insurance premiums where a taxpayer pays 50 percent or more of the cost.
S 2337	Rick Santorum, R-Pa.	Create a refundable tax credit for the purchase of private health insurance (up to $1,000 for an individual and up to $3,000 for a family) and establish state health insurance safety-net programs for uninsurable individuals. Health insurers and HMOs would be required to participate in the safety net program.
S 2888	Paul Wellstone, D-Minn.	Provide federal matching funds to states that provide health care coverage to adults and children with incomes up to $50,000, require that all people receive health insurance benefits equal to the plan that covers members of Congress and provide that the same benefits for mental health and substance abuse treatment as for other medical conditions.

blacks the agency surveyed had no health insurance, compared with 12.2 percent of whites.

Costly Care

The fallout from the uninsured is felt at every level of the health care system. For example, people without insurance often delay seeking medical care in the early stages of a problem, when cures are simpler and less expensive.

Kaiser found that uninsured children are 70 percent less likely than insured children to have not received medical care for such common conditions as ear infections, which, if left untreated, can lead to more serious health problems. Uninsured children are also 30 percent less likely to receive medical attention when they are injured.

When care is given, it is often done in the most expensive setting possible—the emergency room.

According to the American College of Emergency Physicians, three out of every four uninsured patients admitted to U.S. hospitals receive their care in emergency rooms—at a staggering cost. In 1996 alone, hospitals provided $10 billion of uncompensated care, according to a study by the emergency physicians group.

"The emergency department is the ultimate safety net for health care," said Rapp, who practices medicine in suburban Washington. On any given night, he said, 25 percent of the patients in his emergency room are uninsured. The number is probably higher in hospitals that serve poorer communities with larger numbers of uninsured.

Emergency room physicians, knowing that uninsured patients may not have access to specialists, laboratory tests and other medical procedures, may also feel more pressure to admit them to the hospital.

"The problem is: How do we deal with them after they come to the emergency department? Although we have an open door, most of the health care system does not have an open door," Rapp said.

"We see the patient, then we send them out into the brave, new world, and then we don't know what happens to them."

Tax credits are popular with some Republicans and Democrats, but they would not go far enough in reducing the number of uninsured Americans, according to a study in the January-February 2000 issue of the journal Health Affairs. It found that the ability of tax subsidies to reduce the ranks of the uninsured was "uncertain and unproven."

Authors Jonathan Gruber, a professor of economics at the Massachusetts Institute of Technology, and Larry Levitt, director of the Changing Health Care Marketplace Project at the Henry J. Kaiser Family Foundation, found that a tax deduction for non-group health insurance premiums would cost the government under $1 billion annually but cover only about 250,000 people. A refundable tax credit of $1,000 for single adults and $2,000 for families would cost $13.3 billion annually and help 4 million people.

The most expensive option the authors studied, a refundable tax credit that could be used to purchase nongroup and employer-provided insurance, would cover an estimated 12.4 million uninsured—less than a third of those without coverage—and cost a whopping $62 billion a year.

A White House analysis released Sept. 5 reached a similar conclusion. The report by the White House Council of Economic Advisers, found that while tax credits would encourage some individuals to purchase group or individual coverage, they would not be a great incentive and would cost the government more than expanding existing federal health programs or combining any expansions with tax credits.

In the November-December issue of Health Affairs, Stuart Butler, a vice president for domestic and economic policy studies at the conservative Heritage Foundation, and David B. Kendall, senior fellow for health policy at the moderate Progressive Policy Institute, have urged Congress to give states maximum flexibility to use existing funding sources to supplement the value of a federal tax credit and help create stable insurance pools.

Baby Steps?

It is unclear whether Congress will ever make the broad, bold moves—major changes to the tax code, an expansion of existing public health programs or creation of new entitlements—that many experts argue could make health insurance available to the millions of Americans who now lack coverage.

"The steps we've taken have been small steps, not major steps," Diane Rowland, vice president of the Kaiser Family Foundation, said in a Sept. 1 interview. "The incremental strategies everyone knows are going to have a limited reach."

Sen. Paul Wellstone, D-Minn., in July unveiled a sweeping proposal (S 2888) to provide federal matching funds for states to help cover the uninsured.

"All the doctors and all the nurses and all the other health care providers in America cannot solve this problem nor right this injustice, but we in the Congress can," Wellstone said July 19 in floor remarks.

Some Republicans, such as House Ways and Means Health Subcommittee Chairman Bill Thomas, R-Calif., have advocated scrapping the current employer-based system of health care and replacing it with an individual tax credit. Such a dramatic change, however, would take years to evolve.

Piecemeal policy approaches such as CHIP will likely continue no matter which party controls Congress, said David Hebert, director of federal government affairs for the American Association of Nurse Anesthetists.

"I cannot see, in this political climate, the creation of a brand-new program," Hebert said in a Sept. 7 interview. "Those days have gone by."

Congress will likely want to make sure that existing programs have accomplished all they can before lawmakers create new approaches. Such concern is legitimate, because experts say that half of the nation's uninsured children could be covered by either the Medicaid or CHIP programs.

Many welfare recipients and their children still may qualify for Medicaid and CHIP once they have left welfare, but they often are not aware they can keep their benefits; sometimes state caseworkers misunderstand the law as well.

Rapp, the emergency room doctor, offers his own prescription for the dilemma: Start with infants.

Echoing the sentiments of former Democratic presidential hopeful and former Sen. Bill Bradley of New Jersey (1979–97) Rapp suggests that all children be given coverage at birth that cannot be canceled and stays with them their entire lives.

"Everybody likes new babies, right?" Rapp said. "Then in 65 years, we will have it nailed."

'WE ALL (PARTICULARLY POLITICIANS AND THE MEDIA) NEED A CIVICS LESSON.'

A Judge Speaks Out

H. LEE SAROKIN

Democracy in America today faces many seemingly intractable problems—inequality, corruption, political disengagement—but is equally threatened by discrete official acts that eat away at its core institutions. Jesse Helms autocratically denies William Weld a hearing to be ambassador to Mexico. Janet Reno stubbornly drags her feet on appointing an independent counsel on campaign finance abuses. House majority whip Tom DeLay callously calls for impeachment of federal judges who heed a legal "technicality" called the Bill of Rights. These actions feed mistrust of government and must be loudly condemned, as they often are. But in the case of the assault on judicial independence by DeLay, Senator Orrin Hatch and others—which was ramped up during the 1996 elections and continues in an unprecedented stonewalling of President Clinton's nominees to the federal bench—the people who could fight back most eloquently, the judges themselves, are bound by a code of silence.

Judges should be loath to enter the fray, but there are extraordinary circumstances where their rebuttals are warranted, even necessary. When Bob Dole and Newt Gingrich threatened Judge Harold Baer with impeachment in March 1996 because of his decision to suppress evidence in a routine drug case (a decision that, under pressure, he later rescinded), it was inspiring to see four appellate judges publicly proclaim that the criticism had gone too far.

Now, we have the first riposte from one who was a target. Judge H. Lee Sarokin, a courageously independent federal trial and appellate judge for seventeen years in Newark, was for years a favorite scapegoat of those on the right. Last year, battered by increasingly malicious and distorted assault, Sarokin left the bench, saying he no longer wanted his rulings to be fodder for their twisted campaign. While we regretted his decision, we respected it and urged him to break the silence and explain just how corrosive these attacks have become [see "Gavel-to-Gavel Politics," July 1, 1996]. Here is his response.
—The Editors

H. Lee Sarokin is a retired judge of the United States Court of Appeals.

I retired from the federal bench not because my opinions were being criticized but in protest over the politicization (what I characterized as the "Willie Hortonizing") of the federal judiciary. Politicians increasingly mischaracterize judicial opinions and then use them against those who nominated, appointed or voted to confirm the judges involved (like blaming a governor for crimes committed by a paroled prisoner). Not only do such tactics threaten the independence of the judiciary but, more important, they have a corrosive effect on the public's confidence in our judicial system and those who implement it. This is the toll when respected persons in high office constantly contend that judges are not following the law but rather are pursuing their own private agenda. I thought that by stepping down from the court and making my concerns public, I would convey the gravity of this dangerous course.

Now, a year later, I concede that my grand gesture was a complete fizzle, and indeed, rather than dissuade the practice, seems to have emboldened it, since it has been followed by demands, led by Representatives Tom DeLay and Bob Barr, to impeach judges for unpopular decisions. Although the election has ended, the political rhetoric attacking the judiciary has not.

Admittedly, from time to time there will be judicial decisions with which many will not agree. All too often that disagreement arises from the mischaracterization of the opinion and focuses on its result rather than its reasoning. But the validity of a judicial opinion cannot rest on its popularity. Resisting the pressure to please the majority is the strength of the judiciary, not its weakness. Judges who invoke the Constitution to protect the rights of people charged with crimes are not "soft on crime." Judges who declare that a statute or a public referendum violates the constitution are not "legislating" from the bench or "thwarting the will of the majority." They are carrying out their oath of office and following the rule of law.

The verdict in the Oklahoma City bombing trial may have restored some confidence in our judicial system. But a different scenario might illustrate the dangers of the current political vilification of judges and the resulting erosion of respect for our judicial system. Assume that prison guards, angered over the 168 deaths caused by the bombing of the Murrah Federal Building and frustrated by the lack of cooperation from those arrested, decided to beat one of those charged in order to obtain a confession.* As a result, they obtained a statement with sufficient detail so that there could be no doubt as to the knowledge and guilt of the confessor. Furthermore, these details led to the gathering of additional evidence regarding the source of the materials utilized in the making of the bomb, how they were transported, where they were stored, how the bomb was made and how it was ultimately delivered and detonated and by whom.

There are those who would argue, quite reasonably, that the guards should be punished, but that the evidence should be utilized. However, there are some protections that we view as so precious that nothing can be gained from their violation. Under existing law, the confession would not be admissible. In all probability, neither would any of the details, evidence and corroboration obtained as a result. Indeed, the taint of the illegally obtained confession and the fruits thereby gained might have led to an acquittal or dismissal of the charges. One can well imagine and understand the public outrage at such a result. Conservative politicians would be elbowing one another aside to reach microphones to lambaste the "liberal judge" who made such a ruling and decry the use of the "technicality" that made it possible—another example of a judicial system run amok, although there probably is not a judge in the country who would rule otherwise.

But suppose we were to change the above hypothetical scenario as follows: The guilty person beaten by law-enforcement officers was not the first but the tenth. Seven did not confess, because they were not guilty; two other did, even though they were not, just to bring the beatings to an end. One can imagine and hope for an equally vociferous outcry. If public confidence is essential to the maintenance of our judicial system—and it is—what lesson is to be drawn from these two hypothetical instances? What people really desire is two sets of rules and rights: one for the guilty and one for the innocent. People do not want criminals to gain advantage from the assertion of constitutional rights. On the other hand, they want those rights available to and enforced for the innocent. The problem with such an approach is that the determination of constitutional violations is frequently made by a judge before there is a determination of guilt or innocence. Furthermore, for the pre-

*There is no suggestion that any guard would engage in such conduct. The discussion is for illustrative purposes only.

sumption of innocence to have any meaning, a determination of guilt must await a final verdict.

So if it is impossible or impractical to preserve the Bill of Rights for the innocent and deny it to the guilty, should the constitutional protections extended to those accused of crimes be repeated? Has crime become so prevalent and the need to combat it so great that we are willing to sacrifice some of our fundamental rights in order to win this battle? For both practical and principled reasons, the answer should be "no," even if the present atmosphere makes such amendments to the Constitution seem politically possible.

First, we all (and particularly the politicians and the media) need a civics lesson. Have we forgotten our history? The Fifth Amendment is not a "technicality." The right against self-incrimination was considered fundamental and essential to our freedom. Likewise, the restriction on searches and other government intrusions into our private lives was of sufficient importance that our forefathers were prepared to die for it.

Even if one is unmoved by the historical significance of these rights, their enforcement has virtually no impact on crime in this country. If the Bill of Rights were repealed tomorrow, insofar as its protections extend to those accused of crimes, it would not make the slightest ripple in the amount or nature of crime in this country. Law-enforcement officials themselves have repeatedly stated that enforcement of the Bill of Rights has not impeded them, and criminals hardly sit around a kitchen table and say: "If we are apprehended we can invoke our right against self-incrimination, and thus we shall go ahead and rob the corner candy store." They may be street-smart and "know their rights," but that knowledge is neither the catalyst nor cause of their unlawful activity. It probably never enters their thinking, assuming that there is much forethought given to the commission of most crimes.

Most significant, and contrary to the vision portrayed by conservative politicians and media, there is not a group of loony liberal judges out there leaping at the chance to set criminals free. The idea that any judge relishes ruling in favor of a person charged with a crime in the face of evidence of guilt, and particularly after a finding of guilt, is utter nonsense. Those rulings are made with great reluctance, but done because the law compels it. The suppression of the confession referred to earlier in this article would have to be made by any and every judge confronted with those facts. Furthermore, the number of such rulings is minuscule. Roughly, between 5 and 10 percent of all criminal cases are actually tried. In those that are tried, motions to suppress evidence are routinely denied every day, in every court in every state in this country. A dismissal of charges following the granting of a motion to sup-

> *The validity of a judicial opinion cannot rest on popularity. Resisting pressure to please the majority is judicial strength, not weakness.*

press evidence is as rare an event as Senator Orrin Hatch recommending a liberal for a seat on the Supreme Court.

When motions to suppress are granted, those who wish to capitalize on such rulings invariably discuss the heinous nature of the crime or the long criminal history of the defendant, if one exists, neither of which is relevant to the question of whether the defendant's constitutional rights have been violated. Here again, we do not and cannot have two sets of rules—one for bad crimes and criminals and another for those less offensive. The exercise I posed above was chosen because there has been no more horrific crime in the history of this country than the Oklahoma City bombing; but the rights afforded by the Constitution cannot be reduced as the severity of the crime increases.

The law and those who administer it are not perfect. Mistakes are made. That is why we have courts of appeal. But it is essential that the public understand that in large measure the guilty are convicted (indeed, most plead guilty), the innocent are protected and the judicial system and its judges are devoted and dedicated to fairness and justice. Criticism has its place, but truth must have some role in the dialogue. (My nomination to the Court of Appeals was opposed on the basis that I "had a long history of freeing criminals in disregard of the rights of their victims." In fifteen years on the bench two people are free as a result of my rulings—Rubin "Hurricane" Carter, a decision affirmed by the Court of Appeals and left standing by the U.S. Supreme Court after review, and James Landano, who is still awaiting retrial while on bail—hardly a "long history of freeing criminals.") Indeed, granting a writ of habeas corpus orders a new trial and does not free the petitioner unless the state elects not to retry.

The Bill of Rights is meant to protect us all. If in the process a criminal benefits, we must decide whether that detriment outweighs the benefits and freedoms we all enjoy. It is ironic that the criticism leveled at the Bill of Rights and the frequent characterization of its parts as "technicalities" come from conservatives, since the rights enunciated are the embodiment of the conservative philosophy. They codify the fundamental conservative principle of excluding unwanted and unwarranted government intrusion in the private lives of citizens.

Although the critics of "judicial activism" insist that neither the result nor the identity of the judge is what motivates them, the evidence suggests otherwise. There are many former prosecutors who now sit on the judicial benches of this country who were strong advocates of the death penalty. When they rule in favor of capital punishment, none of these critics claim that the judges involved are "activists carrying out their own agendas"; but the personal motives or background of those who vote against the death penalty in a given case invariably becomes relevant. When the Chief Justice of the United States wrote an opinion declaring unconstitutional an act of Congress that prohibited guns within 1,000 feet of schools, there was no cry of "thwarting the will of the people"; if I had authored that opinion, *The Wall Street Journal* editorial world have read: "Sarokin Rules Schoolchildren Can Have Guns!"

The independence of the judiciary is essential to our democracy. Those who seek to tamper with it to gain a momentary political victory for themselves will cause a greater and more lasting loss to the public, and to the confidence in our judicial system, without which the rule of law cannot survive.

The Gipper's Constitution

Republican judges are rewriting the law of the land

BY STEPHEN POMPER

Octuber 13, 1999—Day 6,841 of the Reagan Revolution. The Supreme Court hears an argument in *Kimel v. Florida Board of Regents.* Counsel asks the Court to recognize that state employees have the right to sue their employers for violating the Age Discrimination Employment Act. If not, then state employers will be above the law—immune from damages no matter how egregiously they discriminate on the basis of age. Not only that, but states will have a legal

A growing body of conservative law looks to extend the Reagan legacy well into the next century.

basis to argue that this immunity should extend to private suits under other civil rights laws—like the Americans with Disabilities Act and portions of the Civil Rights Act of 1964. But from reports of the argument, you'd never know what's at stake: Chief Justice William Rehnquist yawns openly. Justices Sandra Day O'Connor and Anthony Kennedy stare into space and down at the bench. And the liberal justices offer up a pittance of supportive questions and fall silent as if to acknowledge that it's a lost cause—why bother?

How did we get here? Twenty years ago the Reagan administration had a conservative social agenda and no way to achieve it. A Democratic House of Representatives stood squarely in the way of the White House on issues like abortion, school prayer, and busing. In *Pursuit of Justices,* a history of the modern Supreme Court appointments process, David Alistair Yalof describes how the administration gave up on Congress and shifted its strategy to redefining the political composition of the federal courts. This was accomplished through careful screening of judicial nominees; Yalof reprints portions of

a 1985 Justice Department memo enumerating the ideal attributes of a Supreme Court Justice, including:

- "disposition towards 'less government rather than more'"
- "appreciation for the role of the free market in our society"
- "refusal to create new constitutional rights for the individual" and
- "respect for traditional values."

It was a brilliant strategy, with long-lived results. At the end of October, even after seven years of a Democratic administration, and the confirmation of 325 Clinton appointees to the federal bench, Republican-appointed federal judges outnumbered Democrat appointees 614 to 571. That imbalance has not been helped by the fact that it now takes roughly 201 days—compared to 38 days during the Carter administration—to shepherd a candidate through the thoroughly partisan Senate confirmation process. (At the end of October there was a backlog of 42 Clinton nominees awaiting confirmation to the federal judiciary.) A once-tenuous 5-4 conservative majority on the Supreme Court has crystallized into a consistent, reliable voting block. And conservative district court judges (the trial court judges who occupy the lowest rung in the federal court system) and circuit court judges (the appellate judges who occupy the middle level between federal trial courts and the Supreme Court) have developed increasingly aggressive tactics to achieve their ends. The result has been a growing body of conservative law which, because it is championed by lifetime-tenured judges and inscribed in precedents that are difficult (sometimes impossible) for legislatures to overturn, looks to extend the Reagan legacy well into the next century.

The most profound changes made by the Republican bench are embedded in a series of highly technical decisions generally grouped under the heading "federalism"—a term that describes legal theories allowing courts to take powers away from the federal government and give them to states. Taken alone, none of the so-called federalist decisions would have earth-shattering impact. Taken together, they have given Republican judges doctrinal cover for redesigning government, picking off civil rights protections, and weakening other federal legislation. And given the political origins of these judges, it comes as no surprise that they are simultaneously making inroads on a conservative social agenda in areas like abortion rights, campaign finance reform, and environmental regulation.

What's more, by advancing the Reagan revolution in discrete, technical steps, conservative judges have given liberals a difficult target to shoot at. "The opinions always give the impression of being one step short of a truly radical decision," says University of Michigan law professor Ellen Katz, while acknowledging that defeat by 1,000 small blows is nevertheless defeat.

Devolution Now, Devolution Forever

Five years ago, Gareth Cook observed in these pages that the devolution of federal powers to local entities is "the core of the modern Republican agenda." ("Devolution Chic," April 1995). Of course even Republican congressmen are capable of loving federal legislation that serves a conservative agenda. (For example, Republican congressmen have recently supported federal legislation on issues like late term abortions and tort reform.) But when it comes to forms of regulation that Republicans inherently mistrust—industry regulation, environmental legislation, and civil rights protections—devolution is still a useful concept for pushing responsibility away from the federal government, down to the states, and perhaps into oblivion.

The Reagan administration of course wanted a judiciary that would support devolution from the bench, which is no doubt the reason for the item in the 1985 Justice Department memo suggesting that the ideal Supreme Court justice would favor "less government rather than more." That objective has been realized, as the Supreme Court (now home to seven Republican appointees—five of whom vote fairly reliably on party lines) has labored for the better part of the past decade to take Congress' powers away.

Some background: Congress gets its general powers to make law from two places—first, the so-called "Commerce Clause" of the Constitution, which allows it to pass laws regulating interstate commerce; second, the 14th Amendment, which allows it to pass civil rights legislation protecting individuals from state abuse. (The Constitution also gives Congress enumerated powers to make law in certain specified areas, for example, bankruptcy). These have been generous sources of Congressional authority. For 60 years, the Supreme Court did not overturn a single law on the grounds that Congress had exceeded its Commerce Clause authority. And the Court also gave Congress a wide berth to define the civil

liberties that required its protection under the 14th Amendment.

As the Reagan Revolution has gathered momentum in the courts over the last decade, however, the rules have changed. The Supreme Court has issued a series of rulings that trim Congressional authority in order to give more power to the states. For example, in two cases (*New York v. United States* and *Printz v. United States*), the Court ruled that Congress cannot force states to implement federal legislation—meaning, for example, that Congress cannot require local police to administer hand-gun checks under the Brady Act. In *United States v. Lopez,* the Court broke with six decades of precedent and said that Congress went outside its Commerce Clause authority when it created nationwide gun-free school zones; this was a matter that states were entitled to regulate. And in *City of Boerne v. Flores,* the Court overturned a federal law that had given religious organizations the right not to observe state laws when they conflicted with religious principles; in so doing, the Court criticized Congress for being too generous with individual rights and not considerate enough of states' rights.

The Supreme Court took the federalist movement to a whole new level, however, with its decision in *Alden v. Maine*—which was decided on the last day of the 1998–1999 Supreme Court term. The *Alden* ruling, combined with a similar decision from two years earlier, says that private citizens cannot sue state governments under Commerce Clause legislation. To be sure, if a state breaks the law, one can still get a court to order a specific person in state government—for example, the governor or a commissioner—to make it stop. But under *Alden,* an injured party cannot sue the state to get compensated for the harm he has suffered, or to give the state a reason for thinking twice before it breaks the law again.

Alden was particularly jarring because it assigned states a right that is not expressed anywhere in the text of the Constitution. In reaching its decision, the federalist majority relied on the "structure" and the "history" of the Constitution—interpretive strategies that were popular with the activist brethren on the Warren Court, but that had long been disdained by the conservative bench. Remember the 1985 Justice Department memo that frowned on "the creation of new constitutional rights for individuals"? In *Alden,* the Republican justices demonstrated that they were in fact willing to create new constitutional rights—when they served the devolutionary purpose of taking authority away from Congress and making states more powerful.

Above the Law

Republicans in Congress do their part to make the federal government smaller by pushing regulatory responsibility down to the states. Republicans on the bench help the cause by making it easier for states to ignore federal regulation, which in turn is supposed to make it easier for the states to do their jobs. But do we really want the states to be unregulated?

After all, states are big business. At the end of 1998, state governments employed over 4.76 million workers, a number that reflects an increase of slightly less than 10 percent in the preceding ten years. (Students of devolution take note: as of year-end 1998, the federal government employed 2.7 million workers, reflecting a decline of slightly more than 10 percent over the same period.) State-run enterprises compete actively and often very successfully with the private sector. And states are sometimes apt to take liberties.

Paul Durham is a case in point. Durham has been an employee of the Iowa Department of Transportation for 34 years, and is responsible for keeping 400 miles of road safe and passable. Starting in 1985, Durham was entitled under the Federal Labor Standards Act (FLSA) to be paid for overtime work at an overtime wage (time-and-a-half). Although he claims that from 1985 though 1995, he generally worked between 700 and 800 hours of overtime a year, Durham says that he never got paid for more than 75 of those hours in any year. Eventually he sued the state of Iowa as part of a class action. In 1996, the verdict came in: his class had won, and according to his attorney's back-of-the-envelope calculations, Durham was entitled to almost $200,000. But before the court could calculate the precise amount of damages, the Supreme Court made states immune from FLSA lawsuits in federal court. Now, under *Alden,* they're immune in state court too. As a result, Durham is out quite a bit of money and the Iowa DOT rides free.

Mary Ann Thomson's case is also instructive. According to the uncontested facts she presented in court, Thomson worked as an administrative assistant at the *Ohio State University Hospital.* When her father was diagnosed with Alzheimer's disease, she asked for unpaid leave and was denied. She then learned that she was entitled to a leave under the federal Family Medical Leave Act, so she asked and was rebuffed again, then sued. It was a strategy that might have paid off for a private sector employee, but unfortunately Thomson worked for a state university. A federal trial court judge, James L. Graham (a Reagan appointee), ruled in 1998 that the state was immune from private suits under the FMLA, and Thomson was out of luck.

But the strangest cases to illustrate this point are a pair that were decided by the Supreme Court at the same time as *Alden—Florida v. College Savings Bank* and *College Savings Bank v. Florida.* In these cases, a private savings bank sued the state of Florida for patent and trademark violations concerning a college investment plan. Without reaching the question of whether there were actually violations, the Supreme Court ruled that the state of Florida was immune from suit under the applicable patent and trademark laws. It was a remarkable ruling given that states—in particular, big state universities—do hundreds of millions of dollars of business each year in technology development. Now, when state research labs borrow the patented materials they need to do their work (a common practice), they can apparently violate the patents on those materials without concern of punishment. "If I'm the state, you can say you'll sue me," says Professor Ronald Mann at the University of Michigan law school. "But I'll laugh and say—go ahead—because in fact, you *can't* sue me."

Federalists argue that states *should* have sovereign immunity against plaintiffs like Durham, Thomson, and College Savings Bank, if only to keep their treasuries from being plundered by lawsuits. But that raises the question: Why should the Supreme Court help states to balance their budgets by denying their employees and business partners access to the courts—compromising their rights and effectively rendering them second-class citizens under the law?

Heedless, Self-promoting Things

One way to gauge the hostility of the Republican judiciary to Congress is by the number of federal statutes that it has overturned in recent years. Since 1995, the Supreme Court has overturned 20 acts of Congress on constitutional grounds. That's more than the total number that were overturned in the previous 20 years combined.

In more balanced times, the Republican bar might have been shamefaced about this sort of judicial activism. The Supreme Court has generally made an effort to defer to Congress, on the principle that Supreme Court justices are not elected and therefore should take a back seat to Congress in deciding how the country is governed.

Those days of judicial modesty are gone. In a *New York Times* op-ed published on the heels of *Alden,* former Reagan administration Solicitor General Charles Fried suggested that the public should be *grateful* to the Court for overturning Congressional legislation in areas like rape protection and gun control because federal laws in this area are redundant with existing state laws and therefore "heedless" and "self-promoting." This is not quite convincing.

Consider, for example, the Violence Against Women Act, which was overturned by a 7–4 majority of judges on the Fourth Circuit court of appeals last spring. (The Fourth Circuit is based in Virginia and comprises seven Republican-appointed judges and four Democratic appointees). The Fourth Circuit's opinion, *Brzonkala v. Virginia Polytechnic Institute,* found VAWA to be outside Congress' Commerce Clause authority. If VAWA was just a heedless, self-promoting act, then perhaps we shouldn't care. But it wasn't. VAWA was enacted because rape crimes were not being adequately prosecuted at the local level. Rape survivors had only a 5 percent chance of seeing their assailants convicted and a 1 percent chance of collecting damages from them on civil charges.

Forty-one state attorneys general signed a letter supporting VAWA's passage, and 17 out of 18 federal trial courts that reviewed the statute before the Fourth Circuit found it to be constitutional.

What end, then, did the Fourth Circuit serve when it delivered a 168-page opinion (an astronomical length by circuit court standards) against plaintiff Christy Brzonkala—a young woman who claimed to have been gang raped during her first week in college, only to see the school fail to meaningfully discipline her assailants and the state fail to press charges? Certainly it set up the Supreme Court (which is reviewing *Brzonkala* this term) to hack back Congress' Commerce Clause powers yet further—advancing the cause of "less government rather than more." But wouldn't it have been preferable if "doing justice for Christy Brzonkala" were the higher priority?

Attack On All Fronts

Looking past the Republican bench's predilection for "less government rather than more," Republican-appointed judges—most notably the Fourth Circuit—have also done a great deal for advancing the conservative agenda on a number of other specific issues in the last two years. In particular:

Abortion. The Fourth Circuit did its part for the pro-life movement, in 1998, by upholding the constitutionality of a law requiring unmarried teenagers to get parental consent before having an abortion and, in 1999, by prohibiting the type of late term abortions referred to as "partial birth abortions." In both cases, the appellate court reversed pro-choice decisions by trial court judges. In the "partial birth" case word leaked out that state authorities had taken steps to ensure the outcome they wanted by maneuvering the case to Judge Michael Luttig, the most outspokenly conservative judge on the appellate court. Luttig returned the favor with an opinion that upheld the anti-abortion law and avoided even mentioning *Roe v. Wade* as a precedent.

Campaign Finance Reform. Campaign finance reform suffered a set-back in *Nixon v. Shrink,* where the Eighth Circuit's Judge Pasco Bowman (a Reagan appointee) ruled that a Missouri law limiting campaign contributions to $1,075 was a violation of the free speech rights of candidates and potential contributors. The ruling undermined the Supreme Court's 1976 decision in *Buckley v. Valeo,* which provides that contribution limits of $1,000 or more are constitutional. (Reformers will recall that *Buckley v. Valeo* said that caps on campaign contributions are constitutional, but that caps on campaign spending are not.) The Supreme Court is presently reviewing Bowman's decision.

Environmental Regulation. The conservative Fourth Circuit undermined the federal Clean Water Act in two notable cases. In *United States v. Wilson,* it refused to punish a Maryland developer for discharging fill into a Maryland wetlands in apparent violation of the Clean Water Act. The court reasoned that because the Clean Water Act was enacted under Congress' Commerce Clause powers, it only applies to "interstate" wetlands. In *Friends of the Earth v. Laidlaw,* the Fourth Circuit declared that a company's mercury dumping violations were "moot" because they were remedied while the case was being litigated, and prevented Friends of Earth—who had prompted the clean up by bringing the litigation—from collecting attorneys' fees. The decision all but destroyed the mechanism for citizens' suits under the Clean Water Act and is now being reviewed by the Supreme Court.

Law and Order. The Fourth Circuit also achieved certain notoriety when it ruled in *U.S. v. Dickerson* that the Supreme Court's venerable opinion in *Miranda v. Arizona* had merely established guidelines for law enforcement officials—meaning that the familiar *Miranda* warnings given by police (the litany beginning with "you have the right to remain silent") may not be constitutionally required. In May of this year, Neil Lewis reported an even more stunning item in *The New York Times*: In 26 consecutive cases where trial courts had granted "habeas corpus" petitions delaying prisoner death sentences, the appellate court reversed every single one—a result that is difficult to justify if one attributes any force to habeas law or assumes that trial court judges are at least minimally competent.

It's How You Play The Game

No discussion of the triumph of the Republican bench would be complete without a nod to extra-legal considerations—the ways in which judges will sometimes depart from convention in order to achieve politically desirable ends. We have already spoken of the new willingness of the Republican bench to create constitutional rights from sources outside the Constitution (but only for states), to aggressively overrule Congress, and to disregard Supreme Court precedent. But this just scratches the surface. Other tactics include:

• *Reaching Out to be Kind.* The Supreme Court gives the appearance of reaching out to review cases from the Fourth Circuit—which has emerged as the most consistently aggressive of the conservative lower courts. By affirming these cases, the Court can render inviolate the Fourth's envelope-pushing conclusions. Reaching out, of course, is hard to prove. But it is worth noting that the number of Fourth Circuit cases that the Court has agreed to take has accelerated just as the Fourth has broken from the pack. At the beginning of the present Supreme Court term, there were already six Fourth Circuit cases on the high Court docket—that's as many cases as the Court agreed to hear from the Fourth in its three previous terms combined.

• *Reaching Out to be Cruel.* If the Supreme Court seems to be reaching out to affirm Fourth Circuit cases, then it seems to be reaching out to overturn decisions issued by the Ninth Circuit—a California-based court dominated by Carter and Clinton appointees and viewed as the last remaining bastion of judicial liberalism. A *Los Angeles Times* article running at the end of the 1997–1998 Supreme Court term—during which the Court overturned 13 of 17 Ninth Circuit decisions—proclaimed triumphantly that "the reviews for the California-based federal appeals court were not all bad at the Supreme Court this year." In the previous term, it had overturned 28 out of 29. Even more unfortunate are rumors in the environmental bar that judges on the Circuit have begun ruling against environmental causes because they feel under attack about their record.

• *Majority Rule.* As a general matter, circuit court decisions are reached by three-judge panels—which may be revisited in "en banc" (group) review by the entire circuit if requested by any of the non-panel judges. The Fourth Circuit, however, has acquired the habit of subjecting all panel decisions that come out the wrong way to en banc review. Lewis' piece in *The New York Times* quotes the University of Pittsburgh law professor Arthur Hellman as saying "There is a conservative majority on the full court, and if they see a panel decision they don't like, they just take it en banc and reverse it. . . No other circuit enforces majority rule the way the Fourth Circuit does."

A Radical Development

It is tempting to hope that the upcoming election will give liberals the break they need to derail the Reagan Revolution in the courts. Four seats on the Supreme Court could open up in the next five years (those currently occupied by Chief Justice Rehnquist and Justices O'Connor, John Paul Stevens and Ruth Bader Ginsburg). Whoever fills those seats will likely have the chance to define the direction of constitutional law well into the next century. In order to be assured of getting the right people on the bench, however, Democrats will need to command the entire appointments process—meaning both the White House and the Senate Judiciary Committee. And that won't be easy. One thing liberal lawyers can do to help is to arouse public awareness of the dangers lurking in recent legal trends.

This will require liberals to voice their concerns even if (to recall the words of Professor Katz from the University of Michigan) the courts remain "one step short of the radical decision." After all, that decision may never come. Meanwhile, in a series of dry, technically devastating opinions, Republican judges have engineered what former Solicitor General Walter Dellinger has referred to as "one of the three or four major shifts in constitutionalism we've seen in the last two centuries."

Dellinger's remark places the Reagan Revolution in the same category as the constitutional changes that attended the Civil War, New Deal and civil rights movement. That's pretty exalted company for a trend that is backward looking, hostile to individual rights, and out of touch with what Americans want and value. There may not be a radical decision behind it, but it's a radical development, and it's something the public should hear about repeatedly and emphatically—before, on the way to, and after the polls next November.

Research assistance provided by Lucinda Vette.

UP FOR GRABS:

The Supreme Court and the Election

by Tom Wicker

Whom do you want to nominate Justices for the Supreme Court in the next four years? No issue is more vital in the race between Democrat Al Gore and Republican George W. Bush—repeat, no issue is more important than the makeup of the next Supreme Court—and therefore the future outlook for reproductive rights, civil rights, campaign finance reform, environmental protection and perhaps much, much more.

No issue is more crucial, for two reasons. First, no matter what the next President or Congress may do or think, among the three branches of the federal government, the Supreme Court is often first among supposed equals, wielding more authority than either of its counterparts through its power to declare unconstitutional the actions of Presidents (such as Harry Truman's seizure of the steel mills in 1952), as well as enactments of Congress or the state legislatures (such as those attempting to validate prayer in public schools).

It was the Supreme Court, of course, that held in *Brown v. Board of Education* in 1954, one of its most historic decisions, that public school segregation violated the Constitution. That decision opened not just the schoolhouse door but the gate to the modern civil rights movement, which in the past half-century has so nearly transformed the nation.

Reprinted with permission from the October 9, 2000, issue of *The Nation*, pp. 11-17. © 2000 by The Nation Company, LP.

The Court resembles a closely balanced scale to which any added weight will tip it conclusively right or left.

It was the same Court, however—different Justices in different times, but with the same powers—that in 1896 upheld a Louisiana "separate but equal" law, ushering in the six long decades of racial segregation that were not effectively ended until *Brown* (and not even then, in some areas). Even earlier, in 1857, the Court's infamous *Dred Scott* decision held that black people had no rights white people were bound to respect and that Congress could not prohibit slavery in the territories. The Civil War followed not long after.

So despite the enmity earned in the twentieth century by the Warren Court in the fifties and sixties for its controversial decisions (*Brown, Miranda, Baker v. Carr*), the Supreme Court has not always been—and need not necessarily be in the future—a bulwark of liberal attitudes. In the thirties, in fact, Franklin Roosevelt undertook his ill-fated "court-packing" scheme because of a series of Court rulings—such as one finding unconstitutional his National Industrial Recovery Act—that he thought were crippling his New Deal programs. In perhaps his worst political defeat, FDR failed to "pack" the Court, but the threat may have achieved his objective in several subsequent decisions—upholding, for example, federal power to prohibit shipment in interstate commerce of goods manufactured in violation of wage-and-hour laws. This was a startling about-face from an earlier ruling.

The second reason no issue is more critical in 2000 than the future makeup of the Supreme Court is that the present Rehnquist Court is so narrowly divided. Sometimes it presents a majority—usually including Chief Justice William Rehnquist—for conservative views; occasionally, it comes to a 5-to-4 or even 6-to-3 ruling for a more liberal attitude. The Court resembles, therefore, a closely balanced scale to which any added weight will tip it conclusively right or left.

A rightward ideological shift of just two votes could swing that 6-to-3 lineup, only rarely existing on the Rehnquist Court, into a solid 5-to-4 majority that in the future would follow the established pattern of Justices Antonin Scalia and Clarence Thomas, the two farthest-right members of the Court. Among other things, that might well doom *Roe v. Wade,* which protects a woman's right to choose. *Three* more Scalia&Thomas-style votes would transform what's now a back-and-forth Court into a conservative bastion that could last for generations—like the one that so frustrated FDR in the thirties.

Yet more conservative votes on the Court are exactly what the Republican candidate says he'd provide. He is on record that he'd appoint more Justices like Scalia&Thomas, those joined-at-the-hip right-wingers. And even if Bush loses the presidency, a Senate that remains in Republican hands—a real possibility—might block, or at least delay, the more liberal nominees a President Gore could be expected to select.

The best guarantee against any such outcomes—a President Bush, a Republican Senate or both—and hence the best hope for a Supreme Court that will not turn back the clock to Scalia&Thomas time, is a big Democratic victory across the board in November. And to those independents—and even some Democrats—who maintain there's so little real difference between the two parties that they'll vote for Ralph Nader of the Green Party or Patrick Buchanan of the Reform Party—the strongest answer is, again, that all-important question: *Whom do you want to nominate Justices for the Supreme Court in the next four years?*

Whatever one may think on other issues, there's a real difference between the candidates and the parties on the question of Supreme Court nominations. Gore's record suggests that his nominees—especially if he gets a Democratic Senate to work with—would be moderate to liberal, rather like those of Bill Clinton (who put Stephen Breyer and Ruth Bader Ginsburg on the Court). If the self-styled "compassionate conservative" wins the presidency and carries in a Republican Senate on his coattails, the next Supreme Court is all but guaranteed to be considerably more conservative than compassionate.

This dire possibility is never far from the minds of the constitutional authorities who review in this issue of *The Nation* the record of the Rehnquist Court in its recently concluded term. It is an ominous review, not only because of decisions already taken but because the narrowly divided Rehnquist Court could so easily—and so soon—be converted into a highly conservative bloc.

In the past thirty-two years, after all, nominations to the High Court have been made principally by Richard Nixon, Ronald Reagan and Bush the Elder, who would have made the situation worse had he known what he was doing when he nominated David Souter. With that choice, Bush didn't

A THOMAS-SCALIA COURT

Putting a Radical Right Team on the Bench

George W Bush has publicly cited Justices like Antonin Scalia and Clarence Thomas as the kind of "strict constructionists" he will appoint to the Supreme Court. Scalia and Thomas have long been the favorites of right-wing religious, political and legal activists eager to see the Supreme Court roll back decades of progressive rulings.

People for the American Way Foundation recently released *Courting Disaster*, the result of a six-month analysis of the concurring and dissenting opinions of the two Justices. It asks, "If these opinions were shared by a majority of the Court, how would that change the outcome of the Court's decisions?" The answer is chilling. If those angry dissents and minority concurring opinions were majority rulings, the result on issue after issue would be a radical, reactionary shift in US law.

Many people are worried about the Court's future rulings on reproductive rights. It's true that Justices Scalia and Thomas are eager to overturn *Roe v. Wade,* and they need only two more votes to do it. Maybe only one—Justice Anthony Kennedy's vote supporting the ban on so-called partial-birth abortion has been interpreted as an indication that he is having doubts about his 1992 vote reaffirming *Roe v. Wade.* But much more than reproductive rights is at stake.

As the contributors to this issue document, the Supreme Court is already dominated by conservative Justices who are aggressively promoting a troubling new theory of federalism and states' rights that is drastically restricting the power of Congress to protect Americans' rights and to address serious national problems. But *even this conservative activist majority* has frequently not been willing to go as far as Scalia and Thomas want. And that's why the prospect of a Scalia-Thomas majority on the Court is so ominous.

Here's just one example: In a 1994 voting rights case, Justices Thomas and Scalia advocated a position that, according to four of the other Justices, was so "radical"

SEYMOUR CHWAST

it would have meant overturning or reconsidering twenty-eight previous Supreme Court rulings that the Voting Rights Act of 1965 should be interpreted to prohibit racial discrimination in all aspects of voting.

There's much more. A Scalia-Thomas majority would exempt elections for state judges from all provisions of the Voting Rights Act, permit sex discrimination in jury selection, eliminate affirmative action, restrict remedies for discrimination while making it harder to prove discrimination in the first place and hold that improper and unnecessary institutionalization of disabled persons would no longer be considered a violation of the Americans With Disabilities Act.

Religious liberty would suffer under a Scalia-Thomas majority hostile to the principle of church-state separation. Such a Court would overturn a series of precedents protecting the rights of students to be free from religious coercion in public school settings. The floodgates would be opened to direct government funding for religious schools.

A Scalia-Thomas majority would weaken the right to strike and bargain collectively, make it easier to fire workers for political reasons and allow employers to deceive workers about the solvency of benefits plans. Scalia has ridiculed laws that protect workers from sexual harassment.

The federal government would be barred from stopping the de-

struction of endangered species on private land. Local governments' power to protect the environment would be restricted.

Campaign finance reform would be virtually impossible under a Scalia-Thomas Court, which would throw out any and all limits on campaign contributions and spending.

Sensible gun control legislation would be struck down.

What is at stake is the legal and constitutional framework under which the nation will operate for decades to come. Radical right leaders know they're just one election away from winning their entire political agenda, and they're mobilizing voters with the prospect of a right-wing-dominated Supreme Court. It was their vocal "no more Souters" campaign that led George W Bush to explicitly name Scalia and Thomas as his models. And it has now been six years since the confirmation of the Court's most recent appointee, Justice Stephen Breyer. Only once in our history—177 years ago—have we gone so long between appointments.

Indeed, the future of the Supreme Court is the most important issue in the most important election year since 1932. Progressive Americans should treat it that way. The radical right does.

—RALPH G. NEAS

Ralph G. Neas is president of People for the American Way. More information about cases cited is available at www.pfaw org.

APPELLATE COURTS

Power Shift Down—The Lower Courts Count

Much of the debate swirling around the upcoming election focuses on the next President's power to shape the Supreme Court—but it would be a mistake to overlook the enormous impact the next President will have on the appellate courts as well. Each year the Supreme Court decides fewer cases. In the seventies and eighties, it routinely heard about 150 cases a year. The typical docket for the Rehnquist Court is less than 100.

This trend toward fewer Supreme Court rulings gives the appellate courts vastly more power. In fact, some experts call the appellate courts "regional Supreme Courts" because so often they become the forums of last resort for plaintiffs bringing civil rights, abortion and environmental litigation.

Appellate court appointments are rarely constrained by the kind of senatorial influence and patronage that frequently govern the selection of district court judges, so the President generally has a freer hand in making these appointments. Conservative activists have long been keenly aware of the importance of the appellate courts. Presidents Reagan and Bush both made it a priority to fill appellate court vacancies quickly, ultimately packing them with right-leaning judges whose agendas were to reverse years of progress on civil rights and the environment. Reagan and Bush appellate court appointees include such well-known ideologues as Robert Bork, Daniel Manion, Douglas Ginsburg, Frank Easterbrook and Alex Kozinski.

Because of the critical importance of the 179 federal appellate seats, Senate Republicans have deliberately delayed confirmation of nominees during the Clinton era. Of the thirty-four judges confirmed last year, only six were to courts of appeals. This year is unlikely to be better; ultraconservatives in the Senate will do everything possible to avoid filling the twenty-two appellate court vacancies until after the presidential election.

Consequently, even after seven years of Democratic rule, nine of the thirteen courts of appeals remain in the control of Republican

SEYMOUR CHWAST

appointees. Many of these judges, such as those on the Fourth and Seventh Circuits, have shown open hostility to civil rights, striking down such crucial protections as affirmative action, the Violence Against Women Act and the 1966 *Miranda* decision.

Judicial hostility to environmental protections is also common. In 1999 two panels of the Court of Appeals for the DC Circuit handed a victory to polluters, overturning longstanding EPA standards reducing the ozone that exacerbates lung disease and asthma. In that case, the Reagan-appointed judges adopted an argument set forth by a conservative lawyer, even though the argument ran contrary to sixty years of legal precedent.

Senate Republicans have also created a judiciary that is shamefully unrepresentative of the public it serves. It wasn't until this past summer that the number of African-American judges serving on the appellate courts reached the same level as when President Carter left office twenty years ago. More than half the country's circuit courts lacked either an African-American or a Latino jurist—or both—at the end of 1999. The conservative Fourth Circuit (which includes Maryland, North Carolina, South Carolina, Virginia and West Virginia) has never had an African-American judge, despite the fact that the region has the largest percentage of African-Americans in the general population of any circuit.

While North Carolina Senator Jesse Helms is notable for actively blocking the nominations of African-American judges to the Fourth Circuit Court, other GOP senators

have contributed to the delays in appointments across the federal judiciary. In the past year the Senate set a record for the longest delay imposed on a nominee: Ninth Circuit Judge Richard Paez, a Hispanic-American, was forced to wait more than four years before the Senate finally scheduled a vote and confirmed him this year.

Unfortunately, in many ways the Clinton Administration has acquiesced in the Senate majority's crusade to strip away presidential appointment power. Clinton's strong desire to avoid confrontation over judicial appointments has led him to draw nominees from a limited pool, for the most part avoiding public interest lawyers and those in private practice with extensive pro bono experience. The regrettable result is that the Clinton Administration has failed to restore balance to the federal court system after twelve years of strongly ideological conservative appointments.

Americans deserve better. We count on federal judges to protect our civil rights, our environment and our most basic freedoms. The next President could well appoint fifty or more circuit judges. We need a President who will appoint federal judges—at all levels—who will advance protections against discrimination and environmental destruction. And we need a Senate that will stop using political gamesmanship to delay and block qualified judicial appointees.

NAN ARON

Nan Aron is president of Alliance for Justice.

get the conservative promised him by John Sununu but suffered the biggest Court surprise since Dwight Eisenhower picked Earl Warren to be Chief Justice.

Nixon, Reagan and Bush the Elder represented eighteen years of middle-to-right conservatism, against only two years of Gerald Ford (who appointed John Paul Stevens, a reliable moderate who is now 80), four years of Jimmy Carter and eight of Bill Clinton. Carter, however, offers a sad example of the vagaries of Supreme Court nominations. In his four years in office, no Justice died or retired, so Carter made zero nominations. Nixon, by contrast, put four men on the high bench, including two Chief Justices, Warren Burger and William Rehnquist—a far more important fact than that Nixon also had two other nominees rejected.

Nor is it only the Supreme Court that's on the line. The trend toward fewer High Court rulings— about two-thirds as many as during the seventies and eighties—has greatly expanded the power of the federal courts of appeal, which Ronald Reagan and Bush the Elder packed with conservative judges. Today, there are no more African-Americans serving on appellate courts than there were under President Carter, whose appointments of women and minorities began to redress the racial and gender imbalances of the lower courts in his time. Long confirmation delays in the Republican Senate have been bluntly focused on minority nominees—for example, Richard Paez, a Hispanic-American, who had to wait four years before the Senate confirmed him for a seat on the Ninth Circuit. Together with Clinton's cautious approach to judicial selection—a Republican Senate gives him little choice but to send up "confirmable" nominations—these delays have helped prevent racial, gender or ideological balance on the appellate bench.

It's not likely that judicial selections by Bush the Younger, to be confirmed in a process dominated in the Senate by chairman of the Judiciary Committee Orrin Hatch and majority leader Trent Lott, will pick up where Carter left off. If Al Gore could send lower-court nominations to a more responsive Senate, however, the federal bench might begin to look more like America.

Again: Whom do you want to nominate Justices for the Supreme Court in the next four years?

The more conservative Court promised by Bush the Younger—who is running on a flatly antiabortion platform—would be a particular threat to a woman's right to choose. This last term the Rehnquist Court, re-examining the broad field of reproductive rights for the first time since 1992, reaffirmed *Roe v. Wade* in *Stenberg v. Carhart,* a challenge to Nebraska's "partial birth" abortion ban, but it did so by a scary 5-to-4 margin. And that decision does little to curb the many restrictions on abortion

rights passed by the states since *Roe* (with lots more still pending in the legislatures).

Also at risk is an important element of democratic choice—campaign finance reform. Ironically, that's at least partially because even the Rehnquist Court has not attacked First Amendment guarantees of freedom of speech. Last term the Court rejected, for example, Congressional efforts to ban casino advertising on television, and the year before it rebuffed Congress's attempt to ban "indecent speech" (whatever that is) from the Internet. When the Rehnquist Court unanimously struck down the effort of an Irish gay group to march in the St. Patrick's Day parade in Boston, it ruled not on moral grounds but on the Court's plausible theory that a parade is an expression of ideas, so that those staging it have a right *not* to express views with which they disagree.

Close Court-watchers nevertheless detect a division among the Justices that could have great impact on campaign finance reform. The perceived split is between Justices who would ban all interference, of any kind, with free speech and those who would permit occasional limitations on the expressions of extremely powerful and/or wealthy interests and people, in order to preserve a marketplace of ideas open to all, regardless of wealth and power. The former group supports the 1976 ruling in *Buckley v. Valeo* that made the crucial distinction between spending on speech aimed at influencing a specific election (funds that can be regulated) and spending for "issue advocacy" supposedly designed only to advance a more general cause (like "democracy" or voter registration). Funds for issue advocacy are considered by the present Court to be free speech; therefore they cannot be regulated—hence "soft money," which effectively bypasses other spending limits, dominates campaign financing today and is the favored target of fundraisers for both parties. If Court appointments in the future strengthen those who support *Buckley*-like views, campaign finance reform is probably a lost cause for years to come.

The distinction in First Amendment attitudes may also affect, eventually, what could be called "subsidized speech"—for instance, public television, professors in public universities and government-supported art institutions. The Rehnquist Court is divided as to what restrictions, if any, government can place on public funds devoted to such public purposes, a famous example being those Mayor Rudolph Giuliani attempted to impose on the city-subsidized Brooklyn Museum of Art.

Moreover, as US media—newspapers, television, motion pictures—consolidate under fewer and fewer owners, can the government intervene to prevent or ameliorate what some would consider dangerous monopolies that threaten free speech? Or would a future Court find such intervention a violation of the First Amendment?

Capital punishment is another pressing subject sure to come before a future Supreme Court. More than 3,600 people are now on death row (mostly sentenced in state courts), with plenty more to come under current standards and procedures. And already the Rehnquist Court has allowed the execution of mentally retarded children, acquiesced in inadequate legal representation, refused federal review of state cases because of minor procedural barriers and excused what the Court—but not necessarily defendants—called "harmless error" in the state courts.

Even in the rare cases in which the Court set aside a death penalty, there were always two familiar dissenters—Scalia&Thomas. What might the Court do with more Justices who would follow their lead? A new expansion of capital punishment would be particularly tragic at a time when public opinion may be swinging—marginally and slowly—to at least a questioning stance on its fairness and utility.

In the long run, the essentially procedural question—are innocent people being executed?—is likely to carry more weight than the moral and religious objections that so far have failed to move the public or the courts. But it's hard to conceive of a Court shaped by Bush the Younger that would outlaw executions on any grounds.

Even without the fresh infusion of conservative Justices that Bush promises, the Rehnquist Court has virtually eliminated federal habeas corpus review—at a time when state-ordered death penalties (and criminal sentences generally) are more than ever in need of such review. These days, a state judge who knows he or she could be voted off the bench at the next election, and who has an unhealthy respect for the right-wing organizations that exercise formidable power in some jurisdictions, might well hesitate in capital cases to rule in ways that might be criticized as "soft on crime." Yet criminal defendants, even those under death sentence, can no longer be sure of federal review by life-tenured judges who might correct injustices perpetrated by elected state judges.

For more on the Rehnquist Court and what could take place after the election, see the following articles. And don't forget to ask yourself, *Whom do you want to nominate Justices for the Supreme Court in the next four years?*

Tom Wicker was a reporter, Washington correspondent and political columnist for the New York Times *from 1960 until his retirement in 1991.*

Turkey Farm

*The government can't afford to keep ignoring the case
for reforming civil service tenure*

BY ROBERT MARANTO

JIM WORKED IN A DEFENSE DEPARTMENT office with an employee whose lack of productivity was matched only by his hostile attitude. Eventually, a good manager with the patience of Job, a mastery of detail to match, and the help of higher management took the time to record, day by day, the offender's record of non-work. After developing improvement plans for the employee and thoroughly documenting his failure to meet them for many months, the incompetent worker was actually fired. Then, the employee appealed before the Merit Systems Protection Board (MSPB). Two years into the appeal, when it looked as if the government would finally win, MSPB threw out the case when one of the team, moving to dismiss the employee, made an offhand remark that "even the people in his neighborhood association think he's unstable." The employee was reinstated with back pay. The agency went through the process all over again. By this time Jim had become boss. With the benefits of hindsight and existing records, the final try took only one more year of work!

Jim's predicament is faced by thousands of hardworking federal employees who must suffer a small number of lazy, incompetent, and, occasionally, dangerous coworkers. For the past three years, I taught high level federal managers at the Federal Executive Institute (FEI). Despite the stereotypes about bureaucrats, the vast majority of federal managers are capable people who take pride in their work. In dedication and smarts, the government bureaucrats I've worked with are more than a match for the college professors I taught alongside during 15 years in the academy. Unfortunately, these good people are thoroughly frustrated by a personnel system which forces them to work alongside (and get the same raises as) a small number of turkeys.

A Broken Personnel System

One of my games in the civil service was to ask a lunch table full of federal managers whether it was possible to fire low-performing employees. Save for the ever optimistic personnel specialists, the usual consensus was that it was

possible, but hardly ever worth the effort. My informal focus groups mirrored public employee surveys.

While career civil servants and political appointees do not always see eye to eye, mail surveys I conducted in the mid-1990s found that each side did agree that the federal personnel system is broken, at least when it comes to separating non-performers. Eighty-eight percent of Clinton political appointees and 83 percent of career managers agreed that "personnel rules make it too difficult to fire personnel"—more than half of each group strongly agreed. This dovetails with the findings of University of Georgia political scientist Hal Rainey. Reviewing years of survey data, Rainey reports that "[r]oughly 90 percent of the public managers agreed that their organization's personnel rules make it hard to fire poor managers and hard to reward good managers with higher pay, while 90 percent of the business managers disagreed."

Since courts have ruled that federal employees have property rights in their jobs, they can only be terminated after lengthy due process and multiple venues of appeal. As a result, managers who decide to use official means to deal with turkeys may face the prospect of spending all their time managing that one person, to the detriment of the rest of the office. As one of my informants, a manager in a regional office, recalled of his one (eventually successful) effort to separate an employee who was both unproductive and breaking the law: "As the year went on, it took more and more of my time and became all consuming. I had to spend a lot of time explaining why I was doing this." Similarly, when asked if he had ever fired a non-performer, one manager told me that he had no intention of becoming like the one person in his agency who had fired several people and "wears that as a badge of honor, but he has no time to do his real work!"

Not only is firing a government employee time-consuming for managers, it is also dangerous. Managers who move against problem employees take serious risks. As Carolyn Ban details in *How Do Public Managers Manage?*, low performers facing personnel actions need not go gentle into that good night. They can make life difficult for months or years. They can take their case to the Merit Systems Protection Board (MSPB). They can file a grievance if they are covered by a union contract. Or if they belong to a protected class (by sex, race, age, or handicap), they can file an Equal Employment Opportunity complaint. Some bring their cases to the Office of the Special Counsel, claiming that they are being fired or otherwise harassed because they are whistle-blowers.

The problem of "low performing whistle-blowers" is particularly vexing for many federal managers, who, on the word of a single employee, can be subjected to prolonged investigations worthy of an independent counsel. Imagine having colleagues and subordinates questioned for months about whether you have ever used the long-distance line for personal calls or have padded the expense account. While the investigations go on, little work gets done and communication between co-workers stops, since everyone is afraid that a random remark could lead to a grand jury. Even when the boss is exonerated, a bad reputation can linger for years. And of course, if all else fails, the employee can simply sue his or her manager.

Not surprisingly, managers who have fired someone describe the process as traumatic. As one of the officials quoted above recalls, "here it is years later, the person has long since left the state, and I still don't want to talk about that sorry episode. It has an impact upon both the office and the family life of the individuals involved. It's something you only do once."

With the deck stacked against them, federal managers tend to avoid using official means of dealing with their turkeys. Phone surveys of managers by the U.S. Office of Personnel Management (OPM), reported in *Poor Performers in Government: A Quest for the True Story*, found that only 7.5 percent of the managers of low performing employees moved to reassign, demote, or remove them, and 77.8 percent of those managers reported that the efforts had no effect. While OPM gives a rough estimate of around 65,000 poor performers in government, from September 1997 to September 1998, only 159 federal employees were removed by performance based personnel actions, with another 1,693 removed for issues other than performance, such as breaking the law. Federal managers suffer low performers or act informally to improve their work and never use the federal personnel system, or only use it as a last resort.

Not infrequently, federal managers use two traditional means of shedding non-performers. By writing glowing letters of recommendation, a boss can get a turkey promoted to a different office. Fortunately, most civil servants are too ethical to use such tactics, and anyway, you can only do that once or twice before your credibility in the bureaucracy is shot. More typically, bosses place non-performers in "turkey farms," "dead pools," or (if it is a single person) "on the shelf." By quarantining non-performers, a good manager can save the rest of the organization from their influence.

The relative inability to act against a small number of poor performers has the effect of making that small number vexing to managers, who are people more used to solving problems than ignoring them. Managers don't like using turkey farms, but many feel they have no choice. At least, when downsizing comes, known turkeys make good candidates for reductions-in-force.

The Costs of Tenure

The sad part is that the vast majority of federal personnel do a good job. OPM's *Poor Performers in Government* report estimates that under 4 percent of federal civil servants are non-performers. One can quibble with OPM's methodology. I suspect that the real figure is a bit higher, but still, the poor performer problem is not nearly as bad as most Americans think. So why deal with it at all?

Aside from inefficiency, there are four huge costs of the federal government's inability to kick turkeys off the farm. First, non-performers themselves never get the message that they have to shape up or ship out and never get the chance for a new start. Instead, they often use the system to pursue old grudges for years. Second, good employees like Jim are forced to work alongside, do the work of, and often get the same raises as a small number of turkeys—a real morale killer.

Third, the low performance problem undermines the image and self-image of the bureaucracy. Business people have no tenure and look down on their government cousins who do. Military officers have an "up or out" promotion system—at key points in their careers officers either get promoted or get discharged. This makes the officer corps, at least at higher levels, a turkey-free zone, giving the brass a certain swagger in their dealings with their protected cousins in the civil service.

Most important, a tenured civil service undermines the legitimacy of the bureaucracy in the eyes of the public. After all, very few voters have tenure, so it is hard to tell citizens why their public servants cannot be fired. It is not surprising that college professors, public school teachers, and government bureaucrats have all come under attack in recent years. The very existence of tenure protects a small number of losers and leads the public to suspect the existence of a large number of low performers in government—a suspicion shared by many public managers.

Originally, the federal merit system was set up in 1884 to keep political parties from using government jobs to reward supporters. Patronage was seen as particularly onerous after President Garfield was assassinated by an insane "disappointed office seeker." Presumably, government would work better if run by technical experts than by political hacks. But on the federal level, at least, the spoils system got a bum rap. Even in the 19th century, a new president and Congress kept most of the incumbent civil servants in place, and only rarely replaced those with special expertise. Politicians have never relished the unpopular task of firing old employees to replace them with political supporters. As politicians have long lamented, each new political appointment provides 10 enemies who themselves wanted the job and one ingrate who got it. Besides, for perfectly sound electoral reasons, politicians cared (and still care) about the efficient management of government. As political scientist Michael Nelson has pointed out, even in the 19th century, more voters sent mail than delivered it. A party that replaces all the mail carriers disrupts service—not a good way to win re-election.

The temptation to "politicize" a bureaucracy in search of pork is even less apparent today. In the old days, political campaigns were won by precinct workers who might welcome a federal job. Today, politicians depend on big kickbacks from campaign contributors rather than small ones from government employees. More important, the greater size and expertise of modern government makes it less susceptible to political takeovers. In the old days, it may have made some sense for politicians to hire friends to deliver the mail, but imagine if a modern president hired precinct workers to run the Pentagon and NIH? To think that politicians would raid the civil service, you have to assume that they have an incredible capacity for both venality and stupidity, and the time to exercise both. In fact, modern presidents can hardly handle the 3,000 political appointments they have now. How could they place more? Sure, presidential political appointments have grown in number since 1960, but not nearly enough to match the growth in congressional staffs, interest groups, and reporters—the people appointees deal with on behalf of their agencies. Unless we downsize the rest of the Washington political class—something not likely to happen—we can't downsize political appointments.

Because of constant scrutiny by opponents, politicians in Washington do not have the sort of vast appointment powers they might have in some states and cities. Presidents are in fact very constrained in who they can appoint to government jobs and how many appointments they can make. The Washington Post test ("How will it look in The Post?") limits what they can do. Congressional scrutiny limits what they can do. Inter- and intraparty battles limit what they can do. Not surprisingly, the worst abuses under spoils were in states and localities with little political competition, not in a two-party, hyperpluralist Washington.

Rebuilding Public Service

To its credit, the Clinton administration has at least acknowledged the non-performer problem, and has begun to act on it. In accord with the Poor Performer study, OPM issued a CD-ROM guide to help managers, Addressing and Resolving Poor Performance. This is more than previous administrations dared try, but probably too little, too late. Not surprisingly, as the longtime guardian of the merit system, OPM's basic inclination is to save a system that should probably be buried. Real change in the merit system requires legislation to simplify procedures, followed by years of culture change inside gov-

ernment, along the lines of the National Performance Review's reforms of government procurement. The White House considered introducing a bill to overhaul the civil service earlier this year but dropped it in deference to public employee unions, an important constituency in the 2000 presidential primaries.

Real change is occurring on an ad hoc basis, however, in the agencies. Currently, the Federal Aviation Administration and Internal Revenue Service are creating their own alternatives to the traditional merit system. The Pentagon and Department of Housing and Urban Development have floated trial balloons proposing to replace most tenured civil servants with contractors and fixed-term employees who can be separated with relative ease—something that is happening incrementally all over government. Further, the rise of Performance Based Organizations, called for by Vice President Gore's Reinventing Government reports, is likely to erode tenure by tying organization budgets and staffing levels to results. Indeed, on all levels of government, the reinventing movement is in part a way to use market mechanisms to get around civil service tenure. Declining demands for an organization's outputs force reductions in force, which in turn push marginal performers out the door.

Many of the most exciting changes are happening in the states. More than 30 states now have serious proposals to reform their civil service systems, but Georgia has gone the farthest. In 1996 Georgia removed tenure from new employees in state agencies. A detailed evaluation of the Georgia experiment does not yet exist, but early work by political scientist Steve Condrey suggests that removing tenure has increased the ability of public managers to manage for accountability. A single Georgia state agency reported terminating nearly 200 employees for cause in the first 20 months after the law came into effect—with no reported challenges or cases of impropriety. Notably, the Georgia civil service reform was developed and pushed through the legislature not by anti-government Republicans but by then Governor Zell Miller, a pro-government New Democrat who sees ending tenure as one way to restore the legitimacy of government.

In short, for the first time in decades, real civil service reform is beginning to happen. For historic context, it took 20 years from 1864 to 1883 to build political support for the original federal merit system, and another 40 years to put it in place. It may take another decade to reform the federal merit system, but tenure now lacks public legitimacy, and the first steps at reform have already been taken. This excites those of us who want to turn "civil service" from an epithet for cumbersome personnel rules into a public service ethic.

ROBERT MARANTO is a visiting scholar at the Curry School of Education at the University of Virginia and co-editor most recently of School Choice in the Real World: Lessons from Arizona Charter Schools.

Finding The Civil Service's Hidden Sex Appeal

Why the brightest young people shy away from government

By Nicholas Thompson

THE COVER OF A BROCHURE GIVEN OUT BY the federal Office of Personnel Management shows a young man in sunglasses crouching like a surfer and holding a model spaceship labeled "United States." The brochure bellows "Look Ma! I'm a Bureaucrat!" in a funky yellow font and notes that the cover model, Dan Ridge, is the 24-year-old program director of the computer crime division at NASA. He "wears jeans to the office" and "uses supercomputing technology to protect NASA's worldwide computer system." The brochure goes on to profile more hip young people working in the public sector, including the new, fast-paced, reinvented government. The message: If you're young, ambitious, and looking to make a difference helping other people and the country, you too can be like Dan Ridge!

But if you call NASA to ask Ridge about his wonderful government job, you'll have some trouble finding him. Turns out he left town not long after posing for the brochure. Now he develops supercomputing technology called Beowulf clusters for Scyld, a startup company in Maryland. He didn't leave because he wanted more money—he's earning about the same amount now—or because he didn't like his job. He left because there just wasn't anywhere to move up to without sticking around for another 10 years. "My work was fantastic. I loved it.

But it was clear that there was no further path for advancement."

Ridge's complaint is all too familiar. Despite the Office of Personnel Management's (OPM's) efforts, time still seems to move more slowly inside the federal government than outside: It takes longer to get hired, it's nearly impossible to get fired, and the promotional fast track moves like molasses compared to the private sector. Although that has been true for at least a century, the problem is getting worse. The private sector has vastly improved at scooping up talented young people, the call to service rings less loudly for young people today, and the civil service seems specifically designed to repel anyone born after about 1970.

The government's recruitment shortcomings threaten to become a national crisis. The flood of people who entered the federal government in the '60s and '70s is getting ready to start collecting social security, and there's a thin bench ready either to replace them or to move up the ranks. Sixty-five percent of the Senior Executive Service, the government's most elite managers, will be eligible to retire by 2004, and only about five percent of the civil service is under 30. That doesn't mean they will all leave, but according to a recent National Academy of Public Administration report, "the flow of high-quality new hires in federal departments and agencies has decreased dramatically while the average age of workers has risen."

It's not time to flee to Canada, but civil-service reform should be an urgent priority for the next administration. The government needs talented new recruits for the sake of people who drink tap water, drive the highways, or buy securities; and the potential consequences of the looming exodus are unnerving. Clinton and Gore should be applauded for making government reinvention a priority, but they didn't shake up the rules in a way that would significantly attract young people. They improved procurement, and they made the government smaller; but they didn't scour the agencies to determine where people are plotting innovative policy solutions, and where they are simply plotting their next conference trips to Maui.

That's a shame because what's going to pull bright young people in won't be a shrunken bureaucracy, or even higher salaries, but a civil service where they can find exciting and useful jobs with real responsibility and high ceilings—just what Dan Ridge wanted.

Kids Today

According to a recent study by Paul Light of the Brookings Institution, the percentage of students from top graduate schools of public policy and management—the folks most likely to be interested in government careers—who go on to work for government has dropped from 76 percent in 1974 to 55 percent in 1988 to 49 percent today, with state, local, and federal government all losing their appeal. The percentage of master's graduates from Syracuse's Maxwell School and Harvard's Kennedy School of Government who actually pursue the careers their schools were designed for has plunged by 50 percent over two decades.

From the inside, the numbers look equally grim. The percentage of Presidential Management Interns who stay in government, the young people on the fastest possible track into the civil service, is stuck at 50 percent; the number of applications to the White House Fellows program has sunk. According to the National Association for Law Placement, the percentage of law school graduates going into the government has declined slowly but steadily for 25 years, from about 20 percent to 13 percent in 1998. If government were a stock, everybody would be selling it short.

These trends in government service partly reflect the generational shift in attitudes toward government itself. Young people don't much trust government, and they don't vote in high numbers. According to a 30-year study of freshman attitudes by Alexander Astin at UCLA, the percentage of students who say that they "want to keep up to date with political affairs" has skidded from above 50 percent in the late '60s and early '70s to below 30 percent today.

But this withdrawal doesn't come, as many critics of Generation X argue, simply because recent graduates are too busy dreaming about hundred-dollar bills, thousand-dollar suits, and million-dollar homes. In Astin's study, for example, the percentage of students who consider it critical, to be "very well off financially" has famously risen from just under 40 percent in 1970 to 74 percent today. But the percentage was even higher in 1986. Plus, there are some trends moving in the direction of civic engagement: The number of young people who perform some sort of volunteer work is at an all-time high and, according to Light's study of graduates from public management schools, only 17 percent said that salary was a very important consideration for their first job. Eighty percent cited the opportunity to do challenging work.

The real reason young people have withdrawn from government is that government has developed a reputation as a place where the wheels spin endlessly and great ideas are filed away into a bottomless heap of paper. According to Greg Wright, a young Stanford honors graduate who wants to work for the government eventually, but went from college to a consulting group and a dot-com instead of joining a dot-gov: "I want to make as big a splash as I can. Government keeps you in the kiddy pool unless you know someone, have a lot of money, or you have been working in the basement for 20 years."

Executive Insufficiency

Wright's attitude shouldn't be surprising considering that the men who have dominated the federal government for the past 25 years have all treated it with something between lukewarm praise and outward hostility. Ronald Reagan set the tone in his inaugural address—"Government is not the solution to our problem. It is the problem!"—and then placed a team of anti-bureaucrats at OPM. Led by Donald Devine, OPM seemed to strangle recruitment efforts, terminating, for example, all promotional material for VISTA, the Great Society program that sent young people into poor areas to teach and work. One OPM official, Terry Cutler, wrote in *The Wall Street Journal* in 1986, "Government's goal should not be employee excellence but employee sufficiency."

Reagan's rhetoric wasn't an anomaly. Every president since Jimmy Carter has come to office by swinging at the bureaucratic bugbear. Clinton's most famous line is "The era of big government is over," and Gore began his report on reinventing government with this zinger: "The federal government is not simply broke; it is broken." Gore's criticism was in the context of useful suggestions for change, but neither that, nor his repeated boasts about how much the government has shrunk in the past eight years, are quite as good an invitation to service as "Ask not what your country can do for you. Ask what you can do for your country."

The recruitment problems aren't simply a failure of rhetoric from the top; they're also a failure of execution in the middle. When Wright was a college senior, the consulting group he eventually joined socked his campus newspaper full of ads every day, interviewed him twice, and then flew him to L.A. for a dream weekend complete with a Mustang convertible. Government recruitment was nowhere to be seen, and if Greg had called its toll-free job line he would have been met by an awkward robotic voice blurting out an endless stream of nearly incomprehensible job numbers. If he had called the Smithsonian Institution, for example, he would have been encouraged to listen to a tutorial on the endless codes, terms, and processes necessary to apply, including "the definition of important technical terms you will need to understand to become a competitive applicant."

To be sure, Al Gore's reinvented government has begun to clean these problems up, and job postings are now available through an extensive Web site. But even these efforts have fallen short—in no small part because the federal personnel workforce, the people in charge of recruitment, has declined by 20 percent from 1991 to 1998.

The Civil Service

Although you wouldn't know it from the toll-free job-hunt line, government can still be a great place to work. And this is where federal public relations efforts really fall short. Rarely do you hear, for instance, that the percentage of federal employees reporting that they are satisfied with their jobs is higher than the comparable number in the private sector, according to a 1999 Reinventing Government survey. For example, Jason Goldwater, a 30-year-old employee of the Health Care Financing Administration (HCFA), has spent the last two years at the Centers for Disease Control and Prevention (CDC) and HCFA designing a common data set of Medicaid users—data that will vastly improve our ability to track the incidence of health problems like asthma. He loves his job both because it's exciting and because, "when I go home, I want to think about what I've done, not just a paycheck." Martin Yeung, 25, left investment banking to join the Office of Management and Budget (OMB) and now works there as assistant to the deputy director of management. That may sound boring, but Yeung has got a great job and he loves his work. The OMB controls how legislation across the government is implemented—from airline safety regulation to federally financed student loans—and sits consistently in the middle of conflicts between agencies, the White House, and Congress. According to Yeung, "It's as fast as 'The West Wing'; it's bare knuckles; it's Olympic wrestling. The only way to outmaneuver opponents is to be on top of everything."

But there aren't enough great jobs like Yeung's and Goldwater's and, unfortunately, far too many young people get stuck in boring ones and leave before they can find real job satisfaction. Out of college, I entered a fellowship program with about 40 other graduates interested in public service careers. We all got jobs with the federal government and lived together in Washington. None of us stayed more than two years. The only two people continuing the work they started with were the only two who didn't join the civil service but instead went to work for Congress.

Government simply deserves part of its bad reputation. The federal civil service remains locked in a structure built in the early 1880s after a disaffected job seeker assassinated James Garfield because so many jobs had been doled out through the patronage system. The solution then was to essentially put the civil service in a lock box. Federal employees are guaranteed stability and consistent, slow promotions—from GS-13 to GS-14 after two years and so on. They can't get fired except through a torturous review process.

This means that the main way to open up jobs is to create new ones, instead of clearing out old ones. And, in the anti-bureaucratic fervor of the past 20 years, that has been nearly impossible. According to Fred Smith, a deputy assistant secretary of defense who has spent his whole career working for the country: "It is extremely difficult, if not impossible, to hire anyone from the outside. We've had maybe four young people come in this year, and all were from the Presidential Management Internship program." Smith has only been able to fire one person in 22 years, and what happened then is instructive. "I tried for three years but two weeks before the process worked through, he chose early retirement and took a $25,000 bonus," said Smith.

In addition, the rules of the civil service don't just block job openings; they also create a bureaucratic mentality that encourages survival over innovation. Agency funding gets renewed every year, even if the work has become obsolete, as long as it can stay below Congress' radar. Salary and rank are based on the number of people supervised, not on the amount of work accomplished. Lastly, once you've left government it's very hard to come back in, a policy that prevents conflicts of interest but also blocks out innovative employees who wanted to step out for a few years and learn about another business culture. In the 1999 government survey of federal employees, only 33 percent said that creativity and innovation were rewarded by the government.

This system limits political meddling and provides safe harbor for saintly civil servants who have been quietly serving for years, but it also makes the civil service singularly unappealing to this generation of young people. In part because of the booming economy and the tremendous opportunities for growth in information technology, this has become the "free agent generation." As Aparna Mohan, a Presidential Management Intern working at the Agency for International Development, says, "Our goal is to have the career be the sum of all the jobs we've had—not to just get one job and make it a whole career."

In short, the advantages of government employment—long-term stability and structure—are the last things that young people seem to care about. The average member of the elite Senior Executive Service, for example, has been working in government for 23 years, more than a lifetime for today's graduates; the average 32-year-old has already worked for nine different companies and is looking around to bounce to a few more. Government just doesn't seem to offer the new thing. As Phil Keisling, the former secretary of state of Oregon and now a vice president at PROdx, a Portland internet consulting firm, puts it, "The rate of change curve is just steeper in the private sector relative to government and the gap is widening."

Uncle Sam Needs You

The government's talent shortage should worry us all. Government employees research asthma at the CDC; they keep planes from crashing at the FAA; and they're the ones who decide when it's safe to set off Forest Service-controlled burns near your house.

Moreover, without top young talent, government is no match for the private sector it is supposed to regulate. Corporations that don't want to pay taxes hire lawyers who compete with the IRS. Mining companies that don't want to pay royalties hire smart lawyers who work wonders with federal law The government is now entering a critical high-stakes battle with the private sector to see who controls the patents to our DNA. Does anyone really want first-rate people on the corporate side and second-rate people on the public's side?

In addition, a great deal of government work is now contracted out—from the administration of welfare programs to the management of private prisons. But contracting work out doesn't preclude the need for smart people in government: You still need smart people to make sure that the public isn't sold a bill of goods. Many of the security problems at the Los Alamos nuclear laboratory in New Mexico, for example, weren't just caused by the Department of Energy, but rather by lax oversight from the University of California at Berkeley, the main contractor running the lab.

This isn't to say that there's something bad about working for corporate America and the private sector. We're lucky that Henry Ford didn't work for the Department of Commerce, just as as we're lucky that executives like IBM's Lou Gerstner and private inventors like Linus Torvalds are improving the ways that America runs. The growth of our private businesses is a primary reason for the current economic boom and its bounties.

The problem is one of balance. A society in which every ambitious environmentalist goes to work for the EPA or a nonprofit would fall apart because there would

be no one to help develop non-polluting effluent systems or to argue internally for the limitation of greenhouse gas emissions. A society in which every ambitious environmentalist goes to work for McKinsey and GE would fall apart because there would be no one to write the regulations and to test pollution levels. Unfortunately, we seem to be shifting to the latter.

Give Youth A Chance

The obvious solution to attracting better people to government is to pay them more. Money does help bring people into government, particularly if targeted to those who need it most, like OPM Director Janice Lachance's recent initiative to allow agencies to pay back student loans as part of the government's often-invoked program to provide relocation, retention, and recruitment bonuses. But even that seems unlikely to reverse current trends. Government will never be able to pay as much as the private sector, no matter how much it tinkers on the margins of federal salary structures. To improve recruitment it needs to rely on its prime advantage: the ability to allow young people to serve others with useful work. According to Lily Batchelder, a 28-year-old law school student who has worked both for a consulting group and the Justice Department: "The problems you try to solve working in government are complex and fascinating. Working in a place where you are focused on profit is like going to a good action movie. It can be fun, but it doesn't hit your soul."

Whether you work in the State Department or the Federal Emergency Management Agency, you have the clear chance to make other people's lives better. This is a powerful incentive, and it's the prime reason that government still attracts as much talent as it does. But the potential to do good doesn't mean much if you can't actually do anything. An idealist who joins an organization only to find her work stifled by rules, regulations, and a boss who comes in at noon, won't stay an idealist for long. If Lily Batchelder finds herself in an agency that's spinning its wheels, she won't stay a government employee for long.

What government needs to do is to improve the ratio of useful to useless work that new employees can do. Fortunately, there are examples right in government—like the White House, the one place in Washington where young people always seem to want to work. In fact, the draw is such that more than 10 million people watch the television program "The West Wing" weekly. They don't watch because they can see the Forest Service and the Bureau of Land Management cross wires. They watch because they can see young people who struggle with moral dilemmas, move quickly, and make everything from the Census to potential war, seem interesting.

In the Clinton White House, similarly, no rules lock employees into place or scuttle promotions, and the days move as quickly as in any dot-com. George Stephanopolous, Rahm Emanuel, and Gene Sperling rose to the top of the hierarchy on plain merit, not because they spent 16 years in the basement of the Interior Department. According to 25-year-old-speechwriter Joshua Gottheimer, who joined the White House after college and a brief stint scooping ice cream at Ben and Jerry's: "There's no defined hierarchy based on age. If you are willing to work hard and put in the hours, you can do almost anything."

In part, the advantage the White House has is that the stakes are higher. It's often only when the work becomes less important that strict hierarchies cement themselves into place. The greatest opportunities for young people in the government came during the New Deal and New Frontier, when they were needed to push forward ambitious and innovative new programs. Even during the arms race, young people were frequently promoted into positions of power. According to James Woolsey, who joined the SALT I negotiating team at age 27 and was counsel to the Senate Armed Services Committee before he turned 30: "Any time there is something brand new like arms control, there are opportunities for young people. The bureaucracy isn't entrenched yet."

The Department of Justice has similar success by placing few limits on the kind of work you can do when you come to it. At the U.S. Attorney's office in Washington, D.C., for example, everyone enters a four-year program that throws them into the middle of important and exciting cases. On Capitol Hill the story is the same. Staffers join their representatives knowing that they can't prepare for 30 years in government because their boss might be booted out in two. If a staff becomes stultified, it's likely their boss would soon be looking for new work.

In the rest of the federal government, the story's different. You can't come and go; you can't move around much; and frequently the good works that you planned to do bear no fruit. But there is hope. Even the Minerals

"The OMB is as fast as 'The West Wing'; it's bare knuckles; it's Olympic wrestling."

Management Service can draw bright people in if reformed the right way. Consider Stephen Warren, the senior budget analyst of the chief financial officer of the District of Columbia, a city job that overlaps with the federal government which has final say over the city's budget. In a sense, Warren's job is just about looking over spreadsheets and developing revenue-collection models. But to Warren, a 28-year-old who worked for Marriott after graduating from Hampton University, it's an opportunity to improve the lives of the people around him. His proudest moment was when a revenue collection model he'd pored over for six months was approved by Congress, sending millions of dollars to the District. "You do a day's work. You can see something happening. You know, it makes you feel good," says Warren.

Warren didn't go into government thinking that he would be locked into a 30-year career with steady promotions and a group of deadwood co-workers. His boss when he started, Tony Williams, now Washington's mayor, "doesn't say that this is the last job you are going to have. He said that he wants this place to be a platform for young people to start their careers and do something good. If you choose to stay, you choose to stay."

Warren has been there for a bit more than four years and he plans to stay a little longer because he's learning, he's using his skills to serve people, and he's doing something important and useful without being stifled by bureaucracy. And, he adds, "when you come right out of school, you're not quite ready to turn your brain off."

Unit 3

Unit Selections

Key Points to Consider

❖ How "democratic" is the American political system compared with others?

❖ Do the Republican and Democratic Parties offer the American people alternatives that amount to a meaningful choice? Explain.

❖ How do the political views of young people compare and contrast with those of their parents?

❖ If you were running for political office, would you use public opinion polls? Focus groups? Talk radio? If so, how?

❖ Do American citizens have satisfactory ways of getting information about their government that do not involve news media?

❖ What effects do you think running for and holding political office have on the individuals involved?

❖ Do you think that our current procedures for choosing the president are good ones? In light of the Florida controversy in the 2000 presidential election, do you think that electoral reforms are necessary? Explain your answer.

 **Links**

www.dushkin.com/online/

These sites are annotated on pages 4 and 5.

According to many political scientists, what distinguishes *more* democratic political systems from *less* democratic ones is the degree of control that citizens exercise over government. This unit focuses on the institutions, groups, and processes that are supposed to serve as links between Americans and their government.

Political parties, elections, pressure groups, and news media are all thought to play important roles in communications between people and government in the American political system.

Changes that are occurring today in some of these areas may affect American politics for decades to come, and these changes are the focus of many of the readings in this section.

The first and second sections focus on politicians, parties, money, and elections. Violence and controversy relating to the 1968 Democratic nominating convention led to a series of changes in the procedures that both parties use to select their presidential candidates. And one of the legacies of the Watergate scandal of the early 1970s was the passage of new laws to regulate campaign financing, which was followed by extensive debate about the impact of those reforms.

In the 1980s, candidates increasingly used focus groups, political consultants, and public opinion polling to shape expensive advertising campaigns, and many observers thought that negative television advertisements played a particularly prominent role in the 1988 presidential campaign. In 1992 more changes in campaign tactics and techniques appeared, including numerous appearances by presidential candidates on television talk shows and a half dozen or so 30-minute paid "infomercials" by third party candidate Ross Perot. In the 1994 congressional elections, Republicans were generally successful in "nationalizing" the competition for 435 House and 30-odd Senate seats, apparently belying the adage that "all politics is local" and winning control of both houses of Congress for the first time since 1954. In 1996, apparently unprecedented amounts of "soft" money from questionable sources fueled President Clinton's reelection campaign, and campaign finance practices became the target of more and more criticism. The 2000 presidential election, of course, will long be remembered for the unprecedented five-week controversy over which candidate had won Florida and, in turn, a majority of votes in the Electoral College. All these events and more underlie the selections in the section.

The third section treats the roles of interest groups in the American political process and their impact on what government can and cannot do. While "gridlock" is a term usually applied to inaction resulting from "divided government" in which neither major party controls the presidency and both houses of Congress, it seems that "gridlock"—and perhaps favoritism in policy-making—also results from the interaction of interest groups and various government policymakers. The weakness of parties in the United States, compared to parties in other western democracies, is almost certainly responsible for the great strength of interest groups in the American political system. In turn, one can wonder whether a possible new era of stronger, more disciplined parties in government will contribute to the weakening of interest groups.

The fourth section addresses news and other media, which probably play a more important role in the American political system than their counterparts do in any political system in the world. Television news broadcasts and newspapers are not merely passive transmitters of information. They inevitably shape—or distort—what they report to their audiences. They also greatly affect the behavior of people and organizations in politics. As already noted, in recent years, especially during the 1992 and 1996 presidential campaigns, less traditional media forums have begun to play bigger roles in politics. Radio and television talk shows and 30-minute "infomercials" have entered the political landscape with considerable effect. Selections in the fourth section provide coverage of how media can shape or distort political communication and the behavior of political actors.

The fifth and last section in this unit treats the 2000 elections. The presidential nominating process, campaign finance, and, of course, the controversy about the presidential election results in Florida are all addressed.

Process of American Politics

RUNNING SCARED

by ANTHONY KING

Painfully often the legislation our politicians pass is designed less to solve problems than to protect the politicians from defeat in our never-ending election campaigns. They are, in short, too frightened of us to govern

To an extent that astonishes a foreigner, modern America is *about* the holding of elections. Americans do not merely have elections on the first Tuesday after the first Monday of November in every year divisible by four. They have elections on the first Tuesday after the first Monday of November in every year divisible by two. In addition, five states have elections in odd-numbered years. Indeed, there is no year in the United States— ever—when a major statewide election is not being held somewhere. To this catalogue of general elections has of course to be added an equally long catalogue of primary elections (for example, forty-three presidential primaries last year). Moreover, not only do elections occur very frequently in the United States but the number of jobs legally required to be filled by them is enormous—from the presidency of the United States to the post of local consumer advocate in New York. It has been estimated that no fewer than half a million elective offices are filled or waiting to be filled in the United States today.

Americans take the existence of their never-ending election campaign for granted. Some like it, some dislike it, and most are simply bored by it. But they are all conscious of it, in the same way that they are conscious of Mobil, McDonald's, *Larry King Live,* Oprah Winfrey, the Dallas Cowboys, the Ford Motor Company, and all other symbols and institutions that make up the rich tapestry of American life.

To a visitor to America's shores, however, the never-ending campaign presents a largely unfamiliar spectacle. In other countries election campaigns have both beginnings and ends, and there are even periods, often prolonged periods, when no campaigns take place at all. Other features of American elections are also unfamiliar. In few countries do elections and campaigns cost as much as they do in the United States. In no other country is the role of organized political parties so limited.

America's permanent election campaign, together with other aspects of American electoral politics, has one crucial consequence, little noticed but vitally important for the functioning of American democracy. Quite simply, the American electoral system places politicians in a highly vulnerable position. Individually and collectively they are more vulnerable, more of the time, to the vicissitudes of electoral politics than are the politicians of any other democratic country. Because they are more vulnerable, they devote more of their time to electioneering, and their conduct in office is more continuously governed by electoral considerations. I will argue that American politicians' constant and unremitting electoral preoccupations have deleterious consequences for the functioning of the American system. They consume time and scarce resources. Worse, they make it harder than it would otherwise be for the system as a whole to deal with some of America's most pressing problems. Americans often complain that their system is not sufficiently democratic. I will argue that, on the contrary, there is a sense in which the system is too democratic and ought to be made less so.

Although this article is written by a foreigner, a Canadian citizen who happens to live in Great Britain, it is not written

From *The Atlantic Monthly,* January 1997, pp. 41-44, 46-48, 52-54, 56-58, 60-61. Adapted from *Running Scared: Why America's Politicians Campaign Too Much and Govern Too Little* by Anthony King. © 1997 by Free Press. Reprinted by permission of Simon & Schuster.

in any spirit of moral or intellectual superiority. Americans over the years have had quite enough of Brits and others telling them how to run their affairs. I have no wish to prolong their irritation. What follows is the reflections of a candid friend.

FEAR AND TREMBLING

POLITICS and government in the United States are marked by the fact that U.S. elected officials in many cases have very short terms of office *and* face the prospect of being defeated in primary elections *and* have to run for office more as individuals than as standard-bearers for their party *and* have continually to raise large sums of money in order to finance their own election campaigns. Some of these factors operate in other countries. There is no other country, however, in which all of them operate, and operate simultaneously. The cumulative consequences, as we shall see, are both pervasive and profound.

The U.S. Constitution sets out in one of its very first sentences that "the House of Representatives shall be composed of members chosen every second year by the people of the several states." When the Founding Fathers decided on such a short term of office for House members, they were setting a precedent that has been followed by no other major democratic

INDIVIDUALLY AND COLLECTIVELY AMERICAN POLITICIANS ARE MORE VULNERABLE, MORE OF THE TIME, TO THE VICISSITUDES OF ELECTORAL POLITICS THAN ARE THE POLITICIANS OF ANY OTHER DEMOCRATIC COUNTRY.

country. In Great Britain, France, Italy, and Canada the constitutional or legal maximum for the duration of the lower house of the national legislature is five years. In Germany and Japan the equivalent term is four years. Only in Australia and New Zealand, whose institutions are in some limited respects modeled on those of the United States, are the legal maximums as short as three years. In having two- year terms the United States stands alone.

Members of the Senate are, of course, in a quite different position. Their constitutionally prescribed term of office, six years, is long by anyone's standards. But senators' six-year terms are not all they seem. In the first place, so pervasive is the electioneering atmosphere that even newly elected senators begin almost at once to lay plans for their re-election campaigns. Senator Daniel Patrick Moynihan, of New York, recalls

that when he first came to the Senate, in 1977, his colleagues when they met over lunch or a drink usually talked about politics and policy. Now they talk about almost nothing but the latest opinion polls. In the second place, the fact that under the Constitution the terms of a third of the Senate end every two years means that even if individual senators do not feel themselves to be under continuing electoral pressure, the Senate as a whole does. Despite the Founders' intentions, the Senate's collective electoral sensibilities increasingly resemble those of the House.

Most Americans seem unaware of the fact, but the direct primary—a government-organized popular election to nominate candidates for public office—is, for better or worse, an institution peculiar to the United States. Neither primary elections nor their functional equivalents exist anywhere else in the democratic world. It goes without saying that their effect is to add a further dimension of uncertainty and unpredictability to the world of American elective politicians.

In most other countries the individual holder of public office, so long as he or she is reasonably conscientious and does not gratuitously offend local or regional party opinion, has no real need to worry about renomination. To be sure, cases of parties refusing to renominate incumbent legislators are not unknown in countries such as France, Germany, and Canada, but they are relatively rare and tend to occur under unusual circumstances. The victims are for the most part old, idle, or alcoholic.

The contrast between the rest of the world and the United States could hardly be more striking. In 1978 no fewer than 104 of the 382 incumbent members of the House of Representatives who sought re-election faced primary opposition. In the following three elections the figures were ninety-three out of 398 (1980), ninety-eight out of 393 (1982), and 130 out of 409 (1984). More recently, in 1994, nearly a third of all House incumbents seeking re-election, 121 out of 386, had to face primary opposition, and in the Senate the proportion was even higher: eleven out of twenty-six. Even those incumbents who did not face opposition could seldom be certain in advance that they were not going to. The influence—and the possibility—of primaries is pervasive. As we shall see, the fact that incumbents usually win is neither here nor there.

To frequent elections and primary elections must be added another factor that contributes powerfully to increasing the electoral vulnerability of U.S. politicians: the relative lack of what we might call "party cover." In most democratic countries the fate of most politicians depends not primarily on their own endeavors but on the fate—locally, regionally, or nationally—of their party. If their party does well in an election, so do they. If not, not. The individual politician's interests and those of his party are bound together.

In contrast, America's elective politicians are on their own—not only in relation to politicians in most other countries but also in absolute terms. Party is still a factor in U.S. electoral politics, but it is less so than anywhere else in the democratic world. As a result, American legislators seeking re-election are forced to raise their own profiles, to make their own records, and to fight their own re-election campaigns.

If politicians are so vulnerable electorally, it may be protested, why aren't more of them defeated? In particular, why aren't more incumbent congressmen and senators defeated? The analysis here would seem to imply a very high rate of turnover in Congress, but in fact the rate—at least among incumbents seeking re-election—is notoriously low. How can this argument and the facts of congressional incumbents' electoral success be reconciled?

This objection has to be taken seriously, because the facts on which it is based are substantially correct. The number of incumbent congressmen and senators defeated in either primary or general elections *is* low. But to say that because incumbent members of Congress are seldom defeated, they are not really vulnerable electorally is to miss two crucial points. The first is that precisely because they are vulnerable, they go to prodigious lengths to protect themselves. Like workers in nuclear-power stations, they take the most extreme safety precautions, and the fact that the precautions are almost entirely successful does not make them any less necessary.

Second, congressmen and senators go to inordinate lengths to secure re-election because, although they may objectively be safe (in the view of journalists and academic political scientists), they do not know they are safe—and even if they think they are, the price of being wrong is enormous. The probability that anything will go seriously wrong with a nuclear-power station may approach zero, but the stations tend nevertheless to be built away from the centers of large cities. A congressman or a senator may believe that he is reasonably safe, but if he wants to be re- elected, he would be a fool to act on that belief.

HOW THEY CAME TO BE VULNERABLE

AMERICAN politicians run scared—and are right to do so. And they run more scared than the politicians of any other democratic country—again rightly. How did this come to be so?

The short answer is that the American people like it that way. They are, and have been for a very long time, the Western world's hyperdemocrats. They are keener on democracy than almost anyone else and are more determined that democratic norms and practices should pervade every aspect of national life. To explore the implications of this central fact about the United States, and to see how it came to be, we need to examine two different interpretations of the term "democracy." Both have been discussed from time to time by political philosophers, but they have never been codified and they certainly cannot be found written down in a constitution or any other formal statement of political principles. Nevertheless, one or the other underpins the political practice of every democratic country—even if, inevitably, the abstract conception and the day-to-day practice are never perfectly matched.

One of these interpretations might be labeled "division of labor." In this view, there are in any democracy two classes of people—the governors and the governed. The function of the governors is to take decisions on the basis of what they believe to be in the country's best interests and to act on those decisions. If public opinion broadly supports the decisions, that is a welcome bonus. If not, too bad. The views of the people at large are merely one datum among a large number of data that need to be considered. They are not accorded any special status. Politicians in countries that operate within this view can frequently be heard using phrases like "the need for strong leadership" and "the need to take tough decisions." They often take a certain pride in doing what they believe to be right even if the opinion of the majority is opposed to it.

The function of the governed in such a system, if it is a genuine democracy, is very important but strictly limited. It is not to determine public policy or to decide what is the right thing to do. Rather, it is to go to the polls from time to time to choose those who will determine public policy and decide what the right thing is: namely, the governors. The deciding of issues by the electorate is secondary to the election of the individuals who are to do the deciding. The analogy is with choosing a doctor. The patient certainly chooses which doctor to see but does not normally decide (or even try to decide) on the detailed course of treatment. The division of labor is informal but clearly understood.

It is probably fair to say that most of the world's major democracies—Great Britain, France, Germany, Japan—operate on this basis. The voters go to the polls every few years, and in between times it is up to the government of the day to get on with governing. Electing a government and governing are two different businesses. Electioneering is, if anything, to be deplored if it gets in the way of governing.

This is a simplified picture, of course. Democratically elected politicians are ultimately dependent on the electorate, and if at the end of the day the electorate does not like what they are doing, they are dead. Nevertheless, the central point remains. The existing division of labor is broadly accepted.

The other interpretation of democracy, the one dominant in America, might be called the "agency" view, and it is wholly different. According to this view, those who govern a country should function as no more than the agents of the people. The job of the governors is not to act independently and to take whatever decisions they believe to be in the national interest but, rather, to reflect in all their actions the views of the majority of the people, whatever those views may be. Governors are not really governors at all; they are representatives, in the very narrow sense of being in office solely to represent the views of those who sent them there.

In the agency view, representative government of the kind common throughout the democratic world can only be second-best. The ideal system would be one in which there were no politicians or middlemen of any kind and the people governed themselves directly; the political system would take the form of more or less continuous town meetings or referenda, perhaps conducted by means of interactive television. Most Americans, at bottom, would still like to see their country governed by a town meeting.

WHY THEIR VULNERABILITY MATTERS

In this political ethos, finding themselves inhabiting a turbulent and torrid electoral environment, most American elective officials respond as might be expected: in an almost Darwinian way. They adapt their behavior—their roll-call votes, their introduction of bills, their committee assignments, their phone calls, their direct-mail letters, their speeches, their press releases, their sound bites, whom they see, how they spend their time, their trips abroad, their trips back home, and frequently their private and family lives—to their environment: that is, to their primary and overriding need for electoral survival. The effects are felt not only in the lives of individual officeholders and their staffs but also in America's political institutions as a whole and the shape and content of U.S. public policy.

It all begins with officeholders' immediate physical environment: with bricks, mortar, leather, and wood paneling. The number of congressional buildings and the size of congressional staffs have ballooned in recent decades. At the start of the 1960s most members of the House of Representatives contented themselves with a small inner office and an outer office; senators' office suites were not significantly larger. Apart from the Capitol itself, Congress was reasonably comfortably housed in four buildings, known to Washington taxi drivers as the Old and New House and Senate Office Buildings. The designations Old and New cannot be used any longer, however, because there are now so many even newer congressional buildings.

Congressional staffs have grown at roughly the same rate, the new buildings having been built mainly to house the staffs. In 1957 the total number of people employed by members of the House and

Senate as personal staff was 3,556. By 1991 the figure had grown to 11,572—a more than threefold increase within the political lifetime of many long-serving members. Last year the total number of people employed by Congress in all capacities, including committee staffs and the staffs of support agencies like the Congressional Research Service, was 32,820, making Congress by far the most heavily staffed legislative branch in the world.

Much of the growth of staff in recent decades has been in response to the growth of national government, to Congress's insistence on strengthening its policymaking role in the aftermath of Vietnam and Watergate, and to decentralization within Congress, which has led subcommittee chairmen and the subcommittees themselves to acquire their own staffs. But there is no doubt that the increase is also in response to congressional incumbents' ever-increasing electoral exposure. Congress itself has become an integral part of America's veritable "elections industry."

One useful measure of the changes that have taken place—and also an important consequence of the changes—is the increased proportion of staff and staff time devoted to constituent service. As recently as 1972 only 1,189 House employees—22.5 percent of House members' personal staffs—were based in home-district offices. By 1992 the number had more than

doubled, to 3,128, and the proportion had nearly doubled, to 42.1 percent. On the Senate side there were only 303 state-based staffers in 1972, making up 12.5 percent of senators' personal staffs, but the number had more than quadrupled by 1992 to 1,368, for fully 31.6 percent of the total. Since a significant proportion of the time of Washington-based congressional staffs is also devoted to constituent service, it is a fair guess that more than half of the time of all congressional staffs is now given over to nursing the district or state rather than to legislation and policymaking.

Much constituent service is undoubtedly altruistic, inspired by politicians' sense of duty (and constituents' understandable frustration with an unresponsive bureaucracy); but at the same time nobody doubts that a large proportion of it is aimed at securing re-election. The statistics on the outgoing mail of members of Congress and their use of the franking privilege point in that direction too. Congressional mailings grew enormously in volume from some 100 million pieces a year in the early 1960s to more than 900 million in 1984—nearly five pieces of congressional mail for every adult American. New restrictions on franking introduced in the 1990s have made substantial inroads into that figure, but not surprisingly the volume of mail emanating from both houses of Congress is still invariably higher in election years.

The monetary costs of these increases in voter-oriented congressional activities are high: in addition to being the most heavily staffed legislative branch in the world, Congress is also the most expensive. But there is another, non-monetary cost: the staffs themselves become one of the congressman's or senator's constituencies, requiring management, taking up time, and always being tempted to go into business for themselves. American scholars who have studied the burgeoning of congressional staffs express concern about their cumulative impact on Congress as a deliberative body in which face-to-face communication between members, and between members and their constituents, facilitates both mutual understanding and an understanding of the issues. Largely in response to the requirements of electioneering, more and more congressional business is conducted through dense networks of staffers.

One familiar effect of American politicians' vulnerability is the power it accords to lobbyists and special-interest groups, especially those that can muster large numbers of votes or have large amounts of money to spend on campaigns. Members of Congress walk the electoral world alone. They can be picked off one by one, they know it, and they adjust their behavior accordingly. The power of the American Association of Retired Persons, the National Rifle Association, the banking industry, and the various veterans' lobbies is well known. It derives partly from their routine contributions to campaign funds and the quality of their lobbying activities in Washington, but far more from the votes that the organizations may be able to deliver and from congressmen's and senators' calculations of how the positions they take in the present may affect their chances of re-election in the future—a future that rarely is distant. Might a future challenger be able to use that speech against me? Might I be targeted for defeat by one of the powerful lobbying groups?

A second effect is that American politicians are even more likely than those in other countries to engage in symbolic politics: to use words masquerading as deeds, to take actions that purport to be instrumental but are in fact purely rhetorical. A problem exists; the people demand that it be solved; the politicians cannot solve it and know so; they engage in an elaborate pretense of trying to solve it nevertheless, often at great expense to the taxpayers and almost invariably at a high cost in terms of both the truth and the politicians' own reputations for integrity and effectiveness. The politicians lie in most cases not because they are liars or approve of lying but because the potential electoral costs of not lying are too great.

At one extreme, symbolic politics consists of speechmaking and public position-taking in the absence of any real action or any intention of taking action; casting the right vote is more important than achieving the right outcome. At the other extreme, symbolic politics consists of whole government programs that are ostensibly designed to achieve one set of objectives but are actually designed to achieve other objectives (in some cases simply the re-election of the politicians who can claim credit for them).

Take as an example the crime bills passed by Congress in the 1980s and 1990s, with their mandatory-minimum sentences, their three-strikes-and-you're-out provisions, and their extension of the federal death penalty to fifty new crimes. The anti-drug and anti-crime legislation, by the testimony of judges and legal scholars, has been at best useless and at worst wholly pernicious in its effects, in that it has filled prison cells not with violent criminals but with drug users and low-level drug pushers. As for the death penalty, a simple measure of its sheer irrelevance to the federal government's war on crime is easily provided. The last federal offender to be put to death, Victor H. Feguer, a convicted kidnapper, was hanged in March of 1963. By the end of 1995 no federal offender had been executed for more than thirty years, and hardly any offenders were awaiting execution on death row. The ferocious-seeming federal statutes were almost entirely for show.

The way in which the wars on drugs and crime were fought cannot be understood without taking into account the incessant pressure that elected officeholders felt they were under from the electorate. As one former congressman puts it, "Voters were afraid of criminals, and politicians were afraid of voters." This fear reached panic proportions in election years. Seven of the years from 1981 to 1994 were election years nationwide; seven were not. During those fourteen years Congress passed no fewer than seven major crime bills. Of those seven, six were passed in election years (usually late in the year). That is, there was only one election year in which a major crime bill was *not* passed, and only one non-election year in which a major crime bill *was* passed.

Another effect of the extreme vulnerability of American politicians is that it is even harder for them than for democratically elected politicians in other countries to take tough decisions: to court unpopularity, to ask for sacrifices, to impose losses, to fly in the face of conventional wisdom—in short, to act in what they believe to be their constituents' interest and the national interest rather than in their own interest. Timothy J. Penny, a Democrat who left the House of Representatives in 1994, put the point starkly, perhaps even too harshly, in *Common Cents* (1995).

> Voters routinely punish lawmakers who try to do unpopular things, who challenge them to face unpleasant truths about the budget, crime, Social Security, or tax policy. Similarly, voters reward politicians for giving them what they want—more spending for popular programs—even if it means wounding the nation in the long run by creating more debt.

America's enduring budget deficit offers a vivid, almost textbook illustration. For nearly a generation—ever since the early 1980s—American politicians have bemoaned the deficit and exhorted themselves to do something about it. However, they have never done nearly enough, even in their own eyes. Why? Part of the answer undoubtedly lies in genuine ideological differences that make it hard for conservatives and liberals to compromise; but much of the answer also lies in the brute fact that every year in the United States is either an election year or a pre-election year, with primaries and threatened primaries intensifying politicians' electoral concerns. In 1985 Senator Warren Rudman, of New Hampshire, reckoned that he and other senators who had voted for a bold deficit-reduction package had flown a "kamikaze mission." One of his colleagues said they had "jumped off a cliff." Twelve years later, not surprisingly, the federal budget remains in deficit.

MORE DEMOCRACY, MORE DISSATISFACTION

NUMEROUS opinion polls show that millions of Americans are profoundly dissatisfied with the functioning of their political system. Consequently, there is a widespread disposition in the United States—at all levels of society, from the grass roots to the editorial conference and the company boardroom—to want to make American democracy "work better," and concrete proposals abound for achieving this goal.

The proposed reforms can be grouped loosely under four headings. First come those that if implemented would amount to the creation of electronic town meetings, taking advantage of technological developments such as CD-ROM, interactive cable systems, electronic mail, and the Internet. *The Wall Street Journal* referred in this general connection to "arranging a marriage of de Tocqueville and technology."

Second, and related, are proposals for promoting democratic deliberation and citizen participation. The Kettering Foundation and the Public Agenda Foundation already organize National Issues Forums that embrace some 3,000 educational and civic groups across America. David Mathews, the president of the Kettering Foundation, considers these modern forums to be directly linked to America's ancient "town meeting tradition." Benjamin R. Barber, a political philosopher at Rutgers University, would go further and create a nationwide network of neighborhood assemblies that could take actual decisions on strictly local matters and also debate and lobby on broader national questions. James S. Fishkin, a political scientist at the University of Texas, likewise seeks to leap the modern barriers to face-to-face democracy by means of what he calls "deliberative opinion polls" (which have been tried, with considerable success, in England).

The third group of proposed reforms is equally radical but more old-fashioned. This group seeks to complete the work of Progressive Era reformers by extending to the federal level the characteristic state-level reforms that were introduced in that period: the referendum, the initiative, and the recall. The political analyst Kevin Phillips, for example, suggests that "the

United States should propose and ratify an amendment to the Constitution setting up a mechanism for holding nationwide referendums to permit the citizenry to supplant Congress and the president in making certain categories of national decisions." He would also like to see congressmen and senators be subject to popular recall once they have been in office for a year. Certainly proposals of this kind have broad public support. Depending on the precise wording of the question, more than 50 percent of Americans support the idea of national referenda and more than 80 percent support both the initiative and the recall.

Finally, many commentators—and the majority of the American public—strongly back the newest and most fashionable item on the "making democracy work better" agenda: the imposition of term limits on both state and federal elected officials, notably members of Congress. But the great majority of those who favor term limits, true to the American democratic tradition, are less concerned with good government and the public interest as such than with the present generation of politicians' alleged lack of responsiveness to the mass of ordinary people. At the center of this argument is the idea that the

> ## WHEN AMERICANS BECOME DISSATISFIED WITH GOVERNMENT, THEY CALL FOR MORE DEMOCRACY. THE MORE THEY CALL FOR MORE DEMOCRACY, THE MORE OF IT THEY GET. THE MORE THEY GET, THE MORE DISSATISFIED THEY BECOME.

United States is now governed by an unresponsive, self-perpetuating, and increasingly remote class of professional politicians, a class that ought to be replaced as soon as possible by "citizen legislators"—men and women who will serve the people simply because they *are* the people. As one advocate of term limits puts it, ordinary people—the proposed citizen legislators of the future—"know things about life in America that people who have lived as very self-important figures in Washington for thirty years have no way of knowing or have forgotten."

Some of the items on this four-part shopping list of reforms are intrinsically attractive, or at least a good case can be made

for them. Nevertheless, taken as a whole, the mainstream reformist agenda, with its traditional American emphasis on agency democracy and its view of politicians as mere servants of the people's will, rests on extremely tenuous conceptual foundations and, more important, is almost certainly inappropriate as a response to the practical needs of turn-of-the-century America. America's problem of governance is not insufficient responsiveness on the part of its elected leaders. On the contrary, America's problem is their hyper-responsiveness. Politicians do not need to be tied down still further, to be subjected to even more external pressures than they are already. Rather, they need to be given just a little more political leeway, just a little more room for policy maneuver. Reforms should seek to strengthen division-of-labor democracy, not to create a still purer form of American-style agency democracy.

THE USUAL SUSPECTS

IF the reformist prescriptions are bad ones, there may be something wrong with the reformist diagnoses on which they are based. What *are* the principal sources of dissatisfaction with the current state of American democracy?

Many commentators have gotten into the habit of blaming Americans' dissatisfaction, in an almost knee-jerk fashion, on "the Vietnam War and Watergate." It is certainly the case that evidence of widespread dissatisfaction began to appear during and shortly after Vietnam and Watergate. *Post hoc, ergo propter hoc?* Maybe. But in the first place, Vietnam and Watergate led to a flowering of idealism as well as cynicism (and to the election, in 1974, of the "Watergate babies," one of the most idealistic and public-spirited cohorts ever to be elected to Congress). And in the second place, it seems strange to attribute the dissatisfactions of the 1990s to events that took place in the 1960s and early 1970s. That distance in time is roughly that between the two world wars; most of today's college students were not yet born when President Richard Nixon resigned. To be sure, subsequent scandals have undoubtedly (and deservedly) damaged the reputations of the White House and Congress, but at least some of the sleaze of recent years has come about because politicians need such enormous sums to finance their re-election campaigns.

Two other hypotheses can be dismissed, or at least assigned little importance. One is that politicians today are a poor lot compared with the intellectual and moral giants of the past. It probably is the case that having to run scared all the time has tended to drive some able people out of politics and to discourage others from coming in. But the phenomenon is a relatively recent one, and for the time being there is no reason to think that the average congressman or senator is in any way inferior to his or her predecessors. The quality of America's existing political class is at most a small part of the problem.

The same is almost certainly true of the idea that divided government—in which one party controls one or both houses of Congress while the other controls the presidency—is to be preferred. Divided government has characterized America for most of the past thirty years, and it has been associated with some of the more spectacular political and policy failures of that period—the Iran-contra scandal of the 1980s (which arose out of a Republican Administration's desire to circumvent a Democratic Congress), and successive shutdowns of parts of the government as Presidents and Congress have failed to agree on timely taxing and spending measures. Other things being equal, divided government is probably to be regretted.

All the same, it is hard to credit the idea that Americans' disillusionment with their politics would be significantly less today if party control had been mainly undivided over the past thirty years. On the one hand, recent periods in which the government has not been divided (the Carter years, 1977–1980, and the first two Clinton years, 1993–1994) were not notably successful (Carter never surmounted the energy crisis, and Clinton failed to reform America's healthcare system even though that reform had figured prominently in his campaign promises). On the other hand, as David R. Mayhew, a political scientist at Yale University, has shown, periods of divided government have often been extremely productive in legislative terms. On balance, divided government appears to be more of a nuisance and a distraction than a root cause of either the government's difficulties or the public's disillusionment.

The idea that the system suffers from the excessive power of interest groups, however, needs to be taken seriously. Jonathan Rauch, in his recent book *Demosclerosis,* argues persuasively that America's interest groups have become larger, more numerous, and more powerful over the past three decades, to the point that they now have the capacity to prevent the government from doing almost anything that would disadvantage or offend any of the clients they represent—taking in, as it happens, virtually the whole American population.

Rauch is probably right; but one needs to go on to ask, as he himself does, what the power of these pullulating and all-encompassing lobby groups is based on. The answer is straightforward: their power depends ultimately on their money, on their capacity to make trouble for elected officials, on the votes of their members (the AARP has more than 30 million members), and on elective politicians' fear of not being re- elected. The groups' power, in other words, depends on politicians' electoral vulnerability; and America's interest groups are peculiarly powerful in large measure because America's elective politicians are peculiarly vulnerable. It is not quite as simple as that—but almost.

It is also important to note the precise timing of the developments described by Rauch and by almost everyone else who has written on this subject. Nearly all these developments date, almost uncannily, from the past thirty years: the rise in the number of interest groups, the growth in their membership and power, the decline in the public's trust in government officials, and the increased sense among voters that who they are and what they think do not matter to politicians and officials in Washington. In other words, the origins of the present era of democratic discontent can be traced to the end of the 1960s and the beginning of the 1970s. It was then that people began to think something was wrong not with this or that aspect of the system but with the system itself.

What happened at that time? It is hard to escape the conclusion that the crucial developments, largely provoked by the Vietnam War and Watergate, were the attempts from 1968 onward to open up the American system, to make it more transparent, to make it more accessible, to make it, in a word, more "democratic." These attempts led to an increase in the number of primary elections, to a further weakening of America's already weak political parties, to increases in the already high costs of electoral politics, and to the increasing isolation, in an increasingly hostile environment, of elective officials. In short, the post-Vietnam, post-Watergate reforms led, as they were meant to lead, to increased vulnerability to their electorates on the part of individual American officeholders.

The paradox that has resulted is obvious and easily stated. Recent history suggests that when large numbers of Americans become dissatisfied with the workings of their government, they call for more democracy. The more they call for more democracy, the more of it they get. The more of it they get, the more dissatisfied they become with the workings of their government. The more they become dissatisfied with the workings of their government, the more they call for more democracy. The cycle endlessly repeats itself.

WHAT, IF ANYTHING, MIGHT BE DONE?

PRECISELY because American politicians are so exposed electorally, they probably have to display—and do display—more political courage more often than the politicians of any other democratic country. The number of political saints and martyrs in the United States is unusually large.

There is, however, no special virtue in a political system that requires large numbers of politicians to run the risk of martyrdom in order to ensure that tough decisions can be taken in a timely manner in the national interest. The number of such decisions that need to be taken is always likely to be large; human nature being what it is, the supply of would-be martyrs is always likely to be small. On balance it would seem better not to try to eliminate the electoral risks (it can never be done in a democracy) but to reduce somewhat their scale and intensity. There is no reason why the risks run by American politicians should be so much greater than the risks run by elective politicians in other democratic countries.

How, then, might the risks be reduced? What can be done? A number of reforms to the existing system suggest themselves. It may be that none of them is politically feasible—Americans hold tight to the idea of agency democracy—but in principle there should be no bar to any of them. One of the simplest would also be the most radical: to lengthen the terms of members of the House of Representatives from two years to four. The proposal is by no means a new one: at least 123 resolutions bearing on the subject were introduced in Congress in the eighty years from 1885 to 1965, and President Lyndon

B. Johnson advocated the change in his State of the Union address in January of 1966.

A congressman participating in a Brookings Institution round table held at about the time of Johnson's message supported the change, saying, "I think that the four years would help you to be a braver congressman, and I think what you need is bravery. I think you need courage." Another congressman on the same occasion cited the example of another bill that he believed had the support of a majority in the House. "That bill is not going to come up this year. You know why it is not coming up? . . . Because four hundred and thirty-five of us have to face election. . . . If we had a four-year term, I am as confident as I can be the bill would have come to the floor and passed."

A similar case could be made for extending the term of senators to eight years, with half the Senate retiring or running for re-election every four years. If the terms of members of both houses were thus extended and made to coincide, the effect in reducing America's never-ending election campaign would be dramatic.

There is much to be said, too, for all the reasons mentioned so far, for scaling down the number of primary elections. They absorb extravagant amounts of time, energy, and money; they serve little democratic purpose; few people bother to vote in them; and they place additional and unnecessary pressure on incumbent officeholders. Since the main disadvantage of primaries is the adverse effect they have on incumbents, any reforms probably ought to be concerned with protecting incumbents' interests.

At the moment, the primary laws make no distinction between situations in which a seat in the House or the Senate is already occupied and situations in which the incumbent is, for whatever reason, standing down. The current laws provide for a primary to be held in either case. An incumbent is therefore treated as though the seat in question were open and he or she were merely one of the candidates for it. A relatively simple reform would be to distinguish between the two situations. If a seat was open, primaries would be held in both parties, as now; but if the incumbent announced that he or she intended to run for re-election, then a primary in his or her party would be held only if large numbers of party supporters were determined to have one—that is, were determined that the incumbent should be ousted. The obvious way to ascertain whether such determination existed would be by means of a petition supervised by the relevant state government and requiring a considerable number of signatures. The possibility of a primary would thus be left open, but those who wanted one would have to show that they were both numerous and serious. A primary would not be held simply because an ambitious, possibly demented, possibly wealthy individual decided to throw his or her hat into the ring.

Any steps to strengthen the parties as institutions would be desirable on the same grounds. Lack of party cover in the United States means that elective officeholders find it hard to take tough decisions partly because they lack safety in numbers. They can seldom, if ever, say to an aggrieved constituent or a political-action committee out for revenge, "I had to vote that way because my party told me to," or even "I had to vote that way because we in my party all agreed that we would." Lack of party cohesion, together with American voters' disposition to vote for the individual rather than the party, means that congressmen and senators are always in danger of being picked off one by one.

BALLOT FATIGUE

WHAT might be done to give both parties more backbone? Clearly, the parties would be strengthened—and elective officeholders would not need to raise so much money for their own campaigns—if each party organization became a major source of campaign funding. In the unlikely event (against the background of chronic budget deficits) that Congress ever gets around to authorizing the federal funding of congressional election campaigns, a strong case could be made for channeling as much of the money as possible through the parties, and setting aside some of it to cover their administrative and other ongoing costs.

The party organizations and the nexus between parties and their candidates would also be strengthened if it were made easier for ordinary citizens to give money to the parties and for the parties to give money to their candidates. Until 1986, when the program was abolished, tax credits were available for taxpayers who contributed small sums to the political parties. These credits could be restored. Larry J. Sabato, a political scientist at the University of Virginia, has similarly suggested that citizens entitled to a tax refund could be allowed to divert a small part of their refund to the party of their choice. Such measures would not, however, reduce candidates' dependence on donations from wealthy individuals and PACs unless they were accompanied by measures enabling the parties to contribute more generously to their candidates' campaigns. At the moment there are strict legal limits on the amount of money that national or state party organizations can contribute to the campaigns of individual candidates. The limits should be raised (and indexed to inflation). There is even a case for abolishing them altogether.

All that said, there is an even more straightforward way of reducing incumbents' dependence on campaign contributors. At present incumbents have to spend so much time raising funds because the campaigns themselves are so expensive. They could be made cheaper. This, of course, would be one of the effects of making U.S. elections less numerous and less frequent than they are now. Another way to lower the cost of elections would be to provide candidates and parties with free air time on television and radio.

THE CASE FOR SWANS

CLEARLY, the idea of term limits also needs to be taken seriously. After all, if American politicians are excessively vulnerable at the moment, one way of rendering them invulnerable would be to prevent them from running for re-election—no impending election contest, no need to worry overmuch about the voters.

As is evident, much of the actual campaigning in favor of term limits takes the form of ranting—against big government, against Washington, against "them," against taxes, against the deficit. Much of the rhetoric of term-limiters is sulfurous, and their principal motive often seems to be revenge. They claim that members of Congress are insufficiently responsive to their constituents, when the evidence suggests that, on the contrary, they are far too responsive. The term-limits movement is of a piece with previous outbursts of frustrated American populism, including the Know-Nothing movement of the 1850s—an essay, as one historian has put it, in "the politics of impatience."

Nevertheless, there is an alternate case for term limits, based not on American politicians' alleged lack of responsiveness to the voters but on their alleged overresponsiveness to the voters and interest groups in order to secure their own re-election. The most persuasive and subtle advocate of this line of argument is the political commentator George F. Will. His goal, Will says partway through his book *Restoration* (1992), "is deliberative democracy through representatives who function at a constitutional distance from the people." He reiterates the point about distance in his final paragraphs: "Americans must be less demanding of government. They must give to government more constitutional space in which to think, more social distance to facilitate deliberation about the future."

THERE IS NO SPECIAL VIRTUE IN A SYSTEM THAT REQUIRES LARGE NUMBERS OF POLITICIANS TO RUN THE RISK OF MARTYRDOM IN ORDER TO ENSURE THAT TOUGH DECISIONS CAN BE TAKEN IN A TIMELY MANNER IN THE NATIONAL INTEREST.

The case for giving American politicians more space and distance is undoubtedly a strong one, but assuming these objectives are desirable, it is still not clear that term limits are a suitable means for achieving them. Three questions arise. Would term limits achieve the desired objectives? Would they do so at an acceptable cost in terms of other American goals and values? Might the desired objectives not be better achieved by other means? The first question is strictly empirical. The other two mix the empirical and the moral.

One way in which term limits might promote deliberation is by causing some incumbent legislators—namely those serving out their final term under term limits—to think, speak, and vote differently from the way they would have thought, spo-

ken, and voted if they had been eligible and running for re-election. In addition, for term limits to affect the behavior not just of certain individuals but of Congress as a whole, it would be necessary for any given Congress to contain a significant number of these final-term members. In other words, congressional lame ducks would have to quack differently from other ducks, and there would have to be a fair number of them on the pond.

It is impossible to be sure, but it seems unlikely that term limits would have significant effects along these lines. In the first place, existing research (along with most human experience) suggests that a final-term congressman or senator, after eleven or twelve years on Capitol Hill, would be unlikely to alter his pattern of behavior in any radical way. He might send out fewer pieces of franked mail and make fewer trips back home, but he would probably not execute many U-turns in the way he spoke and voted. In the second place, although the proportion of senators who would be in their final term under term limits would normally be large (possibly half if senators were restricted to two terms), the proportion of lame-duck congressmen would normally be much smaller (an average of sixty to seventy out of 435 if House members were limited to six terms). The cumulative impact of the lame ducks would thus be much greater in the Senate than in the House, and in both houses it would probably be felt mainly at the margins (though of course the margins can, on occasion, be important).

But those who advocate term limits in fact build very little of their case on the expected future behavior of lame ducks. Rather, they are seeking to create a wholly new class of elected representatives. George Will holds out the prospect that mandatory term limits would have the effect of replacing today's political careerists with noncareerists—in other words, of replacing today's ducks with creatures more closely resembling swans. The new legislators, because they were not careerists, would not be driven by the need to secure re-election, and for that reason they would be more likely to concern themselves with the national interest. Also because they were not political careerists, they would be more likely to have some personal, hands-on understanding of America and its real concerns.

The prospect is undoubtedly attractive. But is it realistic? Would term limits in fact diminish the number of careerists and produce legislators who were more national-minded and disinterested?

The most important difficulties with Will's hypothesis are twofold. One is that modern politics at all levels, local and state as well as national, is an immensely time-consuming, energy-consuming activity that demands enormous commitment from those who are attracted to it. Legislative sessions are long, constituents' demands are exigent, policy problems are increasingly complicated. As a result, politics all over the world, not just in the United States, is becoming professionalized. Men and women in all countries increasingly choose a political career at an early age and then stick with it. It seems likely that even under term limits the great majority of congressmen and senators would be drawn from this professional political class, which has not only the commitment to politics but also the requisite patience, skills, and contacts. To be sure, people's political careers would take a different shape; but they would still be political careers.

The other difficulty is the reverse of the first. Just as politics is becoming more professionalized, so is almost every other occupation. As many women in particular know to their cost, it is becoming harder and harder to take career breaks—those who jump off the ladder in any profession find it increasingly hard to jump back even to the level they were on when they left, let alone the level they would have attained had they stayed. For this reason it is hard to imagine that many upwardly mobile corporate executives or successful professionals or small-business owners would take time off to serve in Congress on a citizen-legislator basis. The citizens who sought to serve on this basis would probably be largely the rich and the old.

VOTER-PROOFING

DESPITE their differences, term limits and the proposals offered here have in common the fact that they seek major changes in America's political institutions—in some cases involving an amendment to the Constitution. But of course America's politicians are free to alter the way they behave in the context of the country's existing institutions. They can try to find alternative ways of insulating at least some aspects of policymaking from the intense campaigning and electioneering pressures they are now under.

Short of taking difficult issues out of electoral politics altogether, there are tactics that could be employed. Most of them are out of keeping with the contemporary American preferences for direct democracy, high levels of political participation, and the maximum exposure of all political processes to the public gaze; but that is precisely their strength. Bismarck is reputed to have said that there are two things one should never watch being made: sausages and laws. Both should be judged more by the end result than by the precise circumstances of their manufacture.

One available tactic might be called "the collusion of the elites." There may be occasions on which the great majority of America's politicians, in both the executive and legislative branches, are able to agree that an issue is of such overriding importance to the nation that it must be dealt with at almost any cost; that the politicians involved must therefore be prepared to set aside their ideological and other differences in the interests of finding a workable solution; and that having found a solution, they must stick together in presenting it to what may well be a disgruntled or even hostile electorate. In order to be successful, the collusion-of-elites tactic requires not only a substantial degree of bipartisanship (or, better still, nonpartisanship) but also unusually small teams of negotiators, complete secrecy (not a single ray of "sunshine" must penetrate the proceedings), and the presentation to Congress and the public of a comprehensive, all-or-nothing, take-it-or-leave-it proposal.

The number of occasions on which politicians will be prepared to set aside their ideological differences and pool their political risks in this fashion will inevitably be small. There

were no signs that such a spirit might prevail when President Clinton and the Republican majorities in Congress wrangled over how to cut the budget deficit last winter. But there have been instances of the successful collusion of elites, even in relatively recent times.

One of them occurred in 1983, when representatives of President Reagan and the two party leaderships on Capitol Hill colluded to save the Social Security system, which at that time was in imminent danger of bankruptcy. Paul Light's classic account of the 1983 Social Security reform, *Artful Work* (1985), is in effect a case study of how to conduct collusion-of-elites politics and of the circumstances in which it may succeed. The so-called Gang of Seventeen that was originally put together to hammer out a deal (and was later reduced to a Gang of Nine) excluded all the more-extreme ideologues and met in circumstances of great secrecy, even using, according to one participant, "unmarked limos."

Of the Gang of Seventeen's activities, Light writes,

> The meetings seemed to inaugurate a new form of presidential-congressional government. The meetings were secret. There were no minutes or transcripts. All conversations were strictly off the record. The gang was free to discuss all of the options without fear of political retaliation. It . . . [existed] completely outside of the constitutional system.

Ultimately, as Light relates, the "secret gang built a compromise, wrapped it in a bipartisan flag, and rammed it through Congress. There was no other way to move. It was government by fait accompli." It was also successful government—and none of the participants suffered electoral damage.

Another possible tactic, with many similarities to the collusion of elites, might be called "putting it into commission." If taking tough decisions is too risky politically, then get someone else to take them. If someone else cannot be found to take them, then make someone else *appear* to take them. The someone else need not be but usually will be a bipartisan or nonpartisan commission of some kind.

Such a commission, the National Commission on Social Security Reform, played a role in the passage of the 1983 act, but an even better example was the procedure adopted by Congress in 1990 for closing redundant military bases. Earlier practice had been almost a caricature of Congress's traditional decision-making process. The Secretary of Defense would propose a program of base closures. Senators and congressmen would immediately leap to the defense of targeted bases in their home states or districts. They of course had the support of their colleagues, who were threatened with or feared base closures in *their* home states or districts. Almost never did anyone manage to close any bases.

Realizing that the process was absurd and that huge sums of taxpayers' money were being wasted in keeping redundant bases open, Congress decided to protect itself from itself. It established the Defense Base Closure and Realignment Commission, which employed an extraordinarily simple formula. The Defense Secretary every two years published a list of the bases he proposed to close, together with a statement of criteria he had used in compiling his list. The commission then examined the list in light of the criteria, held public hearings, and recommended a modified list (with additions as well as deletions) to the President. The President was obliged to accept the commission's list as a whole or reject it as a whole. If, as invariably happened, he accepted it, Congress could intervene only if within forty-five legislative days it passed a bill overriding the President's decision and rejecting the whole list. This it never did.

The formula was a near miracle of voter-proofing. Members of Congress were left free to protest the closure of bases in their home districts or states, but the decision was ultimately taken by the President, who could nonetheless ascribe all blame to the commission, and all Congress had to do for the President's decision to take effect was to do nothing. In the event, hundreds of bases were closed and millions of dollars saved, but no member of Congress ever had to vote—and be seen by his constituents to be voting—in favor of closing a base near home. Beyond any question the results were in America's national interest.

It is not wholly fantastic to suppose that the President in odd-numbered years might, on the basis of advice received from a bipartisan commission, announce a list of "program eliminations," which Congress could countermand only by voting to reject the list as a whole. Presidents would probably prefer to put forward such lists at the beginning of their first term in office—or at any time during their second term—when they, at least, were not up for re-election.

A final tactic, which could also be adopted without major institutional change, might be described as "thinking big." Proposals that are put forward on a piecemeal basis can also be opposed, and in all probability defeated, on a piecemeal basis. In contrast, large-scale, broad-based proposals may have a better chance of success simply by virtue of their comprehensiveness. They can provide something for everyone—conservatives as well as liberals, deficit cutters as well as program defenders, residents of the Sun Belt as well as of the Rust Belt. Gains as well as losses can be broadcast widely. The 1983 Social Security reform and the 1986 tax reform were certainly "big thoughts" of this general type. So, in its way, was the recent base-closure program.

Tactics like these—the collusion of elites, putting issues into commission, and thinking big—all have their virtues, but they also suffer from being tactics in the pejorative as well as the descriptive sense. At bottom they are somewhat cynical devices for getting around the real difficulty, which is the hyper- responsiveness of American politicians that is induced by their having to run scared so much of the time. Although it would be harder, it would be better over the long term to confront this problem directly and try to bring about at least some of the fundamental institutional changes proposed here. The American people cannot govern themselves. They therefore need to find appropriate means of choosing representatives who can do a decent job of governing on their behalf, and that means giving the people's representatives space, time, and freedom in which to take decisions, knowing that if they get them wrong, they will be punished by the voters. In twentieth-century America the airy myths of agency democracy are precisely that: myths. What America needs today, though it does not seem to know it, is a more realistic and down-to-earth form of division-of-labor democracy.

Anthony King, a political scientist who teaches at the University of Essex, and an elections analyst for the British Broadcasting Corporation, is a regular contributor to *The Economist*.

WHO NEEDS POLITICAL PARTIES?

BY RICHARD M. VALELLY

As the major political parties convene this summer, with all the usual noise, pomp, and expense, Americans can be counted on to let out a collective yawn, or maybe a grimace. But not so for political scientists. Academic experts see a lot to like—or at least a lot to study—in the American two-party system. In their considered view, a competitive party system ensures the legitimacy of opposition to government, promotes public debate about policy options, and gets citizens involved in the public sphere. The two-party system never does these things perfectly, but it does them well enough. Without it our system would collapse overnight, leaving gridlock and hyperpluralism—or so most political scientists think.

But if one looks closely at the views of those who are researching, thinking about, and writing about political parties, one finds an interesting division of opinion. One school of thought is that parties are in decline and, consequently, that we have a major problem. The public is right to be irritated. A second view holds that parties have changed dramatically but that they are just as strong as they used to be. The public ought to get used to the transformation and stop griping. A third school, best articulated by David Mayhew of Yale University, is that political scientists have attributed too much importance to party dynamics. They matter, but less so than the professional literature has suggested. In

this light, the public's gripes are beside the point.

To make sense of the disagreement, we must first sift through the ruins of realignment theory. For about 20 years, American government students were instructed in this line of thinking. Its concepts still echo in political punditry. But the theory died a decade ago when it became clear it wasn't explaining with any precision the events of the actual political world.

Still, it was an elegant idea. Realignment theory held that not all elections were the same. In certain highly charged elections or in a string of two or three such elections, big and lasting shifts occurred in how voters behaved. A new voter coalition would assert control over our system, determining policy outcomes for a generation. Walter Dean Burnham, the theory's best-known proponent, suggested such elections might be a uniquely American surrogate for political revolution. Before realignment, there might be a third-party challenge, protests, and even civil disorder. Eventually, ambitious politicians would pick up the pressing issues and make them their own.

With the image of periodic political renewal, there was a soothing message in all this. Realignments allowed the political system to adjust to social and political stress, and to bring those citizens who might otherwise be absorbed in personal concerns into political action. The party

system periodically restored its own vitality and that of the system as a whole.

Burnham explicitly warned, however, that the party system's capacity for "peaceful revolution" was not automatic. If and when the party system lost its ability to adapt, the branches of government would lock up. Governmental remedy as both an ideal and a practice would wither. Gradually, a propensity toward broad-based oligarchy would set in. After all, the wealthy are best protected by government that is deadlocked. Simultaneously, a huge class of unmobilized people would emerge as a "party of nonvoters." Their influence on the system would necessarily be weaker.

Scholars in the "party decline" school have inherited Burnham's worry. They agree that as a party system weakens it tends to pull the rest of the order down with it. Sidney Milkis of the University of Virginia, who is close in spirit to Burnham, makes such a case in *Political Parties and Constitutional Government*, a study of the rise and development of political parties since the founding. While Milkis does not share Burnham's open distaste for markets, capitalism, and social inequalities, he does adopt Burnham's democratic nationalism. For Milkis the weakening of parties has promoted broad discontent with

American government and has generated an anemic civic culture.

In Milkis's account—and this is what makes his work so provocative—the cause of party decline, and thus of public cynicism, is not the depoliticizing force of market values, as Burnham has long argued. Instead, it is the particular development of the presidency. To put Milkis's claim bluntly, FDR killed the parties when he built a government competent enough to run a welfare state. In doing that, he changed the constitutional balance that had been supported by the parties since the time of Madison, Jackson, and Van Buren. Subsequent presidents failed to reverse Roosevelt's legacy.

Party competition first emerged, Milkis argues, when James Madison and Thomas Jefferson sought to develop a political opposition to Alexander Hamilton, John Adams, and the Federalist legatees of George Washington's two-term presidency. Madison, in particular, feared for the future of federalism and the separation of powers if Hamilton's economic nationalism were left politically unchecked. Milkis takes pains to point out that there was a second Madison, one less well-known but just as important as the more familiar Madison who framed the Constitution. The first disliked parties and factions; the second had no trouble embracing them in order to save his overall institutional design. Happily for Madison, the party system that he helped to launch evolved (thanks to the genius of Martin Van Buren) into a stable contest between two large confederations of state and local parties. And happily for the system as a whole, Milkis says, the parties won the political loyalties of voters scattered across a vast geographic expanse.

Americans came to appreciate the full range of national, state, and local institutions contemplated by the founders. Voters liked their town and county governments; they valued their state institutions; and they came to treasure not only the presidency but the Senate, the House, and the Su-preme Court. America's elaborate mix of national, state, and local jurisdictions and offices might never have taken hold without the early development of decentralized but nationally competitive parties. This accomplishment helps to explain the persistence of the Constitution of 1787 despite the extraordinary events of the Civil War and the Reconstruction, and the huge expansion of the republic's size.

But our party system and institutions were never particularly well-suited for strong, positive government, Milkis argues. They were good for participation and office-seeking, but not for supple macroeconomic management or the competent bureaucratic delivery of social benefits, such as old-age income security or work relief. Here Milkis carries forward a long line of thinking about party politics and public administration that dates to the work of Herbert Croly and other progressives in the early decades of the 1900s.

FDR was the first president, in Milkis's view, who was forced to cope with the lack of fit between the institutional forms given to him and new executive tasks. He keenly understood the limits of the party system he inherited, and sought briefly to do something about them, through the ill-fated 1938 "Roosevelt purge" in which New Deal liberals were encouraged to run against reactionary and conservative Democratic incumbents in Congress. He hoped to transform his party into a programmatic, responsible organization. He failed miserably.

FDR did not try again, opting instead for the independent regulatory commissions, new bureaucracies, court-packing, and executive reorganization that he or congressional liberals had already launched or planned before the purge effort. Roosevelt grasped that he could, and probably should, soft-pedal his party as an instrument of executive governance. It was too loaded with southern conservatives and stand-pat careerists. Time was short, and there was much work to be done to save liberal capitalism from its enemies within and without.

But there was a hidden price for this understandable decision. The cost to the polity, one that was not immediately obvious, was reduced voter involvement. As Kennedy, Johnson, and Nixon perfected the New Deal state, they did so on the backs of social movements, professors, experts, and government executives and lawyers. Their mission was not to revitalize the remnants of the urban machines or to reform the conservative state parties and party factions that they scorned. They made the same choice Roosevelt did. So the decentralized system of confederated parties—imagined by Madison and perfected by Van Buren—collapsed, as one ward club or county committee after another (with the notable exception of Chicago) died on the liberal vine. These local institutions were the vital foundation of voter involvement; without them voter turnout began its long decline.

Not all political scientists are alarmed by such developments. In his important 1995 work, *Why Parties?*, John H. Aldrich responds to the passing of the ward heelers by saying, in effect, "so what?" He wants us to face up to a stark proposition: The forms of parties are going to change. As he notes, trenchantly, "The major political party is the creature of the politicians. . . . These politicians do not have partisan goals per se, and the party is only the instrument for achieving them." Politicians run the parties, and they will inevitably change the ways in which parties help them to be politicians.

Aldrich is no iconoclast, to be sure. His book is deeply thoughtful, gently argued, and quite rigorous. At the heart of Aldrich's case lies an extended comparison between two party systems: the system that emerged in the North during the 1820s and 1830s and that lasted until the Civil War, and the more familiar two-party system that has structured our politics since the 1960s. The first was intensely mobilizing and generated sharp increases in voter turnout until it reached extraordinary, indeed uniquely high levels. This was also a period of "team parties," in which politicians subordinated their individual identities to the corporate identity of their party since the path to power lay through making that trade-off.

Today's parties, in contrast, are service-providing organizations. They resemble a franchise for entrepreneurs. The individual candidates of the two parties meet certain programmatic requirements related to party ideology, but in terms of campaigning they act as free-lancers. They have no trouble behaving as highly competitive teams within government, particularly within the House of Representatives, but they do not cooperate with each other to rally voters. Stimulating turnout is up to an individual candidate if he or she chooses.

The point of Aldrich's contrast is not that there has been decline relative to some golden age. Instead, these are fundamentally different systems. Juxtaposed to this claim is a lucid demonstration of the central tendency of any competitive party system, regardless of differences in the campaign styles of politicians. Using simple modeling, Aldrich posits that a party system will solve pathologies that would otherwise plague politicians. Without a competitive party system, politicians could not cooperate around mutual policy gains, which can only come through repeated interaction and binding commitments that hold up across time. They would instead treat all their interactions with each other as one-shot games and thus fall prey to the noncooperative trap epitomized by the "prisoner's dilemma."

Second, without parties' resources and their capacity to stimulate, motivate, and inform voters, politicians could never solve a major dilemma facing voters, i.e., the propensity to

> **Without political parties, our system would collapse overnight, leaving the branches of government tangled and frozen.**

avoid voting and to instead "free ride" on those who take the trouble to vote out of an irrationally strong sense of civic duty. If most of us were freeriders, there could be no genuinely popular electoral system.

Third, without the partisan organization of legislatures and government, politicians could never efficiently restrict the agenda of conflict and debate to a basic set of important issues. They would instead stumble in and out of fragile logrolls that would incorporate many unrelated items. The result would be policy immobility, rendering deliberation and participation beside the point.

Professional politicians in a democracy obviously need parties to satisfy their policy and office-seeking ambitions. But the rest of us also need parties. No parties, no "positive externalities" (in the language of welfare economics)—no streams of consistent and related policies, no agenda for public debate, and little prospect of even a modicum of voter attachment to the polity and its concerns. Thus, our current party system provides essentially the same "positive externalities," Aldrich is saying, as the earlier party system.

But a somewhat different take on the same facts is offered by Steven Schier in *By Invitation Only*. During the golden age of party politics, roughly the period from 1830 to 1890, we had something approaching a genuinely participatory democracy in this country.

Today we have, in its place, a vast congeries of professionally managed "activation," that is, the stimulation and enlistment of thousands of small subsets of the citizenry in service of the ambition of an interest group or a candidate. Several kinds of professional consultancies are available to the well-heeled or the well-organized to accomplish their preferred strategy of activation: pollsters, media consultants, fundraisers, gatherers of demographic data, opposition and issue researchers, speechwriters, schedulers, and so forth. Schier catalogues them all succinctly.

The basic idea here is that parties now compete in a broad marketplace of service providers for the politically ambitious. Their historic monopoly on access to office and influence disappeared with the rise of primaries, referenda, campaign finance regulation, and a privately operated system of broadcast communications.

The loser in the shift toward a competitive market in political techniques is the mass of ordinary citizens. Following politics and getting involved in it is up to them. If they do not have the education, confidence, partisan-ship, or time to do so, no one will ask them. Expending resources to activate the already motivated voters is cost-effective. It is less cost-effective to pursue those who are not listed in the databases of the consultants.

In this way, the political system is a bit like the medical system: technologically advanced, expensive, and replete with a variety of coverages and exclusions. As a nation, we spend a huge amount of money on electoral politics and employ all the latest campaign techniques, but we do not get much average-voter turnout in return.

Schier's final chapter offers an exceptionally thoughtful treatment of possible cures for this state of affairs. The bottom line for reform, he suggests, is making party affiliation more salient to political candidates than it currently is. In response, politicians might have stronger incentives to cooperate with one another in mobilizing voters, rather than worrying only about their own constituency.

We should reorganize campaign finance so that parties control more resources than they do now. And the states could provide ballots that are organized as party slates. More states could do what Maine and Nebraska do, which is to allocate votes in the electoral college to whomever carries a congressional district and give the "Senate votes" to the statewide winner. These are among the most plausible reforms of the many that Schier discusses.

Could it be that such reforms overemphasize the importance of political parties to democracy? David Mayhew is the one leader of the political science profession who has consistently resisted such enthusiasms. In the course of his career, he has helped to show that political parties have little to do with whether Congress works well,

that states with weak parties are not necessarily less generous with social policies (and are sometimes more generous), and that from 1947 to 1990 divided government at the national level simply had no effect on the production of important public policy, budgetary balance, or the frequency or disruptiveness of congressional investigations of the White House or the executive bureaucracies.

It could also be the case that the party system, as Aldrich says, is not in decline but simply has acquired new forms. One might retort that the earlier system made for more active citizens. But cross-national survey research does not show that countries with party systems more like our earlier system have citizens more satisfied with how their democracy works than ours.

Nonetheless, Walter Dean Burnham was right to think as long and as hard as he did about cycles of decline and renewal in American party politics. Perhaps critical realignments never really existed, but political decline and renewal are

hardly fanciful inventions of Burnham's towering intellect. They are the oldest and most important issues of political thought, going back to Aristotle.

For all their faults, political parties have been the essential foundation of both citizen involvement and citizen awareness of the issues facing a democratic polity. Perhaps nothing will come of letting our two-party system continue to become just one among many channels for citizen involvement, rather than the premier channel. It is more likely, though, that good things would come from trying, as Schier suggests, to make our party system more salient for voters and politicians than it currently is.

RICHARD M. VALELLY is a professor of political science at Swarthmore College.

ADDING VALUES

FOR DEMOCRATS TO SOLIDIFY THEIR POLITICAL POWER IN THE POST-CLINTON ERA, THEY NEED TO TALK ABOUT MORE THAN THE ECONOMY. THEY NEED TO PROMOTE FAMILY-CENTERED VALUES.

BY ANNA GREENBERG AND STANLEY B. GREENBERG

Isn't there something puzzling about our current political debate? With a popular Democrat having served two terms in the White House, the nation has seen sustained economic growth with low unemployment and low inflation. A well-qualified vice president is positioned to carry Democratic policies forward. If he were to gain Democratic majorities in Congress, he might be able to confront nagging problems such as inequality in the midst of prosperity.

After all, the public puts more trust in the Democrats on almost everything that matters: securing Social Security's stability, reforming health care, raising education standards, and protecting the environment. Polls show that the public has more confidence in the Democrats to handle the economy and the budget. There is somewhat more trust in the Republicans to handle taxes and crime, but less markedly so than before the Clinton administration. The public turns to the Republicans on few other issues. Yet this seeming mandate for Democrats to take charge of government has so far not altered the balance of forces on the ground. Instead of a cakewalk for Democrats, a competitive election is shaping up—one that might just give Republicans control of the three branches of government. How do we account for this state of affairs?

It goes beyond economics: It has to do with values. This is the one place Republicans hold a decisive advantage. People respect the Democrats for their openness to new ideas, their commitment to community, and their defense of tolerance and individual rights. But at this moment, with families under great pressure, voters are more impressed with the Republicans' insistence on personal responsibility, discipline, and teaching children about right and wrong. Voters want young people to learn norms and limits. And Democrats are more commonly seen to be permissive about such things.

During the 1990s, Democrats changed their standing on these concerns, but the two-year struggle over Clinton's impeachment undermined their progress. At a time when the electorate is increasingly open to the Democrats as a party of sensible investment, the party has lost ground in the battle over values.

This is territory that need not be conceded. For progressives to rediscover America's values, they don't have to embrace the right's version of "family values." The right resents women's changing roles, not to mention abortion rights and sexual freedom. But while the American people are upset with moral decline, they are uncomfortable with solutions that see the family narrowly or that impose a unitary vision of religious belief.

The public discomfort with the right gives progressives an opportunity to re-enter the values debate. Voters want political leaders who put the family at the center of political discussion and who devote themselves to a policy agenda that will help families meet the myriad challenges they face. They are drawn to Democrats who respect the public's religious faith and belief in personal responsibility and who understand the range of economic and social forces undermining parents.

A family-centered progressive discourse on values would free voters to respond to Democrats on the social and economic issues on which Democrats now have a presumptive advantage. Such a discourse could alter the balance of power in the country.

THE EMERGENCE OF DEMOCRATIC VALUES

The historic battles of the 1960s and 1970s broadened rights for blacks, women, and gays, but they also left a scar: the seeming indifference of the left to the decline of personal responsibility. Those who did the right thing—who worked hard and supported their families—

Reprinted with permission from *The American Prospect*, Vol. 11, Issue 19, August 28, 2000, pp. 28-31. © 2000 by The American Prospect, 5 Broad Street, Boston, MA 02109. All rights reserved.

had no special virtues in the Democratic world of values. And for more than three decades, conservatives have warred against the values of the 1960s. A majority of Americans by the 1980s accepted the conservative critique, even if they were reluctant to roll back the gains made by women and minorities. For the right and much of the country, Ronald Reagan personified the nostalgia for the neglected virtues.

The Clinton campaign of 1992 and the Democratic Leadership Council focused on this question of neglected virtues; they wanted Democrats to champion responsibility as well as opportunity. While Clinton offered an ambitious investment agenda, he also proposed welfare reform, supported the death penalty, and promised middle class tax cuts as well as a significant effort to reduce federal deficit spending. He insisted that Democrats would offer opportunity and demand responsibility in return—at all levels, from corporate CEOs to mothers on welfare.

Democrats were becoming part of this family-centered values debate when Monica Lewinsky and a coterie of anti-Clinton right-wing groups took center stage. For two years, the country was forced to come to terms with the president's private sexual behavior and his public defense. Democrats saved Clinton's presidency and even made gains in the 1998 midterm elections, but at a price. The Democrats again were identified with 1960s-style irresponsibility.

You can see the damage by looking at recent public opinion polls on values questions, such as one conducted earlier this year by the Democracy Corps, an independent organization founded to do strategic research for Democrats in the postimpeachment period. In broadest terms, the key question posed was, which party shares your values? Democrats trail Republicans by four points (36 percent to 40 percent) in the electorate as a whole, by 15 points among white voters, and by an alarming 25 points among married white voters. The Democratic values problem deepens when we get to specifics. Democrats trail Republicans by 18 points on knowing right from wrong, by 24 points on personal responsibility, and by 33 points on discipline. Democrats are seen as less interested in teaching people that certain kinds of antisocial actions are not permissible. The Republicans, on the other hand, are seen as championing a kind of individualism that requires learned norms, personal responsibility, and self-restraint.

Thus, when it comes to understanding the demands of parenting and the need for children to learn respect, the public is more likely to look to Republicans: 42 percent of respondents think Republicans understand the need to strengthen families, compared to 28 percent who think Democrats understand this challenge, according to another recent poll.

> Voters are drawn to a candidate's values when he or she speaks out on issues explicitly linked to family needs.

For many people, internalized limits or norms of right and wrong are inspired by a religious world view. Americans are the most religiously observant people in the Western industrialized world, with two-fifths attending church or synagogue at least once a week and two-thirds belonging to a congregation. Two-thirds of poll respondents say they believe religion can answer all or most of today's problems.

But here, too, there is a partisan divide. By an almost two-to-one ratio, the public is more likely to associate Republicans with "faith in God" (40 percent to 22 percent). In the white electorate, the most secular-oriented voters support Democrats by more than two to one, but the more numerous regular churchgoers support Republicans by a like ratio.

Little wonder that voters on the eve of the 2000 elections hold back from the Democrats, even though Democrats seem to have the better approach to government.

THE VALUES PROBLEM

The right is ready to help America's embattled families. But how? By attacking permissiveness and untraditional gender roles, by focusing on character, and by promoting a particular vision of religious belief and religious institutions. And with the left pushed to the sidelines, conservatives have gained yardage.

But the American public does not really think about values in such narrow terms. People want to make a better life for their family without jettisoning the progress we've made on tolerance and civil rights. Alan Wolfe, head of the Middle Class Morality Project, notes that people worry that the changing family structure has not been good for children but that, at the same time, people are not anxious to abandon the gains in personal autonomy and in opportunities for women.

Parents do worry about the breakdown of rules and discipline. In a recent national survey, 45 percent said educating children about rules and respect is the biggest problem facing families today (39 percent said the quality of schools is foremost). And 77 percent expressed con-

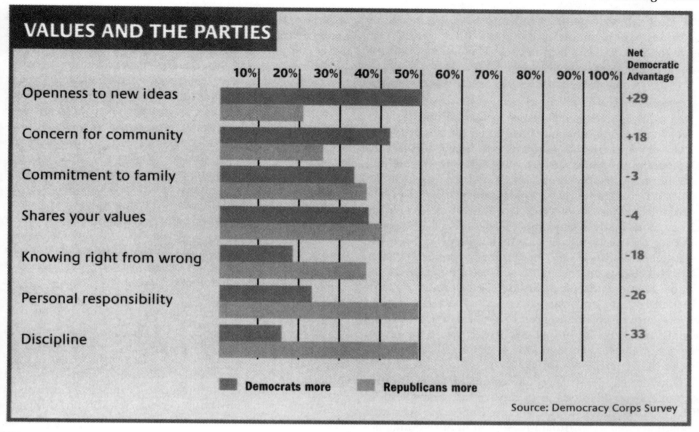

VALUES AND THE PARTIES

	Net Democratic Advantage
Openness to new ideas	+29
Concern for community	+18
Commitment to family	-3
Shares your values	-4
Knowing right from wrong	-18
Personal responsibility	-26
Discipline	-33

■ Democrats more   ■ Republicans more

Source: Democracy Corps Survey

cern that children in America are no longer safe in their schools.

Much of this concern is tied to time and work pressures on parents; according to one national poll, 56 percent worry a great deal that "because of work and other pressures, parents don't have enough time to spend with their children." The vast majority of the public thinks that men's and women's changing roles have made it harder to raise children and maintain a successful marriage.

These are not artificial concerns created by the right. With more single-parent households and more households with both parents working, there are more "latchkey" children. People have real worries about family life, and they are looking for help—from other parents, the community, the church, schools, and even the government. Do progressives have anything to say to these families?

PROGRESSIVE APPROACHES

Many progressives do. There are three predominant schools of thought among progressives who think about values. The first two schools are fairly well-established. The third, more clearly centered on family concerns, reflects policies now supported by Democrats and progressives, but is not always articulated in terms of values. It is this third school that needs to be more prominent.

One established perspective emphasizes material values. It's a credible progressive approach, typified by Ruy Teixeira and Joel Rogers in their recent book, *America's Forgotten Majority: Why the White Working Class Still Matters.* The authors argue, convincingly, that Democrats have lost their majority in the country because they have lost the support of the white working class, particularly men. Democrats have rushed to compete for "soccer moms" while forgetting white workers whose incomes have declined and who cope with the insecurity of the new economy.

These voters, Teixeira and Rogers maintain, bring important value judgments to their political choices. These judgments are "deeply held and broadly shared ones about opportunity, fair reward for effort, the centrality of hard work and individual achievement and social commitment." These values are closely intertwined with work and income. The focus on these "material values" will be an important part of any effort to build a Democratic majority. In fact, the public is more comfortable with this material focus than with one strictly on moral character and religion. According to one recent national survey, voters overwhelmingly prefer a Democratic candidate who emphasizes "families having enough income and affordable health care and education" over a Republican candidate who wants to protect the moral climate and "encourage religion to play a larger role in society."

But the material-values discourse is still separate from faith and family. And the partisan impasse remains. Since the Gingrich Congress, Democrats have been waging battle on health care, education, and the economy, and have made only a small comeback. The national political race remains deadlocked.

There is also a strong progressive tradition that emphasizes social-justice values. From this perspective, Democrats have fought heroic battles to expand rights, and no one need lecture the Democrats on values. Indeed, the battle for rights and equality is unfinished. Representative John Lewis, a battle-tested civil rights leader, personifies this view; it is well reflected also in the voices of the African-American clergy and many Democratic leaders. In his memoir *Walking with the Wind,* Lewis challenges progressives to continue the struggle to "humanize" a political system that still listens to the elites and wealthy but not the "poor, sick and disenfranchised." This country remains divided by race and class, even if this fact is obscured by the current economic prosperity: "a very few people visibly and luxuriantly living in excess while the rest of the nation lives in fear and anxiety. . . two societies, moving farther apart."

Drawing explicitly upon the lessons of the civil rights struggle, Lewis reminds us of the need to promote social justice and equality today. The answer, as he sees it, is both material and spiritual investment in our young people, sparked by efforts from the ground up to force government to respond. Lewis calls for "a revolution of values. A revolution of attitude."

The march for fairness and equality, community and social responsibility, tolerance and change, and individual freedom and privacy has helped solidify Democratic gains with minority voters and with professionals and well-educated women. The affirmation of those values continues to put Republican religious conservatism on the defensive in a wide range of areas.

But affirming those values will not speak directly to the contemporary concerns of families. It will not create any new electoral equation that alters the current balance of electoral forces. For that, one needs a new element.

FAMILY-CENTERED VALUES

More progressives have begun to understand that the future progressive agenda must focus not just on people's work lives but on their family lives. Theda Skocpol in her new book, *The Missing Middle,* offers the clearest formulation yet. She proposes a new politics centered on "the struggles of working mothers and fathers, especially those with modest means." The main policy challenge of that struggle is to "better support parents" in a society that seems to undermine and devalue families. Skocpol argues that "most Americans worry about both the material circumstances *and* the moral climate for family life today." They are receptive to progressive policies that

can become a progressive mission for parents: expanded and intergenerational use of Social Security, ensured child support, affordable child care, a steadily expanding Medicare, and universal access to paid family leave.

Her social goal is to strengthen parents so they can do better both in supporting their children and in giving them moral guidance. Her political goal is to provide social supports for parents who carry so much responsibility for society. In this perspective, the challenges facing families stir progressive passions and shape our discourse. How do parents handle the increasing work pressure and work hours without undermining their responsibilities? How do families find good and safe communities and schools? How do children learn their lessons, but also how do they learn personal responsibility and respect for others? How do people ensure a secure retirement but also keep a family together so it can handle the intergenerational tasks associated with aging?

For a start, Democrats need to honor the religious traditions within their party. Some of their longest-standing supporters—African Americans, Catholics, and Latinos—put religious faith and practice at the center of their family lives. From the Baptist and African Methodist Episcopal churches in Chicago to evangelical churches in Los Angeles to Catholic churches in Detroit and Milwaukee, these Americans practice the lessons of personal responsibility and obligation to others, especially to the disadvantaged. Democrats should feel comfortable with these practices. The progressive left has a proud tradition rooted in the social gospel and the social teachings of the Catholic Church. Moreover, while Americans are religious, it is not in the way the right thinks. The moderate middle does not want to politicize values or religious belief. It wants faith to serve as a source of values, and it wants public officials to embrace such faith. But it does not want to impinge on freedom of religious practice; it does not want to impose values on others.

Progressives also need to rediscover the family. For some three decades, the left neglected to affirm the centrality of the family, especially of two-parent households. The left must give itself permission to recognize the benefit of two-parent families to children. Democrats need to affirm the value of such family structure, even as they redouble their efforts on behalf of single-parent families, whose battles are tougher.

Voters are most attracted to a candidate's values when he or she speaks out on issues explicitly linked to family needs—particularly on health care, education, safety, and retirement. As the Democracy Corps national survey shows, Americans are drawn to candidates who champion affordable health care (64 percent), the education system (61 percent), safe communities (58 percent), and retirement for their parents (57 percent). The least attractive candidates on values, according to the study, are those who forcefully advocate a larger role for religion in society, for example, starting "with the re-introduction of prayer in the public schools" (only 41 percent approval). People are uncomfortable with politicians who rush through this values debate merely by trumpeting the need for greater religiosity.

One more example: When people are asked which candidate they prefer on values—a Republican who sets a moral example and wants religion to play a bigger role in society, or a Democrat who says "young people aren't learning respect for rules, which is why we need to create smaller and safer classrooms where there is more discipline and higher standards"—the Democrat wins by 54 percent to 31 percent.

As it turns out, the best way to win on values is not by pushing religion into public spaces but by creating settings that help parents in their work and by improving places where values can be learned. The classroom is one such place where the Democrats currently have more credibility than the Republicans do.

Democrats can find their voice on values, even in a period when many voters are looking for a return to moral values, a strengthened family, and norms of individual responsibility. To be heard, Democrats must honor religious traditions that teach right and wrong, discipline, responsibility, and respect. Democrats must rediscover the family, where children are nurtured and learn their lessons and values. And finally, Democrats must make clear their motivation in the public realm: to promote policies that help people realize their hopes and dreams for their own families.

ANNA GREENBERG is assistant professor of public policy at the John F. Kennedy School of Government. STANLEY B. GREENBERG is chairman of Greenberg Quinlan Research, Inc., and polling adviser to prime ministers Tony Blair and Ehud Barak.

Making Every Vote Count

Lani Guinier

For years many of us have called for a national conversation about what it means to be a multiracial democracy. We have enumerated the glaring flaws inherent in our winner-take-all form of voting, which has produced a steady decline in voter participation, underrepresentation of racial minorities in office, lack of meaningful competition and choice in most elections, and the general failure of politics to mobilize, inform and inspire half the eligible electorate. But nothing changed. Democracy was an asterisk in political debate, typically encompassed in a vague reference to "campaign finance reform." Enter Florida.

The fiasco there provides a rare opportunity to rethink and improve our voting practices in a way that reflects our professed desire to have "every vote count." This conversation has already begun, as several highly educated communities in Palm Beach experienced the same sense of systematic disfranchisement that beset the area's poorer and less-educated communities of color. "It felt like Birmingham last night," Mari Castellanos, a Latina activist in Miami, wrote in an e-mail describing a mammoth rally at the 14,000-member New Birth Baptist Church, a primarily African-American congregation in Miami. "The sanctuary was standing room only. So were the overflow rooms and the school hall, where congregants connected via large TV screens. The people sang

and prayed and listened. Story after story was told of voters being turned away at the polls, of ballots being destroyed, of NAACP election literature being discarded at the main post office, of Spanish-speaking poll workers being sent to Creole precincts and vice-versa.... Union leaders, civil rights activists, Black elected officials, ministers, rabbis and an incredibly passionate and inspiring Marlene Bastiene—president of the Haitian women's organization—spoke for two or three minutes each, reminding the assembly of the price their communities had paid for the right to vote and vowing not to be disfranchised ever again."

We must not let this once-in-a-generation moment pass without addressing the basic questions these impassioned citizens are raising: Who votes, how do they vote, whom do they vote for, how are their votes counted and what happens after the voting? These questions go to the very legitimacy of our democratic procedures, not just in Florida but nationwide—and the answers could lead to profound but eminently achievable reforms.

§ *Who votes—and doesn't?* As with the rest of the nation, in Florida only about half of all adults vote, about the same as the national average. Even more disturbing, nonvoters are increasingly low-income, young and less educated. This trend persists despite the Voting Rights Act, which since 1970 has banned literacy tests

nationwide as prerequisites for voting—a ban enacted by Congress and unanimously upheld by the Supreme Court.

We are a democracy that supposedly believes in universal suffrage, and yet the differential turnout between high-income and low-income voters is far greater than in Europe, where it ranges from 5 to 10 percent. More than two-thirds of people in America with incomes greater than $50,000 vote, compared with one-third of those with incomes under $10,000. Those convicted of a felony are permanently banned from voting in Florida and twelve other states. In Florida alone, this year more than 400,000 ex-felons, about half of them black, were denied the opportunity to vote. Canada, on the other hand, takes special steps to register former prisoners and bring them into full citizenship.

§ *How do they vote?* Florida now abounds with stories of long poll lines, confusing ballots and strict limitations on how long voters could spend in the voting booth. The shocking number of invalid ballots—more ballots were "spoiled" in the presidential race than were cast for "spoiler" Ralph Nader—are a direct result of antiquated voting mechanics that would shame any nation, let alone one of the world's oldest democracies. Even the better-educated older voters of Palm Beach found, to their surprise, how much they had in common with more frequently disfranchised populations

Given how many decisions voters are expected to make in less than five minutes in the polling booth, it is common sense that the polls should be open over a weekend, or at least for twenty-four hours, and that Election Day should be a national holiday. By highlighting our wretched record on voting practices, Florida raises the obvious question: Do we really want large voter participation?

§ *Whom do they vote for?* Obviously, Florida voters chose among Al Gore, George Bush and a handful of minor-party candidates who, given their status as unlikely to win, were generally ignored and at best chastised as spoilers. But as many voters are now realizing, in the presidential race they were voting not for the candidates whose name they selected (or attempted to select) but for "electors" to that opaque institution, the Electoral College. Our constitutional framers did some things well—chiefly dulling the edge of winner-take-all elections through institutions that demand coalition-building, compromise and recognition of certain minority voices—but the Electoral College was created on illegitimate grounds and has no place in a modern democracy.

As Yale law professor Akhil Reed Amar argues, the Electoral College was established as a device to boost the power of Southern states in the election of the President. The same "compromise" that gave Southern states more House members by counting slaves as three-fifths of a person for purposes of apportioning representation (while giving them none of the privileges of citizenship) gave those states Electoral College votes in proportion to their Congressional delegation. This hypocrisy enhanced the Southern states' Electoral College percentage, and as a result, Virginia slaveowners controlled the presidency for thirty-two of our first thirty-six years.

Its immoral origins notwithstanding, the Electoral College was soon justified as a deliberative body that would choose among several candidates and assure the voice of small geographic areas. But under the Electoral College, voters in small states have more than just a voice; indeed their say often exceeds that of voters in big states. In Wyoming one vote in the Electoral College corresponds to 71,000 voters; in Florida, one electoral vote corresponds to 238,000 voters. At minimum we should eliminate the extra bias that adding electors for each of two senators gives our smallest states. As Robert Naiman of the Center for Economic and Policy Research reports, allowing each state only as many electors as it has members in the House of Representatives would mean, for example, that even if Bush won Oregon and Florida, he would have 216 and Gore would have 220 electoral votes.

Today its backers still argue that the Electoral College is necessary to insure that small states are not ignored by the presidential candidates. Yet the many states— including small ones—that weren't close in this election were neglected by both campaigns. Some of the nation's biggest states, with the most people of color, saw very little presidential campaigning and get-out-the-vote activity. Given their lopsided results this year, we can expect California, Illinois, New York, Texas and nearly all Southern states to be shunned in the 2004 campaign.

§ *How are their votes counted?* The presidency rests on a handful of votes in Florida because allocation of electoral votes is winner-take-all—if Gore wins by ten votes out of 6 million, he will win 100 percent of the state's twenty-five electoral votes. The ballots cast for a losing candidate are always "invalid" for the purposes of representation; only those cast for the winner actually "count." Thus winner-take-all elections underrepresent the voice of the minority and exaggerate the power of one state's razor-thin majority. Winner-take-all is the great barrier to representation of political and racial minorities at both the federal and the state level. No blacks or Latinos serve in the US Senate or in any governor's mansion. Third-party candidates did not win a single state legislature race except for a handful in Vermont.

Given the national questioning of the Electoral College sparked by the anomalous gap between the popular vote and the college's vote in the presidential election, those committed to real representative democracy now have a chance to shine a spotlight on the glaring flaws and disfranchisement inherent in winner-take-all practices and to propose important reforms.

What we need are election rules that encourage voter turnout rather than suppress it. A system of proportional representation—which would allocate seats to parties based on their proportion of the total vote—would more fairly reflect intense feeling within the electorate, mobilize more people to participate and even encourage those who do participate to do so beyond just the single act of voting on Election Day. Most democracies around the world have some form of proportional voting and manage to engage a much greater percentage of their citizens in elections. Proportional representation in South Africa, for example, allows the white Afrikaner parties and the ANC to gain seats in the national legislature commensurate with the total number of votes cast for each party. Under this system, third parties are a plausible alternative. Moreover, to allow third parties to run presidential candidates without being "spoilers," some advocate instant-runoff elections in which voters would rank their choices for President. That way, even voters whose top choice loses the election could influence the race among the other candidates.

Winner-take-all elections, by contrast, encourage the two major parties to concentrate primarily on the "undecideds" and to take tens of millions of dollars of corporate and special-interest contributions to broadcast ads on the public airwaves appealing to the center of the political spectrum. Winner-take-all incentives discourage either of the two major parties from trying to learn, through organizing and door-knocking, how to mobilize the vast numbers of disengaged poor and working-class voters. Rather than develop a vision, they produce a product and fail to build political capacity from the ground up.

§ *What happens after the voting?* Our nation is more focused on elections now than it has been for decades; yet on any given Sunday, more people will watch professional football than voted this November. What democracy demands is a system of elections that enables minor parties to gain a voice in the legislature and encourages the development of local political organizations that educate and mobilize voters.

Between elections, grassroots organizations could play an important monitoring role now unfulfilled by the two major parties. If the Bush campaign is right that large numbers of ballots using the same butterfly format were thrown out in previous elections in Palm Beach, then something is wrong with more than the ballot. For those Democratic senior citizens in Palm Beach, it was not enough that their election supervisor was a Democrat. They needed a vibrant local organization that could have served as a watchdog, alerting voters and election officials that there were problems with the ballot. No one should inadvertently vote for two candidates; the same watchdog organizations should require ballot-counting machines like those in some states that notify the voter of such problems before he or she leaves the booth. Voters should be asked, as on the popular TV quiz show, "Is that your final answer?" And surely we cannot claim to be a functioning democracy when voters are turned away from the polls or denied assistance in violation of both state and federal law.

Before the lessons of Florida are forgotten, let us use this window of opportunity to forge a strong pro-democracy coalition to rally around "one vote, one value." The value of a vote depends on its being fairly counted but also on its counting toward the election of the person the voter chose as her representative. This can happen only if we recognize the excesses of winner-take-all voting and stop exaggerating the power of the winner by denying the loser any voice at all.

Lani Guinier is a professor of law at Harvard Law School. Her latest book is the forthcoming The Miner's Canary: Rethinking Race and Power *(Harvard). Rob Richie of the Center for Voting and Democracy (www.fairvote.org) provided invaluable assistance in the preparation of this essay.*

One Cheer for
Soft Money

The case for strong political parties

BY STEVEN E. SCHIER

TO LISTEN TO JOHN MCCAIN, YOU'D THINK THAT the fate of the republic hinges on the immediate ban of soft-money contributions to political parties. His Web page, www.itsyourcountry.com, boldly asserts: "Ban soft money and your voice will be heard in Washington again." Why? "Without reining in soft money and reducing the role of money in politics, we will never have a government that works as hard for the average American as it does for the special interests."

Translation: national government is corrupt largely because of soft money and by clamping down on soft money, political corruption will shrivel. It's a simple and appealing formula. As with most such formulas, however, it misreads reality and promises more than it can deliver. Though we do need to address any possible corruption resulting from campaign contributions, we need to do it in a way that doesn't damage the ability of our already-weak political parties to add some coherence to America's peculiarly complex, candidate-centered politics.

The Hard Goods on Soft Money

Soft money refers to unlimited contributions directly from corporations, unions, and individuals to party committees. A series of Congressional amendments and Federal Election Commission rulings in the 1970s and 1980s permitted political parties to raise unlimited funds for "election related activities" by state and local parties. These monies, held in "nonfederal" accounts, are not subject to the "hard money" limits of the funds in "federal" accounts. Hard money limits cap annual individual contributions at $25,000. They require interest groups to contribute to candidates and parties through regulated Political Action Committees at a maximum rate of $5,000 per candidate per (primary or general) election and limit individual contributions to $1,000 per candidate per election. Though wealthy individuals, corporations, and unions are thus sharply limited in their hard money contributions, the sky is the contribution limit with soft money.

Since 1980 the parties' national committees and their House and Senate campaign committees have raised increasingly mammoth amounts of soft money, cresting at $262 million in 1996 and $250 million in 1998. Where does all of this money go? Originally, soft money was to be spent on grassroots campaigning by state and local parties for brochures, door knocking, and get-out-the-vote efforts.

The real explosion in soft-money fund raising occurred after a 1995 Federal Election Commission ruling that permitted the parties to spend soft money on "issue advocacy" advertising, an obscure government action that had huge consequences. Though issue-advocacy advertising legally cannot expressly advocate the election or defeat of a candidate, it can link candidates to issues in a way that supports or opposes their election. What is express advocacy? The FEC defined it as any communication that uses phrases like "vote for," "vote against," "elect," or "defeat," and "can have no other reasonable meaning than to urge the election or defeat of one or more clearly identified candidates." Creative campaign minds found all sorts of ways around those restrictions in 1996. The race for soft money to fund issue-advocacy advertising had begun.

The campaign finance scandals afflicting the Clinton presidency in recent years have involved raising soft money from dubious, often overseas sources in large amounts. But the real lesson for candidates from the Clinton experience in 1996 is that soft-money spending works. The Democratic party committees spent over $46.5 million on soft-money-funded ads aiding Clinton's re-election in 1996, many of which appeared early in the election year before Dole and the Republicans were able to respond (they eventually did, but with a comparatively meager $18 million in soft-money ads).

Soft money can spell the difference between victory and defeat, as the 1998 Kentucky Senate race revealed. Pitting two House incumbents, Democrat Scotty Baesler and Republican Jim Bunning, against each other, the race featured an orgy of soft-money spending by the state parties. Though Baesler began the fall campaign with a double-digit lead over Bunning, he was short on funds after winning a competitive primary. Bunning was assisted by over $1.5 million worth of ads paid for by the Kentucky Republican Party, raised with the help of Republican Sen. Mitch McConnell, an outspoken defender of soft money. One GOP soft money ad attacked Baesler for supporting NAFTA, concluding with a stereotypical Mexican saying, "Muchas Gracias, Senor Baesler." The state Democratic Party could only spend one-third of the Republican total for ads. The money disparity helped Bunning earn a narrow victory in November.

What's Bad about Soft Money?

McCain and his fellow reformers have some good arguments against the current soft-money regime. It's not wise to allow corporations and unions to give unlimited amounts to parties. Large corporations give huge amounts to parties to secure or defend favorable governmental treatment. The publicly owned digital television spectrum was recently distributed for free to television broadcasters, who have given $5 million in soft money in recent years. Agribusiness companies have given over $4.5 million in soft-money in recent years, helping to maintain federal ethanol subsidies worth $500 million annually. Even if these actions aren't out-and-out bribes, they certainly present an "appearance of corruption" to many citizens.

We need to keep parties well-funded in some form to ensure they don't have their electoral role greatly diminished. Parties can't prosper without robust national parties at the center of the campaigns.

In addition to bad appearances, the explosion of soft money advertising has increased the "clutter" of messages besieging voters during election campaigns. Political scientist David Magelby, in a recent book on the impact of soft-money and issue-advocacy advertising in the 1998 elections, concludes that in competitive House and Senate races, voters are "inundated" with communications about the candidates and that "the negative tone of many of the noncandidate ads has the potential to reinforce alienation and cynicism among voters." In several states, party ads were more negative than those run by candidate campaigns.

So if soft money contributes to at least the appearance of corruption in national politics, confuses and alienates voters, we should get rid of it, right? That is certainly the conventional wisdom about campaign finance reform in many Washington circles. But it's not entirely correct. We need to keep parties well-funded in some form to ensure they don't have their electoral role greatly diminished. Why? Because, despite the clutter, there are some good arguments for party-based election advertising. Our elections can survive the onset of message clutter, but they can't prosper without robust national parties at the center of the campaigns.

The Virtues of Soft Money

The attack on soft money is appropriately an attack on corruption, but it's also an attack on political parties themselves. Throughout American history, political parties have performed vital services for our democracy. America would benefit from stronger parties, for three reasons. First, strong parties bring people into politics. By distilling the choice among a variety of candidates to a selection between one of two partisan "teams," parties lower information costs for voters, thus encouraging those with less education and less income to vote. In the twentieth century, as ballots have become more complex, it has become harder for many voters to sort their way through the increasing amount of information needed to make an informed decision.

The growing trend of recent decades has been toward more personalism in politics, dominated by candidates selling themselves, not a common party platform. Though Congress is more partisan lately because of the close competitive balance between the parties, the public has turned away from political parties. Political scientist Marvin Wattenberg has found that steadily more members of the public have no views at all about political parties and find them less and less relevant to politics. Accordingly, candidates sell themselves as individuals. Just ask yourself when was the last time you saw a party label prominently displayed in a candidate's general election TV or radio ads? Parties have all but disappeared from candidate communication with general election voters because candidates find the party label less useful in rounding up support.

This sort of politics occurs in Latin American countries such as Peru and Venezuela, where presidents Fujimori and Chavez appeal to the masses first. In both countries, personalism has weakened parties and democracy. Though America is far from the instability of Peru and Venezuela, it shares with them a pattern of declining voter participation and disengagement of large segments of the population from politics. The 49 percent turnout in the 1996 U.S. presidential election was the lowest since 1924, shortly after women got the vote. The 36 percent turnout in the 1998 midterm election was the lowest since the 1942 midterm, which occurred in the middle of a world war.

Second, strong parties can shield lawmakers from the very special-interest influence that many accuse them of surrendering to. As support for parties and turnout in elections has declined, interest-group membership has grown. Now, the proportion of Americans who are interest group members far exceeds the ranks of strong party identifiers. A 1990 survey conducted for the American Society of Association Executives estimated that 70 percent of the public are members of associations, while the number of strong partisans hovers around 30 percent.

As interests grew in numbers and strength in recent decades, lawmakers became more responsive to them.

The number of groups listed in the *Encyclopedia of Associations* mushroomed from 5,000 in 1956 to 23,000 by 1996 and a record number of lobbyists now ply their trade in Washington. From the National Federation of Independent Businesses on the right to the American Association of Retired Persons on the left, national government is beset by hundreds of well-funded, effective, and insistent interest groups. With their resources of campaign money, hired analysts, and memberships that vote, their clout has never been greater.

This cacophony of interests has its costs. Proliferating interest groups do not produce accountable government the way party-based elections can. Worldwide, nations with weak party systems have low participation in elections. Meager electoral participation plays into the hands of organized special interests. In America, these special interests are highly skilled in the art of activating their members to vote and lobby. And with fewer other voters, such groups have a larger voice in electoral outcomes. You need look no farther than the success of Christian conservative groups in promoting the Republican triumph in the 1994 elections to see how well-organized interest groups benefit when others stay home.

Political scientist Robert Putnam correctly argues that accountability to a broad set of interests can only result from heavy electoral participation that exerts influence over the behavior of elected officials. Strong party systems have a global record of facilitating that participation. In America's weak party system, low participation reduces the accountability of those we elect to broad, common interests and enhances their accountability to the narrower set of organized interest groups that help get their favorite candidates elected.

Third, strong and stable parties are essential to the stability of democracy itself. Most of the world's democracies that have survived 25 years or more have had stable party systems with a low number of parties. In most of these nations, parties dominate elections and the operation of government. Many such democracies (and most of the European ones) allow voters to vote only for parties, instead of individual candidates, in elections and have parliamentary systems in which parties gain control of the legislative and executive branches and rule as highly disciplined teams. American parties, in contrast, are a rag-tag assemblage of electoral individualists.

Walter Dean Burnham of the University of Texas summarizes what parties can do for us: "Political parties, with all their well-known human and structural shortcomings, are the only devices thus far invented by the wit of Western man that can, with some effectiveness, generate countervailing collective power on behalf of the many individually powerless against the relatively few who are individually or organizationally powerful." Parties are the best available means for linking majority preferences with governmental action because they help to simplify and clarify voting choices. Choosing between two teams rather than among a plethora of individual candidates makes it easier for more citizens to cast an informed vote. That's one major reason why turnout in just about every other constitutional democracy is well above that of the United States.

To restore this vital party function, we need to make our elections more about parties and their philosophies and less about individual candidates and their personalities. Giving parties more resources with which to do this requires that we not diminish their role in national elections, but rather ensure that they are well funded in ways that minimize apparent or actual corruption.

By encouraging contributions to parties instead of to individual candidates, we can actually limit corruption in American politics. The likelihood of a quid-pro-quo is always greater if the money goes directly to a candidate. By sending money to the parties, we create a "buffer" between campaign contributions and the government officials those contributions seek to influence. The trick is to keep the money from arriving in such large quantities to parties that the buffer virtually disappears, as it has at present.

Reforms to Help the Parties

We need to take several steps to restore parties to a central role in American politics. First, soft-money contributions must be limited to prevent corruption, but preserved to prevent further party decline. A desirable alternative to the McCain-Feingold ban on soft money lies in a bill sponsored by Sens. Bob Kerrey (D) and Chuck Hagel (R) of Nebraska. Their bill caps soft-money contributions of $60,000 per year and indexes hard-money limits for inflation since 1974, effectively tripling them. The soft-money cap will greatly reduce the likelihood of corruption through soft money and the higher hard-money limits will permit larger hard-money contributions to parties.

Second, we need to keep the hard-money individual and PAC contribution limits to candidates low, while raising them considerably for political parties. Hard-money limits are enforced and recorded by the Federal Election Commission. Currently, individuals can only give a maximum of $20,000 a year to political parties. That limit should be raised to $50,000, while keeping the individual contribution limits to PACs and directly to candidates at $1,000. This will cause more funds to flow to parties, reducing the power of narrow interests in elections and curbing the appearance (and, at times, reality) of corruption linked to direct contributions from PACs to candidates. Even with higher hard-money contribution limits for parties, the Kerrey-Hagel cap on soft-money contributions will prevent the "mega-contributions" from unions and corporations to parties that plague our current politics.

Third, to make parties more central to campaigns, we need to allocate large blocks of free airtime to state and national parties for them to use to boost their candidates for national office. This can be a remarkably effective cure for electoral individualism. Campaigns are cash-intensive because of the need to buy TV ads, so giving parties power over ads really hits candidates where they live, making soft-money contributions integral to their success. To make parties more important, the blocks of time allocated to them need to be large. State parties could get one hour for each House candidate they field and two or more hours (pro-rated based on the ratio of Senators to Representatives) for their Senate candidates. National parties each need several hours of network time during the fall presidential campaigns.

Fourth, to weaken the role of interest groups in campaigns, we should ban corporations and unions from direct issue-advocacy electioneering. Those issue-advocacy ads that flood our airwaves during fall elections come straight from corporate and union treasuries, confusing voters and empowering narrow interests at the expense of parties. Such ads seek to aid particular candidates, evading laws passed by Congress that ban corporate contributions to candidates from corporations (in 1907) and unions (in 1947). Courts have upheld contribution bans in the past, so a legislative ban on issue-advocacy ads by such interests might well pass constitutional muster. We need to invite the Supreme Court to reverse *Buckley v. Valeo* on this point.

Fifth, the First Amendment does give individuals the right to run issue ads during campaigns, but the public should have the right to know who is doing the spending. It is difficult to imagine a narrower political interest than a single millionaire or a few wealthy individuals. Elections should involve large, strong parties with broad concerns, not a small number of rich folks with a particular agenda. If we cannot ban that advertising, we can at least strengthen disclosure laws to make it immediately clear who's brought the ads.

These changes will be weak tea for many campaign-finance reformers. Many would like to remove private money from elections completely, or equalize the spending of campaign money through government regulation. Aside from the political improbability of such reforms, such changes would create more problems than they would solve. Figuring out how to equalize expression in campaigns between often little-known challengers and incumbents is an impossible task, the Supreme Court in *Buckley v. Valeo* explicitly rejected governmental regulation to equalize campaign expression on first amendment grounds. Accordingly, any public financing plan would have to be voluntary (as is presidential campaign finance now). New state public financing laws, recently adopted in Maine and Vermont, however, give all the money directly to candidates and sharply restrict the funds parties can raise to influence elections. That is moving in the wrong direction. Instead of creating "a government that works as hard for the average American as it does for the special interests," as John McCain desires, these laws have diminished the electoral power of political parties, the institutions with the best worldwide record of stimulating turnout in elections.

The Maine and Vermont laws reveal an unpleasant truth about many campaign-finance reformers. Like the progressive movement of the early 20th century, they are aggressively anti-party. The progressives pushed through a variety of reforms that drastically curtailed the power of parties in American politics—the direct primary, personal voter registration, and the end of patronage hiring. As party power shrank, elections increasingly became contests between multitudes of individual candidates instead of between two parties. The electoral world became more indecipherable to more Americans. Guess what? Voting turnout dropped. And it's still remarkably low.

During the partisan era of 100 years ago, turnouts of 75 percent were common in presidential elections, far above today's miserable levels, and involving a far less educated electorate than today's voters. Clearly, parties did something right. It's time to give them another chance.

Political parties may be part of the problem with electoral politics, but properly reviving them is very much part of the solution. We need to roll back corrupt practices while strengthening parties. Campaign-finance reformers need to understand that if they want robust campaigns and high turnout, they need to learn how to love political parties, not destroy them.

STEVEN E. SCHIER *is chair of the department of political science at Carleton College and the author of* By Invitation Only: The Rise of Exclusive Politics in the United States.

Government's End

**THE REFORMERS IN THE '80S AND '90S TRIED TO PULL THE FEDERAL
GOVERNMENT TO THE RIGHT OR THE LEFT. BUT, IN THE END,
THEY DID NOT REMAKE GOVERNMENT. IT REMADE THEM.**

BY JONATHAN RAUCH

*S*ince 1980, three waves of reformers have sought to
transform American government. None succeeded.
What went wrong? And what does it mean? In his
new book Government's End: Why Washington
Stopped Working—*extensively revised since its first publication in 1994 as* Demosclerosis—National Journal *senior
writer Jonathan Rauch suggests an answer: The American
public, having accepted limits on government's ability to
change society, must now also accept equally exacting limits
on society's ability to change government. An adapted excerpt
follows.*

To look back upon the 1980s and 1990s is to see
what appears to be, at first blush, a period of quie-
tude following the social and political storms of
the 1960s and 1970s. The Reagan and Clinton years
brought fiscal wars over deficits and culture wars over
abortion and political correctness, but no Vietnam, no
stagflation, no dogs and fire hoses in Alabama, and no
chilling confrontations between democracy and totalitari-
anism. Intellectuals often complained that the Reagan period was complacent and vacuous, and that the Clinton
years brought the abandonment of the activist spirit that
once had energized American liberalism. The appearance, though, was partly deceiving. If American society
was calmer after the 1970s, American government decid-
edly was not, for discontent with society had been displaced by discontent with government.

The era beginning in 1981 and ending, perhaps, in
1996 marks the most concentrated period of governmental reformism since the Progressives swept to power in
Washington and in the cities nearly a century earlier.
There was, however, a difference. The Progressives
largely succeeded in breaking the old cronyist machines

and replacing them with a class of professional ad-
ministrators and a "clean government" ethic (with mixed
effects, by the way). The reformers in the Reagan-to-Clin-
ton years failed. They did not remake government; it remade them.

For the Progressives, the problem had been corruption
and greed and the heavy hands of the bosses, who favored friends and shut out adversaries and thereby (in
the view of the day) created political monopolies as damaging to the public good as were the great economic
trusts. More openness, more access, and above all more
professionalism were the answers. By 1981, when President Reagan took office, the Progressive formula had
been turned on its head, although at that point few people realized the extent of the change. America's government was easily among the cleanest in the world or,
indeed, in history. Endless safeguards of bureaucratic
procedure and legal due process ensured that any decision that was deemed arbitrary or unfair could be challenged, first in administrative rulemaking, then in court,
and finally in Congress. The civil service had been professionalized—and so, more recently and probably more
importantly, had been the political class. It was now not
only possible but common to be a full-time, professional
lobbyist or political consultant.

And access? It was copious, redundant—so copious
and redundant as to transform Washington itself into the
site of a bidding war. With the old congressional seniority system weakened by the post-Watergate reformers of
the 1970s, Congress now consisted of 535 individual entrepreneurs, each member chosen independently of party
and president, each member a canny survivalist who
could be asked to follow where the committee chairman
or whip led but who could not be required to do so. For
the (now) countless thousands of groups that profession-

ally worked Washington, this meant that what you did not get from one member of Congress you could seek from another. The relationship worked the other way, too. When the politicians came calling on the lobbies for campaign money, as they did with growing brazenness, each group knew there were plenty of other lobbies, often competitors and adversaries, eager to help. If the Banking Committee chairman did not get what he wanted from the American Bankers Association, why, the credit union people or S&L people or insurance people or securities people were only too willing to step into the breach. The culture of government, by 1981, was honest and professional and astonishingly transparent; no one hid anything. But the economics of government, by then, was that of a piranha pool, with thousands of small but sharp-toothed and very strongly motivated actors determined not to be the loser at the end of the day. Every actor's activity, of course, drew in yet more actors. The Maryland state lottery, once ran an ad campaign on the theme "If you don't play, you can't win." By the 1980s, Washington had become a kind of demented casino, whose slogan was "If you don't play, you can't win—but boy, can you lose!" Not surprisingly, everybody played.

The public, of course, was angry and disillusioned by 1981. The "trust in government" barometer had collapsed since the early 1960s. Confidence in government had been replaced with cynicism and suspicion. Among conservatives, a reform movement had arisen, in tandem with the change in the government itself. The movement was not progressivism so much as regressivism, but it was equipped with a powerful and sweeping critique of government and with a grand architecture of reform. Some liberals, too, dreamed of sweeping change. Ironically, however, although the liberal reformers and conservative reformers vied to pull Washington in opposite directions, they would soon discover they were trapped together like antagonistic prisoners thrown into the same cell. Both were mostly helpless.

If you view Washington's problems as superficial and transitory—the result of having elected this or that president, or of divided partisan control of government, or what have you—then the answer should be to elect some new leader or to consolidate power. If you think the problem is that the politicians are all the same, all empty suits wedded to the status quo, then the solution should be to elect some revolutionaries who will shake things

PUSH, PULL:
With his ambitious health reform plan, Bill Clinton tried to move government to the left. With his Contract With America, Newt Gingrich tried to move it to the right. Both failed.

up. If you think the problem is that reform in one direction simply goes the wrong way, then the right approach should be to try reform in the opposite direction.

As it turned out, the era of reform proved to be a uniquely useful natural laboratory for diagnosing government's condition, because many of the available permutations were tried. First the Republicans enjoyed effective control of both Congress and the White House, then the Democrats controlled both branches, and then control was divided. Far from electing empty suits, the voters on three occasions brought in strikingly fresh and energetic leaders, leaders who fervently believed in reform and who spared no effort to make it happen. And far from standing pat in moderation, the reform efforts lurched in two opposite directions. Reagan and House Speaker Newt Gingrich had pulled to the right, and had mostly failed (with a few important exceptions, such as Reagan's tax reform and Gingrich's welfare reform); Bill Clinton, with his sweeping health-care reform, had pulled to the left, but fared no better.

Yet, by the end of the 1990s, the reform era had subsided into exhaustion. The voters seemed to have given up, and there was no viable reform movement anywhere in sight. The battlefield was empty, the Bastille untaken, and the adversary little more than inconvenienced. In fact, the Washington establishment was fatter and happier than ever.

A REVOLUTIONARY'S BLUEPRINT

Of the reformers, none showed more energy and promise than Newt Gingrich. In hindsight (always the most discerning kind of vision), Gingrich seems to have been an overweening idealist who pushed his luck too far. But defeat appears inevitable only after the war. Gingrich did not enter office as House speaker without a plan. He explained it in January 1995, and it was not a stupid plan.

Gingrich was no newcomer. He went in with his eyes wide open. The power structure on Capitol Hill, he told *The Washington Times* as he assumed the speakership, had "ossified into a straitjacket. That is not partisan or ideological—these guys and their staffs had networks of power and networks of relationships and habits and things that they weren't going to break for a mere president. They'd ignored Nixon, Ford, Carter. They had blocked Reagan and beaten Bush." Moreover, "every time you mention something which ought to be shrunk or zeroed, twenty-five people who are making money off of it jump up to explain why it is a wonderful institution and they should continue to make money off it."

Gingrich's response, his battle plan, is instructive, because on paper it was plausible. First, he would mobilize his supporters, the fiery voters who had demolished Democrats and tossed out a reigning House speaker to put Gingrich and his reformers in charge. "The point we're going to make to people is, you'd better call your representative and tell them you want them to help pass the constitutional amendment to require a balanced budget—with a tax-increase limit. We're going to use every bully pulpit we have. . . . And we're going to tell every conservative group in the country and every group that wants smaller government, you'd better talk to your representatives." The intensity of the government reformers was high, Gingrich knew, so they could mobilize some of the same merciless spot pressure as the interest groups.

As for the Democrats, the 1994 election had thrown them into disarray. The president sounded chagrined, humbled, the wind knocked out of him. "I agree with much of what the electorate said yesterday," he said the day after the election. "They still believe that government is more often the problem than the solution. They don't want any party to be the party of government. They don't want the presumption to be that people in Washington know what's best. . . . I accept responsibility for not delivering to whatever extent it's my fault we haven't delivered." This humbled president would still wield a veto, but he would be presented with a stream of bills passed on the Republicans' terms in the wake of an election that had given them a mandate. If he refused to deal, he would risk seeming obstructive and deaf to the voters' demands. Anyway (said the Republicans to themselves), this was not a president who had shown a lot of backbone.

The lobbies, of course, could be counted upon to try to block or emasculate everything. Gingrich's response: swamp them. Attack so many programs at once that the Democrats and liberals and establishmentarians would have to choose the programs they wanted to save. The rest, the Republicans would knock off. The Democrats would have to "figure out which fights to stay and fight," Gingrich said. Gingrich was hoping to invert the usual Washington pattern, in which reformers were required to focus their energies on a few programs and let the rest of their agenda slide away. By attacking on a broad front, he would force the *defenders* to concentrate

TRUE TO FORM:

The public wants the government to be leaner, but not at the expense of students, farmers, workers, or retirees.

their fire. The Republicans would not get everything, but they would get a great deal.

Finally, Gingrich knew that at each stage of the process—House deliberations, Senate deliberations, House-Senate conferences, negotiations with the White House, presidential vetoes—he would lose bits and pieces of his agenda. A month or a year wouldn't be enough, a point he went out of his way to emphasize. Instead, he would start in 1995, running a flying wedge through the Washington power structure, and then come back again and again after that, widening the breach. There could be no "Mao-style revolution," he said. "I want to get to a dramatically smaller federal government. I think you do that one step at a time, but you insist on steps every year. . . . The reason I keep telling people to study FDR is if you take fourteen steps successfully you're a lot farther down the road than this guy next to you if he's trying to get all fourteen steps in one jump."

The trouble was, of course, that he never got to the second step. Why?

THE PARADOX OF PARTICULARS

Voters in the polling booth vote for "change" in the abstract. But presidents and members of Congress can't. "In Congress, we don't get to vote on the abstraction," Republican Rep. Vin Weber of Minnesota told Time Magazine in 1992, shortly before retiring from office. "We have to vote for or against actual programs." That means confronting actual constituencies. Gingrich's hope to invert this equation foundered on the fact that in the case of any *particular* program or subsidy or perquisite of whatever sort, there is almost always far more energy on the defensive side than on the offensive side.

Say someone in Gingrich's position as a House leader hoped to reform or abolish a thousand programs. No one of those programs is essential to his effort. If he must, he can always drop twenty or thirty or even a hundred or two. There is no overwhelming incentive to go after any particular constituency. To the defender of the subsidy for left-handed screwdrivers, however, only *one* program matters: his own. He will spare no effort. For that defender, and for each of the others, it's life or death.

Gingrich understood this but thought he could count on his zealous Republicans to hold the line across a broad front. The discipline he was expecting, however, was superhuman. The temptation to help out this one group, or that one, was not Democratic or liberal; it was universal. After all, the clients understood that if one congressman would not help them, another might. Every congressman understood this, too. Why let someone else do the rescuing and take the credit? And every congressman also understood that every other congressman understood. And so, at every stage in the process, Democrats *and* Republicans demanded that this or that program be let off the hook. "I'd love to support you, Mr. Speaker, but I tell you, I am just taking a beating from those left-handed screwdriver people in my district—you've got to cut me a break." Facing this inevitable onslaught, Gingrich found that it was he and his reformers, not the Democrats or liberals, who were swamped.

David Stockman, Reagan's reformist budget director, had run into the same problem, and had reacted with contempt for the gutless Republicans who were all for cutting government except the bits they wanted to save. Stockman, however, missed the point: Given the calculus of the game, the gutless Republicans were doing the only rational thing. The same sort of calculus had wrecked Clinton's health-care package in 1994. In fact, what was remarkable in 1995, arguably, was not how much the reform package was watered down in Gingrich's House (with significant program terminations shrinking by a factor of ten) but how large a tattered remnant actually survived.

Gingrich understood the importance of public mobilization. He counted on it to push his program past the Democrats and Clinton. In Gingrich's case, and also in Stockman's and Clinton's, the reformers depended on the public to rally around when political hackery began to prevail over the spirit of reform. And, sure enough, the public always did rally—but *to the wrong side.*

It turns out to be surprisingly easy for the protectors of programs to spook the public by screaming bloody murder. The public wants the government to be leaner, but not at the expense of students, farmers, bankers, workers, veterans, retirees, homeowners, artists, teachers, train riders, or cats and dogs. The people cannot abide the ghoulish shrieks and moans that are heard the moment the reformers' scalpel comes out. The same narrow focus and intense commitment that make lobbies so adept at defending themselves on Capitol Hill also make them good at alarming the public with "red alert" mailings and scary television ads (as with "Harry and Louise"). When all else fails, there is the old "Don't hurt our children" ploy. In 1993, when Congress managed to abolish the wool and mohair subsidy, the reformers were all the more courageous for having faced down pleas like the one from Nelda Corbell, whose parents raised mohair in Texas: "I am eight years

HARRY AND LOUISE: With their narrow focus, lobbies are adept at defending themselves with "red alert" mailings and scary television ads.

old and I want to know why the government wants to take away our living." What kind of monster would hurt little Nelda?

Now and then, politicians manage to turn public opinion against a particular lobby, or at least they manage to exploit a change in public opinion, as the tobacco lobby found out. But usually they can't even do that. In his 1996 presidential campaign, when Bob Dole tried to mobilize public sentiment against the teachers' unions, he was judged quixotic. The public is nervous, often rightly, when politicians try to demonize some faction or other. Public nervousness makes the climate of opinion flammable; all that remains is to light a spark.

RATIONAL PARANOIA

In May 1981, President Reagan, on Stockman's advice, proposed a package of modest reductions in Social Security: reduced benefits for early retirees, a three-month delay in the cost-of-living adjustment, and so forth. The result was what Congressional Quarterly described as a "tempest in Congress." The Democrats until then had been helpless against Stockman, but they knew that this time he had stumbled onto vulnerable ground. The House Democratic caucus promptly and unanimously passed a resolution denouncing Reagan's "unconscionable breach of faith" and swearing not to "destroy the program or a generation of retirees." Democrats in the Senate promised to use "every rule in the book" to stop the proposal. "Democrats waged their assault with obvious glee," said Congressional Quarterly, and they kept waging it through the 1982 elections, when they gained twenty-six seats in the House and regained effective control there. Painting Reagan and the Republicans as scourges of Social Security received a good deal of the credit (the economic recession received most of the rest).

CHOP, CHOP: With the help of Stockman, Reagan tried to cut government programs, but encountered GOP resistance.

In 1995, Newt Gingrich's Republicans, responsibly and courageously, undertook to propose some modest but significant reforms of the Medicare program for the elderly. That the program's finances were in trouble, and that reductions would have to be made one way or another, were facts known to everybody in Washington, including President Clinton. He proposed reducing the growth of Medicare's costs from more than 4 percent a year for six years to 2.7 percent. The Republican plan, in not exactly sharp contrast, proposed reducing the growth path to 1.5 percent, with some larger structural reforms than Clinton preferred. In dollars, the difference between the plans was about 7 percent in the last year, 2002. But that was enough for the Democrats. Through the 1996 campaigns, they hammered the Republicans for "cutting" Medicare. "The Republicans are wrong to want to cut Medicare benefits," a voice-over intoned in one Democratic ad, as the faces of Bob Dole and Newt Gingrich danced on the screen. "And President Clinton is right to protect Medicare, right to defend our decision as a nation to do what's moral, good, and right by our elderly." The campaign became known as Mediscare, and it was accounted a great success. The public was quite willing to believe that Gingrich and his crew were out to gut Medicare. Despite their pleas of innocence, the Republicans never recovered.

In 1993, Bill Clinton proposed his health-care reform package. In 1994 came the "Harry and Louise" ads and plenty of others like them. Again, opponents had little trouble arousing public hostility to reform. So the trick works for both parties.

It works, you may say, because the public is ignorant and easily frightened. That explanation is right, to some extent. But it fails to give the public quite enough credit, because the public's suspicions were rational in each case. When the Gingrichites tried to make changes in Medicare, they plausibly argued that the (small) pain they were imposing on one group would be more than offset by the benefits to everybody from lower deficits, lower taxes, and a solvent Medicare program. But at that stage, the Democrats and the lobbies, acting as a swing vote, did exactly as the playbook suggests. They recast the debate as group versus group rather than as group versus nation. They stood on a box with a megaphone and warned: "Don't believe those Republicans! They're not going to give anything back to you once they've cut Medicare. They're financing tax cuts for the rich! They're just taking from you to give to their friends!"

Most Americans will sacrifice for a larger public good, but few will sacrifice for a competing group. The larger public loses interest in reducing Medicare, or in reducing anything else, if it believes that the only result will be to shift resources from one group to another. By kindling suspicions that the Republicans were acting in the interests of their favorite clients rather than of the nation as a whole, the Democrats and their allied lobbies had no trouble sinking the Republicans' Medicare deal. On health reform, the Republicans and the plan's other opponents used the same tactic against Clinton and the Democrats. "This plan doesn't mean more care at lower prices," they said. "It means poorer care for you and bet-

ter care for other people, with huge new bureaucracies in the bargain."

Alas, this trick of kindling mistrust can almost always be used by somebody, because the charges, though overdrawn and often misleading, are usually plausible and partly true. The Republicans *were* trying to cut Medicare while also reducing taxes for better-off citizens. The Democrats *were* relying on bureaucratic controls to constrain choices for the middle class and expand health access for the poor. In 1981, the Reagan administration *was* trying to use Social Security reductions to help pay for upper-class tax cuts. In a democracy, parties do not get things done (or win elections) unless they favor their supporters, which means that the other side of any argument can always cry foul. And the voters' cynicism, which admittedly is often justified, makes them quick to believe charges that the system will double-cross them. The cynicism, of course, is self-fulfilling.

ON GUARD: Lobbyists have been successful in perpetuating a stalemate. The borders of the jungle are more or less set.

So here is the conundrum of collective political action. If you assume that everyone else will act in his rational self-interest, you have every reason to support politicians who put dollars or benefits or protections in your pocket, and little or no reason to support politicians who remove them. Although it is certainly possible to neutralize the opposition party and divide the lobbies and win the public's support, no sensible politician or voter ought to expect it to happen. Far more likely is the fate of the reformers of the 1980s and 1990s, who found themselves, after starting out well, suddenly staring at a coalition of opponents that comprised the opposition party, the lobbies, and the broad public. Against that array of forces, there is simply no hope. Reformers are crushed.

In the movie *The African Queen*, a famous scene has the protagonists' boat hopelessly stuck in a marsh—only a few yards, it turns out, from open water. Today's government is in a similar plight. Dissatisfaction ought, by rights, to open the path to comprehensive change. But it does not. The *African Queen* was lifted from the quagmire by the tide. But in the case of the American government, the boat cannot be lifted. The government is, of its nature, inseparable and inalienable from the million commitments it has made and the million interest groups it has spawned. They now form its environment. It cannot lift itself above them. With the replacement of Carter with Reagan, Bush with Clinton, and Clinton (for a while) with Gingrich, the restive electorate outside Washington showed that it could still radicalize politics, at least temporarily, and shake the very ground of the capital. Notwithstanding all the little gray groups and politicians and lobbyists and claques that occupy and ossify the government, the broad electorate proved more than able to coil itself and strike back. What was lacking in the system was not energy or leadership but the ability to focus reformist energy on any *particular* program of reform. Converting the electorate's shuddering waves of discontent into the hundreds or thousands of alterations to programs affecting specific groups is like converting earthquake energy into steam power: possible in theory but elusive in practice.

BORDERS OF THE JUNGLE

In ideological terms, conservatives see government as properly a guarantor of individual rights, and possibly also as a watchman for the interests of enterprise. For 150 years or so, American government conformed largely to their vision. By today's standards, it was very small and very weak, and the country's many associations were of the voluntary, nonlobbying kind that were familiar to Alexis de Tocqueville in the 1830s.

Liberals see government as properly a solver of national problems, and possibly also as a builder of a more nearly ideal society. For thirty or forty or fifty years, beginning around the time of the New Deal, the liberals had their day: The government was ambitious, undertook all sorts of commitments to pensioners and veterans and students and consumers, and seemed often successful in meeting them. But with the growth of the programs came the dense jungle of modern Washington, with all its burrowing and flying and stinging creatures; and with the growing perception of the failure—with farmers being paid not to grow food, the welfare culture expanding, the tax code becoming spaghetti, lawyers and lobbyists overrunning Washington, inflation, deficits, bureaucracies—came the backlash and the era of reform.

And now, at last, comes this, what you see around you: the perpetual stalemate of evolutionary equilibrium, in which the clients and the calculus of collective action will not allow the government to become much smaller or to reorganize its basic functions, while the taxpayers will not suffer it to grow much bigger. The borders of the jungle are more or less as they will be. From a distance, in macrocosm, the jungle seems an immovable mass, unchanging from year to year and impenetrably dense, whereas up very close, in microcosm, it is a constant turmoil of digging and scurrying and eating and mating. But it exists primarily to survive from year to year and to feed its clients. Its clients—we—draw sustenance from it but yield control.

In the end, it is not the conservative vision of government or the liberal vision that prevailed. It is no vision at all that prevailed. The client groups prevailed. And that is the end of government. To see the future, look around.

under the **gun**

The more pressure there is to regulate firearms, the stronger the National Rifle Association becomes. But like the besieged tobacco lobby, the NRA can't resist forever. **by jeffrey h. birnbaum**

If ever there was a time when the gun lobby should be vanquished, it is now. This year alone, there have been Columbine (15 dead, 23 wounded), the Wedgwood Baptist Church in Fort Worth (eight dead, seven wounded), and the North Valley Jewish Community Center near Los Angeles (five wounded). Then Atlanta (nine dead, 13 wounded), and just the other week, Honolulu (seven dead) and Seattle (two dead, two wounded). But the National Rifle Association is not only alive, it is also thriving. Despite the shootings, the NRA is raising record amounts of political contributions, experiencing record growth in membership, and boasting about its strongest financial position in years. "I've been here through good times and bad times," says Wayne LaPierre, the NRA's executive vice president. "We've never been in a better position."

Such is the upside-down world of gun control. The NRA's defenders become most active, inspired, and effective when the right to bear arms is under assault. The organization itself seems to get stronger when its issues are in the cross hairs, even if that means—as it always does—mayhem, destruction, and death. All of which helps explain why in 1999, the worst year in memory for mass shootings, the NRA tied for No. 2 in FORTUNE's Power 25 survey of clout in the capital, its highest rank ever. It was rated No. 1 among Congressmen and their staffs, the people on the frontlines of lobbying.

At the same time, lawmakers and the NRA know that the outlook over the long haul isn't so sunny. Ultimately, shooting people is not good PR. As long as guns are freely available, the NRA is condemned to be in one form of retreat or another. Like the resilient but reviled tobacco lobby, the gun lobby's best hope is to maintain a holding action against forces that won't rest until they get more stringent regulation. No one, not even the NRA, imagines that gun restrictions already on the books will ever be rolled back. Here's how a longtime NRA supporter on Capitol Hill explains the future of the gun-control debate: "We are engaged in a very long, very grim, very hard-fought war. If we are successful, the [gun control] issue will be plaguing our kids and grandkids. If we aren't successful, they won't be dealing with it because we will have lost."

The politics of gun control, in other words, is a constant contradiction. On the one hand, the NRA is permanently under the gun, itself a victim every time there's another mass shooting. In the past few years alone, the NRA has been forced to accept the Brady bill, which imposed a five-day waiting period before a handgun could be purchased, and a ban on 19 categories of assault weapons. Yet day to day, the NRA is a force with few equals in Washington. It is so feared on Capitol Hill that gun-control measures don't come up unless lawmakers are compelled by events to bring them up. Politicians don't want to toy in any way with a group that can make the difference between victory and defeat in hundreds of districts across the land. This story will examine both sides of the NRA: its short-run strength and its long-term weakness.

At the moment, the NRA is keeping losses to a minimum. Despite the spree of killings, it appears to have bottled up for this year a bill that would have required background checks for buyers at gun shows, banned the importation of high-capacity ammunition clips, and required safety locks on all new guns. There's at least an even chance the bill could be stalled next year as well. How is this possible? Because the NRA is famous for being among the very few lobbying groups (the Christian Coalition is another) that can deliver the most important commodity in politics: votes. More lawmakers than are willing to admit it are in Congress today because the NRA mobilized an extra two or three percentage points on election day, which made the difference between winning and losing.

The NRA's power begins with its three million dedicated members and its annual budget of $137 million, numbers that make it one of the nation's largest and wealthiest cause-oriented groups. Of course, not all that money and those people are political. The NRA uses its three magazines—and will soon use an Internet portal—to push the sale of equipment and services like insurance and NRA credit cards, for which it collects a steady stream of royalties. The association's base is composed of hunters, gun collectors, and outdoorsmen who just love their weapons and the rustic way of life that goes with them.

Over the years, though, NRA leaders have kept an eye on legislation and elections, and have carefully sifted their membership lists so that they now have a die-hard group of 175,000 activists to whom they can turn to stump for a candidate or lobby a Congressman. NRA headquarters in northern Virginia features a 30-phone telemarketing center to alert the troops during congressional battles. The association has a Website that is the envy of the Washington lobbying establishment. NRA.org gets 15,000 to 20,000 hits a day and several times more than that when gun legislation is under debate. In order to broadcast its message unfiltered by the national press (which the NRA despises), the Website has a daily netcast of its own version of the news called *NRA Live With Wayne LaPierre*.

Then there's the money. Lots of it. With $7 million to disperse, the NRA's political action committee, confidently called the Political Victory Fund, regularly ranks in the top ten of givers to candidates for federal office, mostly Republicans. Its infamous antigovernment, pro-gun direct-mail solicitations (which once referred to federal employees as "jackbooted government thugs") bring in nearly three times as much money by tapping a loyal band of 900,000 donors. Small but regular contributions from this group help finance lobbying efforts in Washington and in the states by the NRA's fearsome advocacy arm, the Institute for Legislative Action. Lately the NRA has even begun airing a late-night infomercial starring its president, Charlton Heston, to buck up the faithful and recruit new members.

Election time is when the NRA really homes in on its targets. In 1998 it spent $150,000 on behalf of pro-gun Senator Jim Bunning (R-Kentucky). The NRA's PAC also gave the Hall of Fame pitcher $10,000 directly, and Heston hosted a fundraiser that collected even more. At the NRA's direction, 200 activists fanned out across Kentucky putting up signs and visiting gun shows to talk up their man. The NRA even mailed out bumper stickers: SPORTSMEN FOR BUNNING. Every little bit helped; Bunning won by just 6,766 votes out of 1.1 million cast. Because so few people vote (barely half those eligible during the last presidential election and just over a third in the last nonpresidential year), any group that can persuade a few thousand people to support its cause is a major player in Washington. The NRA does that with a vengeance.

Another reason for the NRA's influence is the single-mindedness of its members. Gun-control advocates support candidates who want restrictions on guns, but they rarely cast their votes on that issue alone. NRA members regularly vote one way or the other solely on that issue.

A decade ago few would have predicted the NRA's rise to power. It remains, in fact, an organization in recovery from a series of financial, managerial, and political blows. Over the years managers had allowed the group to atrophy. It was viewed mostly as a men's club that sponsored shooting tournaments. Membership stagnated, and the NRA's imperious black building in downtown Washington was filled with asbestos and antiquated computers; nothing much had been updated since 1958. Worse, the NRA was losing money. According to figures provided by the organization, it had a deficit of nearly $10 million in 1991, $38 million in 1992, and $22

banned weapons

Israeli-made Action Arms **Uzi** assault pistol

TEC-9-type semiautomatic pistol

Street Sweeper revolving cylinder shotgun

AK-47-type semiautomatic rifle

Steyer **ÅUG** assault rifle

Beretta **AR-70** semiautomatic rifle

Modified Colt **AR-15** semiautomatic rifle

million in 1993. "The NRA was decaying and was in danger of dying," LaPierre says now.

In 1991, LaPierre took charge. He and his legislative right hand, a leather-vested, big-game hunter named James Jay Baker, began the long struggle to revive the group and overhaul its physical plant. LaPierre started new programs that targeted women shooters and taught young people and children safety techniques. The NRA also invested in new computers and a new $17 million building.

After two years of rebuilding, the NRA played a major role in the surprising Republican takeover of the House of Representatives in 1994. Its victims included such powerful Democrats as Speaker Thomas Foley (D-Washington State) and Congressman Jack Brooks (D-Texas), chairman of the House Judiciary Committee. NRA members went after both men because they supported the assault weapons ban. Republican leaders acknowledged the gun lobby as central to their victory. President Clinton, too, highlighted the NRA's new prominence, perhaps as a way of stifling it. "The NRA is the reason the Republicans control the House," he told the *Cleveland Plain Dealer*. Hyperbole aside, the NRA clearly had friends in high places.

And that was the problem. The worst thing that can happen to a cause-based group is to get what it wants. After the 1994 election, NRA membership declined, in part because it raised its dues from $25 to $35, but also because its members didn't feel threatened anymore. The apathy led to yet another challenge for the organization: the growing influence of right-wing gun zealots known internally by some as the "crazies." The NRA's lead lobbyist for a time was a hard-core gun advocate named Tanya Mataksa. She would spell her unusual last name this way: "It's 'a-k,' as in AK-47, and 's-a,' as in semiautomatic."

Led by Neal Knox, a militant NRA agitator, the zealots forced the group's policy positions to become more strident. The NRA refused to show any flexibility, for instance, in its stands against banning the most vicious sorts of semiautomatic weapons, "cop killer" bullets, and the use of chemicals that would mark explosives for easy identification. After the 1995 Oklahoma City bombing, when that infamous fundraising letter likened federal agents to "jackbooted government thugs," longtime NRA enthusiasts (including President George Bush) resigned from the organization, and Congressman John Dingell (D-Michigan) left its board. Even police organizations, once among the NRA's closest allies, abandoned the organization as a bunch of nut cases. "People were wondering where the NRA was heading," admits LaPierre.

Once again, the NRA righted itself. After years of losing on the issues, especially the Brady bill (1993) and the assault weapons ban (1994), the Knox wing fell into disrepute, and the moderates (a relative term) began to ascend. Last year LaPierre persuaded Heston to become president, giving the organization a more friendly public face. Who could complain about Moses? James Jay Baker also returned after a five-year exile; as chief lobbyist, he is credited with being a comparatively reasonable voice on Capitol Hill. This year the NRA will have a budget surplus of about $5 million. It rents out enough of its headquarters building to pay its operating costs. And the organization itself has morphed into a fraternal as well as a political organization. The group holds 650 Friends of the NRA dinners yearly that attract between 400 and 1,500 people each. LaPierre is the inspirational speaker at many of them. Parents sometimes bring their children just to get his autograph.

To the extent that the NRA can position itself as the protector of a way of life, the sheer number of its adherents could help it hold out for many years. More than 16 million Americans buy hunting licenses each year; 80 million people own guns; and over 250 million firearms are already in circulation, making confiscation a daunting, if not impossible, task. "We're not the bad guys," LaPierre asserts.

"Oh, yes, you are," reply the advocates of gun control, who regard the NRA not just as bad but as evil. Handgun Control, the NRA's lead accuser, is headed by Sarah Brady, wife of Jim Brady; he was wounded in the 1981 assassination attempt on Ronald Reagan, and the Brady bill is named for him. The group's latest tactic (besides taking political advantage of every new shooting tragedy) is to use the courts as well as Congress in its cause. Its ally in this mission is a group that rivals the NRA in clout: trial lawyers. Gun-control advocates have joined with trial lawyers to sue gun manufacturers on behalf of 24 cities and counties around the country. One gunmaker, Colt, has already said it will stop making certain types of handguns. Gun-control advocates shrug off the decision. They say the company would have discontinued those models anyway because they weren't as profitable as other brands that Colt is making now or plans to market soon.

Handgun Control is also preparing for more combat with the NRA in Congress. It is trying to raise bigger sums for its anemic PAC; its ambitious (and probably unachievable) goal this election cycle is $2 million. And it is beginning to form a network of activists of the kind that the NRA has long had to promote its cause. "We are the ones making progress, not the NRA," maintains Robert Walker,

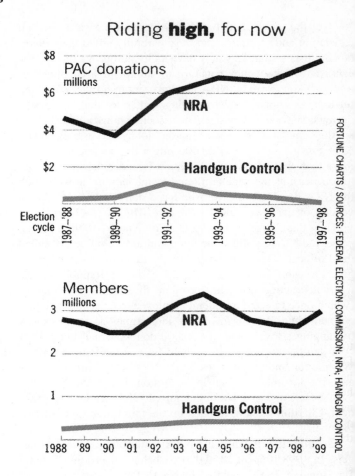

Riding **high,** for now

PAC donations
millions

NRA

Handgun Control

Election cycle: 1987–'88, 1989–'90, 1991–'92, 1993–'94, 1995–'96, 1997–'98

Members
millions

NRA

Handgun Control

1988 '89 '90 '91 '92 '93 '94 '95 '96 '97 '98 '99

FORTUNE CHARTS / SOURCES: FEDERAL ELECTION COMMISSION; NRA; HANDGUN CONTROL

Handgun Control's president. "The NRA is basically running out of gas." Not yet. For now Walker's group is, pardon the expression, outgunned. Despite achieving its highest ranking in three years, Handgun Control still placed 60th in the Power 25 out of 114 groups tested.

Ultimately, the fight over guns is bigger than any single lobbying group, much like the battle over tobacco. The similarities are instructive. Scientists knew the hazards of cigarette smoking for decades before the tobacco companies were finally forced to pay a share of the cost that their product imposed on society. Likewise, gun advocates and manufacturers know the toll firearms take, especially in cities, and have grudgingly given ground to more and more regulation.

As with tobacco, the defeats and concessions never seem to satisfy reformers. President Clinton is pressing yet another suit against the cigarette industry to collect damages he says are owed to the Medicare program because of illnesses caused by tobacco use. (The previous settlements around the country dealt with Medicaid.) Likewise, the suits filed by cities and counties against gun manufacturers are probably only the first wave. "If 25% of these suits are still going forward at this time next year, there'll be a second wave," predicts John Coale, one of the lawyers involved in the early gun cases. "It's like tobacco. Once cities and counties see that these things can happen, the suits will just start rolling." At which point the federal government might join the battle. Coale says federal officials are interested in filing a suit of their own if the local cases make headway. But such a decision would have to await the next President. If a Republican wins the White House, the chances of a class-action suit are nil. But if a Democrat wins, gunmakers had better watch out.

The partisan underpinnings of the battle make it ripe for a protracted conflict. "This is going to be a major issue in the presidential election," says Senator Charles Schumer (D-New York), the Senate's leading gun-control advocate. "It could be George W. Bush's Achilles' heel." In general, Democrats love to depict the NRA as the devil incarnate, while Republicans accuse Democrats of failing to enforce the laws already on the books. Democrats are secretly as eager as the other side to delay action on gun-control legislation through next year—even if compromise were possible—in order to bludgeon Republicans on election day for being in the pocket of that particular special interest. Few things sell better among die-hard Democrats than NRA bashing.

But that strategy misses two key points. First, plenty of Democrats, especially those who represent rural regions, need to keep the NRA's interests in mind; some gun lovers do vote Democratic. Second, no matter how pro-NRA a lawmaker is, he rarely wants to trumpet that fact. Sure, Republicans and a hearty handful of Democrats are often willing to say the next new gun-control idea goes too far. But they mostly say so quietly, and they almost never give a full-throated defense of the organization itself. FORTUNE contacted several lawmakers whose reelections were greatly aided by the NRA; none would speak for the record.

Although NRA membership has been growing lately, overall gun ownership is not. According to the National Opinion Research Center at the University of Chicago, the proportion of men who say they owned a gun dropped from 52% in the 1980s to 38% last year (female ownership has stayed steady at 11%). The U.S. manufacture and importation of guns, while spiking occasionally, has declined by about 20% since the late 1970s. What's more, public sentiment overwhelmingly favors more, rather than less, regulation of guns. A recent national poll by *Newsweek* showed that 74% of the American people support registration of all handguns, 93% back a waiting period for people who want to buy handguns, and 50% of people who don't own firearms favor banning handguns altogether.

The NRA is a pariah even among some of its friends. One well-known lobbyist, who agrees with the association on many issues, never invites it to participate in his legislative coalitions. Its political style is simply too aggressive. "The NRA is anathema to business; its game is always to attack," the lobbyist says. "I don't let tobacco join, either, and for the same reason. If they are members, lots of business groups won't join."

To change its image, the NRA would have to become less fanatical in its devotion to the Second Amendment. But a gentler, more compliant gun lobby would also be a less effective one. Blind faith in the cause and proud inflexibility in the face of an arrogant enemy are what bind the rank and file together. The NRA's right flank may seem scary or even borderline insane to many Americans. But its fervor and single-mindedness are what make it so politically potent. That won't save the NRA forever. But with no dearth of opposition, the gun lobby will be as dangerous as a cornered rattlesnake for a long time to come.

ASSOCIATIONS WITHOUT MEMBERS

BY THEDA SKOCPOL

In just a third of a century, Americans have dramatically changed their style of civic and political association. A civic world once centered in locally rooted and nationally active membership associations is a relic. Today, Americans volunteer for causes and projects, but only rarely as ongoing members. They send checks to service and advocacy groups run by professionals, often funded by foundations or professional fundraisers. Prime-time airways echo with debates among their spokespersons: the National Abortion Rights Action League debates the National Right to Life Committee; the Concord Coalition takes on the American Association of Retired Persons; and the Environmental Defense Fund counters business groups. Entertained or bemused, disengaged viewers watch as polarized advocates debate.

The largest membership groups of the 1950s were old-line and well-established, with founding dates ranging from 1733 for the Masons to 1939 for the Woman's Division of Christian Service (a Methodist women's association formed from "missionary" societies with nineteenth-century roots). Like most large membership associations throughout American history, most 1950s associations recruited members across class lines. They held regular local meetings and convened periodic assemblies of elected leaders and delegates at the state, regional, or national levels. Engaged in multiple rather than narrowly specialized pursuits, many associations combined social or ritual activities with community service, mutual aid, and involvement in national affairs. Patriotism was a leitmotif; during and after World War II, a passionate and victorious national endeavor, these associations sharply expanded their memberships and renewed the vigor of their local and national activities.

To be sure, very large associations were not the only membership federations that mattered in postwar America. Also prominent were somewhat smaller, elite-dominated civic groups—including male service groups like Rotary, Lions, and Kiwanis, and longstanding female groups like the American Association of University Women and the League of Women Voters. Dozens of ethnically based fraternal and cultural associations flourished, as did African-American fraternal groups like the Prince Hall Masons and the Improved Benevolent and Protective Order of Elks of the World.

For many membership federations, this was a golden era of national as well as community impact. Popularly rooted membership federations rivaled professional and business associations for influence in policy debates. The AFL-CIO was in the thick of struggles about economic and social policies; the American Legion and the Veterans of Foreign Wars advanced veterans' programs; the American Farm Bureau Federation (AFBF) joined other farmers' associations to influence national and state agricultural policies; and the National Congress of Parents and Teachers (PTA) and the General Federation of Women's Clubs were influential on educational, health, and family issues. The results could be decisive, as exemplified by the pivotal role of the American Legion in drafting and lobbying for the GI Bill of 1944.

Then, suddenly, old-line membership federations seemed passé. Upheavals shook America during "the long 1960s," stretching from the mid-1950s through the mid-1970s. The southern Civil Rights movement challenged white racial domination and spurred legislation to enforce legal equality and voting rights for African Americans. Inspired by Civil Rights achievements, additional "rights" movements exploded, promoting equality for women, dignity for homosexuals, the unionization of farm workers, and the mobilization of other nonwhite ethnic minorities. Movements arose to oppose U.S. involvement in the war in Vietnam, champion a new environmentalism, and further other public causes. At the forefront of these groundswells were younger Americans, especially from the growing ranks of college students and university graduates.

The great social movements of the long 1960s were propelled by combinations of grassroots protest, activist radicalism, and professionally led efforts to lobby government and educate the public. Some older membership associations ended up participating and expanding their bases of support, yet the groups that sparked movements were more agile

> # The model of civic effectiveness has been upended since the 1960s. Activist groups no longer need actual members.

and flexibly structured than pre-existing membership federations.

The upheavals of the 1960s could have left behind a reconfigured civic world, in which some old-line membership associations had declined but others had reoriented and reenergized themselves. Within each great social movement, memberships could have consolidated and groups coalesced into new omnibus federations able to link the grass roots to state, regional, and national leaderships, allowing longstanding American civic traditions to continue in new ways.

But this is not what happened. Instead, the 1960s, 1970s, and 1980s brought extraordinary organizational proliferation and professionalization. At the national level alone, the *Encyclopedia of Associations* listed approximately 6,500 associations in 1958. This total grew by 1990 to almost 23,000. Within the expanding group universe, moreover, new kinds of associations came to the fore: relatively centralized and professionally led organizations focused on policy lobbying and public education.

Another wave of the advocacy explosion involved "public interest" or "citizens'" groups seeking to shape public opinion and influence legislation. Citizens' advocacy groups espouse "causes" ranging from environmental protection (for example, the Sierra Club and the Environmental Defense Fund), to the well-being of poor children (the Children's Defense Fund), to reforming politics (Common Cause) and cutting public entitlements (the Concord Coalition).

THE FORTUNES OF MEMBERSHIP ASSOCIATIONS

As the associational explosions of 1960 to 1990 took off, America's once large and confident membership federations were not only bypassed in national politics; they also dwindled as locally rooted participant groups. To be sure, some membership associations have been founded or expanded in recent decades. By far the largest is the American Association of Retired Persons (AARP), which now boasts more than 33 million adherents, about one-half of all Americans aged 50 or older. But AARP is not a democratically controlled organization. Launched in 1958 with backing from a teachers' retirement group and an insurance company, the AARP grew rapidly in the 1970s and 1980s by offering commercial discounts to members and establishing a Washington headquarters to monitor and lobby about federal legislation affecting seniors. The AARP has a legislative and policy staff of 165 people, 28 registered lobbyists, and more than 1,200 staff members in the field. After recent efforts to expand its regional and local infrastructure, the AARP involves about 5 to 10 percent of its members in (undemocratic) membership chapters. But for the most part, the AARP national office—covering an entire city block with its own zip code—deals with masses of individual adherents through the mail.

Four additional recently expanded membership associations use modern mass recruitment methods, yet are also rooted in local and state units. Interestingly, these groups are heavily involved in partisan electoral politics. Two recently launched groups are the National Right to Life Committee (founded in 1973) and the Christian Coalition (founded in 1989). They bridge from church congregations, through which they recruit members and activists, to the conservative wing of the Republican Party, through which they exercise political influence. Two old-line membership federations—the National Education Association (founded in 1857) and the National Rifle Association (founded in 1871)—experienced explosive growth after reorienting themselves to take part in partisan politics. The NRA expanded in the 1970s, when right-wing activists opposed to gun control changed what had traditionally been a network of marksmen's clubs into a conservative, Republican-leaning advocacy group fiercely opposed to gun control legislation. During the same period, the NEA burgeoned from a relatively elitist association of public educators into a quasi-union for public school teachers and a stalwart in local, state, and national Democratic Party politics.

Although they fall short of enrolling 1 percent of the adult population, some additional chapter-based membership associations were fueled by the social movements of the 1960s and 1970s. From 1960 to 1990, the Sierra Club (originally created in 1892) ballooned from some 15,000 members to 565,000 members meeting in 378 "local groups." And the National Audubon Society (founded in 1905) went from 30,000 members and 330 chapters in 1958 to about 600,000 members and more than 500 chapters in the 1990s. The National Organization for Women (NOW) reached 1,122 members and 14 chapters within a year of its founding in 1966, and spread across all 50 states with some 125,000 members meeting in 700 chapters by 1978. But notice that these "1960s" movement associations do not match the organizational scope of old-line membership federations. At its post-World War II high point in 1955, for example, the General Federation of Women's Clubs boasted more than 826,000 members meeting in 15,168 local clubs, themselves divided into representative networks within each of the 50 states plus the District of Columbia. By contrast, at its high point in 1993, NOW reported some 280,000 members and 800 chapters, with no intermediate tier of representative governance between the national center and local chapters. These membership associations certainly matter, but mainly as counterexamples to dominant associational trends—of organizations without members.

After nearly a century of civic life rooted in nation-spanning membership federations, why was America's associational universe so transformed? A variety of factors have contributed, including racial and gender change; shifts in the political opportunity structure; new techniques and models for building organizations; and recent transformations in U.S. class relations. Taken together, I suggest, these account for civic America's abrupt and momentous transition from membership to advocacy.

SOCIETY DECOMPARTMENTALIZED

Until recent times, most American membership associations enrolled business and professional people together with white-collar folks, farmers, and craft or industrial workers. There was a degree of fellowship across class lines—yet at the price of other kinds of exclusions. With only a few exceptions, old-line associations enrolled either men or women, not both together (although male-only fraternal and veterans' groups often had ties to ladies' auxiliaries). Racial separation was also the rule. Although African Americans did manage to create and greatly expand fraternal associations of their own, they unquestionably resented exclusion by the parallel white fraternals.

Given the pervasiveness of gender and racial separation in classic civic America, established voluntary associations were bound to be shaken after the 1950s. Moreover, changing gender roles and identities blended with other changing values to undercut not just membership appeals but long-standing routes to associational leadership. For example,

> The styles of civic involvement have changed, especially for women—much to the disadvantage of associations trying to hold regular meetings.

values of patriotism, brotherhood, and sacrifice had been celebrated by all fraternal groups. During and after each war, the Masons, Knights of Pythias, Elks, Knights of Columbus, Moose, Eagles, and scores of other fraternal groups celebrated and memorialized the contributions of their soldier-members. So did women's auxiliaries, not to mention men's service clubs and trade union "brotherhoods." But "manly" ideals of military service faded after the early 1960s as America's bitter experiences during the war in Vietnam disrupted the intergenerational continuity of male identification with martial brotherliness.

In the past third of a century, female civic leadership has changed as much or more than male leadership. Historically, U.S. women's associations—ranging from female auxiliaries of male groups to independent groups like the General Federation of Women's Clubs, the PTA, and church-connected associations—benefited from the activism of educated wives and mothers. Although a tiny fraction of all U.S. females, higher-educated women were a surprisingly substantial and widespread presence—because the United States was a pioneer in the schooling of girls and the higher education of women. By 1880, some 40,000 American women constituted a third of all students in U.S. institutions of higher learning; women's share rose to nearly half at the early twentieth-century peak in 1920, when some 283,000 women were enrolled in institutions of higher learning. Many higher-educated women of the late 1800s and early 1900s married immediately and stayed out of the paid labor force. Others taught for a time in primary and secondary schools, then got married and stopped teaching (either voluntarily or because school systems would not employ married women). Former teachers accumulated in every community. With skills to make connections within and across communities—and some time on their hands as their children grew older—former teachers and other

educated women became mainstays of classic U.S. voluntary life.

Of course, more American women than ever before are now college-educated. But contemporary educated women face new opportunities and constraints. Paid work and family responsibilities are no longer separate spheres, and the occupational structure is less sex-segregated at all levels. Today, even married women with children are very likely to be employed, at least part-time. Despite new time pressures, educated and employed women have certainly not dropped out of civic life. Women employed part-time are more likely to be members of groups or volunteers than housewives; and fully employed women are often drawn into associations or civic projects through work. Yet styles of civic involvement have changed—much to the disadvantage of broad-gauged associations trying to hold regular meetings.

THE LURE OF WASHINGTON, D.C.

The centralization of political change in Washington, D.C. also affected the associational universe. Consider the odyssey of civil rights lawyer Marian Wright Edelman. Fresh from grassroots struggles in Mississippi, she arrived in Washington, D.C. in the late 1960s to lobby for Mississippi's Head Start program. She soon realized that arguing on behalf of children might be the best way to influence legislation and sway public sympathy in favor of the poor, including African Americans. So between 1968 and 1973 Edelman obtained funding from major foundations and developed a new advocacy and policy research association, the Children's Defense Fund (CDF). With a skillful staff, a small national network of individual supporters, ties to social service agencies and foundations, and excellent relationships with the national media, the CDF has been a determined proponent of federal antipoverty programs ever since. The CDF has also worked with Democrats and other liberal advocacy groups to expand such efforts; and during periods of conservative Republican ascendancy, the CDF has been a fierce (if not always successful) defender of federal social programs.

Activists, in short, have gone where the action is. In this same period, congressional committees and their staffs subdivided and multiplied. During the later 1970s and 1980s, the process of group formation became self-reinforcing—not only because groups arose to counter other groups, but also because groups begot more groups. Because businesses and citizens use advocacy groups to influence government outside of parties and between elections, it is not surprising that the con-

In the new electoral arena, where political parties consist largely of direct mailings and fundraisers, advocacy groups can play an influential role.

temporary group explosion coincides with waning voter loyalty to the two major political parties. As late as the 1950s, U.S. political parties were networks of local and state organizations through which party officials often brokered nominations, cooperated with locally rooted membership associations, and sometimes directly mobilized voters. The party structure and the associational structure were mutually reinforcing.

Then, demographic shifts, reapportionment struggles, and the social upheavals of the 1960s disrupted old party organizations; and changes in party rules led to nomination elections that favored activists and candidate-centered efforts over backroom brokering by party insiders. Such "reforms" were meant to enhance grassroots participation, but in practice have furthered oligarchical ways of running elections. No longer the preserve of party organizations, U.S. campaigns are now managed by coteries of media consultants, pollsters, direct mail specialists, and—above all—fundraisers. In this revamped electoral arena, advocacy groups have much to offer, hoping to get access to elected officials in return for helping candidates. In low-turnout battles to win party nominations, even groups with modest mail memberships may be able to field enough (paid or unpaid) activists to make a difference. At all stages of the electoral process, advocacy groups with or without members can provide endorsements that may be useful in media or direct mail efforts. And PACs pushing business interests or public interest causes can help candidates raise the huge amounts of money they need to compete.

A New Model of Association-Building

Classic American association-builders took it for granted that the best way to gain national influence,

moral or political, was to knit together national, state, and local groups that met regularly and engaged in a degree of representative governance. Leaders who desired to speak on behalf of masses of Americans found it natural to proceed by recruiting self-renewing mass memberships and spreading a network of interactive groups. After the start-up phase, associational budgets usually depended heavily on membership dues and on sales of newsletters or supplies to members and local groups. Supporters had to be continuously recruited through social networks and person-to-person contacts. And if leverage over government was desired, an association had to be able influence legislators, citizens, and newspapers across many districts. For all of these reasons, classic civic entrepreneurs with national ambitions moved quickly to recruit activists and members in every state and across as many towns and cities as possible within each state.

Today, nationally ambitious civic entrepreneurs proceed in quite different ways. When Marian Wright Edelman launched a new advocacy and research group to lobby for the needs of children and the poor, she turned to private foundations for funding and then recruited an expert staff of researchers and lobbyists. In the early 1970s, when John Gardner launched Common Cause as a "national citizens lobby" demanding governmental reforms, he arranged for start-up contributions from several wealthy friends, contacted reporters in the national media, and purchased mailing lists to solicit masses of members giving modest monetary contributions. Patron grants, direct mail techniques, and the capacity to convey images and messages through the mass media have changed the realities of organization building and maintenance.

The very model of civic effectiveness has been upended since the 1960s. No longer do civic entrepreneurs think of constructing vast federations and recruiting interactive citizen-members. When a new cause (or tactic) arises, activists envisage opening a national office and managing association-building as well as national projects from the center. Even a group aiming to speak for large numbers of Americans does not absolutely need members. And if mass adherents are recruited through the mail, why hold meetings? From a managerial point of view, interactions with groups of members may be downright inefficient. In the old-time membership federations, annual elections of leaders and a modicum of representative governance went hand in hand with membership dues and interactive meetings. But for the professional executives of today's advocacy organizations, direct mail members can be more appealing because, as Kenneth Godwin and Robert Cameron Mitchell explain, "they contribute without 'meddling'" and "do not take part in leadership selection or policy discussions." This does not mean the new advocacy groups are malevolent; they are just responding rationally to the environment in which they find themselves.

ASSOCIATIONAL CHANGE AND DEMOCRACY

This brings us, finally, to what may be the most civically consequential change in late-twentieth-century America: the rise of a very large, highly educated upper middle class in which "expert" professionals are prominent along with businesspeople and managers. When U.S. professionals were a tiny, geographically dispersed stratum, they understood themselves as "trustees of community," in the terminology of Stephen Brint. Working closely with and for nonprofessional fellow citizens in thousands of towns and cities, lawyers, doctors, ministers, and teachers once found it quite natural to join—and eventually help to lead—locally rooted, cross-class voluntary associations. But today's professionals are more likely to see themselves as expert individuals who can best contribute to national well-being by working with other specialists to tackle complex technical or social problems.

Cause-oriented advocacy groups offer busy, privileged Americans a rich menu of opportunities to, in effect, hire other professionals and managers to represent their values and interests in public life. Why should highly trained and economically well-off elites spend years working their way up the leadership ladders of traditional membership federations when they can take leading staff roles at the top, or express their preferences by writing a check?

If America has experienced a great civic transformation from membership to advocacy—so what? Most traditional associations were racially exclusive and gender segregated; and their policy efforts were not always broad-minded. More than a few observers suggest that recent civic reorganizations may be for the best. American public life has been rejuvenated, say the optimists, by social movements and advocacy groups fighting for social rights and an enlarged understanding of the public good.

Local community organizations, neighborhood groups, and grassroots protest movements nowadays tap popular energies and involve people otherwise left out of organized politics. And social interchanges live on in small support groups and occasional volunteering. According to the research of Robert Wuthnow, about 75 million men and women, a remarkable 40 percent of the adult population, report taking part in "a small group that meets regularly and provides caring and support for those who participate in it." Wuthnow estimates that there may be some 3 million such groups, in-

cluding Bible study groups, 12-step self-help groups, book discussion clubs, singles groups, hobby groups, and disease support groups. Individuals find community, spiritual connection, introspection, and personal gratification in small support groups. Meanwhile, people reach out through volunteering. As many as half of all Americans give time to the community this way, their efforts often coordinated by paid social service professionals. Contemporary volunteering can be intermittent and flexibly structured, an intense one-shot effort or spending "an evening a week on an activity for a few months as time permits, rather than having to make a long-term commitment to an organization."

In the optimistic view, the good civic things Americans once did are still being done—in new ways and in new settings. But if we look at U.S. democracy in its entirety and bring issues of power and social leverage to the fore, then optimists are surely overlooking the downsides of our recently reorganized civic life. Too many valuable aspects of the old civic America are not being reproduced or reinvented in the new public world of memberless organizations.

Despite the multiplicity of voices raised within it, America's new civic universe is remarkably oligarchical. Because today's advocacy groups are staff-heavy and focused on lobbying, research, and media projects, they are managed from the top with few opportunities for member leverage from below. Even when they have hundreds of thousands of adherents, contemporary associations are heavily tilted toward upper-middle-class constituencies. Whether we are talking about memberless advocacy groups, advocacy groups with some chapters, mailing-list associations, or nonprofit institutions, it is hard to escape the conclusion that the wealthiest and best-educated Americans are much more privileged in the new civic world than their (less numerous) counterparts were in the pre-1960s civic world of cross-class membership federations.

Mostly, they involve people in "doing for" others—feeding the needy at a church soup kitchen; tutoring children at an after-school clinic; or guiding visitors at a museum exhibit—rather than in "doing with" fellow citizens. Important as such volunteering may be, it cannot substitute for the central citizenship functions that membership federations performed.

A top-heavy civic world not only encourages "doing for" rather than "doing with." It also distorts national politics and public policymaking. Imagine for a moment what might have happened if the GI Bill of 1944 had been debated and legislated in a civic world configured more like the one that prevailed during the 1993–1994 debates over the national health insurance proposal put forward by the first administration of President Bill Clinton. This is not an entirely fanciful comparison, because goals supported by the vast majority of Americans were at issue in both periods: in the 1940s, care and opportunity for millions of military veterans returning from World War II; in the 1990s, access for all Americans to a modicum of health insurance coverage. Back in the 1940s, moreover, there were elite actors—university presidents, liberal intellectuals, and conservative congressmen—who could have condemned the GI Bill to the same fate as the 1990s health security plan. University presidents and liberal New Dealers initially favored versions of the GI Bill that would have been bureaucratically complicated, niggardly with public expenditures, and extraordinarily limited in veterans' access to subsidized higher education.

But in the actual civic circumstances of the 1940s, elites did not retain control of public debates or legislative initiatives. Instead, a vast voluntary membership federation, the American Legion, stepped in and drafted a bill to guarantee every one of the returning veterans up to four years of post–high school education, along with family and employment benefits, business loans, and home mortgages. Not only did the Legion draft one of the most generous pieces of social legislation in American history, thousands of local Legion posts and dozens of state organizations mounted a massive public education and lobbying campaign to ensure that even conservative congressional representatives would vote for the new legislation.

Half a century later, the 1990s health security episode played out in a transformed civic universe dominated by advocacy groups, pollsters, and big-money media campaigns. Top-heavy advocacy groups did not mobilize mass support for a sensible reform plan. Hundreds of business and professional groups influenced the Clinton administration's complex policy schemes, and then used a combination of congressional lobbying and media campaigns to block new legislation. Both the artificial polarization and the elitism of today's organized civic universe may help to explain why increasing numbers of Americans are turned off by

and pulling back from public life. Large majorities say that wealthy "special interests" dominate the federal government, and many Americans express cynicism about the chances for regular people to make a difference. People may be entertained by advocacy clashes on television, but they are also ignoring many public debates and withdrawing into privatism. Voting less and less, American citizens increasingly act—and claim to feel—like mere spectators in a polity where all the significant action seems to go on above their heads, with their views ignored by pundits and clashing partisans.

From the nineteenth through the mid-twentieth century, American democracy flourished within a unique matrix of state and society. Not only was America the world's first manhood democracy and the first nation in the world to establish mass public education. It also had a uniquely balanced civic life, in which markets expanded but could not subsume civil society, in which governments at multiple levels deliberately and indirectly encouraged federated voluntary associations. National elites had to pay attention to the values and interests of millions of ordinary Americans.

Over the past third of a century, the old civic America has been bypassed and shoved to the side by a gaggle of professionally dominated advocacy groups and nonprofit institutions rarely attached to memberships worthy of the name. Ideals of shared citizenship and possibilities for democratic leverage have been compromised in the process. Since the 1960s, many good things have happened in America. New voices are now heard, and there have been invaluable gains in equality and liberty. But vital links in the nation's associational life have frayed, and we may need to find creative ways to repair those links if America is to avoid becoming a country of detached spectators. There is no going back to the civic world we have lost. But we Americans can and should look for ways to recreate the best of our civic past in new forms suited to a renewed democratic future.

Missed Information

The reporting tool that reporters don't use

By Michael Doyle

THE FREEDOM OF INFORMATION ACT (FOIA) can be a reporter's best friend. But consider this: The Environmental Protection Agency receives about 22,000 FOIA requests annually. One percent come from the media. Or this: In 1998 the Drug Enforcement Administration received more FOIA requests from prisoners than from reporters. Or this: The National Security Agency has received more requests for information about UFOs than for any topic from reporters. Or, symptomatically, this: The apparent 1998 champion for aggressively filing FOIA requests across multiple federal agencies was not a dogged investigative reporter but a political operative seeking dirt on an opponent.

Certainly, a few reporters do use the Freedom of Information Act—sometimes with spectacular results. Reporter Russell Carollo of the *Dayton Daily News* filed more than 100 FOIA requests for the 1998 Pulitzer Prize-winning series on military medicine he co-authored with Jeff Nesmith. But most reporters never use the law at all. Many FOIA-centered stories in newspapers come, not from reporters' initiative, but from special interests who use the law to dig up information that they then feed to reporters. Moreover, although the whole point of FOIA is to dig up the lid on executive branch operations, the few reporters who do use FOIA often couldn't care less about the executive agency they're demanding information from; they want copies of letters sent from members of Congress to various agencies and aren't really probing bureaucracies so much as seeking evidence of congressional muscle. In one small but illustrative example, the Labor Department's Bureau of Labor Statistics received six FOIA requests from the media in 1998. Three of these sought copies of congressional correspondence. Similarly, Transportation Department headquarters received 22 FOIA requests from reporters in 1998; 13 of these, more than half, sought congressional letters. This FOIA-enabled search for congressional letters, however meritorious, reflects the general tendency among Washington-based reporters to concentrate on Congress and

ignore the administrative agencies. More broadly, it highlights just how cramped journalistic FOIA use has become.

Few and Far Between

The law is pretty easy to understand and generally easy to use. In short, the Freedom of Information Act, passed in 1966, establishes a presumption that records in the possession of agencies and departments of the executive branch of the government should be accessible to the people. And usually, to get these records, you don't even need a stamp. Requests for documents from executive agencies—Congress, predictably, excluded itself from the law's reach—can now often be faxed to designated FOIA offices. Professional organizations like the Investigative Reporters and Editors run FOIA workshops, and the Reporters Committee for Freedom of the Press's useful Internet site includes an automatic FOIA letter-generator that makes filing a snap (http://www.rcfp.org/). Recalcitrant agencies can also be prodded by lawsuits. Yes, it can sometimes be a hassle; and, yes, the wait can sometimes be interminable. But the rewards can be abundant; moreover, frequent use of FOIA helps keep bureaucracies on their toes, and helps fend off those who contend the law has lost its Fourth Estate rationale.

"My sense is, it's not being used nearly as much as I think it should be," said Alan Miller, an investigative reporter in the Washington bureau of the *Los Angeles Times*. "I think reporters become discouraged, understandably, by the amount of time it takes . . . it's unfortunate, and it's a missed opportunity."

We know this is so, in part, thanks to the law itself. Using the Freedom of Information Act, I obtained the so-called FOIA logs from about two dozen federal agencies. These are the records of requests made during 1998. The logs themselves are a hodgepodge that highlight how different agencies handle FOIA. The Interior Department and Agriculture Department head-

Reprinted with permission from *The Washington Monthly*, May 2000, pp. 38-40. © 2000 by The Washington Monthly Company, 1611 Connecticut Avenue, NW, Washington, DC 20009, (202) 462-0128.

quarters logs, for instance, were handscrawled, while the Department of Health and Human Services (HHS) headquarters maintained its requests in a handy record-management software package. The federal government may spend $168 million a year coping with 100 million-plus FOIA requests, but a consistent government-wide system has yet to be developed.

Most important, these logs reveal, in varying detail, who's asking for what. They show, for instance, how Alan Miller cast a wide net across various agencies in 1998 with requests for letters from congressional leaders including Senate Majority Leader Trent Lott and Senate Minority Leader Tom Daschle. The logs also show that former Sen. Carol Moseley-Braun (now the Clinton administration's ambassador to New Zealand), Indiana Republican Rep. Dan Burton, and Sen. Mitch McConnell were favorite targets for reporters.

The FOIA logs also reveal, tellingly, that the champion information-seeker wasn't a reporter at all—although her work, properly laundered, might have fed a story or two. With regard to sheer quantity, an opposition researcher from the San Francisco Bay Area named Cara Brown led the pack. Working quietly for the primary campaign of Democrat Al Checchi, Brown filed myriad requests for information on Republican gubernatorial candidate and former southern California congressman Dan Lungren. From the Legal Services Corp., for instance, Brown requested all "letters, memos, telephone log entries, message receipts, notations of conversations, meeting notes, e-mail messages, fax cover sheets, reports, statistics, [and] calendar entries" dealing with Lungren. Nor did Brown limit herself to Lungren's time in public service: Brown wanted Lungren-related files going back to the time he was 18 years old.

"The basic role of the opposition researcher and FOIA is to come up with information that is prejudicial to the object of the search," said Garry South, the senior political adviser to California Gov. Gray Davis. "It can be almost anything, and in a lot of cases, it's a fishing expedition."

South, who identified Brown as one of Checchi's workers, naturally had his own researchers using the same tool. Obnoxious as it may sound, reporters could learn something from these political operatives. Ideally, of course, reporters won't presume that the only worthwhile information will be prejudicial to the target; indeed, FOIA is great at revealing the fascinating nuances of government in action.

Opposition researchers aside, the FOIA logs cumulatively reveal the relative infrequency of media requests. The Drug Enforcement Administration, for instance, received roughly 2,000 FOIA requests in 1998, only 57 of which came from the media. Federal prisoners were far more prolific. Similarly, the Public Health Service received about 520 FOIA requests in 1998. Only 25 came from journalists.

Even worse, take the HHS headquarters. Of the 1,100 FOIA requests it received between Oct. 1, 1997 and Sept. 30, 1998 only about nine percent came from reporters and most of the reporter requests were filed by a handful of journalists or media organizations. Nearly one-fifth of all the media requests to HHS headquarters came from just two trade publications, and, of the requests filed by newspapers, one-third came from the *Los Angeles Times*, *Chicago Tribune* or *Dayton Daily News*. Television reporters filed a grand total of five FOIA requests to the HHS headquarters.

Use It Or Lose It

This all seems a special shame. Journalists, after all, were not just cheerleaders during the long campaign by the late California congressman John Moss to pass the Freedom of Information Act. They were, emphatically, present at the law's creation. "Moss' greatest allies were the press associations," recalled Washington attorney Michael R. Lemov, a former Moss staffer. "Without the press, he never would have gotten that bill."

Moss, who died in December 1997, was a good-government champion with a stubborn streak. He started his FOIA fight in 1955, calling reporters as the first witnesses before his newly formed subcommittee on government information. The beginning stages were certainly bleak. A survey by the journalism society Sigma Delta Chi found that of 3,105 congressional hearings in 1953, 1,357 were closed to the press. Executive branch deliberations were equally closed. Though the Administrative Procedure Act provided for release of government information, exceptions limited release to those persons deemed "properly and directly concerned," and allowed denial of requests simply for "good cause." Neither Republican nor Democratic presidents were sympathetic to Moss' crusade. At one point, representatives of 27 federal agencies testified in opposition to Moss' bill. A blunt and sometimes impolitic man, Moss stuck to his guns for 11 years, and in 1966 Congress finally sent the legislation on for LBJ's reluctant signature.

The Freedom of Information Act, which has been further modified several times since, tightened the exceptions under which information could be kept secret. It allowed, for the first time, people to take agencies to court to compel release of information, and it dropped the requirement that information-seekers be "properly and directly concerned" with the matter at hand. Federal officials would no longer be in the business of judging the appropriateness of a requester's motives. At the same time, lawmakers made clear their expectations about who would be primary users of the new law.

The House Republican Policy Committee in May, 1966 cited the media first in a recitation of FOIA's potential users. The law, GOP members said, would aid "reporters as representatives of the public, citizens in pursuit of information vital to their interests, and members of Congress as they seek to carry out their constitutional functions." Things haven't of course worked out as planned, though.

"Since 1975, the press and research and scientific journal authors and others have largely abandoned the use of the FOIA," William Taft, then-general counsel for the Department of Defense, told a Senate committee back in 1981. "They are encouraged to elicit information through informal channels, and have found those channels to be satisfactory without resorting to use of the formal request."

In reality, the Reagan administration only cared about reporters abandoning FOIA because that could be justification for limiting the law's reach. If prisoners use FOIA and reporters don't, the argument went, then maybe it was time to roll back the law. This was one unintended and potentially dangerous political consequence of reporters not using FOIA. Carollo attributed the disuse in part to "a failure of the journalism schools" to properly train young reporters in the FOIA arts.

Tied Up With Red Tape

Part of the reason that journalists so rarely use FOIA is that agencies can take so long in responding that the information often seems stale by the time it arrives.

In the worst agencies, there's deliberate footdragging; and, for good and bad alike, there's a never-ending batch of requests to cope with. The various agencies of the Department of Veterans Affairs, for instance, receive a mind-boggling 210,000 FOIA requests every year—that's more than 800 every workday. The resulting long delays, and the periodic necessity to haul recalcitrant bureaucracies into court, deter some reporters from using the law at all. For every *Cleveland Plain Dealer,* which used a helpful congressman and the threat of legal action last year to pry open embarrassing records from the stonewalling Department of Housing and Urban Development, there are any number of papers or TV stations that figure the story isn't worth the hassle. Commendably aggressive, *The Washington Post* in April 1995 took the Agriculture Department to court to compel release of certain crop subsidy information. By the time a judge ordered the Agriculture Department to cough up the information, in October 1996, the *Post's* reporter on the beat had gone off to other tasks. The State Department, in particular, is

a notorious black hole; it is the only federal agency whose backlog of unprocessed FOIA requests is larger than the number of requests it receives each year. It claims a median FOIA response time of 444 days; actual delays can extend for several presidential administrations.

"Often, agency staff use the ordinary delays to deter requesters or to persuade them into narrowing the scope of the reporter's request," says Michael Ravnitzky of APBnet, the online crime-and-justice news service, and one of the most prolific filers. "Depending upon the agency, a FOIA request can take anywhere from a few days to as much as eight or nine years, or even more."

The lawmakers who wrote FOIA knew delay and resistance would be standard bureaucratic responses to information-seekers. That's why they included the provision permitting lawsuits. In other ways, though, FOIA's authors couldn't foresee the law's future use. They certainly didn't anticipate some persistently hot topics. The National Security Agency, for instance, received about 830 FOIA requests in 1998; 15 percent of these, the biggest single share, dealt with Unidentified Flying Objects. The second biggest topic for FOIA requests to the nation's secretive code-breaking agency dealt with contract information. Except for the business about UFOs, the National Security Agency is pretty typical. Commercial entities, government-wide, have long since become the greatest user of FOIA. Businesses are filing requests daily to find out who holds government credit cards, who won certain contracts, what competitors are up to, and how decisions are being made. Of all requests to the EPA, 89 percent came from attorneys, environmental consultants or private industry.

This is certainly consistent with the law's intent of opening up government; but, at least judging by the legislative debate, this was not explicitly anticipated by FOIA's authors. That's the nature of groundbreaking legislation, though: The real world always surprises, and you never know what might turn up. The same is true, after a fashion, with a Freedom of Information Act request itself. Reporters who use the law regularly know that the more requests they file, the more likely they are to scare up a story that matters. After all, it's hard to catch fish if you don't go fishing.

MICHAEL DOYLE *is a reporter in the Washington bureau of* McClatchy Newspapers.

www.democracy.com

THERE is a lot of blather about how the Internet interfaces with democracy, but some things make it all seem real. www.scorecard.org is as real as hotdogs. This website, set up a year ago by the Environmental Defence Fund, turns the modern data deluge into a jet hose pointed at polluters. It allows anybody with a modem to find out who is emitting what into his neighbourhood, and to protest instantly. An old lop-sidedness in democracy—big business and big government are better informed than individuals, so win most of the big arguments—is suddenly corrected. It used to be that executives and bureaucrats could assure small-fly citizens that problems had been analysed, scientists consulted, safeguards put in place. Now citizens no longer need to accept those assurances helplessly. They can log on to the Internet and check them, with a few clicks of a mouse.

Scorecard combines a vast reservoir of scientific data with software that makes it accessible to the layman-activist. When you arrive at the website, you can slot in your zip code and get a list of the top ten polluters in your neighbourhood. Click on the worst offender, and you get a draft letter, which you are free to edit, asking why the culprit has failed to bring down its emissions as much as other local firms. Click on the send button, and the letter flies down a fax line to the plant's manager. You can also e-mail the Environmental Protection Agency in Washington, or make contact with fellow greens in your neighbourhood. A cover headline in *Chemical Week* magazine captured the industry's anxious early response to this. "The Internet Bomb", it read.

Ranking neighbourhood polluters is only a fraction of what Scorecard offers. You can rank offenders by industry, or by type of pollution: Scorecard will generate league tables of carcinogen producers, animal-waste dumpers, and so on. If you are suing a big drug company, you can trawl for damning data to leak to the press. If you want to put pressure on your governor to clean up the environment, you can call up a league table ranking states according to green indices: if he protests that he has done all he can to cut pollution, you can point out that others have done more.

David Roe, one of Scorecard's principal creators, preaches the gospel of democratising information. Back in the 1970s and early 1980s, he remembers, environmental legislation floundered: the 1970 Clean Air Act, for example, was meant to result in emissions standards being set for 200 toxic chemicals, but after more than a decade only six had been regulated in this way. Frustrated, environmentalists switched their campaigning efforts in a new direction. Rather than call on government to curb pollution, they called for disclosure of emissions data. In 1986 they won this battle: a federal reporting requirement was enacted, and California passed a ballot initiative that Mr Roe had drafted, requiring another layer of disclosure from state firms. The results are striking. By 1996 emissions of chemicals covered in the legislation had fallen by 72% in California and by 45% in America as a whole.

The question is how far Scorecard will increase this impact. Many expect big changes. Greens in other countries are impressed by Scorecard: Britain's Friends of the Earth has just launched its own website copying it, and a plan is in the works to export the idea to Canada. Activists in other fields put faith in the idea of instant Internet disclosure: a new ballot initiative in California, for example, would require political candidates to report campaign donations over the Internet within 24 hours. In Washington, the lobbyists who schmooze in Congress know that they face a new source of competition. People all over the country are e-mailing their representatives, often pressing them to take positions inimical to those of the lobbyists' corporate clients.

And yet the significance of Scorecard is uncertain. The website attracts a huge amount of traffic—around ten times more than the Environmental Protection Agency's competing site. But quite what people are doing with this data is mysterious. Scorecard's creators reckon that, in peak months last year, the site's users sent about 1,000 protest faxes to polluters. That is a pinprick. Besides, even if the number of protests multiplied, their effect on policy would remain murky, thanks to the political equivalent of Newton's third law.

For every action in American democracy, an equal and opposite reaction can usually be expected. In the case of green e-mail, the reaction will probably come in several versions. Corporations will devise routine responses: they will program their computers to recognise protesting faxes, and to send back stock replies. Meanwhile, corporations will hire consultants to generate artificial grass-roots e-mail in support of their own positions, to balance out the e-mail that congressmen receive from green citizens. Pestered from all sides, congressmen will have difficulty distinguishing between genuine grass-roots indignation and the astro-turf protests paid for by polluters. As a result, they will stop worrying about the contents of their e-mail bags.

Something like this has already befallen traditional letter writing, and this suggests a disturbing theory about Scorecard's eventual impact. In the 1950s and 1960s, letters to congressmen were relatively rare, and so they were taken seriously, just as e-mail is today. But by the 1970s professionally orchestrated letterwriting campaigns began to undermine the letter-writers' impact. The slicker the letter-writers grew, the more congressmen were inclined to dismiss their work as artificial. Over time, politicians grew increasingly cynical about people seeking to influence them one way or the other: if they wanted to know what their constituents were thinking, they called in the pollsters and ignored their mail bags. It would be ironic indeed if the Internet revolution, celebrated now as a catalyst for reinvigorated citizen participation, were likewise confounded: if websites like Scorecard merely ended up enhancing the power of professional consultants and their opinion polls.

The Two-Bucks-a-Minute Democracy

By handing out millions of dollars' worth of Web TV's, two political scientists at Stanford have gathered the most perfect sample of Americans in the history of polling and persuaded them to answer survey after survey, week after week, year after year. It's a marketer's dream. And it just might change how we think about democracy.

By Michael Lewis

Earlier this year, a truly weird and possibly inspired company founded by a pair of Stanford political scientists, Norman Nie and Doug Rivers, finished spending tens of millions of dollars to install Web television sets in 40,000 American homes. The company, called Knowledge Networks, was trying to address the single greatest problem in polling—getting a random sample of Americans to answer questions—by paying a random sample of Americans for their time. In the summer of 1999, Rivers sent out 40,000 letters, most of them containing $10 bills. The money was the teaser for the big offer: spend 10 minutes each week answering his questions over the Internet, and Rivers would give you a free Web TV, free Internet access and a raft of prizes doled out in various contests and raffles. If you were uneasy with new gadgets, Rivers promised to give you not only the TV and the Internet access but also to send an engineer to install the stuff. An astonishing 56 percent of the people they set out to contact took the offer—compared with the roughly 15 per-

cent now willing to answer questions from a stranger over the telephone.

One of those people was Marion Frost. When she received the letter from Rivers, she had just turned 80, which meant she was gold to any pollster looking to build a random sample of Americans. Along with Americans who earn more than $150,000 a year, Americans who have less than an eighth-grade education and Americans who don't speak English, Americans over 75 tend to elude pollsters. Frost has lived in the same quaint cottage for 46 years, nestled in a middle-class Silicon Valley neighborhood doing its best to avoid being overrun by property developers. The only hint of frailty about her was the cast on her left wrist, which she had broken, absurdly, on her way back from the D.M.V., where she had gone to obtain a handicapped parking sticker. The only sign that she found it odd for a complete stranger to show up at her house to watch her watch television was that she had invited a friend over to join us. The three of us—me, Frost and her friend, Yvette Reyes—settled down to a spread of pizza, cookies and coffee in a living room that doubled as a shrine to bygone values. The furniture would be familiar to anyone who had grandparents in the 1960's; the television was one of those giant oak cabinets with chrome dials that they stopped making back in the 1970's. "My husband died 18 years ago," Frost said, "and we bought the TV at least 15 years before that." The single anomaly in the place was the black Web TV box on top of the television cabinet. With its infrared ports, flashing lights and miniature keyboard, the thing was as incongruous as a Martian.

It was the night of the second Bush-Gore debate, and CBS was using Knowledge Networks—and by extension Marion Frost—to conduct two kinds of polls. One, which Dan Rather was calling "a snap poll," would measure who won the debate. The other, which Dan Rather would never mention, since CBS was still testing it, would seek to understand *why* he won. Twenty minutes before the debate, the red light on top of Frost's black box began to flash, its way of saying that it was waiting for her to switch on her TV and answer a few questions from Knowledge Networks.

Among the many things I was curious to know was why Rivers had been so successful at luring Americans into being the rats in his massive laboratory experiment. I assumed that in all cases he had appealed to the rats' insatiable lust for money and freebies. I was wrong.

"How did these people talk you into taking their surveys?" I asked Frost.

"They just called me out of the blue," she said. She sat toward the edge of her chair, her arm in a dark blue sling. All around her were photographs of children. She had reared three of her own, adopted another and taken in seven foster children.

"But you got their letter with the $10 in it?"

"They never sent me a letter with $10 in it," she said. "I got a letter from Doug Rivers but no $10." Yvette chuckled softly on the sofa beside me. "You come cheap, Marion," she said.

I motioned to her $249 Web TV. The box enabled Knowledge Networks to send polls and surveys to her over the Internet, which then could be displayed on her TV screen. Once each week, the red light flashed to tell Frost that questions awaited her answers whenever she had 10 minutes to spare. Tonight's poll was an exception in that it required Frost's presence at an appointed time. "So," I said, "what do you use that for?"

A hint of discomfort flashed across her impossibly sweet face. "The truth is, I haven't figured out how to use it."

"Then how do you take the surveys?"

"Oh," she said, "I do all the surveys. When the light comes on, I call Robert, and he comes over and turns it on and feeds in the information." Robert is Frost's 45-year-old son.

"When I get the cast off, I think I'll learn how to use it," Frost added, trying and failing to raise her broken arm.

"But you still answer the surveys?" I said.

"Oh, yes," she said, brightening. "Mostly all the questions are about products. Juice. One I remember was the different kinds of juice. They wanted to know what was my opinion of cranberry juice. Would I mix it in with other juices. I don't know. I figure they want to dilute the cranberry juice with other juices. I told them my opinion."

No $10 bill, no interest in the Web TV or the free Internet access or the raffles and contests. No sense whatsoever that she was being paid to answer questions.

"I don't understand," I said. "Why did you agree to be in this survey?"

She was at a loss for an answer, which was O.K., since Yvette wasn't. "Because," she said, with a tone that put an end to further questions, "she's a good person."

On that note, we settled back and waited for Knowledge Networks to begin measuring Marion Frost's opinions.

EVER SINCE THE INTERNET WENT BOOM, PEOPLE HAVE BEEN trying to figure out how to use it to open a window on the American mind. One curious subplot of this year's presidential campaign has been huge, inexplicable swings in the polls. There are a number of possible reasons for these—inept pollsters, fickle voters—but the most persuasive is the growing reluctance of Americans to take calls from pollsters. In the past decade, the response rate to telephone polls has fallen from as high as 40 percent to 15 percent. If the 15 percent of our population still willing to be polite to people who interrupt their dinners were representative, this trend would not be a problem for pollsters. But they aren't, so it is.

Onto this scene, the Internet seems to have arrived just in time. It gives new hope to people who believe that human behavior can be studied and explained scientifically. Internet polling enjoys several obvious advantages over old-fashioned survey techniques: it's potentially more scientific than chasing down people in shopping malls, it's less blatantly intrusive than phoning people at dinner and it carries video to those polled so that ads, movie trailers and product designs can be tested directly. But maybe as important as all these combined is the ease with which an Internet pollster can create a new kind of dialogue with the people he polls. In what Doug Rivers calls "a virtual conversation," the pollster with easy, steady access to a cross-section of the population can unspool a detailed story about the population's tastes and habits.

But the Internet has one huge disadvantage for pollsters: not quite half the U. S. population uses it. In the summer of 1998, Rivers and his Stanford colleague, Nie, both of whom had made distinguished careers studying polling techniques, discovered that they shared an outrage at the sham polls of the "general population" conducted on the Internet. They got to talking about ways that the Internet might be used to poll properly, short of waiting the years it would take for the technology to trickle down. They decided to go out and identify a random sample of Americans and persuade them to go on-line, for free.

Of course, it costs a fortune to dole out tens of thousands of Web TV's. So Rivers, who wound up running the business, was forced to neglect his original interest in political polling and acquire an interest in market research. Corporate America spends $5 billion a year for market surveys. Companies pay roughly $2 for every minute that randomly selected Americans spend answering questions of people who pester them at dinner time. The reason you are worth $120 an hour while you scratch yourself and talk on the phone to a pollster is that pretty much anyone with anything to mass-market—packaged goods, media come-ons, financial products—longs for detailed portraits of the consumer. A network of tens of thousands of Web TV's randomly distributed across the population would represent not just a statistical improvement. It would create a new genre of portraiture.

Typically, the relationship between the American Observer and the American Observed has been a one-night stand. A pollster calls and insists on pawing you a bit, and then you never hear from him again. Knowledge Networks was after something more. Its Web TV's would follow the same people, easily and cheaply, and measure not just their responses to surveys but also their behavior on the Internet. And it would be able to divine patterns in that behavior that companies could then exploit. As Knowledge Networks expanded, it would become possible to poll random samples of tiny populations—people who drank expensive tequila, say, or voted for Pat Buchanan. "Try finding a random sample of Jews by phone," Rivers says. "Jews are 2 percent of the population. Do you know how many randomly generated phone numbers you need to call to find 400 Jews?"

Interestingly, all parties to this new and seemingly intrusive relationship shared a financial interest in it becoming ever more intrusive. There might be people like Marion Frost who don't think of their time as money, but they are a rare breed. By enriching the information he mined from the brains of his random sample, Rivers raised the value of those who spent time answering his questions. The more their time was worth, the more goodies they got, and the more goodies they got, the more willing they would be to answer questions.

It took Rivers just three days to raise the first $6 million he needed from Silicon Valley venture capitalists. The only question they had was why Rivers was sending $10 to people before they agreed to his deal. "The V.C.'s said things like, 'If you sent that to me, I'd just keep the money and not do the surveys,'" Rivers says. "I had to tell them that most people weren't like venture capitalists." Once Rivers had proved to his backers that his system worked in a few hundred homes, he went back and asked for another $36 million so he could install many,

many more Web TV's. The V.C.'s promptly handed that over too.

By the spring of this year, 100,000 Americans were spending 10 minutes each week answering Rivers's questions, often e-mailing him with extra ideas and comments and news about their lives. ("Mr. Rivers," wrote one, "Terrence cannot answer the questions this week because he is in jail.") By the end of the summer, the system was running at full capacity. So Rivers has gone back once again to the venture capitalists for as much as $60 million more to install another 60,000 black boxes. By the end of next year, 250,000 Americans will be engaged in Knowledge Networks' virtual conversation—the fastest, biggest and quite possibly most accurate tracking poll ever conducted. Each person will remain in the sample for three years, at which point they are considered too overexposed to polls to be accurately polled.

Even by Silicon Valley standards, this is a fairly sensational financial story. Among other things, it tells you a great deal about what might be called the public opinion of public opinion. Between 1876, when the last new polling technology, the telephone, was invented, and the 1960's, when the phone was sufficiently widespread to allow for random sampling, it occurred to no one to go out and install 100,000 telephones in American homes. The telephone didn't become a polling device until it had spread on its own into every nook and cranny of American life. But the world is no longer willing to wait for a more accurate self-portrait. Offered even the slightest chance to, as Rivers puts it, "get inside people's minds and find out what's there," investors have proved willing to pay whatever it cost.

The ever-evolving relationship between American consumers and producers inevitably spills over into American politics, which is why a Stanford political scientist has wound up, at least for the moment, testing cranberry juice cocktails for a living. A better view of the public opinion of juice soon becomes a better view of the public opinion of issues and ads and phrases and candidates. Once investors had poured in tens of millions of dollars to create an elaborate mechanism designed to obtain a "360-degree picture of the mind of the American consumer," Rivers knew it wouldn't be long before some enterprising political consultant used it to enter the mind of the American voter. "But the thing we've found," he says, "is that the political people are slower on the uptake than the businesspeople. In part, it's because they don't have the same money to spend. But it's also that the sort of people who become pollsters to presidential campaigns don't like to hear the answers to honest polls. They're believers in a cause."

He is able to say this with detached amusement rather than despair because he assumes that the political people will come around—and how could they not? Politics is a competitive market. Better polls give politicians who follow them an edge. Those who don't will wind up being put out of business by those who do.

PEOPLE WHO BOTHER TO IMAGINE HOW THE INTERNET might change democracy usually assume it will take power away from politicians and give it to the people. It's easy to see how the Internet might lead inexorably to the same extreme form of democracy that has evolved in California, where the big issues often are put directly to the people for a vote. Sooner or later, it will be possible to vote online. And sooner or later, it will be possible to collect signatures online. Together, these changes might well lead to a boomlet in direct democracy, at least in states like California where citizens can call votes on an issue simply by gathering enough signatures on its behalf. At which point someone asks, Why can't we do the same thing in Washington? One constitutional amendment later and—poof—we're all voting directly to decide important national questions rather than voting for politicians and leaving the decisions up to them.

This line of futurology has history on its side. Every step taken by American democracy has been in an egalitarian direction. The direct elections of U.S. senators, the extension of the vote to blacks, women and adolescents, the adoption of initiative and referendum in the vast majority of states, the rise of public opinion polling—all of this pushes democracy in the same direction. It forces politicians to be more informed of, and responsive to, majority opinion. It nudges American democracy ever so slightly away from its original elitist conception and moves it toward something else.

The Knowledge Networks poll offers a glimpse of what that something else might be, a world in which politicians become so well informed about public opinion that there is no need for direct democracy.

It was with something like this in mind that George Gallup began his campaign in the 1930's to make political polling scientifically respectable. Gallup thought that democracy worked better the better-informed politicians were of majority opinion. Rivers does not exactly share this view. He created Knowledge Networks because he believed that inaccurate polls are a danger to democracy and an insult to good social science—but that is a long way from Gallup's original utopian vision. Rivers says he believes that Internet polling is inevitable, so that it might as well be done honestly. But he also believes that his faster and cheaper opinion-gathering machine will provide politicians with a more detailed snapshot of public opinion, and thus give rise to an even more constipated politics. The more perfectly informed politicians are about public opinion, the more they are chained to it. "The problem right now isn't that politicians in Washington are out of touch," Rivers says. "The problem is that they're too closely in touch. And this will make the problem worse." In short, you may believe that politicians could not be more automated than they are now. Just wait.

But it isn't just the politicians who are changed by the technology. The more perfectly watched that voters are, the less they have to pay attention to politics. After all, there's no point in anyone but a revolutionary participating in a system of majority rule when the will of the majority is always, and automatically, known.

OF COURSE, IT TAKES A WHILE FOR AN ENTIRE CULTURE TO get used to the idea that there is no point in participating in democracy unless you are paid to do so. It takes even longer for it to figure out that its participation is worth two bucks a minute. For old ideas to die, the people who hold them must die first. And Marion Frost wasn't quite ready for that. Fifteen minutes before the second presidential debate began, her doorbell rang. It was a young man from Knowledge Networks, who had driven an hour to switch on her Web TV. (Frost's son was traveling, and I couldn't figure it out.) The screen, previously given over to Dan Rather's face, went blue. Onto it came a message: "Please try to have fun while being as serious about this test as possible."

It went on to ask several long, pro-forma questions, which Frost insisted on reading aloud before turning her attention to the alien keyboard. Yvette sighed. "This is going to be a long night, Marion." This was my cue to take her son's place at the keyboard. When we had finished with their questions, the picture came back on the screen, with a long measuring rod at the bottom of it. The rod had a plus sign on one end and a minus sign on the other. Frost was meant to signal what she thought of whatever Bush and Gore said, as they said it, by moving a tiny rectangle back and forth between the two. Instead, she told me what she thought, and I moved the rectangle for her. Her stream of opinions would flow into a river through Knowledge Networks' computers and into CBS studios in New York.

Anyone with anything to mass-market longs for more detailed portraits of the consumer. A network of tens of thousands of Web TV's represents not just a statistical improvement. It creates a new genre of portraiture.

The debate started. I waited for Marion Frost's first command. "I like that Jim Lehrer," she said.

Lehrer had asked Bush a question about foreign policy, and Bush talked for as long as he could on the subject, then did his best to think up some more words to fill the time. Frost said nothing. The little rectangle didn't budge.

"I don't know about Bush," she finally said, "but I'm glad Jim Lehrer's going to be there." Al Gore then went off on his usual relentless quest for a gold star, and Frost listened to all of what he said intently, but again failed to respond. She seemed to want to think about what he said, but the new technology didn't want thought. It wanted quick.

"I don't know," she finally said, as Bush took over. "I'm confused. I think they're both right on some areas." She was growing ever so slightly distressed at her inability to give the black box what it wanted. Finally, Bush said something that caused Frost to say: "I like that. Go ahead and make it positive." But it was as much out of a concern for the little rectangle than actual deep feeling. In any case, her reflex was too slow to hit its mark; by the time I'd moved the rectangle, Gore had again butted in. This didn't seem to bother Frost. She was too busy trying to make sense out of the arguments Bush had made about the I.M.F. "That's the International Monetary Fund," she said—for my benefit, I think.

Yvette sighed and headed for the kitchen. "I get to take a break," she said. "You two can't move."

Frost looked at me with concern and asked, "Would you like a cookie?" The debate heated up again. Gore began to attack Bush's record on health care. Frost became irritated. " 'I believe he has a good heart,' what kind of statement is that?" she said. Hearts were something she knew about. The implications for the rectangle were unclear.

"Should I make it negative?"

"A little," she said.

On this went for an hour and a half, much like the debate itself, defying any possibility of the reflection or deliberation that Frost was intent on supplying. The joy of watching her with her Web TV was her insistence on layering old and dying habits of mind onto the new, supercharged process. Her opinions were being monitored as closely as political opinions have ever been monitored, and yet she didn't really allow the monitoring to interfere with her idea of how to watch a political debate. She avoided making snap judgments just as she had somehow avoided getting paid for offering them. She watched without much interest Dan Rather announce that Bush had won the snap poll—52 percent to 48 percent. She just did what she did because she entertained some notion of her social obligations above and beyond her economic interests. Either that, or she simply could not believe that a citizen is meant to be paid for her services.

Michael Lewis is a contributing writer for the magazine. He is the author, most recently, of "The New New Thing."

BUSH AND GORE: PERFECT WINNERS OF A PERFECT RACE. ALMOST

Jonathan Rauch

can't imagine a worse process, can you? Three more months of meaningless primaries! Eight months until the general election! It all drags on and on and costs so much, and what's the point? The candid candidates are out; the real winners aren't George W. Bush and Al Gore, but big money and party machines. I tremble for my country, darling. Do pass me one of those delightful little canapé things."

On the contrary, I said, passing the little canapé things. I can hardly imagine a better process.

"You're joking, right?"

Not at all. The primary campaign of 1999 and 2000 was as perfect a nominating contest as American democracy has yet produced—which is to say, not too bad.

"Surely you don't defend this crazy primary system? Why, it isn't a system at all."

It is senseless, of course. But so is politics and so is life, and so, above all, is the presidency, which requires its holder to negotiate four to eight years of surprises, reversals, frustrations, foul-ups, and dirty tricks. Thanks to being dragged through the nominating process, the greenhorn Texas governor and the wind-up Vice President became distinctly better at managing senselessness; former Sen. Bill Bradley showed that senselessness isn't his métier; current Sen. John McCain lost his cool under pressure and made mistakes. The crazy system is a magnifying glass that exposes flaws mercilessly. If New Hampshire didn't exist, we would have to invent it.

"But the race started too early and then finished before most states could even vote. The British finish their campaigns in six weeks."

Actually, this was the year when America's parties blundered their way toward a home-grown equivalent of the British system. In a parliamentary system, the parties choose leaders, often in sharp contests between the center and the edges. The leaders then spend months organizing their parties and sharpening their messages before finally facing the electorate. In practice, Tony Blair campaigned for years, not months, before finally winning the British election of 1997.

The process in America this year did something quite a lot like that. First the party insiders chose their favorites, and then the favorites

From the *National Journal*, March 18, 2000, pp. 847-848. © 2000 by National Journal Group, Inc. All rights reserved. Reprinted by permission.

faced stiff challenges, and now both nominees will build their platforms, organize their parties, and probe each other's weaknesses—just what British party leaders do between elections. By November, any voter who cares at all will know as much as any political system could reveal about George W. Bush and Al Gore.

"They're Tweedledee and Tweedledum, you know. You call this a choice?"

I do. The primary process offered every conceivable kind of candidate, plus Alan Keyes. You could have a tax cut, no tax cut, a flat tax, or no tax; you could have gays in the military, gays in the closet in the military, or gays driven out of the military with a sharp stick. If you wanted a candidate who pandered to racist whites, this was your lucky year; and if you wanted one who pandered to racist blacks, this was also your lucky year.

The two winners aren't alike, either. Far from it. They can't both be right about abortion, or school choice, or the budget surplus, or gays in the military, or—most important—humanitarian intervention in conflicts abroad. You want a Big Choice? Gore has called America's involvement in Kosovo a "moral test." "Our strategic interests are important," he said in 1999, "but so are our moral interests." Phooey, says Bush: "We should not send our troops to stop ethnic cleansing and genocide in nations outside our strategic interest." Bush has said pointblank, twice, that he would not send U.S. troops to avert a genocide in Rwanda; Gore's boss has effectively apologized to the Rwandans for not having intervened. If that's not a choice, I've never seen one.

"You know, though, it was all about money in the end. Bush didn't beat McCain; the money did."

Oh, money mattered, all right, as it always has and always will; but the pleasant surprise was that so many other things mattered more. Bradley attained financial parity with Gore early on and held it through the race, and in the crucial

> THE PRIMARY CAMPAIGN WAS AS PERFECT A CONTEST AS DEMOCRACY HAS PRODUCED— WHICH IS TO SAY, NOT TOO BAD.

last quarter of 1999 he outraised and outspent Gore by a wide margin— all to no avail. And Steve Forbes' $40 million got him . . . where?

As for Bush, his $72 billion— sorry, million—gave him an enormous head start, but it also gave John McCain his opening. The Senate Commerce, Science, and Transportation Committee chairman, a full-time Washington insider since 1982, became the "outsider" in no small part because of the flood of big money into Bush's treasury. The irony was that Bush really is an outsider, a newcomer. But he lost that claim when he became a walking cash register and the favorite charity of shadowy Texas zillionaires. This time around, money often worked against itself.

According to a McCain adviser, by the way, McCain spent about $40 million, all told, which isn't peanuts. Would more money have put McCain over the top? After he called religious-conservative leaders "evil"? Maybe, but I doubt it.

"If money didn't count, why would they spend so much of it? Have you seen these spending totals?"

Yes, but the reason is no mystery: Communicating with voters is expensive. Michael J. Malbin, the executive director of George Washington University's Campaign Finance Policy Forum, added up the amounts spent by the most-recent winning Senate candidates in all the states that held presidential primaries this year as of March 14. Grand total: $145 million. Which is more

than the winning presidential nominees spent. Conclusion: That is what politics costs. Deal with it.

"It's all such a turnoff. So few people even bother to vote."

Turnout in the Democratic primaries was the second lowest in 40 years, with only about 10 percent of the voting-age population going to the polls, according to Curtis Gans, the director of the Committee for the Study of the American Electorate. But then, the Democratic race became dull as soon as Al Gore beat Bill Bradley in New Hampshire. Republican-primary turnout, according to Gans, was 13.6 percent of the voting-age population, the highest level since Barry Goldwater electrified Republicans in 1964. Voters came out for, and against, John McCain.

Gans warns that the record turnout for (and against) McCain was not a sign of political health, because McCain tapped into voter disaffection. "It's precisely the opposite of euphoria," Gans told reporters. "It was unhappy people looking for hope." See? Low turnout is a sign of disaffection, whereas high turnout is a sign of disaffection.

W ell, that's one way to look at it. Or you could say that McCain was an inspiring, hell-raising figure who made politics fun again. And he was! And he did!

"But so much of the campaign was negative."

Postmodern negativism ruled: anti-negativity negativism, otherwise known as pre-emptive whining. The idea is to be the first to go negative by attacking the other guy's negativism, preferably before he actually goes negative. Well, I say *nyet* to negativism about negativism! Give me the old-fashioned kind any day. Attack ads are useful, as long as they are approximately truthful. If Barry Goldwater tells jokes about dropping bombs into the Kremlin men's room, why shouldn't LBJ call him trigger happy? If George W. Bush goes out of his way to appear at rabidly anti-Catholic Bob Jones University, why shouldn't McCain nail him?

"Yes, but a lot of the ads this year were not 'approximately truthful.' "

Ah, there you have a point. If the primary race fell short, it was because a fair amount of lying went on, and the winners were the two candidates who did the most lying. Gore told a national television audience that Bradley "went 17 years in the United States Senate before he ever sponsored a campaign finance reform bill," when in fact, as Robert B. Reich notes in *The New Republic,* Bradley sponsored reform bills in six straight Congresses. Bush's brazen ad that falsely accused McCain of opposing breast-cancer research will live in infamy. The candidates who tried not to do this sort of thing, McCain and Bradley, got shellacked.

"Well, then. You see. That's bad."

Yes. That is bad. But don't forget the bigger picture. The voters had no trouble picking out the four best men in the race (though I retain a soft spot for Orrin Hatch), and each of the final four had the makings of a perfectly adequate President, or perhaps even quite a good President. Besides, a certain amount of ruthlessness, within reason, is not a bad thing in politics. Neither Bush nor Gore is pure, but neither of them is a Nixon, or even a Clinton. Remember the four basic rules of presidential politics:

1) Be honest.
2) Be smart.
3) Don't be too smart.
4) Don't be too honest.

Bush and Gore fill the order pretty well.

The Last Straw Poll

Seven things from Campaign 2000 to eliminate

KATE O'BEIRNE

BEFORE the reform-minded spirit of this year's campaign gives way to the practical realities of governing, the most irritating features of the 2000 presidential race should be noted and reformed out of existence. Any "not to do" list for the next slate of White House contenders should include the Iowa straw poll, the New Hampshire primary along with open primaries in other states, the Commission on Presidential Debates, focus groups of "undecided" voters, tracking polls, and "ad watches" by media referees.

Iowa's greedy GOP takes two big bites of the nomination apple by conducting a **straw poll** that candidates typically dare not ignore. Because the media join the hype, this fundraising stunt can shrink the field of candidates a full year before the party's convention. Happily, John McCain's atypical campaign benefited by ignoring this season's straw poll, as well as the state's January caucus. Conventional hindsight holds that Bill Bradley should also have headed straight to New Hampshire. If Iowa's loss in the political marketplace prompts future candidates to follow McCain's strategy, the caucuses will no longer test the field, and reporters will be spared spending January in Des Moines—and August in Ames.

This year, **New Hampshire** again failed its own political marketplace test. John McCain enjoyed a huge win in New Hampshire that bore no relation to how he fared in later primaries. Four years ago, Pat Buchanan was unable to duplicate his success in the Granite State. Why should New Hampshire continue to enjoy its preeminent status when the state has become the "Worst in the Nation" at picking GOP nominees? The disproportionate attention paid to New Hampshire voters—demonstrated by the tiresome quadrennial jokes about locals being undecided because they had only met a certain candidate five times—has made them too obnoxiously self-aware to provide a valid test of candidates. With independents free to vote in the GOP primary in numbers that outstrip registered Republicans, the state's voters now just seem to enjoy letting challengers without broad party appeal rough up the GOP frontrunner.

All of the other state parties ought to restrict their primaries to party members. When independents and Democrats vote in **open primaries** (like those in Michigan), the results don't represent the nominee party members favor. Agnostics who reject the creed shouldn't dilute the will of the party faithful. The media fawns over "thoughtful" nonaligned voters, but political partisans who are informed and engaged on the issues are the most responsible members of the electorate, and the parties should be doing everything possible to encourage party membership.

This year it became clear that the **Commission on Presidential Debates** has gotten too big for its bipartisan britches. The Commission has been hosting the face-offs since 1988, when its bossy predecessor, the League of Women Voters, refused to modify its debate demands to suit Vice President Bush. In January, the Commission announced the number, dates, sites, and times for the fall debates. In June, it dictated the lengths and the single-moderator format. When George W. Bush had the temerity to suggest alternative debate forums, he found that the private bipartisan group had achieved some weirdly official status that had the unprecedented effect of preventing any modifications by the candidates. (As recently as 1996, Bill Clinton got away with debating only twice.) So, in the high-stakes debates, Jim Lehrer alone decided every question posed, even screening those offered by the "undecided" Missouri voters the Commission had rounded up. Since 1976, the leading presidential candidates have taken part in nationally televised general-election debates, and voter expectations will ensure that candidates debate in 2004—without the Commission.

The tiresome, predictable **undecided voters** at the Missouri town-hall debate did fairly represent the ill-informed, detached voters whose views the media examined ad nauseam this season. Basking in the TV lights, these debate watchers invariably told Wolf that they were still torn between candidates who hadn't yet matched their own precise positions on education, health care, or the environment. Maybe if they weren't so busy being interviewed, they could watch the news, read a newspaper, or check a website to find out everything they'd care to know about candidates who broadly reflect the philosophical positions their parties have represented for the past 40 years.

With so many of this year's **polls** embarrassingly inaccurate, let's hope the media and their pollsters enter a trial separation. Over one recent four-day period, Gallup's tracking poll found a 15 point swing in the presidential candidates' support, which commentators gamely tried to attribute to some development or other on the campaign trail. Of course, there had been no such wild fluctuation, but the four frequently contradictory national polls that were in the field during October drove media coverage in the campaigns' final weeks. Polling

expert Karlyn Bowman of the American Enterprise Institute is dismayed with the attention paid to every purported blip in polls; it makes the poll numbers appear much more precise than they really are. She notes that one study found that about 25 percent of voters don't firmly make up their minds until the last two weeks of the campaign, "These polls are often probing opinions that are nonexistent," Bowman explains. She recalls that the first question about the 2000 race was asked in 1995, attempting to measure the support Colin Powell would enjoy should he elect to run. Before the Iowa caucuses this year, there had been 1,000 polling questions on the presidential race. And the daily bombardment won't end because the campaigns are over. Rasmussen Research has announced that "for the first time in history, the new president will have his approval ratings measured every day." Stop them before they poll again.

Finally, media **"ad watches"** should stick to policing the intentionally false accusations made against candidates, such as being complicit in the death of a nursing home resident or opposing research on breast cancer, rather than nitpicking the typical campaign fare. One ad analysis in the *New York Times* complained that Bush's claims about his education record were "selective and broad." Imagine that: "selective and broad" statements in a political TV commercial! Another *Times* ad analysis faulted a Republican TV spot that mentioned the Buddhist temple for ignoring Al Gore's admission that he was "an imperfect messenger," on campaign finance reform. The ad was said to represent "a certain desperation" on the part of Republicans. Does that sound like an objective judgment?

With the 2004 campaign season beginning on November 8, 2000, it's not too soon to start getting rid of these irritants.

Selling America to the Highest Bidder

IT HAS been a week of dramatic surprises. But, looking at the campaign as a whole, one of the unexpected delights of this election is how a subject that was once the prerogative of Beltway bores kept threatening to turn into a popular crusade. Campaign-finance reform popped up at the start of the process, when Bill Bradley and, particularly, John McCain shook their parties' establishments. It popped up at odd points in the middle of the campaign (as when Rick Lazio tried to cajole Hillary Clinton into signing a pledge to ban soft money). And it popped up at the end, when Ralph Nader, the most prominent ranter against money politics, drained votes from Al Gore.

Now it should be central to any post-mortem on the election. There are many admirable things about the American political system, not least its ability to force politicians to get to know every part of their sprawling country. But there is no doubt that the campaign-finance system is badly broken. A country that regards itself as an international torchbearer of democracy would be wise to make sure that its own political system is not rotting from within.

This year's election has been the most expensive in American history. An estimated $3 billion has been spent on presidential and congressional races—including millions of dollars by unaccountable outside groups—and an additional $1 billion or more has been spent on state contests. Expenditure is up nearly 50% from the 1996 election, a contest that supposedly set an all-time low in money-grubbing and rule-bending.

George W. Bush raised an astonishing $100m for his primary campaign: so much money that he decided to do without federal matching funds and the limitations that went with them. Jon Corzine, a former head of Goldman Sachs, spent around $60m of his $400m fortune to become a senator from New Jersey—and succeeded. The influence of money could be seen everywhere in politics, from the lavish feasts that special interests put on for their hired shills during the political conventions to the free cigarettes that Democratic enthusiasts gave to homeless people in Wisconsin in an attempt to persuade them to vote.

The most dramatic feature of the election was the increase in "soft money"—political contributions from companies, unions and fat cats that escape federal rules because they go to party organisations rather than particular candidates. Common Cause, a think-tank, points out that the Democratic and Republican national party committees raised a record $393m in soft money in the first nine months of this year, compared with $207m in 1996.

This rising tide of soft money has all but eroded the three pillars of America's campaign-finance system: the ban on corporate contributions, strict limits on individual donations and public financing for the presidential campaign. Companies and unions may be barred from making direct political donations, but they can spend unlimited amounts of soft money on issue ads. All candidates may be banned from taking contributions of more than $1,000 from individuals or $5,000 from political action committees in any election cycle; but they can take unlimited sums from outside sources by establishing separate soft-money committees. When Bill Clinton and Bob Dole introduced the idea of soft money in 1996, they seemed to have discovered a novel way to get round the election rules. Now soft money has become just another part of the American political landscape.

The underlying reason why Americans spent so much on politics in 2000 was in part because they had so much money to spend. Special interests, such as the trial lawyers, are flush with tobacco loot and determined to keep the good times rolling. The ever-growing battalions of the mega-rich are also looking for intriguing ways to use their money. Jane Fonda gave almost $12m to a new abortion-rights group in September. Tim Draper, a Silicon Valley venture capitalist, spent $20m on a school-voucher initiative, though it still got trounced this week.

But two other things also increased the conspicuous consumption. The first was that so much rested on a knife-edge: not just the presidency, but also control of both houses of Congress. The second was the Clinton factor. It is no accident that two of the most expensive races in the election—the $80m Senate race in New York and the $10m congressional race in California's 27th district—featured Bill Clinton's wife (who won) and his enemy, James Rogan, one of the House managers during the impeachment crisis (who lost).

Does this matter? Why shouldn't Mr Corzine, a rather benevolent bearded cove, be allowed to spend a fragment of his fortune on his nice new hobby? Why shouldn't the nation's taxidermists, trial lawyers (or whoever it may be) express their heartfelt opinions on "issue ads"?

Because it is bad for democracy. Money politics reduces the quality of candidates for high office by giving an unfair advantage to three groups of insiders: "legacies", such as the sons and wives of presidents, who don't need as much money to "build name recognition", but also find raising the stuff easier than their "unbranded" rivals do; the mega-rich, who can finance their own campaigns (the Democrats cleverly recruited five multi-millionaires to stand for expensive seats); and incumbents, who can sell, sorry parlay, the power of their office into political contributions. In this year's House races, incumbents spent nine times as much money as their challengers did. Nobody invests millions of dollars in a politician without expecting a payback: hence the much vaunted "iron triangle" of legislators, lobbyists and fundraisers.

Wander around Washington, DC, and there is no shortage of people—not all of them lobbyists or incumbents—who will explain that translating this vague sense of unease into concrete reform remains extremely difficult. Money has a way of getting round the rules, and the Supreme Court does not help by (mistakenly) equating freedom of speech with freedom to spend money *ad libitum* on getting elected. But there is a growing sense that those explanations remain excuses rather than decent reasons. Without action, campaign-finance reform will surely play an even greater role in the next election. And nobody should be surprised.

Ten Observations on the 2000 Presidential Election Controversy in Florida

By Bruce Stinebrickner

1. POLITICS AIN'T BEANBAG

After a long, intense season two teams compete with each other for the national championship. At the end of regulation time the score is very close, with the official scorebook showing ambiguities in the final total of points for each team. The coaches and their assistants huddle with the referees. A widening circle of game officials, team representatives, and league officials become involved in the protracted dispute. Spectators, almost equally divided in their loyalties, return to their seats, while television networks provide continuous coverage of the dispute. Each team badly wants to win and each side employs virtually every conceivable line of argument in the intense and emotional proceedings. After consultation with the highest authorities, the referees accept the original score showing one team to be one point ahead and declare that team the winner.

The foregoing sports story can provide a context for understanding a first, elementary observation about the protracted controversy surrounding the 2000 presidential election in Florida: it was not surprising at the time, nor is it surprising in retrospect, that presidential candidates George W. Bush and Al Gore and their supporters each postured, argued, and litigated as if they wanted to win at all costs. A great deal was at stake for the two candidates and their supporters, and the psychological investments of each side in winning the presidency were enormous. As the old adage suggests, "politics ain't beanbag." (Or, as Al Gore might add, "close only counts in horseshoes.")

2. HYPOCRISY

I know of no supporter of candidate George W. Bush who sided with candidate Al Gore's position that a manual recount of some—or all—Florida ballots was essential. Similarly, Gore supporters lined up virtually unanimously *against* the Bush campaign's efforts to stop such a manual recount.

Perhaps you wonder whether it was pure coincidence that virtually all Bush supporters opposed a manual recount and all Gore supporters advocated one. Ask yourself whether James A. Baker II, Bush campaign point man during the Florida election controversy, would have been so adamantly opposed to a manual recount if *his* candidate had been the one behind in the original machine-counted totals. And ask yourself a parallel question about William Daly, Gore campaign chairman, who intoned repeatedly that all votes should be counted. Would Daly and Gore have favored "counting all the votes" if Gore had led Bush by a razor-thin margin after the initial machine count and re-count?

There was plenty of hypocrisy on display in the post-Election Day controversy in Florida. One only had to note that every Bush and Gore supporter interviewed by journalists adopted a procedural stance that conveniently favored the chances of that supporter's preferred candidate. This correspondence between individuals' procedural stance on manual recounts and preference between the candidates was not a matter of sheer coincidence.

3. CLOSE ELECTIONS ARE INEVITABLE

Hotly disputed election results are not unprecedented in the United States or in other functioning democratic political systems. Indeed, if enough elections to fill enough government positions are held in *any* political system, some close results are virtually inevitable.

And close results often bring out the worst in candidates and their supporters.

With one national, fifty state, and more than 80,000 local governments, the United States probably has more elective government offices and more frequent elections for those offices than any other political system. Thus, the odds are that the United States will have a significant number of close elections, with the Florida presidential contest in 2000 being the most noteworthy example of late.

The challenge in a modern democratic political system of the size and complexity of the United States is to ensure that election machinery, broadly construed, can produce vote tallies that are accurate and reliable *and* widely viewed as such. Constructing voter rolls, writing voter instructions, designing ballots, and counting (and re-counting) votes all are tasks that must be done fairly and well. For a country that can send people to the moon, shoot ballistic missiles accurately over thousands of miles, provide ATMs on seemingly every street corner, and invent such medical marvels as MRI machines, substantially improving the reliability and obvious fairness of election machinery should not be a daunting task. Government officials responsible for running elections in the USA should upgrade election machinery so that a Florida-like controversy does not embarrass the nation again.

4. THE CULT OF THE CONSTITUTION AND CONSTITUTIONAL CRISES

It seems that Americans love to talk or hear talk of a "constitutional crisis." Media commentary as the Florida controversy unfolded often focused on just such talk.

Just what was the essence of the "constitutional crisis" to which commentators referred? (i) That who would and should succeed Bill Clinton as president was not immediately clear? Hardly a crisis when the scheduled date for the succession was two months away. (ii) That the candidates and their aides were exhausting all legal and procedural avenues to try to win the election and become president? This seems only natural. (See Observation 1 above, "Politics Ain't Beanbag," and Observation 5 below, "Lawsuits and the Rule of Law.") (iii) That the popular vote winner was not the Electoral College winner and thus it seemed that candidate George W. Bush would become president even though more people had voted for candidate Al Gore? But that is how the Electoral College system is structured, and much of it is set forth in the Constitution. Anyone with an elementary familiarity with the Electoral College system knows that such an outcome is possible, so such an outcome should not constitute a constitutional crisis.

Many Americans embrace what foreign observers are fond of calling "the cult of the Constitution." That is, Americans seem to endow the Constitution of 1787 and its amendments with the status of a sacred text. As a more realistic alternative, why not view the Constitution as a statement of basic governmental procedures (e.g., how a bill becomes a law, how a president is elected) and policies (e.g., freedom of speech should be protected as far as practicable, the manufacture and sale of alcoholic beverages are illegal) that can be changed through a set of procedures specified in the document itself?

The "cult of the Constitution" predisposes Americans to view a "constitutional crisis" as something akin to a collective Judgment Day for a whole nation of individual souls. Such a conception can seem a bit laughable in the political realm, but it certainly served to spice up initial reporting and commentary about the hotly contested results of the 2000 presidential election.

As the post-Election Day controversy wore on, some media commentators began to wonder whether the USA was indeed in the throes of a "constitutional crisis." Rather than ask a Bush or Gore representative about legal and public relations activities occurring or being contemplated, journalists asked whether a "constitutional crisis" still loomed. In response, otherwise capable and intelligent individuals presented an appropriately furrowed brow, adopted just the right intonation, and pontificated solemnly on a distinctively American preoccupation.

5. LAWSUITS AND THE RULE OF LAW

As Alexis de Tocqueville suggested in the 1830s, the American political system and American society are very litigious, i.e., prone to use legal proceedings to settle disputes that in other political systems and other societies would be settled in other ways. Why, then, be surprised or concerned that a hotly contested presidential election winds up being litigated in both federal and state courts? Resort to courts to settle all sorts of disputes, large and small, is part and parcel of American life. That the hotly contested results of the 2000 presidential election were litigated *ad nauseum* should not come as a surprise. Nor should it be a cause for public hand-wringing.

The term "rule of law" was frequently intoned in post-Election Day pronouncements. Bush spokesperson James Baker was one of its most fervent advocates, *until* a key court decision or two went against his candidate. Then Baker and other Bush partisans were heard to lament the Gore team's resort to litigation to try to get a manual recount of some—or all—votes in Florida. (It was also Baker who said in the first day or two after Election Day that the Bush side would not take action in the courts, right before the Bush campaign under Baker's leadership filed the first of more than forty lawsuits that the two candidates—and others—eventually filed in connection with the Florida election results. See Observation 2, "Hypocrisy.")

The "rule of law" can be made into a fairly complex topic, though there is no evidence to suggest that Bush or Gore partisans who mouthed the term were familiar with its philosophical complexities. In essence, "rule of law" seems to refer to the finality—and public acceptance of the finality—of fair and appropriate legal proceedings in resolving whatever disputes arise in a political or social system. Understood thus, the "rule of law" is a necessary ingredient in a properly functioning democratic political system. The 2000 presidential election controversy showed that, in the litigious American political system, arrival at a final determination under the "rule of law" often involves multiple legal proceedings in state and federal courts, with the U.S. Constitution sometimes being invoked. (See Observation 4, "The Cult of the Constitutional Crises.")

It is noteworthy how completely and quickly candidate Al Gore and his partisans accepted the 5-to-4 U.S. Supreme Court rulings that doomed his presidential hopes. First the Court stopped the manual recounting of ballots that had been ordered one day earlier in a 4-to-3 ruling of the Florida Supreme Court and then it declared that no satisfactory and timely manual recounting procedure was possible under the circumstances. After much litigation in state and federal courts, the "rule of law" can be said to have prevailed.

6. AMERICAN DEMOCRACY AT WORK

How about a look at the bright side of all the post-November 7, 2000, fuss?

First, neither candidate nor his supporters threatened or even hinted at the prospect of using force to gain the presidency. (See discussion of the "rule of law" under Observation 5.) Although there were a few demonstrations in Florida—one of which may have influenced a county canvassing board to stop its recounting at a critical juncture—there were no riots in the streets threatening to take over the government through violence. Nor did anyone in the U.S. military issue threats to put a preferred candidate in the White House.

Second, the public relations battle between the Gore and Bush camps shared center stage with proceedings in various courts, county canvassing boards, and the Florida state legislature. The reactions and anticipated reactions of Americans were clearly important to both camps. In particular, candidate Gore declined to pursue certain legal options available to him (e.g., law-

suits aimed at declaring invalid thousands of absentee ballots because Republican party functionaries had been allowed to remedy deficiencies in Republican absentee voters' applications and legal action stemming from the confusion and invalidation of ballots caused by the so-called butterfly ballot in Palm Beach County) because of his belief that the public would not approve of those particular legal tactics. Such public relations considerations should not, of course, have substituted for concerns about fair, accurate, and complete counting of ballots. Yet the interest that both camps showed in what the public was thinking does not suggest that democratic values and responsiveness to the public were being altogether ignored.

Third, as suggested in Observation 5 above, "democracy" cannot exist in isolation from other important organizing principles of government such as "the rule of law." As already noted, through all the public relations posturing, name-calling, and, yes, litigation in the tumultuous post-election events of November, 2000, the rule of law ultimately prevailed. The declared loser conceded (Gore said that he "accepted" but did not "agree" with the U.S. Supreme Court's critical ruling), the declared winner became president-elect (and later president), and the rule of law prevailed in determining a successor to President Bill Clinton. While a great many Americans harbor doubts about whether the outcome of the 2000 presidential election was accurately determined, the whole process of determining a nation's chief executive can be—and often is—much less democratic, as *coup d'etats* illustrate.

7. PERSPECTIVES FROM ABROAD

Observing elections in other countries and monitoring them for "fairness" has been almost a cottage industry for some Americans. In the 1960s, teams of American election specialists observed elections in South Vietnam during the ill-fated Vietnam War and reported that the elections had proceeded fairly and appropriately. Former president Jimmy Carter has reportedly led teams to observe no fewer than thirty national elections in foreign lands since he left the presidency.

The irony of all this was apparently not lost on foreign observers, prominent and obscure. Russian President Vladimir Putin remarked shortly after the Florida controversy erupted that Russia's commissioner of elections, already in the United States on other business, should perhaps go to Florida to ensure electoral fair play! India's commissioner of elections said that he would never have approved the infamous and confusing "butterfly" ballot used in West Palm Beach. A well-known Australian political scientist expressed astonishment at the woeful procedures in place to handle the recounting of close election results in Florida. And a cab driver in Namibia had a good laugh at Florida's expense when an American traveler admitted that she hailed from the Sunshine State.

8. ELECTORAL MECHANICS I: VOTING MECHANICS

- In 1988 the U.S. Bureau of Standards issued a report on the mechanics of voting and vote-counting in the USA and recommended that punch-card machines be abandoned because of inherent deficiencies. Yet in 2000 more than one-third of USA voters used punch cards to record their preferences among presidential candidates.

- Each of Florida's 67 counties reportedly designed their own ballots for the elections of November, 2000. As anyone who followed news media reports at the time knows, Palm Beach County used its notorious "butterfly" ballot, which apparently confused many voters and led a substantial number of them to invalidate their votes by accidentally casting preferences for *both* candidate Gore *and* candidate Buchanan.

- A partisan elected official, Republican Florida Secretary of State Katherine Harris, who had served as co-chair of George W. Bush's Florida campaign effort, was the government official charged with overseeing the Florida presidential election vote certification process.

One result of the 2000 presidential election will likely be a substantial overhaul of procedures used by voters to record their preferences among candidates. Change may occur through congressional enactment of federal funding for the improvement of states' electoral equipment. A standard national ballot for all presidential and congressional elections would also seem a good idea. So would standardized procedures to be followed if a recount is deemed necessary, and perhaps the establishment of a professional, nonpartisan agency of the national government to implement appropriate procedures in elections for president and congress and to minimize the likelihood of a controversy such as occurred in 2000.

9. ELECTORAL MECHANICS II: MEDIA COVERAGE

Arising anew in the aftermath of the 2000 presidential election controversy was a concern over the effect of journalists' premature declarations of election results. On the nights of November 7/8, TV commentators first reported that Gore had won Florida, next called the state for Bush (prompting a telephoned concession from Gore to Bush, which Gore soon thereafter withdrew), and then declared that Florida was "too close to call." The announcement that Gore had won Florida was broadcast even before the polls were closed in the western (i.e., panhandle) part of Florida, not to mention states farther to the west.

Central to this problem is the use of exit polls, usually in conjunction with early returns in selected precincts, to facilitate such predictions soon after the polls close in a particular state or in particular parts of a state.

Election commentators are understandably eager to "call" states as early as possible. And commitments to freedom of speech and freedom of the press as well as fair elections lead some Americans to simultaneously defend and criticize such potentially disruptive election predictions. Yet the well-accepted practice of prohibiting campaigning within a certain distance of polling places may suggest a way to undermine the accuracy of exit polls and thus minimize or eliminate troublesome early prognostications. After taking the relatively simple step of preventing any ballot counting until all polls across the nation are closed, why not prohibit asking any voter within, say, one-quarter mile from a polling place how he or she voted? This would enable enough voters a chance to "escape" unquestioned so as to render exit polling unreliable. (The increased incidence of mail and absentee balloting may itself render exit polls as we know them anachronistic.) In turn, the problem of early and generally reliable TV prognostications would probably fade away, even as the First Amendment and the important commitment to free speech, free press, and fair elections would, in my judgment, survive essentially undisturbed.

10. ELECTORAL MECHANICS III: THE ELECTORAL COLLEGE

Before November 7, 2000, respected election analysts suggested that George Bush might win more popular votes than Al Gore but still lose in the Electoral College. As it turned out, Gore lost in the Electoral College, but, as of this writing, seems to have won the national popular vote. Big deal. This lack of coincidence between popular and Electoral College results had already happened at least three times in American history. Either you support an electoral system that permits someone other than the popular vote winner to win the presidency or you don't. That the Electoral College "misfired" in 2000 is not much of a reason for opposing the system anew. The possibility of such a "misfiring" is inherent in the system, whether it happened in 2000, will happen again in 2004, or will not happen again for a century.

The Old College Try

How we pick the prez

BYRON YORK

I BELIEVE strongly that in a democracy we should respect the will of the people, and to me that means it's time to do away with the Electoral College," said New York senator-elect Hillary Rodham Clinton shortly after Election Day. She wasn't alone. A Gallup poll conducted a few days after the voting showed that 61 percent of Americans agree with Mrs. Clinton—a sentiment that's sure to give at least temporary new energy to the old cause of getting rid of the College. In fact, public opposition has been constant for years; in 1944, Gallup found that 65 percent of those polled wanted to do away with it.

What the polls cannot show, however, are the ways in which eliminating the Electoral College would change the nature of our political campaigns. For an idea of what those changes might be, just look at how the 2000 presidential campaign would have played out if George W. Bush and Al Gore had been trying simply to win the popular vote, rather than crafting their strategies to capture a majority in the Electoral College.

Start with the candidates' schedules. In the closing days of the campaign, Bush and Gore spent most of their precious time stumping in those famous "key battleground states"— places like Pennsylvania, Michigan, Florida, Wisconsin, and Missouri, which had enough electoral votes to attract a lot of candidate attention. In practical terms, that often meant going to relatively small cities in an effort to lock up a state's electoral votes. In early November, Gore paid visits to towns like Ames, Iowa, Las Cruces, N.M., and Huntington, W. Va., while Bush spent time in places like Duluth, Minn., Albuquerque, N.M., and Little Rock, Ark.

Would they have done that in a popular-vote system? No. The Electoral College gives smaller states a boost by awarding them electors based on their representation in Congress. Each state gets two votes to begin with, for its two senators; then, each state is given one vote for each congressional district it contains. Thus Iowa, which has five House seats, has seven electoral votes—a touch more influence than its population warrants. Those state boundaries would disappear in a popular-vote system; instead of concentrating on individual states in order to win electoral votes, candidates would focus on metropolitan areas and regions where they already have strong support as they try to build up their popular-vote totals. "Gore would probably have been in California more; he would have been in Massachusetts, he would have been all over the Northeast, and not in Michigan and Pennsylvania and Wisconsin and Missouri," says Democratic strategist Steve McMahon. "He would have been up and down the West coast and up and down the East coast, with a stop in Chicago."

At the same time, George W. Bush would have tried to run up the score on his home turf. "Bush did not push for a large turnout in Texas," says David Israelite, political director for the Republican National Committee. "If the election were based on the popular vote, I'm sure he could have generated tens of thousands or hundreds of thousands more votes there." Bush would also have spent more time in urban areas in the South and the Great Plains, which, while not having the concentration of votes found in the Northeast, are solidly Republican. And the closer the race, the stronger the temptation to stick to one's

From *National Review*, December 4, 2000, pp. 24–26. © 2000 by National Review, Inc., 215 Lexington Avenue, New York, NY 10016. Reprinted by permission.

base—Ames, Iowa, could forget about seeing any presidential candidates.

A popular vote would also change the candidate's advertising strategy. In the current state-based system, the campaigns buy air time on hundreds of local television stations, concentrating on the areas that are most hotly contested and offer the most electoral votes. Those advertising campaigns are designed to dovetail with candidate visits to create the maximum combination of free and paid media. But places that each candidate has in the bag receive little or no attention. For example, viewers in the nation's two largest television markets, New York and Los Angeles, saw no commercials from the Democratic candidate. "The Gore campaign didn't communicate with them at all," says Steve McMahon. "They were wholly taken for granted because they were in the 'D' column automatically." Likewise, the Bush campaign didn't waste its money on television advertising in Dallas, Houston, and San Antonio—or New York, for that matter.

In a popular-vote system, the candidates would instead buy much more time on the national networks, both broadcast and cable. That would create a split between where the campaign poured advertising money and where the candidate actually traveled, a difference between what political professionals call the "media strategy" and the "body strategy." "The body would go to major media markets where you could meet the most people," says McMahon. "The candidate would physically appear in the top 50 markets, but his media would appear everywhere."

A switch to a popular-vote system would change much more than the style of campaigning. The issues that candidates choose to stress would also be transformed. Without the Electoral College, each candidate would likely emphasize issues important to his base in an effort to build up support from core voters. "Both Bush and Gore avoided gun control and abortion for the most part, which are defining issues of the two parties," says Michael Barone, coauthor of *The Almanac of American Politics*. "The problem was that in the target states, there is close to a balance on those issues, so you alienate as many voters as you enthuse. If it were national, Gore would be running on gun control to turn out urban voters."

Local issues would also disappear. In September, Bush traveled to Monroe, Wash., to stand in front of the Haskell Slough salmon-recovery project, which he praised as a model of local environmental-protection efforts. As with so many other issues, Gore covered some of the same territory, promising more than Bush; on his own visits to Washington, the vice president promised to convene a "Salmon Summit" devoted to increasing fish population and preserving dams on the Snake River. Would candidates chasing a majority of voters nationwide spend much time on questions like that? Probably not. "Those are issues that might be ignored in a national campaign," says David Israelite.

Finally, getting rid of the Electoral College would change the contours of the two-party system itself. If amassing the most votes were the only standard for election, it's likely we would see more third- and fourth-party candidates. "Unless you get a third candidate like Ross Perot who was competitive, and that's been rare," Barone says, "the Electoral College works very much to their disadvantage, because you always get back to the 'wasted vote' theory." Most voters don't want to throw away their votes on a candidate who can't win, and the public tends to move away from lesser candidates as Election Day approaches. They know full well that the electoral system does not reward even the strongest third-party candidate; in 1992, Perot received 19,741,048 popular votes and not a single vote in the Electoral College.

Of course, Perot was highly eccentric, to say the least, which limited his vote-getting appeal. Where a change in the system might really have an effect is with a candidate who is intensely popular with the hard-core base of one of the parties and who is able to generate high turnout in high-population areas.

Which brings the issue back to New York's senator-elect. It seems highly unlikely that Hillary Rodham Clinton could run a winning campaign for president under the Electoral College system; she would be too unpalatable to voters in the battleground states. But under a popular-vote system, one in which Mrs. Clinton could concentrate on the Northeast, the West Coast, and Chicago, she might well have a chance. Just one more reason to revere the wisdom of the Founding Fathers.

Mr. York is *The American Spectator*'s senior writer.

Unit Selections

Key Points to Consider

❖ What do you think is the single most important social welfare or economic policy issue facing the American political system today? The single most important national security or diplomatic issue? What do you think ought to be done about them?

❖ What factors increasingly blur the distinction between foreign and domestic policy issues?

❖ How would you compare President Clinton's performance in the areas of social welfare and economic policies with the way he has handled national security and diplomatic affairs? What changes has he tried to make in each of these areas? What about President George W. Bush?

❖ What policy issues currently viewed as minor matters seem likely to develop into crisis situations?

❖ What do you think is the most significant policy failure of American national government today? The most significant policy success?

❖ What do you think about the idea of devolution, which means giving state and local governments *more* responsibility for policy making and policy implementation and the national government *less*? What reasons are there to expect that state and local governments will do a better—or worse—job than the national government in such areas as welfare and health care benefits for the old and the poor?

 **Links** ## www.dushkin.com/online/

These sites are annotated on pages 4 and 5.

"Products" refers to the government policies that the American political system produces. The first three units of this book have paved the way for this fourth unit, because the products of American politics are very much the consequences of the rest of the political system.

Dilemmas and difficulties in one policy area are often reflected in others. Indeed, tensions between fundamental values lie at the heart of much public policy making in all spheres: equality versus freedom, reliance on the public sector versus reliance on the private sector, collectivism versus individualism, internationalism versus isolationism, and so forth.

The health of the American economy is always a prominent policy issue in the American political system. One of the most remarkable consequences of 12 years (1981–1993) under Presidents Reagan and Bush was enormous growth in budget deficits and in the national debt. Moreover, the nation's economy had entered a recession by the halfway mark of President Bush's term. During the Clinton presidency the country enjoyed the longest period of continuous economic growth in U.S. history, accompanied by relatively low unemployment and inflation rates. Indeed, a healthy economy was the foundation of President Clinton's popularity in public opinion polls and of his successful reelection campaign in 1996. Continuing economic growth increased tax revenues to such an extent that the long-sought goal of a balanced budget was reached in 1998 amidst predictions that the entire national debt would be eliminated within a decade or so. In the last months of the Clinton administration, however, some signs of an economic slowdown appeared and it remains to be seen whether prosperity will continue unabated during the Bush presidency.

Domestic public policy usually involves "trade-offs" among competing uses of scarce resources. During his 1992 campaign Bill Clinton called attention to many such trade-offs in the area of health care. For example, are we as a nation content to spend a greater proportion of our national income on health care than any other industrialized country? If not, are we willing to limit medical spending when that may mean that sophisticated and sometimes life-saving treatments become less available to middle-class and poor Americans? Do we want to extend medical insurance to those millions of less affluent Americans currently uninsured, even though this might result in higher costs and/or less medical treatment for those who are already insured? As president, Clinton introduced a comprehensive health care reform proposal late in 1993. Congress never voted on that proposal, and, while various minor changes were made in the nation's health care delivery system during the Clinton administration, no comprehensive overhaul was ever achieved.

Other domestic policy areas also involve trade-offs. To what extent should we make the unemployed who are receiving welfare payments work, and what responsibility should the government take for preparing such citizens for work and for ensuring that jobs are available? (The landmark 1996 welform reform act, the result of a compromise between President Clinton and House Speaker Newt Gingrich, addressed several of these issues in fairly direct ways.) How much are cleaner air and other environmental goals worth in terms of economic productivity, unemployment, and so forth? Such trade-offs underlie debate about specific tax policies, social welfare programs, immigration policies, environmental problems, and the like.

For at least three decades, the United States and the Soviet Union each had the capacity to end human existence as we know it. Not surprisingly, the threat of nuclear war often dominated American diplomacy and national security policy making. Since World War II, however, the United States has used conventional forces in a number of military actions—in Korea, Vietnam, Grenada, Panama, and the Persian Gulf area. In 1991 the Soviet Union dissolved into 15 independent republics. This change left the United States as the world's sole remaining superpower. This has greatly affected world politics and U.S. foreign policy ever since. Questions about the appropriateness of U.S. intervention in disparate places such as Bosnia-Herzegovina, Somalia, Haiti, Iraq, Kosovo, and even Russia were at the forefront of foreign policy concerns during the Clinton administration. The threatened proliferation of nuclear weapons in North Korea also posed a difficult problem for the Clinton administration.

The foreign and defense policy process in the United States raises a host of related issues. One of these stems from the struggle between legislative and executive branches for control of foreign and defense policy. Conflict between the branches sometimes takes place today in the context of the War Powers Resolution of 1973, which is itself a legacy of the Vietnam War. In 1991 Congress authorized war with Iraq, which was the first time since World War II that there has been explicit and formal congressional approval prior to commencement of military hostilities by the United States. In late 1995, President Clinton committed the United States to sending troops to Bosnia-Herzegovina as part of a multinational peacekeeping force. Despite some opposition in Congress, resolutions supporting the troops were passed. Toward the end of 1997, President Saddam Hussein of Iraq obstructed UN weapons inspection teams in his country. President Clinton responded by increasing the readiness of U.S. military forces in the Persian Gulf. In late 1998, in response to what the U.S. considered further provocation, there were several days of U.S. air strikes on Iraq. Two other issues in the foreign policy process involve the legitimacy of covert action and the recurring question of the relationship between foreign policy and democracy.

The traditional distinction between domestic and foreign policy is becoming more and more difficult to maintain, since so many contemporary policy decisions (for example, passage of NAFTA in 1993) seem to have important implications for both the foreign and domestic scenes. President Clinton's emphasis on the connection between domestic and international economic issues in maintaining what he called national economic security reinforced this point.

Products of American Politics

Welfare Reform, Act 2

ACT 1 WAS A HIT, BUT IT STILL HAD GLITCHES. THIS TIME, LOOK FOR A FOCUS ON HELPING THE WORKING POOR.

By Marilyn Werber Serafini

THE NEXT ROUND

Republicans and Democrats agree that the landmark 1996 law that over-hauled the nation's welfare system did exactly what it was supposed to do—that is, move people from welfare to work. Since the law's enactment, states have cut their welfare caseloads nearly in half (from 12.2 million people in 1996 to 6.6 million in 1999). Sixty percent to 80 percent of those leaving welfare have entered the work force, and 80 percent of those people were still working three months later, according to the Health and Human Services Department.

That's the good news. Here's the rest of the story.

• Many of the people still on welfare have serious problems, such as substance abuse and mental illness, standing between them and employment. A recent Urban Institute study found that 41 percent of the adults receiving assistance in 1997 hadn't graduated from high school, 43 percent had last worked three or more years ago or had never worked, and 48 percent reported poor general or mental health.

• Within the next few years, welfare recipients will begin running up against the law's five-year time limit for receiving federal cash assistance, and it's unclear how many will be cut from welfare without first having a job.

• Many people leaving welfare are filling low-wage positions, and most of them are not subsequently getting better and higher-paying jobs. (Only 23 percent of people who left welfare for work in 1999 received a raise after six months, according to HHS.) Recent studies show that these people sometimes don't have enough to eat. Despite being eligible for food stamps, Medicaid, and other government programs that are supposed to ease the transition to work, families aren't receiving aid.

Expect to hear more about these problems in the next two years as Congress prepares to undertake Act 2 of welfare reform. Congress must reauthorize key welfare programs in 2002, including the Temporary Assistance for Needy Families block grant, the cash assistance program that replaced Aid to Families with Dependent Children. Congress will also have to reauthorize the food stamps program; the child care block grant; and the abstinence educa-tion block grant, which provides money to educate children to postpone sexual activity.

Unlike Act 1, Act 2 is expected to focus as much on what happens after people leave welfare as on getting them off the rolls. Specifically, policy-makers will be looking at how to improve the prospects of low-income workers. In addition, some key lawmakers want to extend to fathers some of the assistance that's now available to mothers to help them develop job skills, encourage marriage, and discourage illegitimacy.

"The new face of welfare reform is work support," said Rep. Nancy L. Johnson, R-Conn., chairwoman of the Ways and Means Human Resources Subcommittee, which will have the lead in Act 2. Johnson has fought to maintain funding for states' work-support programs such as child care.

Rep. Benjamin Cardin of Maryland, the ranking Democrat on Johnson's subcommittee, said that Congress must be willing to spend money to take the next step in welfare reform. "I look at poverty as one of the major responsibilities of the federal government," he said. "We should certainly re-evaluate our objectives, re-evaluate the expectations and the ways in which we can judge progress being made, but we shouldn't diminish our presence."

Battle lines are already forming. For starters, governors are determined to fend off efforts by congressional appropriators to repossess federal welfare money that states haven't used. The governors say they need time to put support programs, such as child care assistance, in place, and that they want to save some of the unused dollars in case an economic downturn swells their welfare rolls.

Some welfare advocates from liberal think tanks say that programs that help the working poor need more money. Although states have the flexibility to pull money from their TANF block grants for such purposes, state officials say they have been reluctant to do so because they fear funding shortfalls during a recession.

Recent surveys show that the American public is more willing to spend taxpayer money to help people in low-income jobs than to help people on welfare. In a May poll conducted by Democratic pollster Celinda Lake, the president of Lake Snell Perry & Associates, more than three-quarters of respondents said they favored giving tax cuts to people who work but do not earn enough to keep their families out of poverty, even if the tax cuts meant an increase in government spending. And nearly 70 percent said that the government "should continue to help low-income people even after they find jobs by offering things like additional training or help with child care, so they can succeed in their jobs."

THE IMMOVABLES

Policy-makers acknowledge that they have no easy answers for what to do with people who can't seem to get off welfare. Give them more time on welfare rolls? More job training? Better programs to handle such obstacles as substance abuse and child care?

A recent Urban Institute study hints at the challenges ahead. The authors identified six potential obstacles to success and looked at whether they were more prevalent among those leaving welfare or among those still on the rolls. The obstacles were: Had the person dropped out of high school? Did her physical condition limit her work? Did

her mental condition limit her work? Did she have a child under the age of 1? Was a child of hers receiving disability benefits? Did she have to speak Spanish when interviewing for jobs? The study found that 42 percent of those who left welfare in 1997 faced no obstacles, 35 percent faced only one obstacle, and 23 percent faced two or more obstacles. In contrast, only 22 percent of those still on welfare had no obstacles, but 34 percent had one obstacle, and 44 percent had two or more.

"This underscores that the barriers to work are more significant for those still receiving welfare than for those who left," said Mark Greenberg, the senior staff attorney of the Center for Law and Social Policy, a liberal think tank. "It's not to say that employment is impossible [for those still on welfare], but the difficulties are more serious."

Ron Haskins, the staff director of the House Ways and Means Subcommittee on Human Resources, says he's concerned about these "floundering families. Moms at the bottom have not responded, and we have to figure out how to work well with those mothers." Indeed, he said, "we may need additional federal legislation."

But, he said, the answer is not to change the law that bars states from exempting more than 20 percent of their welfare recipients from the five-year time limit on federal cash assistance. Some welfare analysts say the 20 percent limit may need to be relaxed because most of the easier-to-move people have already left welfare.

"Most people did not envision caseload reductions like anything that's happened," said Greenberg. "Twenty percent is now 20 percent of a much smaller number. If a state had a caseload of 100 in 1994, and it's 20 now, the law would allow the state to allow exemptions for 20 percent of its remaining cases, even though the state may have the view that all of the families still receiving assistance have great barriers to employment."

Rather than concentrating on the 20 percent exemption, key Democrats and Republicans are suggesting that the focus should be on removing obstacles to leaving welfare. "We have to keep up the assumption that every parent can support children," Haskins said.

Cardin, for his part, does not rule out trying to expand the 20 percent exemption, but says he would rather try appro-

priating more money to help people get off the rolls. "If you don't provide the money, you have to increase the 20 percent," he said. "There are some people who aren't going to succeed. . . . But I think we can succeed with a lot of the hard-core people, if we're willing to make an investment."

While Cardin is suggesting adding federal money to help with these problems, Republicans such as Johnson are talking about continuing the current federal commitment and making sure that states have the flexibility to funnel federal block-grant dollars into social programs, such as ones dealing with substance abuse. "Right now we're saying that until you've fallen apart, we can't help you," Johnson said.

Haskins added: "All of our programs to deal with substance abuse, mental health—they're puny. We need to give states flexibility. Make sure they have the flexibility and resources to . . . deal with these problems. That's why we have to make sure to protect states' money."

BREAKING OUT OF POVERTY

To the extent that the next round of welfare reform focuses on the working poor, it has the potential to affect even more people than the first round did. One out of six people are now part of working-poor families, according to Gregory P. Acs, a senior research associate at the Urban Institute.

"Too many hardworking families are still having trouble making ends meet," said Jared Bernstein, an economist at the Economic Policy Institute. "We need to close the gap between family income and need." Some possible solutions, he said, are to create new training programs, raise the minimum wage, and expand work-related subsidies.

"We should put states on notice that we're concerned about poverty," said Wendell Primus, the director of income security at the Center on Budget and Policy Priorities, who resigned from a top position at HHS to protest President Clinton's signature on the welfare reform bill. "A lot of mothers are working more, but they haven't increased their disposable incomes."

Indeed, while overall poverty levels have declined, some evidence indicates that the situation is worsening for those who remain poor. "For the kids we're leaving behind, we're leaving them

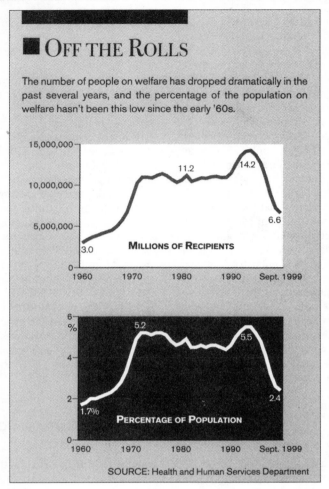

OFF THE ROLLS

The number of people on welfare has dropped dramatically in the past several years, and the percentage of the population on welfare hasn't been this low since the early '60s.

15,000,000

11.2   14.2

10,000,000

5,000,000

6.6

3.0   **MILLIONS OF RECIPIENTS**

0

1960   1970   1980   1990   Sept. 1999

6
%

5.2

5.5

4

2

2.4

1.7%   **PERCENTAGE OF POPULATION**

0

1960   1970   1980   1990   Sept. 1999

SOURCE: Health and Human Services Department

deeper in poverty," said Primus, who described a poverty gap that he says is widening. In 1995, he said, it would have taken $1,471 to bring each child in poverty up to the federal poverty level, but by 1998, it would have taken $1,604. (The poverty level for a family of four is $17,050, according to HHS.)

The Urban Institute surveyed people who had left the food stamps program and found that about two-thirds reported worrying that food would run out. One-third reported skipping meals or running out of food.

"Our food banks are being inundated with requests for emergency food—and it is becoming a torrent of need which we cannot meet," said Deborah Leff, the president and CEO of America's Second Harvest, a hunger relief organization with a network of more than 200 food banks. It distributes food to 26 million Americans each year.

"Although we distribute more than 1 billion pounds of food annually, 45 percent of the agencies with which we work still must stretch food supplies to

keep up with demand. And, in the worst cases, we are forced to turn hungry people away—nearly 1 million hungry people last year—because the cupboards are bare."

The Central Union Mission in Washington, which provides food for 130 families a week, has experienced a 25 percent increase in demand since last year, mostly from young people, according to Henry Holland, the food service director. "There are women off of welfare that now get minimum-wage jobs, and that doesn't take care of all their needs."

One problem is that people entering low-wage jobs aren't advancing very quickly. A new study of Wisconsin's welfare program looked at families that left welfare in late 1995. The study, conducted by the Manpower Demonstration Research Corp., a nonprofit research organization, found that the families' median earning was $8,608 in the first year. In the second year, it was $9,627, and in the third year, $10,924, still below the poverty level.

Even workers whose incomes are well above the poverty level can have a hard time making ends meet. Consider the experience of Elizabeth Jones, who is now a police officer in Washington earning $41,000 a year. The single mother of three left welfare in 1996 to take a $22,000-a-year job as a receptionist, but says she felt the squeeze of poverty. Her job offered no benefits. She was cut off from food stamps when she left welfare, and then from Medicaid after six months. She tried to get child support from her kids' three fathers, but welfare caseworkers were no help.

"That's when my kids decided to break an arm and a leg," she said, and that saddled her with $3,000 in medical bills because she had no insurance. "It was real hardship," she recalls. "I had to pay child care. The kids were going to an after-school care program that cost $400 a month."

A HELPING HAND

When Jones left welfare, she received little help from the programs that were supposed to ease her transition to work. Congress is likely to devote a significant amount of time in the next round of welfare reform to examining whether programs such as food stamps and Medicaid are adequately serving low-income people.

The early evidence is that these programs are not getting to as many people as they should. In some cases, people don't realize they're still eligible when they leave welfare. In other cases, state officials don't know who's eligible, and they wrongfully terminate benefits. And there is the question of what to do about low-income people who earn too much to qualify for benefits but are still needy. Republicans and Democrats generally agree that low-income workers need more support than they are getting.

Red tape is one large obstacle people must overcome to receive benefits. In many states, recipients must show up at a government office every 90 days, during business hours, to maintain food stamp benefits. (If a state pays benefits to too many ineligible people, it could face a federal fine, so states often require people to appear in person to verify their frequently changing income status.) Medicaid has had the same constraints, but some states have made it

DOWN, ACROSS THE BOARD

Some states recorded declines of 60 percent or more in their welfare caseloads between January 1994 and June 1999. Only four states, Rhode Island, Hawaii, New Mexico, and Minnesota registered drops of less than 30 percent.

Washington -41%
Oregon -60%
Montana -60%
North Dakota -49%
Minnesota -29%
Maine -41%
-34%
Vt.
Idaho -85%
South Dakota -56%
Wisconsin -89%
Michigan -60%
N.H. -56%
Wyoming -87%
New York -36%
Mass. -55%
R.I. -20%
Nevada -48%
Nebraska -33%
Iowa -54%
Pennsylvania -48%
Connecticut -43%
Utah -47%
New Jersey -51%
California -33%
Colorado -68%
Illinois -52%
Indiana -50%
Ohio -59%
Delaware -46%
Maryland -56%
W.Va. -73%
Virginia -54%
Washington, D.C. -33%
Kansas -58%
Missouri -47%
Kentucky -49%
Arizona -52%
New Mexico -24%
Oklahoma -61%
Arkansas -54%
Tennessee -49%
North Carolina -58%
Alaska -34%
Texas -62%
Miss. -74%
Alabama -62%
Georgia -63%
South Carolina -68%
-58% Louisiana
Hawaii -21%
Florida -71%

☐ 0 to 30% decrease ▨ 31% to 61% decrease ■ 61% and greater decrease

SOURCE: Health and Human Services Department

possible for eligible people to apply by mail.

"People must reapply for food stamps every 90 days in person," said Robert Greenstein, the executive director of the Center on Budget and Policy Priorities. "If a family doesn't show up, they're gone. It's not work-friendly. You can wait in a welfare office for hours."

One way to encourage a worker-friendly program may be to turn the food stamp program into a block grant, Haskins said. Republicans attempted to enact such a switch in 1996 but failed. Haskins said he would like to see a demonstration project in two or three states. It would have to be an entitlement to satisfy Democrats, he said, but the states could decide how to administer individual programs.

But as a financial matter, states may not be interested, Greenberg said. Because of the sharp decline in welfare caseloads, states might get smaller block grants than they would have gotten in

1996, he said. However, he added, "certainly, states want to have more control over food stamps."

In addition to making sure eligible people have access to food stamps, Greenstein says that Congress should focus on people who were cut from the food stamp rolls in 1996, and those who simply are earning too much to qualify. (People qualify for food stamps if their earnings are less than 130 percent of the poverty level.) From 1996–98, the food stamp program shrank by 6.2 million people—about 25 percent of the caseload. (During the same period, 4.4 million people left cash assistance—36 percent of the caseload.)

"The economy partially explains some of the reduction in the proportion of people receiving food stamps," Greenstein said. In addition, in 1996, immigrants became ineligible, although eligibility has been partially restored. Congress also lowered the maximum food stamp benefit.

Greenstein argues that attempts to save money drove the food stamp cutbacks and that because of the good economic times, Congress should rethink its decisions from 1996. "It's important to remember that this started out as part of the budget discussions," said Greenstein. "TANF was not a budget saver, so the Agriculture committees had to save big amounts in food stamps. According to Congressional Budget Office scoring, the welfare act saved $54 billion over six years, and $27 billion was in food stamps. Here we are, four years later, and we don't have a budget deficit, but surpluses that are supposed to get very big. Given that these across-the-board cuts are no longer needed to balance the budget, we should be rethinking some of the food stamp changes that were unrelated to the core welfare reform goals," he said.

Members of Congress have already begun to address the issue. Sen. Edward Kennedy, D-Mass., introduced the Hunger Relief Act last year with Sens. James M. Jeffords, R-Vt., Arlen Specter, R-Pa., and Patrick Leahy, D-Vt. The act would restore 10 percent of the cuts made by the 1996 welfare reform legislation. "Working families should at least be confident that their children will be fed," the four Senators wrote in a Feb. 4 letter urging the Republican and Democratic leaders of the Senate Agriculture, Nutrition, and Forestry Committee to conduct a hearing on the bill. "Especially in this time of economic prosperity, there is no reason that either children or adults should be going hungry anywhere in America."

Some members are also concerned that too many families, including those who qualify for Medicaid, have no health insurance. The House Ways and Means Committee held a hearing on May 16 to explore why the number of children on Medicaid declined in 1997, after five years of growth. Medicaid experts told the panel they suspected the decline resulted from the 1996 welfare act, which uncoupled Medicaid and welfare. Before the welfare act, AFDC recipients were automatically enrolled in Medicaid. But that's not the case for TANF recipients, even though the writers of the welfare law didn't intend to downsize the program. "We worked very hard to make sure no poor child lost eligibility for Medicaid," Johnson said.

The Urban Institute analysis shows that many parents who have left welfare have entered low-wage jobs in service, sales, and trade industries, which are among the sectors least likely to offer health coverage to employees. A significant portion of parents who left TANF have disabilities or health conditions that may affect their ability to succeed in the workplace if they lose health coverage, said Barbara Lyons, a vice president of the Henry J. Kaiser Family Foundation, a policy institute that analyzes health care coverage and access for the low-income population. Families leaving welfare are often unable to retain health coverage, she said. Forty percent of women and 25 percent of children previously on Medicaid were uninsured one year later.

One problem may be that Medicaid isn't a priority for welfare caseworkers, who are concentrating on moving people into the work force. Nevertheless,

those caseworkers are important because eligibility is still determined through the welfare offices. And that means the caseworkers are in the best position to ensure that families leaving welfare apply for health benefits.

A WELFARE RE-FORM GLOSSARY

TANF—Congress must reauthorize the Temporary Assistance for Needy Families block grant (cash assistance) in 2002. Republicans and Democrats generally agree that the block-grant structure is working and shouldn't be changed.

CHILD CARE AND DEVELOPMENT FUND—There's general agreement that this block grant is underfunded and that states need more money specifically for child care; that way, they won't have to use TANF money for child care and worry that it may disappear when it's needed again for cash assistance.

FOOD STAMPS—Republicans may again try to turn the food stamp program, which is supposed to be reauthorized in 2002, into a block grant. Democrats may try to expand eligibility. Both parties want to lessen the administrative burden on working recipients.

HARD-CORE RECIPIENTS—Some poverty analysts will push for Congress to allow more than 20 percent of welfare recipients to bypass the five-year time limit on federal cash assistance. Others want to see more money spent helping these people find work.

MEDICAID—Congress is likely to examine whether the 1996 law caused Medicaid enrollment to fall and how to get states to do a better job of enrolling eligible people.

SUPPLANTATION—Congress may create mandates or additional oversight mechanisms to prevent states' misuse—or "supplantation"—of federal welfare dollars.

Another problem is that the eligibility requirements are too stringent, said Diane Rowland, the executive vice president of the Kaiser Family Foundation. In 32 states, a person working at the minimum wage earns too much to qualify for Medicaid.

COMING: ACT 2

Members of Congress are just now beginning to think about the form that a second round of welfare reform should take. One key legislator—Johnson—said she would even consider putting off the second round, to give states more time to get their various programs and ideas up and running. Cardin, however, argues against a delay. "The problem with Congress's delaying reauthorization is that a year or two becomes five years," he said. "It's important for states to be able to plan."

In the meantime, some legislators, including Johnson and Cardin, are getting a head start by touting the need to help fathers more. "We've been neglecting men, said Wade Horn, the president of the National Fatherhood Initiative, a membership group that promotes marriage and live-in fatherhood. "Children do worse in one-parent households. We have to bring fathers back into the picture. They're not deadbeat dads, but dead-broke dads."

Johnson and Cardin co-sponsored a fatherhood bill that passed the House in November, but the Senate has not acted on the measure. The bill would extend to fathers some welfare benefits that are now available only to welfare moms. The idea is to get the dads both working and into better jobs so that they can help support their families. Johnson said she wants the bill to pass *before* the 2002 reauthorizations. But, if it doesn't, it's likely to be part of the debate in 2002.

Of course, much will depend on the outcome of the November elections and which party will control Congress and the White House.

Both Texas Gov. George W. Bush, the likely Republican presidential nominee, and Vice President Al Gore, the likely Democratic presidential nominee, have outlined general poverty plans, but neither has specifically addressed the reauthorizations that will be an early issue of the next Administration.

Looking to the next step in welfare reform, Bush said that the government should turn first to faith-based organizations and community groups to help people in need. "We will make a determined attack on need by promoting the compassionate acts of others," he said. "We will rally the armies of compassion in our communities to fight a very different war against poverty and hopelessness."

Bush proposed $8 billion in new tax incentives to encourage giving and to support charities and private institutions that address human needs. His poverty plan also seeks to raise the performances of low-income schools. And he has proposed exempting 6 million low-income families from income taxes.

Bush would help low-income working families acquire basic health insurance through a family health credit that would pay for 90 percent of the cost of an insurance policy, up to $2,000 a year, for families earning less than $30,000. He has also recommended giving states more flexibility in covering the uninsured under the state Children's Health Insurance Program. Some states have sought such flexibility to cover the parents of uninsured children, for example, or to make more children eligible.

Helping low-wage earners buy homes is another goal. Bush says he wants to help these families use some rent subsidies to make down payments on their own homes.

To encourage savings to get an education, buy a home, or start a business, Bush advocates individual development accounts that would provide tax credits for low-income people.

Gore has identified fatherhood as the "critical next phase of welfare reform and one of the most important things we can do to reduce child poverty." As part of that goal, he said at a June 2 speech in Washington, he wants to "crack down on deadbeats who abandon their children."

He proposed requiring all fathers who owe child support to pay or go to work. He also seeks to strengthen child support enforcement; make it harder for parents who owe child support to get new credit cards; and increase the amount of income a married couple can earn and still receive the full earned-income tax credit. Regarding poverty, Gore has said he wants to close the "opportunity gap" by making changes in education and income policies.

For starters, he wants to make sure that disadvantaged children get an adequate education by ensuring access to preschool for all children, improving teacher quality, using new technology to increase educational productivity, adopting a new focus on discipline and parental involvement, and creating savings accounts to make college and job training more affordable. He also wants to hold school districts accountable for dropout rates.

Clearly, both candidates and both parties want to help people escape poverty. Still, it's not clear how this issue will play out in the welfare reauthorizations in 2002 and whether big partisan battles will ensue. "Tell me who's going to control Congress and the White House, and I'll answer that question," said Cardin.

$80,000
AND A DREAM

A SIMPLE PLAN FOR GENERATING EQUAL OPPORTUNITY

America has become a three-class society. While more than 25 percent
of its children now graduate from four-year colleges, the lowest
20 percent inhabit a world of low wages and dead-end jobs.

BY BRUCE ACKERMAN AND ANNE ALSTOTT

And then there is the vast middle. Despite the economic boom, real wages for men have declined, and only the massive entry by women into the workplace has prevented many families from sinking to income levels lower than in the 1970s. Trickle-down economics has failed to trickle. Globalization will only make these divisions worse.

Our politics has not caught up with this three-class reality. While the college-bound elite reap large subsidies, we have done little to aid the vast middle—and we target the underclass with diminishing amounts of assistance.

The result is simmering resentment and a receptive audience for the protectionist nostrums of Ross Perot and Pat Buchanan. The current boom may hold these economic nationalists in check—while it lasts. But it is past time to search for a more constructive response to economic inequality. How can we use the benefits of globalization to ensure that every American gets a fair start in life?

One way is to give every young American adult a stake of $80,000 as a birthright of citizenship. The stake should be financed by an annual wealth tax, equal to 2 percent of every individual's wealth in excess of $180,000. Under this "flat tax," the wealthiest 1 percent of Americans will pay 40 percent of the entire bill. (This proposal, as spelled out in our book *The Stakeholder Society,* includes an $80,000 exemption for each taxpayer, but this is on the basis of data for 1995 collected by the Federal Reserve Board at a time when the Dow was at 4,500. In January 2000, the Fed released 1998 data, which we have begun to analyze. Preliminary estimates suggest that an exemption of $180,000 will be fiscally responsible.)

Stakeholders should be free to use their money for any purpose they see fit: to start a business or pay for higher education; to buy a house or raise a family or save for the future. Their triumphs and blunders will be their own.

At the end of their lives, stakeholders should repay the $80,000 at death if this is financially possible. The stakeholding fund, in short, will be enriched each year by the ongoing contributions of the wealthy and by a final payback at death.

Stakeholding's broad political appeal should be clear. How many young adults start off life with $80,000? How many parents can afford to give their children that kind of head start?

Stakeholding liberates college graduates from the burden of debt and offers unprecedented opportunities for the tens of millions who don't go to college. For the first time, high school graduates lacking a college degree will confront the labor market with a certain sense of security. The stake will give them the independence to choose where to live, whether to marry, and how to train for economic opportunity. Some will fail, but fewer than today.

We should structure the program to maximize the successes. No stakeholder should be allowed free use of his $80,000 without completing high school and passing a state or national qualifying examination. High school dropouts will have their stakes held in trust, spending only the $4,000 or so in annual interest. Since only three-quarters of Americans have high school degrees by the age of 21, this single requirement will prevent massive "stakeblowing" by those least capable of handling adult responsibilities. It will also provide a beacon of hope to kids locked in rural poverty or urban ghettos. Stay in school and graduate, and you will get a solid chance to live out the American dream of economic independence.

Timing is crucial. High school graduates should get immediate access to their money if they want to spend their $80,000 on college. But those choosing other paths should get some real-world experience before they can obtain their stakes—in $20,000 annual payments between the ages of 21 and 24.

The result will change the way young people think about themselves, their options, and their obligations to society. Begin with the college-bound. Poor kids confront hardships unknown to their better-off peers—juggling schoolwork, jobs, and scholarship applications in ways that overwhelm self-confidence. Students in two-year colleges are even harder-pressed: A much higher percentage live at home, hold a job, and work more hours. It should be no surprise that lower-class kids are much more likely to delay enrollment, and less likely to earn a degree, than their richer peers: 51 percent of students from families in the top income quartile earn bachelor's degrees, compared to 22 percent of middle-status students and only 7 percent in the lowest socioeconomic quartile. Stakeholding will allow all men and women to focus their energies on academic work and compete with their peers on relatively equal terms.

Stakeholding will also inaugurate a new era of healthy competition in higher education. Every student will enter the market with significant resources and an incentive to shop carefully. No longer will state universities or community colleges have a captive pool of in-state or low-income students without other options. These people could now choose a school in another community, or across the country, or even overseas.

The prospect of stakeholding might initially tempt colleges to raise tuition, but competition among schools should keep increases down. And because colleges must compete with other uses of the stakeholding dollar—like home buying and entrepreneurship—the academic sector as a whole cannot hope to capture the stakeholding program as it might a more conventional education subsidy.

At present, two-year junior colleges provide much smaller subsidies to their students than do more traditional universities. But under the new system, students at two-year colleges will have the same buying power as their more academically inclined age-mates. To be sure, they won't spend their entire $80,000 on a couple of years of post-high school education. But their stakes will create new incentives for serious two-year colleges to craft programs that will appeal to these students' distinctive concerns. Over time, two-year colleges will emerge from the shadow of their bigger brothers and build their students' skills and self-confidence with increasing imagination and vigor.

Finally, consider the millions of Americans who decide that even a two-year college isn't for them. These are today's forgotten Americans. Many of them have been denied the decent high school education that should be a fundamental right. They are then tossed unaided into the marketplace, while their upwardly mobile peers win federal scholarships and state-subsidized tuitions.

This is just plain wrong. Jane Worker is every bit as much of an American as Joe College. Under the stakeholding system, her claim to equal citizenship will be treated with genuine respect. High school graduates not going to college will have to wait until their early 20s before staking their claim to $80,000. Indeed, some may want to require these young adults to wait until they are 25. We would be happy to compromise, so long as the

> **STAKEHOLDING WOULD CULTIVATE CROSS-CLASS, CROSS-GENERATIONAL SOLIDARITY.**

basic principle remains intact. All Americans have a fundamental right to start off as adults with a fair chance at making a decent life for themselves.

Of course, some people face multiple social problems—inadequate education, drug or alcohol abuse, a propensity to violence—that will leave them ill-equipped to handle financial responsibility for their stake. But by any reasonable estimate, this constitutes less than 1 percent of the population, almost all of whom will be excluded from full control of their stake by the requirement of high school graduation.

We also propose a cautious use of stakeholding as a sanction in the criminal-justice system. Instead of sentencing 19-year-old drug traffickers to lengthy prison terms, we could threaten them with the loss of $20,000 (or more) of their stakes. No longer will high school dropouts taunt their age-mates with luxury cars and expensive clothes. Kids will learn fast that civil behavior and a high school degree provide the sure track to a real stake in America.

To a very large degree, the institutional infrastructure for a stakeholder society is already in place. Despite efforts to demonize them, both the IRS and the Social Security Administration are full of competent professionals whose tasks might readily be broadened to encompass the jobs of identifying eligible stakeholders and paying out benefits. Unlike a comparable reform of, say, education, stakeholding builds on institutions we already have.

Equal opportunity doesn't come cheap. Using conservative assumptions, the annual cost of stakeholding today would be about $255 billion—a little less than we spend on national defense. This is a big number, but we have made comparable commitments in the past: After World War II, wealthy taxpayers were a lot poorer than they are today, and they were paying far heavier taxes—yet they did not seek to evade their obligation to give the rising generation a fair start in adult life in the form of the GI Bill of Rights.

The GI Bill represented the payment of a debt for the sacrifices that our soldiers made during the war. Today the ties that bind older to younger are less obvious—but no less important. If the younger generation is denied a fair start, how can the rest of us expect its members to reciprocate as the need requires?

For the rest of their lives, stakeholders will know that their $80,000 contributed to their individual pursuits of happiness. This will prompt a deeper loyalty to the country. The Declaration of Independence's promise of equality and freedom will take on a new meaning, encouraging stakeholders to take their responsibilities as citizens more seriously and make America a better place for their successors.

But isn't stakeholding a political pipe dream? If we can't even expand medical coverage to embrace the tens of millions of the uninsured, can we possibly enact a program that carries a quarter-trillion-dollar annual price tag?

Yes, because stakeholding strikes at the heart of the problem that has pushed progressives to the margin of American politics. Republicans have for years succeeded in portraying liberal Democrats as concerned only with the fate of the bottom 20 percent, and not with the large number of folks who have graduated from high school but have failed to share in the great prosperity gained by successful college graduates. Unless and until we come up with a big policy initiative that speaks to middle America, Reagan Democrats will continue to react skeptically to liberal initiatives. Why should economically pressed middle-class families fork over their hard-earned tax dollars to help those below them?

Stakeholding decisively changes this political equation in a way that makes sense to average voters. Most people quickly turn off the tube when earnest liberal politicians sing the praises of the EITC (Earned Income Tax Credit) or some other technocratic acronym; the average voter assumes that he or she is about to be taken for a chump. But $80,000 for each kid—that would make voters sit up and take notice!

The average couple of 40-year-olds, blessed with two children of 10 and 12, know realistically that they won't likely be able to give their kids a stake of $80,000 apiece for college in a decade or so. But if a national stakeholding policy were to be implemented, they wouldn't have to; their kids would be able to pay for college on their own. Yes, these two 40-year-olds may retire in 30 years with more than $360,000, in which case they would have to pay a small wealth tax. But wouldn't most parents consider this future tax worth the chance to give their kids a solid start in life?

Obviously, the calculus will look a lot different to older Americans. Though we have exempted all Social Security payments from our wealth tax, the economically successful will be facing a new tax bill. But we hope that not everybody's position will be determined by a narrow economic calculus focusing on self and family. As in all political exercises, each voter will come to judgment after filtering self-interest through a sense of civic obligation. Some will vote against stakeholding even though their kids might profit mightily—simply because they think it's an awful idea. And vice versa.

But, you may ask, won't the wealth tax be an alien concept to most citizens? While the idea may be new to Americans, they already pay taxes on capital gains and real estate. It is only one step further to a wealth tax, which has been a long-standing feature of European systems. Taking a broader perspective, our overall proposal falls squarely within the American tradition that gave us the Homestead Act in the nineteenth century and the GI Bill in the twentieth.

It also builds on recent initiatives throughout the world. When Margaret Thatcher became prime minister of England, 32 percent of all English housing was publicly owned. Though bent on sweeping privatization, Thatcher refused to sell these vast properties to big companies. Instead, she invited residents to buy their own homes at bargain rates. With a single stroke, she created a new property-owning citizenry and won vast popularity in the process.

In the aftermath of 1989 in the Czech Republic, former Prime Minister Vaclav Klaus confronted a state sector containing 7,000 medium- and large-scale enterprises, and 25,000 to 35,000 smaller ones. How to distribute this legacy of communism?

Klaus saw his problem as an opportunity to create a vast new property-owning class. Through "voucher privatization," each Czech citizen was encouraged to subscribe to a book of vouchers that could be used to bid for shares in state companies as they were put on the auction block. An overwhelming majority—8.5 out of 10.5 million—took up Klaus's offer and claimed their fair share of the nation's wealth as they moved into the new free market system.

The citizens of Alaska have made stakeholding a regular part of their political economy. The original occasion, as in England and the Czech Republic, was the distribution of a major public asset, the revenues from North Slope oil. Rather than using it all for public expenditures, the Republican leadership in the state designed a stakeholding scheme that is now distributing about a $1,000 a year to every Alaskan citizen. The system has become broadly popular, with politicians of both parties regularly pledging that they will not raid the symbolically named Permanent Fund.

In our view, there is no good reason to limit stakeholding to cases involving physical assets like housing or factories or oil. Americans have created other assets that are less material but have even greater value. Most notably, the "free market" requires heavy public expenditures on police, courts, and much else besides. Without billions of voluntary decisions by Americans to respect the rights of property in their daily lives, the system would collapse overnight.

All Americans benefit from this cooperative activity—but some much more than others. Those who benefit the most have a duty to share some of their wealth with fellow citizens whose cooperation they require to sustain the market system. This obligation is all the more exigent when the operation of the global market threatens to split the country more sharply into haves and have-nots.

This moral judgment gives our proposal a different ideological coloration than that of the more conservative initiatives pioneered by Margaret Thatcher and Vaclav Klaus. Nonetheless, their example suggests that the first progressive politician who takes up stakeholding would find herself appealing to the very concrete interests of a massive majority of Americans. Stakeholding would also give the lie to neoconservative banalities about the inevitability of government failure and help re-establish a faith in our collective capacity to redeem our fundamental ideals. Of course, the fate of our proposal will depend not only on the vision of the political leader who seizes the moment, but on how ordinary men and women answer some basic questions: Is America more than a libertarian marketplace? Can we make this a place where all citizens have a fair shot at the pursuit of happiness?

BRUCE ACKERMAN and ANNE ALSTOTT are professors at Yale Law School.

Yes and No to Gun Control

By Gary Rosen

GUN CONTROL is hardly a new issue in American politics, but its current prominence—with the presidential candidates staking out positions on such esoteric matters as trigger locks and the "gunshow loophole"—would seem to require some explaining. After all, the U.S. continues to enjoy an unprecedented downturn in the crime rate. For eight consecutive years and across every major category of crime, the country has grown considerably safer, with the most impressive gains coming in urban areas. In New York City, to take just one much-celebrated example, the incidence of rape has dropped by 35 percent, aggravated assault by 37 percent, and robbery by 62 percent; having suffered some 2,200 murders as recently as 1990, the city recorded fewer than 700 in each of the last two years.

What such statistics fail to register, of course, is the shock and outrage caused throughout the country by one small subset of violent crimes: the mass shootings that have recently occurred with bloody regularity in corners of American life usually spared such things. Last year alone, there were highly publicized attacks at a brokerage firm in Atlanta, a Jewish community center in Los Angeles, and a church in Fort Worth. Still more disturbing have been the more than a half-dozen episodes since 1997 in which students have opened fire at their own schools, the deadliest of these assaults being the one at Columbine High School in Littleton, Colorado, where two teenage gunmen killed twelve of their classmates and a teacher before taking their own lives. As the number of these shootings has mounted, so, too, has public concern. How have such young, or deranged, or racist malefactors been able to acquire the lethal instruments of their rage?

For the proponents of gun control, the answer is simple: the country is awash in firearms, and, thanks to the obstructionism of the National Rifle Association (NRA) and its political allies, we have not done nearly enough to keep weapons out of the hands of the most dangerous members of society. Moreover, they add, for all the recent progress in fighting crime, the U.S. remains the most violent of Western societies, with a death toll from gun-related incidents vastly exceeding that of nations with more stringent regulations and fewer firearms. What the country thus desperately needs, it is said—in the joint rallying cry of this past spring's "Million Mom March," of advocacy groups like Handgun Control, Inc. (HCI), and of a swelling chorus of sympathetic politicians and editorialists—is a full range of "sensible" or "commonsense" gun laws.

OWNERSHIP OF guns is extraordinarily widespread in the United States, and has been for some time. Indeed, since the late 1950's, when surveys on this question were first done, the share of American households reporting at least one firearm has remained fairly constant at just under 50 percent. Needless to say, this does not mean that there is a gun-owner behind every second door in any American community. Guns are much more common in the Rocky Mountain states, South, and Midwest; in every region of the country, they are most likely to belong to middle-class, middle-aged men who live in rural areas or small towns. A useful shorthand for all this demography is that the average American gun-owner, both today and in the past, has tended to be a hunter or target-shooter.

What has changed dramatically over the last several decades is the size and composition of the American gun stock. The total number of firearms in circulation across the country has expanded at an astonishing rate, from about 75 million in the late 1960's to some 230 million today. At the same time, and despite the continuing predominance of the "long" guns (that is, rifles and shotguns) favored by sportsmen, an ever-increasing share of these firearms has consisted of handguns, whose primary use, as the supporters of stricter controls like to say, is against people. Such weapons have proliferated both among criminals, who use them in more than four out of five gun-related crimes, and among law-abiding citizens, especially urbanites, concerned about self-protection. As a result of these trends, Americans are now thought to possess somewhere in the neighborhood of 80 million handguns.

This shift in the character of ownership has taken place against a complicated legal backdrop, the basic feature of which at the federal level is the Gun Control Act of 1968. Passed in the aftermath of a spate of inner-city riots and the assassinations of Martin Luther King, Jr. and Robert Kennedy, the act was something of a catch-all, its provisions ranging from restrictions on machine guns to new federal penalties for the criminal use of a firearm. Its central aim, however, was to establish, for the first time, certain national standards concerning how guns are sold, and to whom. Dealers were required to obtain a federal license, to keep records of their sales (including the serial numbers newly mandated for all guns), to limit their interstate business, and to put an end to mail-order deliveries. More importantly, they were obliged to refuse guns to minors and to several categories of people now prohibited by federal law from possessing them, including convicted felons, fugitives from justice, drug abusers, and anyone with a history of serious mental illness.

The chief addition to this original set of federal controls has been the Brady Act, which went into effect in 1994. Named for James Brady, the White House press secretary gravely wounded in the attempt on President Reagan's life in 1981, the law requires licensed dealers to run a background check on prospective buyers, who previously had only to sign a form declaring that they did not fall into any of the prohibited groups. To make such investigations more practical—and less onerous for purchasers—the legislation also created a computerized "national instant check system" for criminal records. Under the supervision of the FBI, this system has been in operation since 1998.[1]

Far outnumbering federal regulations are the various local and state laws that have long been the principal source of firearms control in the U.S. As one might expect, these vary widely, according to the political tendencies and "gun culture" of different parts of the country. Even before passage of the Brady Act, about half the states, but especially more urbanized ones with higher crime rates, were already conducting background checks on purchasers, usually as part of a state-run system of licensing or registration. A few states also ban an assortment of semiautomatic "assault" weapons (thus supplementing a less comprehensive federal ban), and others have passed "child-access-prevention" laws, making it a crime to leave a gun within easy reach of a juvenile.

But where the states diverge most among themselves is in their treatment of handguns. Several have set a limit of just one purchase a month or have outlawed the cheap, smaller guns popularly known as "Saturday-night specials," and a substantial minority impose a waiting period of their own, typically seven days or less, before a sale may be completed. A number of localities, including New York City, Chicago, and Washington, D.C., have gone still farther, passing ordinances that are so restrictive as to make the legal acquisition of a handgun virtually impossible. In most of the country, however, such firearms are essentially available on demand to any federally qualified buyer. In addition, more than 30 states, from Oregon to Florida to Maine, allow anyone who meets certain basic requirements to receive a concealed-handgun permit, entitling its holder to keep a weapon at the ready in a holster, pocket, or purse; the legislation giving Texans this right was signed into law in 1995 by Governor George W. Bush.

To the critics of this patchwork regime of local, state, and federal laws, its gross inadequacy is best seen in the high number of lives regularly lost to firearms in the U.S. Thanks to the "nation's porous gun laws," the *New York Times* declared in a recent editorial, "more than 80 Americans, including about a dozen children, continue to die every day from gun violence." For Handgun Control, Inc., the largest and most influential of the gun-control lobbies, the cumulative figures from this carnage suggest a damning analogy. "In 1997, 32,436 Americans were killed with firearms," the group notes. "In comparison, 33,651 Americans were killed in the Korean war, and 58,148 Americans were killed in the Vietnam war."

What is perhaps surprising about these gun fatalities is how few of them, relatively speaking, are the result of homicide. As HCI and its sister organizations emphasize, firearms pose a threat to "public health" that extends well beyond their role in the commission of violent crimes. Of the deaths in HCI's alarming tally, almost 13,000 were murders—but some 17,500 were suicides and nearly 1,000 were accidents. "The nexus is inescapable," according to an analyst for the Violence Policy Center. "The more accessibility to guns you have, the higher the rates of gun-related death and injury."

The senselessness of this human destruction is compounded, in the eyes of gun-control advocates, by the fundamental delusion that persuades so many Americans to own firearms in the first place. "It is important to remember that the belief that handguns are useful for self-defense is misguided," warns the Coalition to Stop Gun Violence, reporting an oft-cited study's conclusion that "a firearm in the home is 43 times more likely to be used for suicide or murder than self-defense." Worse, because so many guns kept in the home are stored recklessly or lack safety features, children have frequently been their special victims, inadvertently doing grievous harm to themselves and others. As HCI starkly puts it, presumably with a view to the suburbanites who are among its prime supporters, American parents have too often dropped off a child "at a friend's house for an afternoon play session or a sleep-over party not knowing that the car ride would be the last time they would see their child alive."

For the proponents of gun control, any solution to America's gun problem must be, like the problem itself, national in scope. Left to their own devices—and to the grassroots machinations of the NRA—too many states, they argue, have failed to pass adequate regulations, thereby endangering not just their own citizens but those of other states as well.

One broad set of remedies proposed in recent years—and pursued both on Capitol Hill and through lawsuits against the firearms industry—has focused on design and manufacture. Under these supply-side measures, gun-makers would be required, among other things, to stop producing "Saturday-night specials" and to add various safety features to their other handguns, from trigger locks meant for the protection of children to "smart" technology that, when fully developed, would allow a weapon to be fired only by an authorized user.

As for the demand side of the equation, gun-control groups have called for new laws that would place further barriers in the path of criminals and other people prohibited from buying firearms. At the top of this list, particularly after investigators discovered where the weapons used in the Columbine massacre were obtained, has been closing the "gun-show loophole." As matters now stand at such events (more than 4,000 of which are held each year), private collectors and hobbyists—unlike the licensed gun dealers who set up their wares alongside them—do not have to run background checks on potential buyers, and as a result, critics contend, they have become a key source for criminals and the illegal gun trade.

Much more ambitious, if less of-the-moment politically, is the idea of a national system of registration and licensing. The most fully articulated plan of this sort, a bill introduced in the Senate to coincide with the Million Mom March, would require anyone selling a handgun or semi-automatic firearm, whether a dealer or a private citizen, to provide the government with a record of sale, including a serial number. In addition, anyone wishing to buy such guns—or anyone owning older versions of them—would have to obtain a federal firearms license, a process that would include an extensive background check, a written safety test, and a thumbprint. Such a system, a spokesman for HCI told the *Atlanta Journal and Constitution*, "would make sure that the wrong people don't get a hold of guns; make sure that people know how to use guns properly; [and] make it easier for police to trace crime guns and detect gun traffickers."

THAT THOSE urging the adoption of these laws would present them as simple expressions of "common sense" is understandable. There is no denying the large number of Americans killed by gunfire each year. More to the point, there seems to be something obvious, even self-evident, in the idea that the general availability of guns goes a long way toward explaining the country's high rates of violence, or that placing further limits on manufacturers, dealers, and owners would help to save lives.

Commonplace as these intuitions may be, however, and central though they are to the abiding popular appeal of gun control, they deserve scrutiny—at least if the ultimate objective is indeed a truly "sensible" set of policies. A useful place to begin is with the "firearm facts" routinely deployed by the advocates of gun control. These, as it happens, are frequently either incomplete or misleading, and especially so with respect to children, whose vulnerability to random gun violence has been grossly exaggerated in order to score political points.

Of the "dozen children" killed by guns each day, for example, about ten are older adolescents, aged fifteen to nineteen, and most of them perish as a result of involvement in drug or gang activity.[2] Preteen children, by contrast, are rarely the victims of fatal gun accidents, the overall incidence of which has been dropping steadily for decades. Although trigger locks and "child-access-prevention" laws may avert a few of these domestic tragedies (and are arguably worthwhile for that reason), as accident risks go, particularly among the children solicitously delivered to "afternoon play sessions" and "sleep-over parties," backyard swimming pools should be a much greater cause for concern: despite being present in far fewer households than are guns, they take many times the number of young lives.

As for suicide, there is no reason to think that its likelihood is higher because of the widespread availability of firearms. To the contrary, despite a three-fold increase in the number of guns in the U.S. over the last three decades, the total suicide rate has remained fairly constant. *Gun* suicides have occurred slightly more often—they now account for over half the firearm deaths in the country—but when guns are less readily to hand, people who are determined to kill themselves just resort to other equally lethal means.

Much the same logic applies to the acts of criminal violence that are most troubling to the public and to policy-makers. As recent history demonstrates—with gun ownership on a steep rise while rates of murder, robbery, and assault have dropped precipitously—the total volume of violent crime in the U.S. is unconnected to the prevalence of guns in American society at large. Guns certainly make such violence as we have more deadly, but they in no sense *generate* that violence, and still less do they explain the dispiriting fact that we murder one another much more often than do Europeans or the Japanese. Alas, we do so in every category of homicide, whether the instrument is a gun, a knife, or a fist. Instructive too in this regard is a comparison to countries like Switzerland, Norway, and Israel, where household gun ownership is very common but violent crime is not.

CONSIDERABLE MODESTY is also in order when it comes to the utility of gun laws for preventing further mass shootings. "No more Columbines" may be a rousing slogan, but the perpetrators of the Columbine massacre—like their counterparts in a number of similar incidents—would not have been stopped by the new regulations that have been proposed. Although it is true that the guns used in the Colorado attack were bought from private collectors at gun shows and that neither of the "straw" purchasers who obtained them for the killers underwent a background check, had they been required to do so, both would have been approved, their records having been completely clean.

Or consider the case of Larry Gene Ashbrook, the forty-seven-year-old loner who killed seven people, including four teenagers, at a Fort Worth church last September. Though irascible and mentally unbalanced according to neighbors and police, he had never committed a felony or undergone psychiatric treatment, and was in no way barred by law from buying the pistol used in his murderous rampage. If a federal license had been necessary for this purchase, he would have had no trouble qualifying for one. As *Newsweek* commented at the time—and as one can say of mass shootings in general, considering how utterly atypical they are among gun murders—"the hard lesson of Ashbrook's spree was that there are some dangers against which society might just not have a clear defense."

Finally, there is the issue of self-protection, perhaps the most important in the entire gun-control debate and the one concerning which proponents of gun control tend to be at their most disingenuous. As Iain Murray of the nonprofit Statistical Assessment Service observes, the endlessly repeated claim—or some variation of it—that "a firearm in the home is 43 times more likely to be used for suicide or murder than self-defense" has been "discredited completely," for it depends "on the very rare instance of someone actually shooting dead, as opposed to scaring off or wounding, an intruder." When the defensive use of firearms is defined more reasonably to include, in particular, its most common form, which is the simple display of a gun, the picture that emerges is radically different.

The most comprehensive research on this issue, conducted by the criminologist Gary Kleck of Florida State University, suggests that Americans use guns to ward off a criminal aggressor as many as 2.5 million times a year—a figure roughly three times higher, Kleck points out, than the number of gun-related crimes committed each year. Far from being foolhardy or dangerous, as skeptics contend, such resistance makes it less likely that would-be victims will lose their property in a robbery or be injured in an assault. Surveys of imprisoned felons confirm that the possibility of confronting an armed victim is among their biggest worries.

A narrower, if more provocative, case for the deterrent effect of private gun ownership has been made by John R. Lott, Jr., a research scholar at Yale Law School. In his much-discussed 1998 book, *More Guns, Less Crime*,[3] Lott analyzed the state laws allowing most citizens to qualify for a concealed-handgun permit—a privilege that gun-control advocates have derided, and fought, as a sure recipe for Wild-West-style shootouts. Not only, he found, have such "right-to-carry" laws failed to spark irresponsible gun use, but they have driven down rates of violence, with the most dramatic progress often occurring in those urban jurisdictions, like Pittsburgh and Atlanta, that saw

the largest increase in the number of permits issued. Lott's conclusion: the carrying of concealed handguns is "the most cost-effective means of reducing crime."

DOES ALL this mean that the opponents of gun control and in particular the NRA are right? To some extent, it does. Despite their often incendiary rhetoric—"From my cold, dead hands!" intoned NRA president Charlton Heston, hoisting a musket over his head at the group's annual convention in May—they do keep the national debate honest. This is not because they are necessarily honest themselves, but because the view they espouse is so intransigently at odds with the anti-gun prejudices of the country's educated elite and major media organs. With close to 4 million members, the NRA is a standing reminder that, however distasteful firearms may be considered in Manhattan or Georgetown or Beverly Hills, a great many ordinary Americans own and value them for a range of perfectly valid reasons.

It is therefore all the more unfortunate that these legitimate interests have been translated, as a practical matter, into a virtually absolutist rejection of any proposal for the regulation of firearms. The usual starting point for the NRA is the Second Amendment, which declares, in its much-fought-over 27 words, "A well-regulated militia, being necessary to the security of a free state, the right of the people to keep and bear arms, shall not be infringed." For advocates of gun control, the amendment's introductory phrases about the militia render it little more than an 18th-century curiosity, a constitutional anachronism best left to historians of the early republic. For the NRA and its sympathizers, it is the main clause that counts, describing in unequivocal language an individual right no less fundamental than those enshrined in the First Amendment.

But even if this latter view is basically correct—and I believe that it is—it is a far cry from a general prohibition on laws regulating the sale and ownership of firearms. Short of banning most guns or denying them to certain individuals without cause—measures that would strike at the core right "to keep and bear arms"—the government would seem to have a substantial degree of latitude under the Second Amendment. As the legal scholar Nelson Lund recently wrote in the *Weekly Standard*, urging the courts to take this part of the Bill of Rights more seriously, "most existing federal regulations . . . would probably survive such scrutiny because they are sufficiently well tailored to achieve sufficiently important government purposes."

As for the many specific measures that the gun lobby has invariably resisted over the years, some have been worth combating and others have not. There is, for instance, every reason to oppose efforts (like that of Vice President Gore) to ban "Saturday-night specials." Though criminals show no special preference for these small, inexpensive guns, they are often the only ones that the law-abiding poor can afford for self-defense. It is worth noting in this connection that the idea of singling out such weapons originated in the Jim Crow South as a means of disarming blacks; the name for them comes from the racist epithet, "nigger-town Saturday night." Similarly, the imposition of costly "smart-gun" technology on firearms manufacturers would have the effect—if it should ever get off the drawing board—of pricing many low-income people out of the market.

What of restrictions on machine guns and "assault" weapons, plastic guns and armor-piercing bullets? It is here that the supporters of gun rights have displayed an astonishing and self-destructive obtuseness, even as they have sometimes acceded to such measures under political duress. Their argument that these weapons and munitions are seldom used in crime (which is in fact the case) is quite beside the point. Such menacing firearms are widely, and rightly, viewed as falling outside any reasonable recreational or protective need—as HCI asks, "Who needs an AK–47 to go duck-hunting?"—and the simple prospect of their availability is perceived as a threat to public safety. Even if the stakes involved are largely symbolic, symbols matter.

There are problems, too, with what is perhaps the most formidable argument of the gun lobby: that gun control is pointless because, in the words of one NRA brochure, "criminals do not bother with the niceties of obeying laws—for a criminal is, by definition, someone who disobeys laws." This is certainly true, but not in an unqualified sense. Gary Kleck, whose *Targeting Guns* (1997)[4] is an encyclopedic scholarly critique of the key assumptions of gun control, agrees that "many criminals will ignore gun laws and get guns anyway." But as he notes, this is hardly "decisive regarding the desirability of gun control, since it does not address the number of successes of gun control. . . . It is even conceivable that if just 1 or 2 percent of potentially violent persons could be denied a gun, the resulting benefits might exceed the costs of whatever measure produced this modest level of compliance." The question, then, is how this calculus plays out with a given policy.

FOR THE system of background checks that is now the centerpiece of federal gun-control law, the benefits are not difficult to see. In 1999, according to the Justice Department, more than 200,000 gun-sale applications were rejected because the buyer was disqualified in some way, overwhelmingly for a felony conviction or indictment. Since the Brady Act went into effect in 1994, such rejections have numbered well over a half-million. It is true that a small fraction of these, especially early on, resulted from bureaucratic foul-ups. Moreover, the fact that individuals with a criminal record were unable to get a gun from a licensed dealer tells us nothing about whether they were *ultimately* able to get a gun, a problem highlighted by a widely reported study of the Brady Act published last month in the *Journal of the American Medical Association*. Still, for the price of making everyone submit to a slight administrative inconvenience, hundreds of thousands of high-risk bad guys have been denied weapons at the moment they wanted them.

Should the requirement of running background checks apply to the hobbyists and collectors who set up shop at gun shows? Those opposed to the notion point with some justice to its arbitrariness, since it would not affect the private sale of firearms at any other venue: to skirt the new law, private sellers could just arrange to complete their transactions elsewhere. But such critics draw the wrong conclusion. What the "gun-show loophole" really illustrates is the need to extend the terms of the Brady Act to *every* private transfer of a firearm, whether at a gun show or not.

Gun-owners would squawk, but the requirement would not be especially burdensome. It would merely mean having to use a licensed dealer as a broker for private firearms transactions—of which there are some 3 million each year—in order to ensure a proper background check. The arrangement already prevails on the Internet, where sales of guns—as of everything else—have grown exponentially in recent years. Would many people evade this system? Certainly. But enough would make a good-faith effort at compliance to hinder the immediate acquisition of firearms by criminals, who are much more likely to get their guns in a private exchange—or from theft—than from a licensed dealer.

An even more promising way to keep firearms from falling into dangerous hands, it is said, would be a federal system for registering guns and licensing gun-owners. This idea is supported, according to opinion polls, by a sizable majority of Americans. The NRA, however, is vehemently opposed, seeing registration in particular as the first bureaucratic step toward the eventual banning of firearms, as indeed it was in the de-facto prohibition of handguns now in effect in Washington, D.C. and Chicago.

But the more serious objection to any national scheme of registration is of an opposite complexion: not that it would be too irresistibly efficient but that it would be almost completely irrelevant. As even the rather visionary proposal recently introduced in the Senate concedes in its details, no viable system of registration could apply retroactively—that is, to existing firearms; the expense and administrative complications would be too great, not to mention the political grief of persuading (or compelling) current gun-owners to cooperate. What this means is that, under the bill, registration would apply, at most, to the 5 or 6 million handguns and semiautomatic weapons that are sold new or privately transferred each year—leaving the rest of America's 230 million guns untouched. Such limited information may be worth having in order to discourage illicit sales, but even decades from now it would make a negligible difference in solving all but a tiny handful of gun crimes.

As for insisting that every gun-owner obtain a federal license, there is again the question of efficacy. The research that has been done on licensing, as well as on waiting periods, suggests that whatever impact these measures have on reducing violent crime is owed to the background checks that they entail. If such checks are expanded, as they should be, to cover *all* gun transactions, licensing would merely duplicate the effort. A better use of time and money would be to improve the accuracy and accessibility of both the FBI's "national instant check system" and the similar screening operations run by many of the states.

"Common sense," in short, should indeed be our guide in devising gun laws, but its dictates are not as clear as the advocates of further regulations would have us believe. Banning whole categories of firearms amounts at most to a reassuring gesture (as with "assault" weapons) but can also interfere with the legitimate right of self-defense (as with "Saturday-night specials"). Safety measures like trigger locks may save a few lives on the margins, but allowing law-abiding citizens to carry handguns may do even more in this regard. And background checks are a helpful tool—but they are only that, not a solution for the "gun problem," whose dimensions, in any event, have little to do with our society's possessing so very many firearms.

IT HAS often been observed that, though generally well disposed to gun control, the American public doubts such laws will have much of an effect on stopping crime. Far from being contradictory, this view strikes a nice balance, reflecting as it does not only the reasonable belief that having *some* effect on stopping crime is no bad thing but also a realistic assessment of the result of most gun regulations.

Arrayed on either side of this sober consensus, however, are the true believers, the noisiest participants in what B. Bruce-Briggs, writing in the *Public Interest* in the mid-1970's, could even then call "the great American gun war." The NRA plays its part, defending a nearly unconditional right "to keep and bear arms." On the other side, HCI, the "Million Moms," and the *New York Times* play

theirs, waving a bloody banner after each new outburst of gun violence and declaring "if only there had been a law." Neither side is right, but, at this particular juncture, it is the latter group, the devotees of gun control, that stands to do more harm.

This is not because the gun controllers will see their agenda fully realized, but rather because their extravagant rhetoric, magnified by the powerful forums available to them, has begun to shift the terms of a more fundamental debate, the one over *crime*, in an ominous direction, away from the strategies that have made the U.S. so demonstrably safer a place in recent years. For those who have never been happy with aggressive policing, or high incarceration rates, gun control has become a useful diversion, explicitly targeting a colorful array of "rednecks" and "gun nuts" but implicitly placing under moral suspicion anyone who owns or uses a firearm. To the degree that this hysteria over guns causes the rest of us, including public officials and the police, to lose sight of the real crime problem— and the criminals behind it—it is a dangerous and deeply worrisome development.

Notes

1. In the four years before the "instant" system was available, the Brady Act provided a waiting period of up to five days for the completion of a background check and applied exclusively to handguns; it now covers all firearms bought from a licensed dealer.
2. Even the figure of a "dozen," based on data from 1997, is no longer accurate; statistics released in July by the federal Centers for Disease Control and Prevention put the daily toll of "children" at ten for 1998, continuing the downward trend of recent years.
3. It has recently been reissued in an updated paperback edition: University of Chicago Press, 321 pp., $12.00.
4. Aldine de Gruyter, 450 pp., $26.95 (paperback).

GARY ROSEN *is the managing editor of* COMMENTARY *and the author of* American Compact: James Madison and the Problem of Founding.

Musclebound:

The limits of U.S. power

By Stephen M. Walt

AP/WIDE WORLD

Operation Desert Fox: A U.S. destroyer launches a cruise missile from the Persian Gulf

THE END OF THE COLD WAR LEFT THE United States in a position of preponderance unsurpassed since the Roman Empire. It has the world's largest and most advanced economy, and its military forces now dwarf those of any other country. Although the collapse of the Soviet Union left it without a major rival, the United States continues to spend more on defense than the next five largest military powers *combined*. English is the language of choice in science and in world business, American media and popular culture are increasingly pervasive, and the ideals of free market democracy have found new converts around the world. The international position of the United States may not be perfect, but Americans could hardly ask for much more.

Yet this extraordinary position of power does not guarantee that the

Reprinted by permission from *The Bulletin of the Atomic Scientists,* March/April 1999, pp. 44-48. © 1999 by the Educational Foundation for Nuclear Science, 6042 South Kimbark, Chicago, IL 60637. A one-year subscription is $28.

United States can achieve its foreign policy objectives. Wherever one looks, in fact, there is abundant evidence of the limits of U.S. influence. In the Middle East, for example, the Israeli–Palestinian peace process has stagnated despite repeated U.S. proddings and President Bill Clinton's personal intervention at Wye Plantation. In Iraq, neither eight years of crippling economic sanctions nor a punishing series of U.S. air strikes have been able to remove Saddam Hussein from power, and the inspections regime established at the end of the 1991 Gulf War is now in tatters.

> **Even the most powerful state in the world will not get its way on every issue and it may sometimes find itself thwarted at every turn.**

In the Balkans, the peace agreement negotiated at Dayton has failed to quell ethnic suspicions and only the continued presence of NATO troops prevents a new round of ethnic bloodshed. The situation looks even worse in Kosovo, where the cease-fire arranged by U.S. envoy Richard Holbrooke in October 1998 is unraveling rapidly, and the killing continues.

In Asia, explicit U.S. warnings and the threat of economic sanctions failed to halt India's and Pakistan's decision to test nuclear weapons; meanwhile, China continues to ignore U.S. concerns about its human rights practices and its sales of sensitive military technology.

Relations between the United States and Russia remain edgy at best, and Moscow has re-emerged as a persistent critic of U.S. policies in Eastern Europe, the Middle East, and the Balkans. All things considered, being the world's sole superpower may not be so wonderful after all.

If the United States is so powerful, then why doesn't it get its way more often? Is it due to a failure of will, as some of President Clinton's critics contend, or is it the result of pursuing the wrong goals at the wrong time with the wrong strategy? If the United States is really the "one indispensable power," to use Madeleine Albright's self-flattering phrase, then why does its recent track record seem so discouraging?

The belief that the United States is both all powerful and impotent rests on a fundamental misunderstanding of the nature of power in international politics. For starters, the United States does get its way a good deal of the time, but Americans rarely notice when other states do what the United States wants without making a fuss about it. Focusing on the most difficult or persistent problems inevitably understates U.S. influence, because it ignores all the problems that were avoided because other states followed the U.S. lead, and it omits all the disputes that have already been resolved.

More important, the inability of the United States to get its way on every issue should not be surprising, because that is not how power works in the international system. Being bigger and stronger gives a state more influence, to be sure, in the sense that strong states can do more to weaker states than weaker states can do to them. Thus, the United States has a larger overall impact on world affairs than, say, Bolivia, Pakistan, or Denmark. Moreover, a powerful country like the United States can pursue a more ambitious range of goals than can a weaker state, and it will be better equipped to deal with unforeseen events. For these reasons, states prefer to be strong rather than weak.

Yet even the most powerful state in the world will not get its way on every issue and it may sometimes find itself thwarted at every turn. The reasons are many.

Who cares more?

One obvious reason why the United States does not always get its way is that other states care more about certain issues than the United States does. The United State lost the Vietnam War in large part because the North Vietnamese cared more about unifying their country than Americans cared about preventing unification. Similarly, the United States worries about the possibility that Iraq might acquire weapons of mass destruction, but it is a safe bet that Saddam Hussein cares more about Iraq's strategic situation than the United States does. He is willing to endure far more punishment than Americans are, just as Americans would be willing to run greater risks and bear greater costs if their security were more directly at stake.

In the same way, U.S. influence over Israel and the PLO is limited by the fact that they care more about the final peace terms than most Americans do. Both sides are willing to stand up to U.S. pressure when disputes arise, even if opposing the United States is costly.

The tendency for other states to care more than the United States does is a direct result of the favorable position the United States enjoys. In addition to being wealthier and stronger than any other state, the United States is insulated from the other major powers by two enormous oceans and protected by a large and robust nuclear deterrent. Although no state is perfectly safe from harm, the United States is easily the most secure great power in history. Other states have to worry a lot about how certain issues are resolved; the United States can often take a more sanguine view.

That condition leads to something of a paradox: Although solving many global problems requires active U.S. involvement, Americans do not see them as vital to their own interests and they are unwilling to

AP/WIDE WORLD

There are limits to U.S. influence: Despite President Clinton's personal intervention at Wye River Plantation, the Israeli-Palestinian peace process appears stalled.

expend much effort addressing them. U.S. officials were visibly reluctant to send U.S. troops to the Balkans, and they were clearly

> **Americans would like to coerce others to do what they want, but they aren't willing to risk much blood or treasure to make sure they do.**

aware that public support would evaporate if there were even a modest number of U.S. casualties. Similar concerns explain why economic sanctions and air strikes by *unmanned* cruise missiles have become the preferred tool of U.S. diplomacy. Americans would like to coerce others to do what they want, but they aren't willing to risk much blood or treasure to make sure they do.

This tendency is not caused by a lack of vision, leadership, or courage within the U.S. government. Rather, it is a direct result of the favorable international position that the United States now occupies. The reluctance to "bear any burden" also reveals the tacit recognition that the problems the United States is trying to solve may not be worth an extraordinary level of effort. The bottom line is clear: When other states care more about an issue than does the United States, Washington won't use all the power at its disposal—and it will be less likely to get what it wants.

It's lonely at the top

A second reason why U.S. influence is less than one might expect follows from the familiar principle of the balance of power. In a world in which each state must ultimately provide for its own security, the most powerful state in the system will always appear at least somewhat threatening to others. This tendency will be muted if the strongest state appears to be fairly benevolent (and especially if its interests are generally compatible with those of

the other major powers), but it never vanishes entirely. Even when a strong state seems relatively benevolent, other states may try to keep it from becoming even stronger and may band together to contain its influence.

The well-known tendency for states to "balance" against the strongest power helps explain why France and Russia have joined forces to undercut U.S. efforts to pressure Iraq, and why Russia and China have been working to improve relations as well. The desire to free Europe from its subordination to the United States is one reason why many Europeans favor continued progress towards European economic and political union.

Efforts to balance against the United States have been restrained thus far. This is partly due to the legacy of good relations established during the Cold War, but an even more important factor is America's geographic separation from the other major powers. Just as the Atlantic and Pacific oceans have long protected the United States from potential rivals, they also protect the Eurasian powers from the possibility of U.S. domination. Although European and Asian elites may resent U.S. high-handedness and worry about American cultural hegemony, they don't have to worry about the United States conquering them militarily. Further, the United States has been a relatively well-behaved great power, which makes it less likely to provoke others into joining forces to keep it in check.

Nonetheless, there are growing differences between the United States and a number of its traditional allies, and these differences are partly the result of the preponderant U.S. position. For example, the United States has dragged its heels on many environmental issues, in part because it fears being forced to pay a disproportionate share of the costs. It also stood apart from its allies over the proposal to create an International Criminal Court to try human rights violators and over the treaty to ban landmines, largely because U.S. officials feared that these initiatives might impair their ability to meet important military commitments both now and in the future.

A similar desire to preserve its own superiority and freedom of action explains why the United States seeks to keep countries like India and Pakistan from acquiring their own nuclear arsenals, while steadfastly preserving its own nuclear deterrent and opposing proposals for NATO to adopt a no-first-use doctrine.

Other states are more willing to oppose U.S. policy because they have less need for U.S. protection. During the Cold War, for example, differences between the United States and its allies were muted by the larger objective of preserving Western unity in the face of the Soviet threat. Now that the Soviet Union is gone, traditional allies are more willing to line up against the United States when they do not agree with its position. Despite—or more precisely, *because*—the United States is so obviously the biggest kid on the block, even its traditional allies may be looking for ways to keep U.S. power in check.

Dreaming impossible dreams

The apparent gap between U.S. power and U.S. influence also reflects the nature of the goals that American leaders have chosen to pursue. The euphoria that accompanied the end of the Cold War encouraged them to adopt an ambitious set of international objectives, and if anything that policy has intensified during the Clinton administration. Americans have always been inclined to remake the world in their own image, and that temptation is especially hard to resist when the United States seems to possess so many advantages.

Since the end of the Cold War, the United States has tried to broker a peace settlement between Israel and the PLO, sought to prevent the spread of nuclear weapons to other states (including several with active nu-

clear programs), and worked (successfully) to reduce the Russian nuclear arsenal and to disarm the former Soviet republics of Kazakhstan, Ukraine, and Belarus.

It has also committed itself to expanding NATO eastward and enlarging the sphere of democratic rule around the world, and it has provided the military and diplomatic muscle behind the prolonged campaign to eliminate Iraq's residual weapons capability. Finally, the United States also took on the mission of trying to reconstitute a stable, multi-ethnic society in war-torn Bosnia, while simultaneously trying to foster a solution to the simmering conflict between Serbs and ethnic Albanians over Kosovo.

This is a breathtaking array of foreign policy goals, and some of them were clearly quixotic from the beginning. Take Bosnia, for instance. As John Mearsheimer, my colleague at the University of Chicago, has pointed out, history offers not a single case where contending ethnic groups have agreed to share power in the aftermath of a civil war. Yet the 1995 Dayton agreement committed the United States to achieving this historically unprecedented outcome.

In much the same way, the effort to deny nuclear weapons to states like Iraq, North Korea, India, and Pakistan flies in the face of the powerful norm of national sovereignty and it ignores the powerful incentives that each of these states has for acquiring such a capability. It is also transparently hypocritical, given U.S. reluctance to give up its own far larger nuclear arsenal. Slowing the spread of nuclear weapons is a good idea, and U.S. policy has clearly helped achieve this goal, but it is not surprising that it did not achieve 100 percent success.

Knitting with one hand, unraveling with the other

The U.S. position as the sole superpower creates a final constraint on the effective exercise of U.S. influ-

ence. The United States is actively engaged in an enormous array of issues and in virtually every area of the globe. As just noted, many U.S. objectives are quite ambitious, and one would probably expect a low success rate under the best of circumstances. Unfortunately, given the number of goals the United States is trying to pursue, it is virtually inevitable that its efforts in one area will undermine its efforts somewhere else.

For example, the U.S.-led campaign to expand NATO is intended to help to defuse potential tensions within Europe and to nurture the new democracies in Poland, the Czech Republic, and Hungary. This is a laudable goal, but it directly undermines the equally laudable goal of improving relations with Russia and the related objective of obtaining Russian adherence to the START II arms control agreement. A similar example is the contradiction between U.S. efforts to promote trade with China, its desire to improve human rights conditions there, and its equally strong desire to build a more cordial political relationship with the Chinese government.

In the same way, U.S. leaders are strongly committed to supporting Israel, yet they also want to hasten a peace settlement, which requires putting pressure on Israel. They also want to avoid becoming the target of terrorist attacks, which are partly a reaction to close U.S. ties with Israel. No matter what the United States does, it will be difficult to achieve all these objectives simultaneously.

All states face tradeoffs between different goals, but they are likely to be more numerous and more complicated for a state that has its fingers in lots of different global problems. Paradoxically, America's extraordinary capacity for action is sometimes self-defeating. The more successful it is in one area, the more elusive success becomes somewhere else.

How much is enough?

In the immediate aftermath of the Cold War, many Americans rejoiced

AP/WIDE WORLD

But sometimes U.S. influence works: Former U.S. Sen. George Mitchell, shown here with Irish Prime Minister Bertie Ahern and British Prime Minister Tony Blair, helped broker a peace agreement for Northern Ireland.

at the prospect of a "new world order" in which international conflict would be consigned to the dustbin of history. Instead of debating which weapons to buy, national security experts began to discuss how the country could convert defense industries and spend the anticipated "peace dividend."

Some eight years later, the much-ballyhooed "end of history" has yet to materialize. Although defense spending and weapons levels have fallen steadily since 1989, international conflict did not cease and U.S.

military forces have been extremely busy. Indeed, President Clinton recently proposed the first real increase in U.S. defense spending since the Reagan era, to ensure that the United States could still meet its current level of commitments. Americans are discovering what other imperial powers learned long ago: the world is a complicated and messy place and trying to run it is a costly and difficult business.

This situation raises awkward questions for those who simultaneously believe that the United States

is still spending too much on its military and that U.S. foreign policy should seek more than the pursuit of selfish national interests. International influence cannot be had on the cheap, and those who want to use U.S. power to deter aggression, halt genocide, or discourage proliferation will have to provide U.S. leaders with the means to ensure that their voice is heard and their actions are felt. In doing so, however, they must remember that even enormous advantages in relative power will not get the United States everything it wants.

Similarly, those who favor continued reductions in U.S. military power must confront the fact that U.S. influence would be even smaller if this policy were followed. Reasonable people can disagree about which course the United States should take; but we should begin by recognizing that there is a very clear choice to be made.

Stephen M. Walt is a professor of political science at the University of Chicago and a member of the Bulletin's *Board of Directors.*

UNITED STATES

The longest war

WASHINGTON, DC

Vietnam was a defeat. Was it therefore a mistake? And if it was, can America avoid repeating it?

ON MARCH 29th 1973, South Vietnam's President Nguyen Van Thieu bade farewell to the last American combat troops leaving his country. "When the emotions aroused by this long war have calmed down," he said, "the world will acknowledge by consensus that you have played a great role in the elaboration of peace in freedom and that you have shaped history for the better. God bless you."

Two years later, on April 30th 1975, the last American helicopter lifted off the roof of the Saigon embassy. For most of the past quarter of a century, Mr Thieu's hope has been dashed. The emotions aroused by the conflict may have calmed but few people have argued that the Vietnam war—the longest conflict America has ever fought—has shaped history for the better.

It is not surprising. America lost 58,000 soldiers and failed to stop North Vietnam over-running the South. Even now, two-thirds of Americans think the war was a mistake, but cannot agree what the error was. One group—the majority, probably—thinks it lay in becoming involved in the first place. To them, Vietnam was an unnecessary and unwinnable conflict. It presented

Americans with the image of their country not as a defender of democracy but, it seemed, as an imperial power. Others think the mistake lay in getting out. President Ronald Reagan declared that American soldiers had been "denied permission to win", and ever since then, conservatives have argued that Vietnam was a failure of political will, not of geopolitical or military strategy.

Either way, the conflict has remained too painful for agreement. Henry Kissinger gloomily concluded that the war destroyed "the once near-universal faith in the uniqueness of our values and their relevance around the world". To its opponents, he wrote, defeat came about not because of "errors in judgment but moral rot at the core of American life."

It would be too much to say that the passage of time has transformed opinions about the war. Yet there are signs that Americans are at last beginning to come to terms with the legacy of Vietnam. Thanks to the ending of the cold war, the conflict in Kosovo, and new historical evidence, the longest war is starting to emerge less as a unique event—either uniquely bad or uniquely bungled—and more as an under-

standable defeat in what turned out to be, over the longer run, a winning cause.

The most striking recent evidence that public attitudes may be changing was the unexpectedly strong performance in the presidential primaries of Senator John McCain. Mr McCain was not the first Vietnam veteran to run for president. But his campaign seemed to elicit popular responses that went beyond mere admiration for a military hero. As Mary McGrory of the *Washington Post* put it to a recent conference at the Brookings Institution:

> "John McCain's candidacy for some reason or other had a mysteriously healing effect on the country. He made it possible for people who were irreconcilably still against Vietnam and all it represented [to] look at him, [to] admire him, [to] like him and [to] vote for him. Because, although he brought back bad memories, he had survived it and he was not bitter. And I think people thought, 'Well, if he can digest it, if he can handle it, why can't we?' "

A second and more indirect example of changing public attitudes came last year, during the war in Kosovo. For the first time since the

Vietnam war, some members of the left supported the use of military force abroad. Presidents Kennedy and Johnson had sought to justify their intervention in South Vietnam by arguing that it would save a threatened people from a brutal communist-nationalist regime which most of them did not want. Defeat discredited that argument for a generation. (President George Bush, for example, justified the Gulf war largely in terms of national self-interest.) But in Kosovo a group of "liberal hawks" returned to the humanitarian argument for military action, suggesting that part of the left is overcoming its Vietnam-era loathing of military action.

Third, for the first time since the war ended, there are signs of a historical revisionism to challenge the entrenched views of left and right about the war. Two recent books exemplify the change: Michael Lind's "Vietnam: The Necessary War" (The Free Press, $25) and Lewis Sorley's "A Better War" (Harcourt Brace, $28).

Mr Sorley, a former teacher at West Point, attacks the conservative view that the war was lost because of political meddling. Rather, he shows, America's initial "search and destroy" policy—which boiled down to trying to kill as many Viet Cong and North Vietnamese as possible—received reasonably consistent support from the Johnson administration, even though it was doomed to fail against an enemy which specialised in avoiding open battle.

Mr Lind attacks the widespread view "that it was a mistake to intervene in Indochina at all, but once the United States had intervened, it should have used unlimited force to quickly win an unqualified victory." Rather, he claims, the war was worth fighting because Indochina was one of the most important fronts in the cold war, along with Korea and West Germany. It was not worth sacrificing hundreds of thousands of lives for, however, because that endangered America's broader commitment to containing communism.

Indeed, America, in Mr Lind's view, should have pulled out earlier.

Neither analysis has created a new orthodoxy about the war. But the striking thing is that they were written at all after so many years of predictable left- or right-wing comment. Along with Mr McCain's campaign and the liberal hawks of Kosovo, they show that new views of the conflict are starting to break through. Do these views still suggest that the war did more harm than good?

A tyranny of exaggeration?

That question revolves around two issues—the extent to which the war disrupted American domestic politics, and its effect on the world in general. At home, the war divided the country more profoundly than any conflict except the Civil War of 1861–65. David Halberstam, one of the first reporters to cover the conflict, called it a second civil war. The conflict destroyed two presidencies (forcing Johnson not to seek re-election and maiming Nixon even before Watergate). It also seemed to tear apart an entire generation of Americans.

Yet, a quarter of a century later, these claims are beginning to seem exaggerated. The strength of the opposition to the war was certainly striking. But every war in America has generated strong opposition, and this opposition was rarely typical of the country as a whole. Surprisingly, opinion polls taken while the Vietnam war was going on showed that the most enthusiastic supporters of the war were younger Americans, not older ones. The peaceniks of Vietnam were no more proof that young Americans hated the war than the recent demonstrators against the World Bank and IMF meetings in Washington are evidence that all young Americans oppose globalisation.

Similarly, Vietnam and Watergate frequently get the blame for broad social changes such as the undermining of Americans' belief in the

competence and integrity of their government. Yet similar things happened at the same time in Europe. If the war is to be blamed for anything, the blame must be more specific. The two best arguments are, first, that it destroyed American support for liberalism; and, second, that it divided the Democratic Party so badly that you can still see the scars.

Many people have argued that Vietnam was "liberalism's war" and that liberalism (social democracy to non-Americans) paid the price of failure. It is indeed true that the escalation of American military involvement in Vietnam happened at the moment of liberal triumph. In the first two years of Johnson's presidency his administration passed more domestic reforms than most two-term presidents. The Voting Rights Act, the Civil Rights Act, the Economic Opportunity Act, the Elementary and Secondary Education Act: these formed the basis of the "Great Society" of the 1960s and 1970s.

It is also true that those who opposed the war soon turned on the Great Society and on Johnson, its architect. The result discredited liberalism. As E.J. Dionne of the *Washington Post* has pointed out, "Liberalism itself attracted derisive adjectives. It became corporate liberalism, or establishment liberalism." And now it has become merely a synonym for left-wingery.

Yet much of the reaction against the Great Society was happening anyway and would probably have turned the tide against liberalism regardless of Vietnam. In the 1960s, people, jobs and political influence were starting to move from the bastions of liberalism in the north-east to the more conservative south and west, where first Barry Goldwater and then Ronald Reagan were shaping the new forces. And, in the south, the governor of Alabama, George Wallace, exposed a deep fault-line in the old liberal alliance between blue-collar whites and blacks. Johnson himself said that the Voting Rights Act of 1965 turned the south over to the Republican Party for a generation.

The bigger domestic impact of the war was on the Democratic Party. Vietnam sullied its reputation for toughness on foreign affairs for a generation or more. From 1940 to 1970, the Democrats had often been the party Americans trusted on national security. They had led America into the second world war against the opposition of many Republicans. Vietnam changed that.

So-called "cold-war liberals"—the type represented by Truman, Kennedy and Johnson—found themselves marginalised while opponents of the war took over much of the party. In the 1970s and 1980s, Democrats opposed building any new weapons systems. Most voted against the Gulf war. Even under President Clinton, the "New Democrats" have been less successful in defining what they stand for in the outside world than on economic or social matters.

So the influence of Vietnam on domestic American politics has been strong in one party but exaggerated in general. The same can be said for the war's influence on the world in general.

At the time, one of the most common assertions about Vietnam was that defeat would break up the cold-war consensus in the democracies in favour of standing up to communism. A humiliated and defeated America, it was feared, would abandon its allies to a resurgent communism. American public support for containing Russia would melt away. And defeat would unleash a new wave of American isolationism.

It is not quite true to say that none of this came to pass: the 1970s were a period of successful Soviet expansion in Africa and elsewhere. Yet, for all the hair-tearing, it is clear that defeat in Vietnam had none of the long-lasting effects that were predicted.

Consider Asia itself. Not only did the dominoes of Thailand and Malaysia stay upright, but America has remained the pre-eminent foreign power in the region. Its alliance with Japan is intact. It has even re-established diplomatic relations with Vietnam and, though these are uneasy, that has more to do with the still largely Marxist Vietnamese government's hostility to foreign investment than with the ancient enmities of conflict. America lost the battle in Vietnam, but won the war in South-East Asia and the cold war itself.

Nor did Vietnam plunge America into isolationism. Americans supported the Gulf war even though their generals, including Colin Powell, feared there might be thousands of casualties. They were also more enthusiastic about the operation in Kosovo than anybody had expected. At one point opinion polls showed that 50% of Americans favoured using ground troops there, even though the administration did not.

Caspar Weinberger, Mr Reagan's secretary of defence, commissioned a study to work out the cast-iron military lessons of Vietnam. It dutifully reported that, if America were ever to go to war again, there should be a clearly defined national-security interest at stake, and strong political support at home and in Congress; and, once a decision had been made to intervene, America should go in with guns blazing, with victory the only acceptable outcome.

These conditions were met in the Gulf. But Vietnam has not prevented American involvement in other places, where its national-interest concerns were less than vital. Indeed, the Gulf apart, all the wars that America has fought since Vietnam, notably in Bosnia and Kosovo, have been confrontations in which America has had the luxury of choosing when and whether to get involved. In most of these interventions, diplomacy—not to mention reality—has imposed limits on all-out military action. When it came to a fight, though, it was win or bust; and, in the 1990s, victory came.

It is true that Vietnam has altered the way foreign policy has been conducted in America, by increasing the extent of congressional oversight. Largely because of the reaction against the "imperial presidency" that was accused of taking the country into Vietnam, Congress has stopped deferring so readily to the president. Its new activism was in evidence in Kosovo, during the Gulf war and in the recent shooting down of the Comprehensive Test Ban Treaty. But even this can be overstated. In practice, Congress was not extending its power in new ways after Vietnam. Rather, it was returning to the pre-war arrangement in which the legislature, as well as the executive, got engaged in the grand issues of war and peace. The atypical period was that of the early cold war, until about 1965.

In short, Vietnam has had surprisingly little geopolitical impact, either in the world at large or in American foreign policy. Why? Conservatives inevitably return to the argument that the seriousness of the defeat in Vietnam was mitigated only by Ronald Reagan. The other explanation, which carries more weight, was first advanced by several opponents of the war within the Kennedy and Johnson administrations, including George Kennan and George Ball and, in the Senate, William Fulbright, chairman of the Senate Foreign Relations Committee.

They agreed that America ought to try to contain communism's spread. But going to war in Vietnam was a disproportionate response to the threat of Soviet or Chinese expansionism. And, because Vietnam was a side-show, it follows that defeat there did not really affect America's core anti-communism. So it could recover quickly from defeat. China, North Vietnam and Cuba all became communist without America's cold-war alliances collapsing. If American credibility was at stake in Vietnam, it was because Kennedy and Johnson made it so.

Yet it is still doubtful whether they could have avoided doing what they did, at least without causing problems for America elsewhere. For most of the evidence that has emerged since the end of the war in Vietnam has tended to buttress the other view: that Vietnam was merely one campaign in a bigger struggle.

It turns out that there was much more Soviet and Chinese support for North Vietnam than anyone had suspected: at one point China had 170,000 soldiers in Vietnam. There was also communist unity at the start, even if China, the Soviet Union and North Vietnam fell out later: in 1950, Stalin, Mao and Ho Chi Minh met in Moscow to map out how to take over Indochina. America's enemies—Mao in particular—certainly saw Vietnam as a cold-war confrontation.

Given America's position in the world, then, intervention in Vietnam looks, in hindsight, hard to have avoided. And if it was still a mistake—given the scale of the slaughter and the fact that the communists won—it is one that America could easily come under pressure to make again.

Consider the parallels with Kosovo. That too is a poor part of the world, without obvious American security interests but close to long-standing American allies, and threatened by a communist-nationalist dictator supported by a big rival of liberal America. The Kosovo war too saw communists defy an American ultimatum, and wage a low-intensity campaign on difficult terrain where outsiders have frequently come to grief. It too put American credibility at stake because allies were ready to interpret retreat as a sign of weakness.

In the event, modern air power enabled Mr Clinton to avoid in Kosovo the fatal decision that Johnson took in Vietnam in 1965, to send in more troops. But, considering the pressure Mr Clinton came under to do the same thing in Kosovo, it seems unreasonable to dub the Vietnam war a uniquely foolish piece of adventurism, or to condemn Kennedy and Johnson for making decisions that looked, at the start at least, remarkably like the ones Mr Clinton took in Kosovo.

Defeat in Vietnam has not changed the aims or values of American foreign policy. At most, as Mr Kissinger put it recently, it may have created a new generation "in search of the riskless application of our values."

Test Your Knowledge Form

We encourage you to photocopy and use this page as a tool to assess how the articles in **Annual Editions** expand on the information in your textbook. By reflecting on the articles you will gain enhanced text information. You can also access this useful form on a product's book support Web site at **http://www.dushkin.com/ online/.**

NAME: DATE:

TITLE AND NUMBER OF ARTICLE:

BRIEFLY STATE THE MAIN IDEA OF THIS ARTICLE:

LIST THREE IMPORTANT FACTS THAT THE AUTHOR USES TO SUPPORT THE MAIN IDEA:

WHAT INFORMATION OR IDEAS DISCUSSED IN THIS ARTICLE ARE ALSO DISCUSSED IN YOUR TEXTBOOK OR OTHER READINGS THAT YOU HAVE DONE? LIST THE TEXTBOOK CHAPTERS AND PAGE NUMBERS:

LIST ANY EXAMPLES OF BIAS OR FAULTY REASONING THAT YOU FOUND IN THE ARTICLE:

LIST ANY NEW TERMS/CONCEPTS THAT WERE DISCUSSED IN THE ARTICLE, AND WRITE A SHORT DEFINITION:

ANNUAL EDITIONS revisions depend on two major opinion sources: one is our Advisory Board, listed in the front of this volume, which works with us in scanning the thousands of articles published in the public press each year; the other is you—the person actually using the book. Please help us and the users of the next edition by completing the prepaid article rating form on this page and returning it to us. Thank you for your help!

ANNUAL EDITIONS: American Government 01/02

ARTICLE RATING FORM

Here is an opportunity for you to have direct input into the next revision of this volume. We would like you to rate each of the 48 articles listed below, using the following scale:

1. Excellent: should definitely be retained
2. Above average: should probably be retained
3. Below average: should probably be deleted
4. Poor: should definitely be deleted

Your ratings will play a vital part in the next revision. So please mail this prepaid form to us just as soon as you complete it. Thanks for your help!

RATING

ARTICLE

1. The Declaration of Independence, 1776
2. The Constitution of the United States, 1787
3. The Size and Variety of the Union as a Check on Faction
4. Checks and Balances
5. What Good Is Government?
6. Chomp!
7. The New Power
8. America's Ignorant Voters
9. American Federalism: Half-Full or Half-Empty?
10. Vigilante Justices
11. Guns and Tobacco: Government by Litigation
12. Drawing Legal Lines
13. Speech Isn't Cheap
14. Disability Act's First 10 Years and the Challenges Ahead
15. Gone Are the Giants
16. Hooked on Polls
17. Did Clinton Succeed or Fail?
18. Trivial Pursuits: Clinton's Record
19. Crackup of the Committees
20. King of the Roads
21. Can It Be Done?
22. Uninsured Americans Linger on Congress' Waiting List
23. A Judge Speaks Out
24. The Gipper's Constitution
25. Up For Grabs: The Supreme Court and the Election
26. Turkey Farm

RATING

ARTICLE

27. Finding the Civil Service's Hidden Sex Appeal: Why the Brightest Young People Shy Away From Government
28. Running Scared
29. Who Needs Political Parties?
30. Adding Values
31. Making Every Vote Count
32. One Cheer for Soft Money: The Case for Strong Political Parties
33. Government's End
34. Under the Gun
35. Associations Without Members
36. Missed Information: The Reporting Tool That Reporters Don't Use
37. www.democracy.com
38. The Two-Bucks-a-Minute Democracy
39. Bush and Gore: Perfect Winners of a Perfect Race. Almost
40. The Last Straw Poll: Seven Things From Campaign 2000 to Eliminate
41. Selling America to the Highest Bidder
42. Ten Observations on the 2000 Florida Controversy
43. The Old College Try: How We Pick the Prez
44. Welfare Reform, Act 2
45. $80,000 and a Dream: A Simple Plan for Generating Equal Opportunity
46. Yes and No to Gun Control
47. Musclebound: The Limits of U.S. Power
48. The Longest War

(Continued on next page)

NO POSTAGE
NECESSARY
IF MAILED
IN THE
UNITED STATE

BUSINESS REPLY MAIL
FIRST-CLASS MAIL PERMIT NO. 84 GUILFORD CT

POSTAGE WILL BE PAID BY ADDRESSEE

**McGraw-Hill/Dushkin
530 Old Whitfield Street
Guilford, CT 06437-9989**

Illııılllıılıılıılllıılllıılılıılılıılılıılılılıılılıl

ABOUT YOU

Name   Date

Are you a teacher? ☐ A student? ☐
Your school's name

Department

Address   City   State   Zip

School telephone #

YOUR COMMENTS ARE IMPORTANT TO US !

Please fill in the following information:
For which course did you use this book?

Did you use a text with this *ANNUAL EDITION*? ☐ yes ☐ no
What was the title of the text?

What are your general reactions to the *Annual Editions* concept?

Have you read any particular articles recently that you think should be included in the next edition?

Are there any articles you feel should be replaced in the next edition? Why?

Are there any World Wide Web sites you feel should be included in the next edition? Please annotate.

May we contact you for editorial input? ☐ yes ☐ no
May we quote your comments? ☐ yes ☐ no